THE POWER
TO PERSUADE

THE POWER TO PERSUADE

A Rhetoric and Reader for Argumentative Writing

THIRD EDITION

Sally De Witt Spurgin
Southern Methodist University

PRENTICE HALL, Englewood Cliffs, New Jersey 07632

Library of Congress Cataloging-in-Publication Data

Spurgin, Sally De Witt.
     The power to persuade : a rhetoric and reader for argumentative
writing / Sally De Witt Spurgin. —3rd ed.
        p. cm.
     Includes bibliographical references and index.
     ISBN 0–13–221185–8
     1. English language—Rhetoric. 2. Persuasion (Rhetoric)
3. College readers. I. Title.
PE1431.S68 1994   93–2233
808'.0427—dc20   CIP

Acquisitions editor: Alison Reeves
Editorial/production supervision and
   interior design: P. M. Gordon Associates, Inc.
Copy editor: Debra E. Soled
Cover design: Violet Lake Design
Prepress buyer: Herb Klein
Manufacturing buyer: Bob Anderson

© 1994, 1989, 1985 by Prentice-Hall, Inc.
A Simon & Schuster Company
Englewood Cliffs, New Jersey 07632

Printed in the United States of America
10 9 8 7 6 5 4 3 2 1

ISBN 0-13-221185-8

Prentice-Hall International (UK) Limited, *London*
Prentice-Hall of Australia Pty. Limited, *Sydney*
Prentice-Hall Canada Inc., *Toronto*
Prentice-Hall Hispanoamericana, S.A., *Mexico*
Prentice-Hall of India Private Limited, *New Delhi*
Prentice-Hall of Japan, Inc., *Tokyo*
Simon & Schuster Asia Pte. Ltd., *Singapore*
Editora Prentice-Hall do Brasil, Ltda., *Rio de Janeiro*

To my niece and nephews, college students present and future, with love:

> *Ann Thornton (Texas, Class of 1996)*
> *Ryan Thornton (Baylor, Class of 1996)*
> *Christopher De Witt (Class of 2010)*
> *William De Witt (Class of 2011)*
> *Andrew De Witt (Class of 2013)*

Contents

Preface   *xv*

1   **Argument and Persuasion**   **1**

  The Ethics of Persuasion   *2*
  The Need for Argument   *4*
Relationships in Argument   *5*
  Verbal Signals of Argument   *7*
  EXERCISE 1–1   *8*
  Assumptions   *9*
  EXERCISE 1–2   *10*
  Limiting Arguments with Qualifiers   *11*
  EXERCISES 1–3 AND 1–4   *12*
Logic, Emotion, and Ethos *in Argument*   *14*
  The Logical Appeal   *14*
  The Emotional Appeal   *15*
  EXERCISE 1–5   *17*
  The Ethical Appeal   *18*
  EXERCISES 1–6 AND 1–7   *20*
Readings   *23*
  "What So Proudly We Hailed?" (Student Essay), Debbie Sapp   *23*
  "Thinking and Rethinking" (Student Essay), Lindsay Moran   *25*
  "Celebrate Free Speech: Say What You Think," Ellen Goodman   *27*
Suggestions for Writing and Further Discussion   *29*

2   **Creating Arguments**   **31**

The Rhetorical Context   *32*
  Consider Your Purpose   *33*

Consider Your Audience   *33*
The Invented Reader   *35*
EXERCISE 2–1   *37*
Working Toward a Thesis   *37*
Invention Strategy: Using Topical Checklists   *38*
EXERCISE 2–2   *40*
Invention Strategy: Finding and Resolving Contradictions   *41*
EXERCISE 2–3   *44*
Invention Strategy: Examining Influences and Consequences   *44*
The Enthymeme as Thesis   *46*
Shaping the Argument   *50*
EXERCISE 2–4   *52*
Readings   *53*
"Group Discussions Are Beneficial" (Student Draft)   *53*
"Pay Equity Is Unfair to Women," Linda Chavez   *55*
Suggestions for Writing and Further Discussion   *58*

3   **Developing Arguments: Defining Terms   59**

How to Define   *60*
Reportive Definitions   *60*
Stipulative Definitions   *61*
How to Judge Definitions   *62*
EXERCISE 3–1   *63*
The Roles of Definition in Argument   *65*
Using Definition to Clarify   *66*
Using Definition to Control   *67*
Persuasive Definitions   *68*
Readings   *69*
"If It Isn't Censorship, What Is It?" Linda Waddle   *69*
"What Lasts" (Student Essay), Ann Taylor Haun   *71*
"Born to Be Mild," Paul Rudnick   *73*
Suggestions for Writing and Further Discussion   *77*

4   **Developing Arguments: Finding and Evaluating Evidence   79**

Creativity in Research   *79*
Finding Evidence for Arguments   *81*
Kinds of Evidence   *81*
Locating Background and Historical Evidence   *85*
Locating Current Evidence   *86*

Selected Database Sources   *89*
Personal Knowledge and Research   *90*
EXERCISES 4–1 AND 4–2   *93*
Evaluating Evidence   *94*
Recent Evidence   *95*
Primary Evidence   *95*
Unbiased Evidence   *96*
Representative Evidence   *98*
Sufficient Evidence   *99*
EXERCISES 4–3 THROUGH 4–5   *99*
Using Evidence in Documented Essays and Research Papers   *102*
Summarizing, Paraphrasing, Quoting   *102*
Incorporating Quotations   *103*
Citing Sources   *107*
Avoiding Plagiarism   *107*
Citations in the Humanities   *109*
Citations in the Social Sciences   *112*
Citations in the Natural Sciences   *113*
Readings   *114*
"Reports, Inferences, Judgments," S. I. Hayakawa   *114*
"The Problems with Television News" (Student Essay),
Dequa Thompson   *120*
Suggestions for Writing and Further Discussion   *132*

5   **Testing Arguments: Inductive Reasoning**   **134**

Patterns of Inductive Reasoning   *134*
Arguing from Analogy   *137*
Literal Analogy   *137*
Metaphorical Analogy   *138*
Evaluating Arguments from Analogy   *138*
EXERCISES 5–1 AND 5–2   *139*
Arguing from Cause or Effect   *142*
The Post Hoc Fallacy   *145*
EXERCISE 5–3   *146*
Arguing from Examples   *148*
Evaluating Arguments from Examples   *148*
EXERCISE 5–4   *150*
Limiting Generalizations   *151*
EXERCISE 5–5   *151*

Readings   153
   "Is Business Bluffing Ethical?" Albert Z. Carr   153
   "Why I Want a Wife," Judy Brady   156
   "Concealed Weapons Can Save Lives," Suzanna Gratia   159
Suggestions for Writing and Further Discussion   161

6   Testing Arguments: Deductive Reasoning   163

Deduction in Fiction and Fact   163
Induction and Deduction   164
Validity, Truth, and Soundness   166
Distribution of Terms   167
   EXERCISE 6–1   *170*
Testing Validity: The Syllogism   171
   EXERCISES 6–2 AND 6–3   *172*
Formal Fallacies   173
   EXERCISE 6–4   *176*
The Limitations of Logic: Toulmin's Corrective   176
The Enthymeme   177
   EXERCISES 6–5 AND 6–6   *178*
If/Then and Either/Or Arguments   180
   EXERCISE 6–7   *183*
Readings   185
   "Should We Abolish the Presidency?" Barbara Tuchman   185
   "We'll Never Conquer Space," Arthur C. Clarke   190
   "A Few Kind Words for Affirmative Action," Hosea L. Martin   196
Suggestions for Writing and Further Discussion   198

7   Testing Arguments: Fallacies   200

Why Study Fallacies?   200
Kinds of Fallacies   201
Fallacies in Arguments   201
   Appeal to Pity   201
   Appeal to Popular Sentiments   203
   Begging the Question   204
   False Dilemma   204
   Faulty Analogy   204
   Guilt by Association   205
   Hasty Generalization   205
   Post Hoc Fallacy   205

Fallacies in Counterarguments   206
　　Lack of Contrary Evidence   206
　　Oversimplification   206
　　Personal Attack   207
　　Shifting Ground   207
　　Straw Man   208
　　Trivial Objections   208
Detecting Fallacies   209
　　EXERCISES 7–1 THROUGH 7–4   210
Readings   215
　　"The Checkers Speech," Richard M. Nixon   215
　　"Lies, Fallacies, and Santa Claus" (Student Essay), T. J. Stone   219
　　"The Language of Advertising Claims," Jeffrey Schrank   221
　　Advertisements for Analysis   228
　　"Love Is a Fallacy," Max Shulman   232
Suggestions for Writing and Further Discussion   240

8　　*Revising Arguments: Completeness and Coherence*   **242**

The Aims of Revision   243
Macro-Revision: The Draft as a Whole   244
　　Testing for Unity and Completeness   244
　　Checking Organization and Development   245
　　EXERCISES 8–1 THROUGH 8–6   257
Micro-Revision: Paragraphs and Sentences   262
Revising for Paragraph Unity   262
Revising for Paragraph Completeness   263
Revising for Coherence   265
Avoiding Repetitiousness   268
　　EXERCISES 8–7 THROUGH 8–12   272
Readings   275
　　"Conformity and Nonconformity: The Prices Paid for Each"
　　　(Rough Draft)   275
　　"Nonconformity: The Price and the Payoff" (Student Essay),
　　　Kathy Taylor   276
Suggestions for Writing and Further Discussion   278

9　　*Revising Arguments: The Power of Style*   **280**

What Is Style?   280
The Elements of Style   282
　　EXERCISES 9–1 AND 9–2   283

Sentence Style   284
    Sentence Types   *284*
    Sentence Length   *285*
    Sentence Openers   *286*
    Syntactical Patterns   *287*
    EXERCISES 9–3 AND 9–4   *288*
    Sentence Logic   *290*
    EXERCISE 9–5   *291*
Word Choices   292
    Level of Diction   *292*
    EXERCISE 9–6   *296*
    EXERCISES 9–7 THROUGH 9–11   *298*
    Tropes   *300*
    EXERCISES 9–12 AND 9–13   *302*
    EXERCISES 9–14 AND 9–15   *305*
Readings   306
    "War and Reason," William James   *306*
    "Sculptures in Snow," Lewis Lapham   *310*
Suggestions for Writing and Further Discussion   313

10   *Readings for Further Discussion*   315

Voting   316
    "Let's Not Get Out the Vote," Robert E. Coulson   *316*
    "For Compulsory Voting," Alan Wertheimer   *319*
    "Throw the Rascals Out," Meg Greenfield   *320*
Censorship   322
    "Pornography, Obscenity, and the Case for Censorship,"
      Irving Kristol   *322*
    "Defending Intellectual Freedom," Eli M. Oboler   *325*
    "Censorship and Its Aftermath," Nadine Gordimer   *327*
AIDS Testing   329
    "We Need Routine Testing for AIDS," William J. Bennett   *329*
    "AIDS: The Legal Epidemic," Arthur S. Leonard   *332*
    "How *Not* to Control the AIDS Epidemic," Mathilde Krim   *336*
Christianity   339
    "Why I Am an Agnostic," Clarence Darrow   *339*
    "What Are We to Make of Jesus Christ?" C. S. Lewis   *344*
Women's Roles   347
    "The Case for Equality," Caroline Bird   *347*
    "Paid Homemaking: An Idea in Search of a Policy,"
      William J. Byron, S. J.   *351*

Minorities' Rights   *357*

    "A Call for Unity," Members of the Birmingham Clergy   *357*

    "Letter from Birmingham Jail," Martin Luther King, Jr.   *358*

The Middle East   *367*

    "Sharing the Land and the Legacy," Rami Khouri   *367*

    "Maps of Revenge," Meron Benvenisti   *370*

Selected References   *373*

Acknowledgments   *377*

Index   *381*

Preface

Some years ago the idea for this book arose out of the interest and encouragement of three people. First, when I was a graduate student, Professor M. L. Lawhon taught me how to teach argument to my composition students, and the value of doing so. Later, my colleague William R. Barr urged me to write a book to fill what was then a near-total void in the field. Finally, Philip Miller of Prentice Hall believed in the concept and the book at a time when other publishers thought there was no interest in and no market for argument texts.

In the last decade these three all have been proven right. As composition instructors have discovered what the study of argument can do for students' writing and critical thinking, enthusiasm for this approach to composition has grown most gratifyingly. Many colleagues now share the conviction that practice in argumentative writing and critical reasoning gives students writing and reasoning skills they need both in college and beyond.

With all this enthusiasm for teaching argument, we can lose sight of our first aims and find ourselves teaching "informal logic" courses. But we must not. Our objective is that students become more confident and able *writers,* that they learn how to plan, develop, and revise a written argument. This book aims to keep the focus on writing and on evaluating written arguments. To strengthen that focus, in the third edition the chapters have been reordered so that they more closely follow the writing process: from creating arguments to developing them more fully, testing their soundness, and revising them.

What else is new in this edition? First, boxes summarizing key information make important points easier to remember. Second, the text has been simplified throughout. Third, many new examples and exercises and additional student passages and essays provide "user-friendly" illustrations of each chapter's concerns. Throughout the book new readings cover important ideas ranging from personal issues to global concerns. This book includes enough readings (more than forty) to provide plenty of choices and flexibility for instructors, but not so many that it loses its primary focus as an argumentative writing text.

The Power to Persuade can be used by instructors who prefer the traditional rhetorical terms first applied by Aristotle more than two thousand years ago, or by instructors who prefer the terminology developed by British philosopher Stephen Toulmin in the 1950s. The two are not antithetical. Toulmin did not propose a non-Aristotelian logic; he aimed to simplify the language and to emphasize the probable, rather than certain, nature of rhetorical argument. (In this, Toulmin follows Aristotle's discussion of the enthymeme in the *Rhetoric*.) The fundamental concepts are the same; the labels are different, and instructors can use the labels they prefer in a course that includes this book. My aim has been to use relatively little technical language while still providing students with the tools they need to evaluate their own and others' arguments.

Chapter 1, "Argument and Persuasion," offers students the basic tools they need to begin writing arguments. It distinguishes argument that is only persuasive from argument that is genuinely convincing. It offers a nontechnical introduction to the concerns of argument: how relationships between ideas make up arguments; how assumptions underlie arguments; how language limits, defines, and slants arguments; and how logical, emotional, and ethical elements imbue arguments.

Next, Chapter 2, "Creating Arguments," shows students how to develop argumentative theses they can support. It focuses on the importance of thinking about audience and purpose. The chapter offers specific advice on three key invention strategies, with plenty of illustrations and examples.

Once a working thesis is planned, the next two chapters help writers find ways to develop arguments fully. Chapter 3, "Developing Arguments: Defining Terms," shows students not only how to define key terms but also how to evaluate definitions. It discusses the two primary roles definition plays in argument, and how to use definitions appropriately to fulfill those roles. Then Chapter 4, "Developing Arguments: Finding and Evaluating Evidence," shows students how to find material beyond their own life experiences with which to support their claims. It includes a new section on personal research through polling and other means, updated lists of helpful computer databases, and current print resources listed according to how frequently they are updated. One section explains in some detail how to incorporate evidence and quotations into students' own arguments.

Once a written argument begins to take shape, students need skills with which to evaluate the soundness of their reasoning. If they understand what makes an argument sound, they can adjust faulty support or illogically organized arguments. They may even find that they have to rethink their conclusions. Chapters 5 through 7 address these concerns. Chapter 5, "Testing Arguments: Inductive Reasoning," explains through examples and simple analysis how analogy, cause-effect reasoning, and examples function in sound arguments. Chapter 6, "Testing Arguments: Deductive Reasoning," is much shortened and simplified from the second edition, while still showing student writers how to draw connections logically and how to construct if/then and either/or arguments that will carry conviction. This chapter includes a section on "Toulmin's Corrective" to the certitude of formal logic. Last, Chapter 7, "Testing Arguments: Fallacies," is greatly simplified from the second edition. Just fourteen of the most common fallacies of reasoning are described, in two groups: fallacies we most commonly commit when we construct arguments, and fallacies we most commonly commit when we refute others' arguments. The emphasis is on understanding the errors in reasoning rather than on merely assigning labels to fallacies.

The next part of the text focuses on what is for many student writers the hardest part of the writing enterprise: revising and finishing written arguments. These two chapters have been reorganized and simplified to make them more appropriate for beginning writing students. The chapters now include lists of questions students can ask to help them revise their essays, along with boxes summarizing key points. Chapter 8, "Revising Arguments: Completeness and Coherence," offers students specific suggestions for completing key parts of their essays and for revising paragraphs and sentences to achieve unity and coherence throughout. Many examples, particularly student examples, have been added to this chapter. Next, Chapter 9, "Revising Arguments: The Power of Style," now addresses the stylistic needs of the beginning writer rather than only those of more advanced students. The major concerns of the chapter are sentence style and word choices. Again, new examples and exercises have been added throughout.

Chapter 10, "Readings for Further Discussion," includes essays with particular (and varied) strengths in argument or persuasion or both. Because several of these essays are relatively long and complex, they can provide a fitting final unit to a course in critical thinking and argumentative writing. What better way to end a course in argumentative writing, after all, than with King's "Letter from Birmingham Jail"? The essays also can be used with earlier chapters: For example, C. S. Lewis's "What Are We to Make of Jesus Christ?" illustrates the *a priori* ideas discussed in Chapter 1. Meron Benvenisti's "Maps of Revenge" shows the power of style that Chapter 9 describes. If students are intrigued by Linda Waddle's argument, "If It Isn't Censorship, What Is It?" in Chapter 3, they can turn to more arguments on the subject in Chapter 10. The Instructor's Guide suggests applications to earlier chapters for each essay in Chapter 10.

The Instructor's Guide for this book is not just an "answer book." It includes teaching suggestions, rhetorical analyses of essays in each chapter, biographical notes on the authors of readings, and additional references and materials for classroom or instructor's use. With the graduate teaching fellow or new instructor in mind, it does suggest approaches to the exercises and the discussion questions following each reading. One aim of the Instructor's Guide is to anticipate writing and reasoning issues that are likely to arise as students work through the material. The Guide not only suggests ideas for integrating readings into the concerns of each chapter, but also identifies outside readings and other materials that can provide additional material for student discussion and writing. It includes a number of supplementary exercises and discussion questions as well. The Instructor's Guide can be further supplemented, at no charge to adopters of *The Power to Persuade*, by the ABC News/Prentice Hall Video Library for Composition and the *New York Times* Supplement for Writing.

I began by naming three people to whom I am grateful in connection with this enterprise that now enters its third edition. Those three begin the list of my indebtedness, but they by no means exhaust it. No mere mention in a preface can adequately discharge the debt I owe to several people: to Alison Reeves, Executive Editor in English at Prentice Hall, who enlisted the help and hard work of the wonderful people whose names follow here, and who saw this project to fruition; to Joyce Perkins, a gifted developmental editor; to Peggy Gordon of P. M. Gordon Associates, Inc., a talented and keen-eyed production editor. Heartfelt thanks to each of them. I owe as well particular thanks to developmental editor Leslie Taggert, who inspired many of the changes in and additions to this edition.

I am also most grateful to the many students, both named and anonymous, whose hard work and willing revisions provided many of the writing samples in this book. Graduate student Phyllis Lambert was particularly helpful as my research assistant, and I thank her for her long and late hours at the library. The reviewers for this third edition provided many helpful suggestions: Elizabeth Novinger, Tallahassee Community College; Eugene Hollahan, Georgia State University; and Pam Pittman, University of Central Oklahoma.

Finally, Bob, Alice Ann, and Steve Spurgin, and Hester and Bill De Witt once again showed me—as I worked for two years on this project—that the love and support of family are the greatest treasures on earth. Of that I am not only persuaded, but convinced.

THE POWER
TO PERSUADE

1

Argument and Persuasion

> [T]he most obvious truth about rhetoric is that its object is the whole man. It presents its arguments first to the rational part of man, because rhetorical discourses, if they are honestly conceived, always have a basis in reasoning. Logical argument is the plot, as it were, of any speech or composition that is designed to persuade. Yet it is the very characterizing feature of rhetoric that it goes beyond this and appeals to other parts of man's constitution, especially to his nature as a pathetic being, that is, a being feeling and suffering. A speech intended to persuade achieves little unless it takes into account how men are reacting subjectively to their hopes and fears and their special circumstances.
>
> —**Richard M. Weaver**

To many people *argument* connotes unpleasantness: quarrels and disagreement, raised voices and smashed vases. But just as *rhetoric* meant simply "the art of persuasion" long before the word acquired connotations of political doubletalk and empty verbal flourishes, so *argument* (as we will use the term) leads not to discord but ideally to harmony. In the rhetorical art of persuasion, an **argument** is supposed to be a reasoned consideration of an idea. It is through argument that we try to make sense of what we don't understand, try to refute ideas we believe are mistaken, try to determine appropriate policy for future actions. Rhetorical argument is—or at least, should be—the search for truth.

While *argument* as we will use the term does not mean *quarrel*, it does imply the existence of misunderstanding or disagreement. We do not argue about things that can be verified readily or that are true by definition; we do not argue that 24 plus 17 equals 41, that the return of Halley's comet was first predicted in 1682, that St. Paul is the capital of Minnesota. People may *quarrel* about such things, of course, when their memories of experiences differ, but such disagreements are pointless. They may be resolved simply by consulting an encyclopedia, an almanac, or any other appropriate authority. The issues of rhetorical arguments may not be resolved so easily, for there is likely to be more than one possible way of treating the question, and often more than one plausible answer. Was Kennedy responsible for initial U.S. involvement in Vietnam, or was it really Eisenhower? Can the Social Security program be saved? Should Ellen accept the job offer in Kansas City or the one in San Diego? Is there life elsewhere in the universe?

Just as the possibility for doubt or disagreement must exist to warrant argument, so the arguer must want to search for an answer or to persuade the reader or listener, although persuasion and argument are not quite the same thing. To **argue** is to make a case for a judgment or opinion, while to **persuade** is to bring about a desired response in a reader or listener. The difference is that argument is logical; persuasion, psychological. This book will consider some of the psychological elements of persuasion as well as the logical: style, fallacies, and the persuasive power of the **persona** (the image the arguer creates of himself or herself).

The Ethics of Persuasion

Because persuasion can work by fair means or foul, by fallacious and manipulative appeals as well as by logical and just appeals, we must consider the problem of ethics that persuasion raises. If we study persuasion, do we not show the unscrupulous how better to manipulate their audiences?

Even among the scrupulous, opinions regarding what is ethical and relevant in argument may differ. In *The School of Athens,* Raphael illustrates the ethical dilemma the study of persuasion creates. In the center of the painting stand Plato and Aristotle, debating; Plato points heavenward, toward the realm of ideas, while Aristotle's hand gestures out toward the world of men and women (including a number of renowned philosophers and scientists) below them. In these gestures Raphael has captured the essential difference between the two thinkers: Plato advocates the pursuit of the True in an Ideal world; Aristotle advocates the pursuit of truth in the world of human beings. Neither man, the viewer notes, seems by his stance or expression to be winning the debate. Raphael has depicted Plato and Aristotle as equally in the right.

And so they are: Unadorned truth should be sought and accepted on its merits alone, as Plato would have it; in the real world, however, persuasive skills can work even without the support of truth, as Aristotle recognizes. Even Plato acknowledges this dimension of argument in words he ascribes to Socrates in the *Phaedrus* (Jowett trans.):

> Whatever my advice may be worth, I should have told him to arrive at the truth first, and then come to me. At the same time I boldly assert that mere knowledge of the truth will not give you the art of persuasion.

Knowledge of the truth does not seem "mere" to most of us, of course, but we probably agree that truth alone is all too often not sufficient to persuade. We hope

that our arguments are persuasive, but we cannot guarantee it. And we hope that we are persuaded only by sound arguments, but we suspect differently. There are forms of persuasion beyond logic, as every consumer of shampoo, deodorant, or detergent, and every person ever intimidated by a large bully or a determined aunt, well know.

We should not infer, of course, that all nonlogical appeals are without merit. People arrange to donate organs after death out of pity for those in need of livers, kidneys, or corneas. We give toys and roast turkeys to poor families at Christmas in response to perfectly valid appeals to our emotions. But we could all testify also to the abundance of persuaders who distort or abandon the truth and yet enjoy tremendous success in persuading the rest of us to do what they wish: buy their product or their swampland, vote for them, overlook their misdeeds, and otherwise behave as they want us to. These people have mastered the art of persuasion but have failed to assimilate a system of ethics that makes the truth the basis for persuasion.

As you study argument and persuasion, you will necessarily consider ethical issues. Argument requires value judgments: Is what is argued true or false, good or bad, effective or ineffective, practical or impractical? And, if value judgments are made, a system of values must precede and inform those judgments. In later chapters you will study the ways in which fallacious arguments are developed: What is to prevent you from deliberately employing fallacious arguments yourself? If your persuasive aim is a good one, might not any means to that end be justifiable? For that matter, who is to say that deliberate fallacies, simply because they are illogical, are also unethical? You will need to consider all these ethical questions.

The Need for Argument

If all ideas have equal merit, there is no need for argument. In that case, your assertion that Puerto Rico should be made the fifty-first state and your cousin's assertion that even its status as a territory should be taken away are equally true and acceptable ideas. But, in the real world, such is fortunately not the case, for how chaotic life then would be! We care about our ideas and we want other people at least to understand them, if not to accept them. Issues come in black, white, shades of gray—and a number of other colors. Opinions on those issues are just as varied as the issues themselves and are not all of equal value or merit. We *can* assert opinions and construct arguments to back them up. And we should try to make sense, to search for truth, in doing so.

We look for the truth not only in the explicit statements of argument but also in the unspoken assumptions that the arguer makes about the audience, the subject, and the relationship of the two to each other and to the arguer. For example, consider the argument, "Taking swimming lessons is a waste of time and money; don't do it." The arguer assumes, among other things, that the hearer or reader considers time and money important (and more important than future safety on the water), that learning how to swim is not an essential skill, or that swimming can be learned without lessons. Some of these assumptions are questionable; their truth may be challenged.

All arguers also reflect in their arguments assumptions about the nature of the world and of life itself. They may have a particular religious faith or philosophy of life, for instance, that informs and colors the premises of their arguments. Such assumptions are nonlogical; their truth is taken on faith by those who hold them. We call these assumptions **a priori** (in Latin, "before the fact") **premises.** Writers need to consider their own and their readers' *a priori* beliefs in choosing their line of reasoning. In attempting to persuade an agnostic that abortion is not an acceptable form of birth control, for instance, a Christian or Jew should not limit arguments to appeals to Biblical authority. Otherwise, the arguments are likely to fall on deaf ears and the discussion will be sidetracked to the one individual's *a priori* acceptance of Biblical authority and the other individual's *a priori* rejection of it.

Therefore, while the need for argument is real, some values must be shared between writer and reader, arguer and audience, if argument is to reveal truth and resolve disagreement. *A priori* beliefs are rarely fruitful subjects of argument because they are outside the realm of reason. The strained relationships between culturally or politically dissimilar nations—as seen in Iraqi and American confrontations in the Middle East and in competing Chinese and Taiwanese claims to represent all the Chinese people—illustrate the difficulty of arguing any issue concerning which *a priori* premises differ. Even individuals living side by side may find that they have *a priori* differences: One believes that a clean house or dormitory room is a sure sign of a misspent life, while the other is just as certain that cleanliness is at least next to godliness, if not greater.

Nor are matters of personal taste profitable subjects of argument. One person may prefer the color yellow to pink, American primitive furniture to Danish modern, chocolate to butterscotch. Another person may have entirely different tastes. Neither is likely to have logical grounds for those preferences, and neither is "wrong."

All the same, some matters of personal opinion can be argued. If *a priori* standards of value and judgment are shared, even questions of esthetics are arguable. After all, the conclusion to any argument is a statement of opinion, a judgment. But how often have you heard people say, "Of course, that's just my opinion"? Some people act as if such a disclaimer absolves them from any need to offer reasons for their assertion. They seem to think that all opinions have the same—little—worth. Not so. Reasoned opinions have merit, and the opinions of experts speaking in their fields have particular merit.

Appropriate subjects of argument are many, and range from the merits of a musical composition to the best plan for economic stability in a nation. We may argue our reasons for moving to Buffalo or for buying a Chevrolet instead of an import. We may argue about the past (What really happened? What was important? What factors contributed to our subject issue or event?), the present (What is the present state of our subject? What is its value? What are its proper functions?), or the future (What should we do? What will our subject be like in the future? What will be the consequences of our subject?). We may argue about the abstract, wrestling with philosophical and imaginative problems; or we may argue about the concrete—advocating, for example, that a stoplight be installed at the corner of Maple and Thornton streets. We all have opinions regarding all kinds of subjects—about some of which we have expert knowledge, about many of which we do not—and those opinions need only to be supported by sound argument to merit a hearing.

RELATIONSHIPS IN ARGUMENT

But what constitutes sound argument? Indeed, what constitutes argument of any kind? To begin with the second question, **all argument centers on the relationships between ideas or observations.** That is, an argument does more than offer an opinion; it gives reasons for that opinion. An argument is a statement of opinion or judgment (also called an **assertion**) offered together with at least one other statement that supports it. The statement of opinion or judgment toward which the argument moves is the **conclusion** or **claim.** Statements offered in support of the conclusion are called **premises** or **grounds.** If the relationships drawn between the grounds and the claim are clear, consistent, and complete, we say that the argument is a sound one. Its statements are all true, and they are related to each other in a logical way.

An assertion unrelated to supporting grounds does not constitute argument of any kind, either sound or unsound. If I say, "It will rain later today," I have offered an assertion but not an argument. You may nod sagely and say, "You're probably right"; you may simply disagree with a brusque "I doubt it" or "No, it won't"; or you may disagree and also offer an argument in support of your own conclusion: "No, it won't rain. Those are high clouds, and the humidity is low. Besides, the weather forecast mentioned no chance of rain until Thursday." But even if your imagination races on to consider all the reasons why I might have offered such an assertion (perhaps, like the White Queen in Looking-Glass Land, I have resolved to believe six impossible things every morning before breakfast), my single claim, without support, is an assertion—not an argument—until I express at least one of those reasons.

An assertion is arguable if it can be supported by reasons or evidence. It is not arguable if it is simply a statement of personal taste or a verifiable report. Given that distinction, determine which of the following propositions are arguable assertions.

1. I like pistachio pudding.
2. The board of directors will meet next Thursday.
3. The situation in the Middle East is not resolvable by Western intervention.
4. Margaret dislikes the color red.
5. Spiders are not insects.
6. Every college needs a career-counseling office.

Sentences 2, 4, and 5 purport to be reports, not expressions of opinion, and as such are in principle verifiable, not arguable. They are "statements of fact," even if the facts are in error. The board of directors actually may be scheduled to meet on Friday, not Thursday, but I could check with the chairperson's secretary to verify the day. Sentence 4 is tricky, because it looks like an unarguable opinion. Nevertheless, while Margaret's own assertion, "I dislike the color red," would be an unarguable personal opinion, the statement "Margaret dislikes the color red" is a *report* of that opinion. Sentence 5 is true by definition. Scientists long ago decided that spiders, having eight legs rather than six, require a separate category in the animal kingdom. Despite the capitulation of some dictionaries, spiders are arachnids, not true insects. The other statements in the list are assertions; they express opinions.

Statements do not become part of an argument until they are related to other ideas. Suppose we say,

> Harry, worthless bum though he may be, is a citizen of this country. He ought to get out of his lawn chair and go to the polls.

Here we have inferred a relationship between citizens in general, Harry in particular, and the act of voting. The proposition "All citizens should be legally obligated to vote" has become an implicit premise that, together with the stated premise that Harry is a citizen, supports a conclusion about what Harry ought to do. Together they constitute an argument.

An ordinary sentence can become either a claim or grounds for a claim when we begin to relate it to other statements. Take the statement, "All citizens should be legally obligated to vote." That sentence could be a premise in a variation of the argument about Harry:

> All citizens should be legally obligated to vote. Therefore, Harry should be legally obligated to vote.

And if other relationships were being examined, "All citizens should be legally obligated to vote" might appear as a conclusion:

> Because voting is a right of all citizens and an important responsibility, citizens should be legally obligated to vote.

In both cases, relationships between three things are under examination: voting, citizens' rights and responsibilities, and legal obligations. These components of statements are called **classes**. A class is a unit of things or ideas considered together. "Citizens" is a class, clearly enough. So is "important responsibilities." Less obviously, "Citizens' rights and responsibilities" is a single class—a class of all things pertaining to citizens' rights *and* to their responsibilities. From the relationships drawn among the three classes in the arguments about voting, we infer a conclusion. Examining relationships and inferring conclusions about those relationships is the process of argument.

Verbal Signals of Argument

In order to understand and evaluate arguments fully, we must be able to recognize arguments readily and distinguish premises from conclusions. To do so, we rely on common sense and on transitional words and phrases that signal logical relationships. We begin by looking for the writer's claims, both large and small. If the claims are supported by reasons and evidence, we have found arguments to evaluate, to accept or reject. A single paragraph may contain several supporting arguments, with the conclusions to minor arguments functioning as support for the paragraph's main argument. If a claim makes what seems to be the main point of the entire essay, article, or presentation, we have located the thesis. The **thesis** is the controlling concept in the essay and the conclusion to its principal argument. (The next chapter centers on developing workable theses for your own written arguments.)

Claims—conclusions to arguments—may appear before, after, or between supporting statements. Usually writers give verbal signals, but at times you must simply depend on the meaning to determine what is a claim and what is support. In all three of the earlier arguments about voting, the conclusion appears last, but the first argument provides no signal word to identify either claim or support. The second contains the typical conclusion-signal *therefore*. The third includes a premise-signal, *because*. When you write arguments, usually you will include such signals to make your meaning clear to your reader.

Verbal signals that conclusions follow include words and phrases such as:

therefore	consequently	accordingly
hence	as a result	in conclusion
then	thus	so

Verbal signals that premises follow include:

since   because   if   given that

You should bear in mind three notes of caution about verbal signals of argument:

- **Signals of argument must be earned.** A causal relationship must exist between two statements before a *therefore* can link them. The verbal connector does not *create* the logical connection; it calls attention to a logical connection that already exists.
- **Verbal signals are not completely interchangeable.** There can be major or minor differences in meaning. *Accordingly* and *consequently*, for example, signal slightly different kinds of relationships. Be as precise as possible in the verbal signals you choose.
- **What may appear to be verbal signals of argument occasionally may be no such thing.** *Because* can preface an explanation rather than an argument: "He came because I asked him." *Since* can indicate simple chronology: "We have been playing croquet ever since our friends arrived."

Verbal signals are invaluable to both writer and reader, but they must be understood accurately in the contexts in which they are used.

EXERCISE 1–1

Using your common sense about relationships between ideas and statements, locate the conclusions in the following arguments. Underline any conclusion-signals.

1. I don't care if you don't like the name. I'm serving Watergate cake for dessert because I like the pistachio pudding that goes with it. So there.
2. The board of directors will meet next Thursday, and I always find its meetings dreadfully dull. Accordingly, I will plan to be out of town that day.
3. Westerners fail to understand the Middle Eastern mindset, mores, or even the Muslim religion. They also fail to understand Middle Eastern distaste for outsiders' intervening in internal political affairs, despite protests to the contrary by some Christian Lebanese leaders. Consequently, it seems likely that the situation in the Middle East is not resolvable by Western intervention.

4. Margaret is bound to dislike the color red. She hates all bright colors.
5. Spiders look like insects, but they have eight legs—so they can't be insects.
6. The reputation of a college is enhanced if its graduates readily find good jobs in their fields. Therefore, every college—no matter how small—needs a career-counseling office.

Assumptions

In the three arguments about voting presented earlier, one statement relating two of the three classes is implied but not stated. It is an **assumption** made by the arguer about the subject at hand. We tend to assume, rather than state, those parts of arguments that seem to us self-evident or sure to be familiar to and accepted by our audience. Often we are right to leave unstated those obvious relationships among the terms of our argument: How boring and long-winded we would seem were we always to spell out every assumption underlying and justifying our arguments. Instead of saying only that "Harry, worthless bum though he may be, is a citizen and, as such, ought to vote," our full argument would go something like this:

All citizens ought to vote.	(implied premise)
Harry is a citizen.	(stated premise)
Therefore, Harry ought to vote.	(conclusion)

The implied premise is obvious enough. And the second argument—"All citizens should be legally obligated to vote. Therefore, Harry should be legally obligated to vote"—holds an even more obvious assumption: "Harry is a citizen." The full argument could be spelled out in this way:

All citizens should be legally obligated to vote.	(stated premise)
Harry is a citizen.	(implied premise)
Therefore, Harry should be legally obligated to vote.	(conclusion)

We hardly need to have all that spelled out in order to understand and respond to the argument.

But the third argument, which draws a conclusion identical in meaning to a premise in the argument just above, shows the importance of paying attention to the assumptions that link terms together in argument. When we say, "Because voting is a right of all citizens and an important responsibility, citizens should be legally obligated to vote," we are assuming that what is a right should also be a legal obligation. But is it fair to bury that claim as an unstated assumption? Hardly. It warrants argument itself. When we set out the full argument,

Rights of all citizens should also be their legal duties.	(implied premise)
Voting is a right of all citizens.	(stated premise)
Therefore, voting should be a legal duty of all citizens.	(conclusion)

we can better examine both the truth of the implicit and explicit claims of the argument and the logical relationships among the terms of the argument. How to evaluate the truth of premises will be our concern in Chapter 4; how to evaluate the logical relationships in the argument—the ways premises are related to conclusions—will be our chief concern in Chapters 5 and 6. In the meantime, watch those assumptions, both in your own arguments and in those you read. If there is a weakness in an argument, more often than not it lies buried in what is assumed by the arguer.

EXERCISE 1–2

All of these sentences and passages make—or imply—claims, and all of them reflect the writers' assumptions about their subjects and perhaps about their readers. Identify the assumptions underlying each passage. Be careful to focus on the writers' assumptions, not your own.

1. The feminist movement is over, because equality has been achieved.
   —Student essay

2. Fuel economy has been mandated, but won't smaller, lighter cars lead to more traffic deaths?

3. Computer keyboards are laid out like typewriter keyboards, so people who can type can use a computer successfully.

4. More energy is required to recycle coated paper cups than styrofoam cups, so our company was wrong to stop buying the latter in favor of the former.

5. The results of a prototype math test, released in early June, showed that 54 percent of high-school seniors couldn't do seventh-grade math. Only 5 percent were truly ready for college. . . . [However,] 81 percent of college freshmen had a B average or better in high school.
   —Robert J. Samuelson, "The School Reform Fraud"

6. The great danger is not that Americans may make too little of history but that they will make too much of it. In politics, dubious policies have a far easier chance of winning public support when they are defended on historical grounds. Support for the decision to go into Vietnam, for instance, was considerably strengthened when it was explained that fighting communism in Asia was analogous to fighting Nazism in Europe.
   —Richard Shenkman, *I Love Paul Revere,*
   Whether He Rode or Not

7. [I]t is perhaps unsurprising that whereas FBI statistics indicate that about half of America's murders are committed by blacks, in TV-land the proportion is around 3 percent. Instead, 90% of TV murderers are white, with seven out of ten from "a generic northern European background." But why does one out of every four TV Hispanics commit a crime, including twice as many murders as any other identified ethnicity?
   Which is still better than businessmen. Although they make up only about 8% of TV characters, businessmen are responsible for about a fifth of all

TV crimes and a third of the murders—considerably more murders, in fact, than TV's professional criminals. And an extraordinary one in three of the crimes committed by TV businessmen are violent.

—Peter Brimelow, "TV's Killer Businessmen"

8. Did you know that, according to the National Science Teachers Association, the standard high school gym can accommodate about 200 science fair projects? Did you know that 199 of them are likely to be volcanoes? Did you know that out of 89 Nobel Prize and Medal of Science winners recently polled on the subject, only two had taken first place at a science fair?

—Judith Stone, "Under the Volcano"

9. I remember being summoned by the assistant housemaster at The Lawrenceville School in New Jersey. In his eloquent Scottish accent he began, "It is the opinion of the housemasters that you are involved in so many activities at Lawrenceville because you want to prove that black people are as good as white people. That is not in the spirit of the prize." He was referring to the fourth-form prize for scholarship and citizenship, and explaining why I had been passed over, despite my high grades, honors, and activities in sports, the glee club, newspaper, and drama club.

—Marcus Mabry, "The Bounds of Blackness"

Limiting Arguments with Qualifiers

The relationships among parts of an argument are also affected by the degree of certainty expressed in the premises and conclusions. We cannot push a tentative premise or a limited one to a sweeping conclusion. With that point in mind, it's easy enough to see which of the following arguments is more acceptable logically:

> Utility stocks usually perform well, so you are sure to make money if you invest in Tennessee Utilities.

> Utility stocks usually perform well, so you stand a fair chance of making money if you invest in Tennessee Utilities.

Both arguments use the same premise to reach their conclusions, but the second conclusion is clearly more sound than the first—and all because of the degree of certainty claimed. Adverbs and adjectives such as *usually, often, never, many, a few, some,* and the like are **qualifiers:** that is, they limit the extent of the claim a statement makes. In the arguments above, the qualifier *usually* in the premise automatically limits the degree of certainty we can claim in the conclusion; the first conclusion is too sweeping ("sure to") and the second is more appropriately qualified ("a fair chance").

Now, there is such a thing as too much caution in qualifying arguments, although that is a problem we see less often than unwarranted boldness. An arguer with strong premises should not draw a conclusion weaker than it need be just to prevent a challenge. It would be silly to argue,

Utility stocks usually perform well, so you may or may not make money if you invest in Tennessee Utilities.

How could that argument help a potential investor make a decision? Such pointless caution trivializes an argument.

A good rule of thumb as you write is to make your premises as strong as you can support—and your conclusion as qualified or as emphatic as your premises warrant. And as you *read*, check to make sure that arguments are appropriately qualified. Arguments should be stated as firmly as reason and evidence permit, but they must not press further.

EXERCISE 1–3

Look for qualifiers in these passages. Decide whether the claims and supporting reasons are modified appropriately or inappropriately. Change those that are too sweeping or too tentative to appropriately qualified statements.

1. Many cases of asthma develop because of severe allergies, so we can eliminate asthma by aggressively treating allergies and their symptoms.
2. Preferential admissions of minority group members to colleges and universities is discriminatory. Because discrimination is wrong, such preferential admissions must be eliminated.
3. Gallup polls have shown that single, childless people tend to be more liberal politically than are married people with children. Your friends are mostly single and childless, so they are probably liberal in their political thinking.
4. "Videophones" are now commercially available. With them people can see as well as hear the party with whom they are speaking on the telephone. But videophones are very expensive—about $3,000 initially—and are useless except in communication with other videophones. The picture quality is poor and the video image arrives several seconds *after* the words do, making conversations hopelessly out of sync. Moreover, many people do not want to be seen as well as heard over the telephone. The concept may fail commercially.
5. In a 1991 study of just over 100 Michigan high school valedictorians and salutatorians from a decade earlier, researchers found that only one in four had achieved substantial career success. A stronger indicator of future success turned out to be participation in at least two extracurricular activities during high school. Evidently, high school students would do better to sign up for yearbook staff and student council than calculus and honors chemistry.
6. Gabriel is from Mexico, so he must speak Spanish.
7. Gabriel is from Mexico, so he must be Catholic.
8. People who pledge fraternities tend not to be environmental activists, so it is unlikely that Philip—who is president of the local chapter of Greenpeace—is a member of a fraternity.
9. Majors in the hard sciences are tougher than majors in the humanities, so hardly anyone is attracted to majoring in chemistry, physics, and the like.

However, jobs in the hard sciences are abundant, and jobs for humanities majors are scarce. So students who take the long view will major in one of the hard sciences.

10. The trouble with environmental questions is that they do not yield to simplistic answers. Banning styrofoam cups will not remedy the landfill crisis. Mandating an end to freon use will not preserve the ozone layer. We cannot legislate "magic bullet" solutions.

EXERCISE 1–4

Do the following arguments offer reasonable support for their claims? Do they make fair assumptions? Discuss the strengths or weaknesses of the arguments. (Try not to be affected by your personal feelings, if any, about the issues on which they center.)

1. Executions are counterproductive. They are not a deterrent and actually cause more killing. The state and our leaders are role models for our behavior. When they use killing to solve society's problems, they make it easier for us to kill our neighbors.

   For every execution, we probably promote three or more murders. Society comes down to the lowest level of the murderer when we kill. We should try to raise civilization a few notches instead of going to the lowest level.
   —Letter to *Dallas Morning News,* 17 July 1991

2. [T]he worst thing that happened to Bill Clinton in the [1992] Democratic presidential primaries was not being hit with allegations of cheating on Hillary [his wife] and dodging the draft. Nope, the worst thing was the consequence of those allegations, both of which Clinton denies, both of which everybody else believes to be true. But don't jump to the wrong conclusion. The consequence I'm referring to isn't the spate of polls showing that a huge chunk of Democrats and a solid majority of overall voters think Clinton lacks the honesty and integrity to be President. I'm referring to something more specific: the South. The allegations all but wiped out Clinton's chance to win a Southern state outside Arkansas—and made Arkansas iffy. And since a Democrat has to win some Southern states to capture the presidency, Clinton is practically a goner.
   —Fred Barnes, rev. of Earl Black and Merle Black,
   The Vital South: How Presidents Are Elected

3. As long as the media refuse to look at AIDS on a worldwide scale, heterosexuals will continue to feel they are not at risk. Your graphics show that only 5.7 percent of reported AIDS cases in America resulted from heterosexual transmission. Worldwide, however, 75 percent of AIDS cases have been transmitted heterosexually, and in some areas of central Africa one-third of the people are infected with HIV. Looking in that mirror to see our future should scare the hell out of all of us in this country.
   —Letter to *Newsweek,* Nov. 1991

4. [I]t would be a simple matter to get rid of organized crime if we wanted to. All we would need to do is make legal all of the illegal services that mobsters provide. That would not only eliminate—by definition—the "crimes," say of prostitution and gambling, but also the necessity of making the invidious payoffs that mobsters make to police and politicians, payoffs that corrupt the system. Organized crime only appeared in the United States when the big cities in the middle of the nineteenth century began establishing police departments. Before there were police departments there was no one to pay off. This removed an essential ingredient in the recipe for syndicated crime.

—Richard Shenkman, *I Love Paul Revere,*
Whether He Rode or Not

The U.S. decision to drop two atomic bombs on Japan during World War II saved Japanese lives and deterred the outbreak of subsequent wars. It saved lives because it forestalled an American invasion that was anticipated to cost hundreds of thousands of lives on both sides. It deterred the outbreak of subsequent wars because the stakes became too high with the advent of the atomic bomb.

LOGIC, EMOTION, AND *ETHOS* IN ARGUMENT

Argument consists not only of what you say and how you say it, but also of what you imply or omit. And arguments must offer more than dry logic formulas, for they are developed and presented not in a vacuum but among people with varying knowledge and biases. In fact, argument is at least three-dimensional and, in a sense, four-dimensional. The dimensions of argument are the **logical appeal,** the **emotional appeal,** and the **ethical appeal;** and, since argument is couched in words, its fourth dimension, on which the others depend, is the verbal—the words we choose and how we arrange them. All are essential to argument that is both persuasive and convincing.

The Logical Appeal

We often think of the logical appeal as preeminent. It concerns relationships among statements and ideas, as discussed above and, more specifically, in Chapters 5 and 6. But much of what we will discuss in those chapters is already part of your reasoning skills: what we unglamorously call "common sense." You already are able to ask questions such as these of arguments you read and hear:

Is there evidence? Is there enough? Is it believable?

What are the assumptions and implications? Are they fair?

Does this conclusion follow reasonably from the premises offered in support of it?

And you should ask such questions, not only of others' arguments, but also of your own as you revise and work on them. For without a sound logical foundation, the most eloquent and vivid language will not make an argument acceptable to a discerning audience.

Logical appeals abound in professional journals, newspaper editorial pages, and well-written arguments of all kinds. How do you know one when you see one? The argument will avoid inflamed language, and it will carefully connect its claims to supporting reasons and evidence. Here, for example, is the first sentence of a New Hampshire Supreme Court opinion:

> This is a domestic relations case in which the Trial Court (*King,* J.) transferred four questions that raise the issue of whether a stepparent has a duty to support his step-children to the same extent as his natural children, and if so, whether evidence of such support and evidence of the ability of others owing a duty to support the same children can be introduced in a support modification hearing.

In this sentence Justice Brock of the New Hampshire Supreme Court establishes the logical framework for his analysis: Either A or not-A; and if A, either B or not-B. Either a stepparent is obligated to support stepchildren to the same extent as natural children or he is not. The New Hampshire legislature has determined that a stepparent *is* obligated to support stepchildren to the same extent as natural children. And if a stepparent is so obligated, it must follow that such financial obligations can be considered in a support modification hearing.

The argument is logical.

Of course, the logical appeal is not restricted to judicial opinions, philosophical treatises, or the *New York Times.* Here are some everyday arguments that rely on the logical appeal just as much as any judicial opinion does:

> If Miriam takes two more science courses, she will meet the final requirements she lacks for admission to medical school. If she meets the requirements for admission to medical school, she will surely enroll. So, if Miriam takes two more science courses, she'll enroll in medical school.

> Because taxol has been granted FDA approval for use in treating ovarian cancer, its only natural source, the Pacific yew tree, may become an endangered species.

> This place is in poor repair. Either we must fix it up and paint it, or we must find another apartment. But we'll never find another apartment for such a reasonable rent. So get ready to fix up and paint.

The logical appeal is valuable. But because we are not solely rational beings, it also has its limits. Miriam may yearn to be an artist. Cancer patients may be more important than trees. Some people have no "fix-up" skills and would rather die than paint ceilings. The New Hampshire child support case outlined above reveals some of the limits of logic: The perhaps unfortunate result of this eminently logical argument was that a parent with stepchildren could use that fact to provide less support to his or her own children.

The Emotional Appeal

The emotional appeal in argument is no less powerful than the logical. Although frequently abused, the emotional appeal is a legitimate aspect of rhetorical argument, for we want our audiences to care about the issues we address. The most effective ways for an ethical writer to achieve that end are through the use of vivid (but accurate) illustrations and examples and through a clear, graceful, and appropriately emphatic writing style. To begin, you can make sure to include specific and concrete examples and details in your arguments. Try never to make a point without illustrating it, never to make a claim without giving an example to make it clear and memorable. For example, suppose your claim is that Hong Kong's return to Chinese control in 1997 will lead to economic disaster. Statistics on the numbers of workers who say they are likely to leave Hong Kong will be helpful. Numbers of foreign corporations and business operators who fear Chinese control will be similarly useful. But specific descriptions of and quotations from people who live and work in Hong Kong will add a legitimate emotional appeal to your claims that will help readers grasp your arguments all the better.

Second, you can hone your writing style. A style that is both distinctively your own and pleasing to readers comes slowly, with much writing and rewriting, with much reading of well-written prose, and with a heightened awareness of all your verbal options, as Chapter 9 will demonstrate. For now, you can do wonders for your writing style simply by showing concern for and courtesy to your readers. That is, express your ideas as simply and clearly as possible. The more complicated the ideas, the more important this point becomes.

Slanting The particular illustrations and the specific language used in an argument involve choices that can distort unfairly even as they heighten the emotional impact of the argument. Choosing one example means omitting others, after all. And if the example a writer chooses is atypical, selected for its emotional impact only, the argument is skewed unfairly through that **selection** of untypical evidence. If the writer describes someone or something in unflattering terms when more neutral or even favorable language would have been more accurate, the argument is again skewed, through that **charged language.**

Slanting an argument through selection and charged language may not be fair, but it is pervasive. In the following passage, for example, the claim is implied rather than stated, but the implicit claim is clear enough, thanks to the word choices and selection of particular details:

> Spike Lee has made his reputation as a film innovator by posturing as a free-floating radical, as a spokesman for the nation's oppressed, as a fulminator against convention and bourgeois morality. He is also a spokesman for the Nike Corporation, and you can regularly see this daring and revolutionary young filmmaker on prime-time TV, selling an extraordinarily expensive athletic shoe.
> —T. C. Frank, "Buy Hip," *Utne Reader*, July/Aug. 1992

Notice the word choices: *posturing, free-floating radical*. What other word choices are emotionally weighted against filmmaker Spike Lee? And notice the choice of detail: The one fact we learn about Lee in this passage is that he advertises "an extraordinarily expensive athletic shoe."

Even ostensibly objective newspapers and magazines slant what they report. Notice the different impressions the next two passages create, even though they report the same event:

Clarence Thomas was sworn in as the 106th justice of the Supreme Court last week and began by asking the nation to "look for what is good in others." But now that he had been confirmed by the Senate he once accused of a public lynching, no one seemed interested in his advice. The fight had moved beyond Thomas and his accuser, Anita Hill, transformed into a spectacle of blame and revenge: women's groups charging Democrats with betrayal; Democrats charging Republicans with dirty tactics; Republicans worrying about alienating young women voters; voters disgusted by the entire display. Senators pledged to change the process—and voters promised to limit congressional terms. It was a backlash of infinite possibility.

Advice and consent had little to do with the ascendancy of Clarence Thomas to the Supreme Court. Once Hill's charges of sexual harassment against him leaked into public view, the fight escalated into a drama with all the intensity of the last days of a political campaign. It was grueling, unfair and open to manipulation. Without substance, the fault lines were drawn first over character, then over character assassination. "Clearly we Democrats didn't learn anything from losing the last election," complains party strategist Bob Squier.

—"The Swearing Never Stops," *U.S. News & World Report*, 28 Oct. 1991

Don't be surprised if Clarence Thomas wakes up with the flu on Dec. 11. On that Wednesday, the U.S. Supreme Court will hear a case on sexual harassment, so it's a good bet the newest justice would rather stay home and tend tulips. Nonetheless, Thomas will likely take his place on the far right side of the bench, even if he lets his more experienced—and less tarnished—brethren do the questioning. If he does pipe up, expect his every utterance to be parsed by pundits, his every twitch captured by courtroom sketch artists. Anita Hill's allegations that Thomas sexually harassed her in the early 1980s didn't cost Thomas his seat on the high court, but that seat will be very uncomfortable. So much so that, for now, his credibility—and that of the court—are damaged. Nothing, Thomas himself said, could ever "give me my good name back."

Thomas doesn't officially take over until this week, yet his troubles already have disturbed the quiet work of the court. The electronic images of Thomas and Hill blared in offices throughout the building as secretaries, law clerks and the justices themselves tuned in the Senate mudfest. *Newsweek* has learned that two conservative justices who watched the hearings told their clerks that they thought Thomas lied to the Judiciary Committee.

—"An Uncomfortable Seat," *Newsweek*, 28 Oct. 1991

These are the first two paragraphs from the same week's edition of two national news magazines. Neither is unbiased. Notice in both cases what is omitted and what is stated—and how it is phrased. As readers of arguments, we would do well to be alert for such subtle emotional manipulation masquerading as reporting. As writers, we would do well to avoid slanting as much as possible, for readers who recognize it will be offended and lose faith in our arguments altogether.

EXERCISE 1–5

A. Examine these passages for slanting. Identify the slanting you find as either charged language or selection of details.

B. Rewrite one of the passages in language slanted to convey an impression opposite to that in the version printed.

C. Rewrite the same passage in language as neutral as possible. Add or change details to eliminate slanting through selection.

1. There ought to be a shelf of books on Frances Lear's lurid life. Adopted by a vindictive mother and molested repeatedly by a stepfather, she later had three marriages (one to TV producer Norman Lear), countless affairs, numerous addictions and bouts of therapy. Yet she managed to climb the garment-industry ladder and found *Lear's* magazine. So why does [her autobiography] *The Second Seduction* . . . seem so enervating at a mere 190 sparsely printed pages? For one thing, she never describes the horrors of drugs or the excitement of creating a magazine. For all her vaunted feminism, she is too absorbed in self-pity to make her story real or dramatic to others. Or the answer may be simpler and sadder: the eloquence needed to share a complex life was far beyond her capacity to write.

—Unsigned *Time* book review, 22 June 1992

2. Virtually alone among progressive intellectuals, sociologist Orlando Patterson loudly warned against making street hustlers the standard-bearers of black cultural authenticity: "The 'street culture' of petty crime, drug addiction, paternal irresponsibility, whoring, pimping, and Super Fly inanity," he wrote bitterly, "all of which damage and destroy only fellow blacks, instead of being condemned by black ethnic leaders, has, until recently, been hailed as the embodiment of black 'soul.'"

—Mark Naison, in African-American opinion
journal, *Reconstruction*, 1.4 (1992)

3. I've seen the best bands of my generation, and they have nothing to say. The rock 'n roll dream is alive and well among twentysomethings, and many groups have an abundance of imagination and passion when it comes to expressing themselves musically. But lyrics are a different story.

Rock lyrics today come in three varieties: furious, clichéd, and non-existent. Angry young bands such as Nirvana and Babes in Toyland virtually explode with rage, but it's almost impossible to figure out what they're screaming about. Sonic Youth is reinventing rock guitar and Teenage Fanclub retools the best of '70s rock for the '90s, but lyrically both resort to pop-culture trivia, tired truisms, and simply admitting they have nothing to say. (Sonic Youth's latest album included a non-ironic tribute to Karen Carpenter, and the deepest Teenage Fanclub gets is this: "There are things I'd like to say / But I'm not sure if I'll say them to you.") And while such bands as Ride, Dinosaur Jr., My Bloody Valentine, and the Pixies are musically innovative, the lyrics are buried so deeply in the mix they might as well not be there.

—Jim DeRogatis, *Utne Reader*, July/Aug. 1992

The Ethical Appeal

Your readers must have faith in the integrity of your arguments. They must trust you and what you say. This is the third dimension of argument: what the Greeks called *ethos*, the ethical appeal. The logic of your argument and its emotional strengths actually contribute to your ethical appeal. If your readers know you personally, they know if you are fair-minded and a scrupulous researcher. If they do not know you personally, they still make unconscious judgments about whether you are believable and trustworthy, based on how and what you write. Aristotle considered the ethical appeal the single most crucial element of any argument. In his day, if a speaker was known to be a person of intelligence and integrity, his audience was likely to be receptive to his arguments. If, on the other hand, the audience distrusted him, it was unlikely to accept even his most eloquently expressed and rational assertions.

Sometimes the entire purpose of a paper or speech is to create or redefine the audience's sense of the writer or speaker. Political campaign speeches and press releases by celebrities' agents offer fine (and often creative!) examples of ethos-centered prose. Closer to everyday contexts, letters to in-laws or pen pals, "personal statements" on college applications, letters proposing friends for membership in clubs, and autobiographical statements required of prospective parents by adoption agencies may all share as their primary purpose the creation of an appealing and trustworthy image. This image, or **persona,** is *the writer as perceived by the reader*.

Even when the primary purpose of a written message is something other than image building, the persona you create through choices of words and examples determines whether or not the arguments will be persuasive. When you read another's argument, you form conclusions, either consciously or otherwise, about the writer's believability and trustworthiness. If the writer seems biased, for instance, or less than candid, you may reject the argument. Similarly, readers may reject *your* arguments if your persona troubles them.

The persona is the sum of many parts, all as perceived by the reader: the writer's knowledge of the subject, apparent bias or lack of bias toward that subject, accuracy or sloppiness, precise or inappropriate vocabulary, humor or earnestness, degree of candor, and more. The persona is the least tangible element of any piece of writing—yet it can make or break an argument.

And it can mislead a reader. Indeed, the possibility of a discrepancy between the persona created in a written message and the actual character and personality of the writer is suggested by the very word *persona*—Latin for "mask." Sometimes the writer does try to create a mask behind which to hide. But the effective, honest writer does not try to seem an entirely different person. Instead, the writer tries to demonstrate such a regard for the subject and the readers' needs that what is conveyed through the message are qualities of integrity, good sense, and good will, as well as the particular features of the writer's own style and personality that prevent the writing from appearing nondescript and impersonal. That "appropriate image," then, is not a mask applied over the writer's real face—one's convictions and biases nearly always show through—but a filter that enhances what is really there, in much the same way that a camera filter reduces glare, intensifies colors, and sharpens the photographic image. The creation of an effective persona is almost incidental to the writer who has done two things: He or she has carefully considered potential readers' needs and has just as carefully considered the issue at hand. Let these be your own considerations if you aim to be both an effective and an ethical persuader.

EXERCISE 1–6

A. Identify each of the following as an argument or non-argument.
B. Identify the unstated assumptions, if any, in the arguments. Write them out. Are they as readily acceptable as the arguer assumes? If not, explain why not.
C. Convert the non-arguments into arguments by altering and/or adding to their content.

1. Polly can't be trusted. She cheats at Monopoly.
2. The Vikings beat Columbus to America, so they say.
3. I can't go to the concert because Thursday night is my TV night.
4. Willy: "The street is lined with cars. There's not a breath of fresh air in the neighborhood. The grass don't grow anymore, you can't raise a carrot in the back yard. They should've had a law against apartment houses."
   —Arthur Miller, *Death of a Salesman*
5. Because uneducated and even illiterate people are capable of rational thought and can make themselves understood, it is wrong to say that poor writing reflects poor thinking.
6. The 1987 nomination of Judge Robert Bork to the Supreme Court was successfully opposed by people who questioned his concept of "judicial restraint." The 1991 nomination of Judge Clarence Thomas to the Supreme Court was unsuccessfully opposed by people who questioned his treatment of women. These cases show that the members of the United States Senate regard judicial restraint as a more important issue than sexual harassment.
7. Burglar bars may be more dangerous than burglars. They often prevent people from escaping fires in their homes.
8. Dignants are wuffles, and all wuffles garbit. Therefore, dignants garbit.
9. Sometimes people call me an idealist. Well, that is the way I know I am an American. America is the only idealistic nation in the world.
   —Woodrow Wilson
10. The more is given the less people will work for themselves, and the less they work the more their poverty will increase.
    —Leo Tolstoy, *Help for the Starving*
11. We can help the environment in a small way by picking the best type of coffee cup to use in the campus snack bar. The obvious choices are ceramic, coated paper, or styrofoam cups. Ceramic cups use up heated water when they are washed. Coated paper cups, because of the coating, do not recycle easily. Styrofoam cups use the smallest amount of energy of the three to manufacture, can be recycled, and are inert, harmless matter in landfills. Therefore, we can help the environment in a small way by using styrofoam cups in the campus snack bar.

12. Small children who collect rocks, bugs, and other junk tend to grow up into adults with hopelessly cluttered homes and offices. No doubt, Uncle Chris was a childhood junk collector.

13. David and Howard are playing gin rummy. After the first hand is dealt, Howard asks, "Are aces high or low?" David reasons: Either Howard has an ace or he is very crafty. But he isn't crafty at all. Therefore, Howard has an ace.

    —Howard Pospesel, *Arguments: Deductive Logic Exercises*

14. Dependency, by its very nature, creates self-doubt, and self-doubt can lead all too quickly to self-hatred.

    —Colette Downing, *The Cinderella Complex*

15. All publicity is good, you say? Well, this review attacking your latest movie is publicity. So, according to your reasoning, this review is good!

16. All things worth doing are worth doing well, so washing dishes is worth doing well.

17. Elisha Gray and Alexander Graham Bell invented the prototype of the telephone almost simultaneously. Therefore, we should give them equal credit.

18. Australia needs a supplemental source of pure drinking water, and icebergs could be such a source. Therefore, we must find a way of transporting icebergs to Australia.

19. Sex and reproduction are natural and nonproblematic for all animals except Man. Females come into heat, males are attracted to them, and the species is maintained. Nothing could be simpler. Compare that to the sexual tensions existing among human beings: the teenage girl who waits for a boy to call her, feeling shunned and unattractive; the college student who cannot concentrate on his studies and is contemplating suicide because his girlfriend has broken up with him; the pregnant unmarried career woman who does not believe in abortion but is not sure what other choice she has; the severely depressed housewife whose husband has left her for another woman; the victims of rape, the patrons of pornographic movies, the furtive adulterers, the self-hating promiscuous "sexual athletes." Sex is so simple and straightforward for animals, and so painful for the rest of us (unless we are willing to behave like animals), because we have entered the world of good and evil.

    —Harold S. Kushner, *When Bad Things Happen to Good People*

20. [W]hy, you may ask, has the enormous increase in complexity of our recent technological environment not had a measurable physical impact on our brains? (Our industrialized brains, after all, are not demonstrably different from those of contemporary hunter-gatherers.) Simply because there has not been time; none of us need go back many generations in our family trees before we find that most of our forebears were peasants leading simple lives quite free of fax machines and the IRS. The rate at which we are changing our environment now has outstripped even the fastest biological evolution. We basically still have peasant or hunter-gatherer brains in a high-tech world.

    —Christopher Wills, "Has Human Evolution Ended?"
    Discover, Aug. 1992

EXERCISE 1–7

Write a paragraph in which you apply to the editor of the campus newspaper for the position of sports editor; or to the college president for the job of assistant director of fundraising for the school; or to your former rhetoric instructor for the job of grader and teaching assistant. After writing and revising the paragraph, label your conclusion and the premises supporting it, and underline words showing logical relationships and qualifications, such as *because* and *however*.

This chapter has briefly introduced the concepts that the rest of the book will develop more fully. After studying this chapter, if not before, you know the difference between argument and persuasion and the ethical dimensions of both. You understand that everyone holds some fundamental, *a priori* ideas about the world and that *a priori* beliefs affect both your own arguments and how you regard others' arguments.

And you know quite a bit about the nature of argument—that it draws relationships among what you know and what you surmise about ideas, places, people. You know that the basic elements of any argument are a claim and at least one other statement directly supporting that claim—and that unstated assumptions about the subject and the audience underlie every argument. Moreover, you understand that our imperfect knowledge rarely allows us to make unqualified arguments, so you take special care that your claims and supporting statements are appropriately qualified (with words like *often, most, typically*). Your claims must never extend beyond what the support for them warrants.

Finally, you are aware of the three dimensions of argument: the logical, emotional, and ethical appeals. You understand that logic provides the framework for a well-expressed and clearly organized argument, but that logic alone lacks the human qualities that the emotional and ethical appeals provide arguments. You know that the emotional appeal gives arguments a human quality, but that it must not replace reasoning—and it must not be used, as in deliberate slanting, to manipulate readers. And you realize that readers judge an argument in part according to how trustworthy they find the writer. You must take care to argue in a reasonable tone, to document claims carefully and accurately, to give credit to other viewpoints when credit is due. Your readers then will trust you and believe what you say.

But all this is only a beginning. The next chapter takes up ways to develop a strong working thesis; the two following chapters offer advice for supporting that thesis through careful definitions of key concepts and through the evidence you muster to support your claims. Then Chapters 5–7 show you how to test the logical framework of your argument, and Chapters 8 and 9 suggest specific ways to revise and complete your argument drafts. All along, of course, you will write arguments. And you know more than enough to do so.

READINGS

WHAT SO PROUDLY WE HAILED?

Debbie Sapp
(Student Essay)

1   God bless me, my country, and its flag: I am not a Communist, and by most people's standards I am not even a radical, but I am angry because I stand with a healthy majority of my fellow Americans who cannot sing—standing *or* seated—our national anthem. Folks, to face facts, "The Star-Spangled Banner" (or SSB) is a real SOB to sing. There. It's been said. I have spoken my vicious, unpatriotic piece. I do not like the national anthem, and I hold that there are plenty of reasons and a good number of alternatives that would justify a change.

2   The exact range of the SSB is nineteen half-steps. The average range of the human singing voice is from one and one-half to two octaves, or eighteen to twenty-four half steps. Those below-average people or those on the lowest end of the "average" voice range are destined never to sing allegiance to their country, at least not without risking a few close friendships. The average people who might be able to fit the SSB into their range are only so lucky when the band starts on the right note. And those few above-average people who can actually sing the anthem well, and can hit "land of the free" on the money every time, are resented by the rest of us who have to stand close to them at football games.

3   Of course, a national anthem is more than just music. The lyrics should express the deepest sympathies of the people who sing it. In the case of the SSB, these people represent an entire nation. So I ask: Does the entire nation hold a grudge against England, and does everyone wish to revel continually in the victory over our British cousins? "The rocket's red glare, the bombs bursting in air . . . !" Is this the appropriate way to begin every sporting event, or to welcome visiting foreign dignitaries (even those from England)? The song in its original form celebrates more than a battle and a flag—it resorts to downright name-calling. In the second, third, and fourth stanzas, of which many people are completely unaware, several offensive lines hold the potential to ignite an international incident, if not a whole new war between the United States and Great Britain, such as: "Their blood [that of the English] has washed out their foul footsteps' pollution." A wonderful tribute to a country that is now our staunchest ally!

4   These words are strong, to say at least; but then, this is powerful poetry. It must be powerful poetry because it is largely unintelligible, and most of us seem to require of our best poetry that it be beyond our comprehension. I admit, although with embarrassment, that until the middle of my freshman year in high school I thought one of the final lines read: "Oh, Sadists! That

star-spangled banner yet waves. . . . " And I'm afraid even to guess at the number of Americans with no idea what a *rampart* might be, or what it means to be spangled, with stars or anything else. Thank heaven we are not expected to know the last three stanzas of the song; half the country would be puzzling over the metaphoric message in "foul footsteps' pollution."

5   Now is a crucial time. Although it is none too soon to change our national anthem, neither is it too late. If we Americans are shrewd and quick, the students of the year 2025 will read with a yawn this brief note in their history texts:

> On March 3, 1931, "The Star-Spangled Banner," written in 1814 by Francis Scott Key, was officially adopted as the National Anthem of the United States. Over sixty years later, after having been deemed too difficult to sing, too esoteric in vocabulary, and too belligerent in its attitude toward England, it was replaced by _____.

6   The blank is yet to be filled, but the possibilities are numerous. Perhaps "America the Beautiful" would do, despite its failure to distinguish the U.S.A. from all of South and Central America, Mexico, and Canada; for at least "America the Beautiful" is more specific than the vague flourish of "the land of the free and the home of the brave." Or we might use "America" (also called "My Country, 'Tis of Thee"), changing its melody so that it would no longer be identical with that of "God Save the Queen." Or how about a good, rousing George M. Cohan song like "Grand Old Flag"? If none of the existing possibilities seems just right, then a new national spirit of patriotism and unity could be ignited by the announcement of an anthem-writing competition. Barry Manilow, are you listening? The time has come for all true-blue Americans (and even those in off-shades) to sing together without embarrassment, pain, or bewilderment. Our nation changes as it grows, with unfair or outdated laws and traditions replaced by new and better ones. Just as blacks were emancipated, just as women were given the vote, so, too, must American vocal cords be enabled to sing every note of their patriotism.

QUESTIONS AND IDEAS FOR DISCUSSION

1. (a) What main point (thesis) does this essay argue? State it in a sentence. Then state the main supporting points (premises) in one sentence each. Do the premises support the thesis well? Comment. What, if anything, has the writer failed to consider?

    (b) Identify any verbal signals of argument that you find. Are they sufficient in number and appropriate in meaning?

2. What ideas does the writer appear to hold *a priori* about her subject?

3. What assumptions does the writer appear to have made about her readers? You are one of her readers: Were her assumptions correct in your case? If she were to revise this argument for a broader audience (all the readers of this

text as well as her own rhetoric class), what would you suggest she do differently?

4. Of the three appeals—logical, emotional, and ethical—which is strongest in this essay? Why? Does that emphasis seem appropriate?

5. What do you like best about this essay? What do you like least? If this essay were your own next-to-last draft, how would you change it? What would you add, delete, or alter? Explain your reasons.

THINKING AND RETHINKING

Lindsay Moran
(Student Essay)

1   When I was a sophomore, I attended the march on Washington, defending the pro-choice movement. My parents live in the D.C. area, so I called home just before boarding the bus in Cambridge.

2   "How 'bout meeting me for dinner?" I asked my father.

3   "Sure," he said, "I'll just look for you on the steps of the Capitol."

4   I tried to explain to my father—who is politically conservative, who does not believe in marches, and who (under any other circumstances) would avoid a mass of raving feminists, that this event was going to be a big deal.

5   Ten buses were coming from Harvard alone. At least 20,000 women and men were expected to be in Washington by 9 a.m. the next day. The chances of my father just running into me were slim to none. He did not seem to understand.

6   "See you on the steps of the Capitol, sport," he said before he hung up.

7   The next day, the march went as planned, but I did not see my father.

8   When I arrived back in Cambridge the following night, I turned on the 11 o'clock news.

9   "People of all types showed up for the march on Washington today," the anchorwoman said.

10   A short clip of footage appeared on the screen. There—standing on the steps of the Capitol, looking lost amidst a group of chanting women—was Dad. Dad (like every other father, I suppose) has learned to accept a lot of things, to support me even when his better judgment tells him not to.

11   My roommate co-chairs the campus pro-life group. We did not get stuck together. We chose to live together, and we have for two years. We have had some terse discussions, a few vituperative arguments; but mostly, we've had really good talks.

12   If I have not accepted her point of view, I have certainly rethought mine—not just about abortion but about religion, racism, freedom of expression and feminism—everything that each of us has inevitably questioned during our years at Harvard.

13   I have realized that maintaining one's individuality, in both thought and practice, is one of the most difficult tasks in college. I do not go to marches anymore. My feelings toward abortion are more complicated than those conveyed in a rally. In the few that I attended, I retrospectively felt as if I had relinquished part of my individuality, surrendered myself to the conformity of pseudo-activism.

14   We are all well aware of the pressures that exist here, particularly the pressure to conform to certain social and political standards.

15   As seniors, many of us feel pressure to go to a top-notch grad school or find a high-paying job. Recently, we have created another pressure, one which systematically destroys the remnants of individualism—that is, the pressure to be politically correct.

16   The pressure to be politically correct tends to dichotomize the campus into opposing factions. It diminishes the diversity of our ideas; it oversimplifies our complex attitudes.

17   The only way to remain unencumbered by the pressures that accompany a Harvard education is for each of us to preserve his or her individuality.

18   Harvard is an open forum for individuals. We can talk about anything we want. And we do. At meals, we talk because we don't want to get up from the table and do our work. In class, we talk just to hear ourselves talk. The best thing about Harvard is that no matter what we say, someone will listen and most will think we know what we are talking about. We are the Milli Vanillis* of academia.

19   I do not agree with my roommate about a lot of issues. I do respect her point of view; I would never challenge her right to express it. On this campus, she represents a minority of people who oppose abortion rights. In this respect, she is one person who has not compromised her individuality.

20   It is my hope that as we leave Harvard each of us will influence a particular community and that we will benefit our society, not by shouldering the expectations of others but by remaining faithful, foremost, to ourselves.

QUESTIONS AND IDEAS FOR DISCUSSION

1. What is this essay about? That is, does it have a central argument and, if so, what is that argument? Is it consistently developed throughout the essay—or does the author indulge in side excursions and detours? Comment.

2. An anecdote involving Moran's father and a description of Moran's roommate take up at least half the essay. Why is the anecdote so prominent—what role do the father and the roommate play in the essay?

---

*In 1988 the pop/rap duo "Milli Vanilli" received a Grammy award in the "Best New Artist" category. The award was later revoked when it was discovered that the Milli Vanilli performers were frauds: They lip-synched to others' singing.

3. If this were a draft for your own speech to your fellow college students, what changes—additions, deletions, reordering of points—would you make? Why?

4. How important is a title? When this essay was originally delivered orally, it had no title. A newspaper editor assigned it the title "The Pressure to Conform on Campus." Here it is entitled "Thinking and Rethinking." Which title suits the essay (and you, the present audience) better? Suggest a couple of others, and settle on the best choice. Explain your reasons.

CELEBRATE FREE SPEECH: SAY WHAT YOU THINK

Ellen Goodman

1   Some years ago, I clipped a cartoon out of the *New Yorker* that showed two couples seated in a living room while a giant furry beast loomed over them. The host couple amiably explained the creature's presence to their guests this way, "We deal with it by talking about it."

2   I kept the cartoon as a reminder of the humor and the hubris in the idea that we can talk every problem down to size, verbally wrestle all monsters to bay. After all, I have had an abiding faith in the value of what the college course catalogues now call "communication." This belief in words has been the chicken and egg of my life as a journalist. Not to mention my life as a mother, wife and friend.

3   But lately I've had an urge to rewrite the caption. I sense that we are a country living with great monsters, and we are dealing with them by not talking about them. I am struck by the reticence, the unwillingness on the part of everyday people to say what they think.

4   This Sunday, we are celebrating the 200th anniversary of the Bill of Rights. The most fundamental of these rights is that of free speech. Under its protection, we have been largely free of the fear that still inhibits citizens of other countries. But we value that freedom much more than we exercise it.

5   I can offer up any number of moments when this self-censorship seemed clear to me. This fall, during the Clarence Thomas hearings, I told a class of college students what I thought and heard a nervous and yet relieved titter through the room. The truth was, the students said later, they hadn't felt free to offer an opinion in public and didn't really expect to hear one.

6   Then last week, I was watching a television reporter ask people on the street for their views. It seemed to me that the answers were not spontaneous, open speech. What I heard were the practiced imitations of sound bites, carefully excised of controversy. Or candor.

7   At a business meeting, in a dorm, during a dinner party, among strangers, it seems to me that people speak without speaking up. In a public forum, it is even rarer to find a politician remotely "outspoken."

8   Why are people who don't have to worry about the police knocking on their door late at night so reticent? Our inhibitions seem to be internal. This spring, the American Society of Newspaper Editors presented a survey of attitudes toward the First Amendment. It found that Americans believe that we believe in free speech more than we do in fact. But the greatest inhibitor of free expression wasn't the fear of the state or even the boss, but the fear that we might offend someone else. The people polled worried most that "saying what's on your mind may harm or damage other people" and that "speaking your mind may hurt the feelings of those you care for."

9   The priority that we put on civility, on sensitivity to others, is not exactly a flaw in a democracy as diverse as ours. It inhibits the use of fighting words, keeps the lid on name-calling and epithet-throwing.

10   The good news is that it may stop a bigot from yelling "nigger" or "bitch" in a crowded theater. The bad news is that it may stop any candid conversation about, say, affirmative action or abortion.

11   The monsters in our living rooms do not carry placards that read "tax policy." They are labeled race, gender, values, sexuality. Stuff that needs a good talking about.

12   But while campus administrators worry over speech codes that place a civil framework around debate, it's hard to find the debate. While children learn in grade school to read and write, they often unlearn how to speak their minds. And while our leaders sit on couches, comfortably chatting, they talk around the monsters.

13   The First Amendment, that amendment that leads off the entire Bill of Rights, was not just the founders' gift of gab to the country. It grew out of the belief that only an informed people could make their own laws, form and reform their society, govern themselves. Words were fundamental to keeping democracy alive. We had to deal with "it" by talking about it.

14   So for the 200th anniversary party, celebrate free speech the old-fashioned way. Mix together civility and candor. Say what you think.

QUESTIONS AND IDEAS FOR DISCUSSION

1. What is Ellen Goodman's thesis in this essay? How does it resemble or differ from the argument put forward by college student Lindsay Moran in the previous selection? Does the professional writer, Goodman, use any techniques in developing her subject that Moran or you might do well to employ in future arguments? In what ways, if any, does Moran succeed in engaging your interest in her argument more effectively than does Goodman?

2. Goodman wrote this essay on the occasion of the 200th anniversary of the Bill of Rights in December 1991. Is its argument still relevant or not? Discuss, offering specific illustrations from your own knowledge and experience.

3. What are "sound bites" and why does Goodman take pains to distinguish them from reasoned argument? Do your own written (or voiced) arguments

ever resemble sound bites? Do your friends' arguments ever resemble sound bites? Comment.

Suggestions for Writing and Further Discussion

1. Like the student author of "What So Proudly We Hailed?," argue for a change in an existing situation. Your audience is your classmates: Show them why they should take an interest in the subject and why they should agree with your proposal regarding it. You may choose a campus tradition or residency requirement, employers' rules, the burden of income taxes on college students, or your own pet peeve. The possibilities are many.

2. Assume that a friend in another state is planning to buy a car, and, although she is knowledgeable about engines, she recognizes that she has no sense of taste and fears that she will be persuaded to buy something gaudy or ugly—a choice that she will later regret. She asks your advice. Write an essay in which you argue a set of esthetic (as opposed to mechanical) standards by which to judge automobiles, so that your friend will know what to look for.

3. In an essay entitled "How Do You Know It's Good?," art critic Marya Mannes argues that some values *are* absolute, that not everything is relative, limited to context. If you disagree with this assertion, write an essay supporting your belief that all values are relative, giving specific examples (perhaps from the fields of music, art, literature, politics, advertising, or the like) to support your case. You may find it helpful to first read "How Do You Know It's Good?," which comprises a brief chapter in Mannes's *But Will It Sell?*

4. In a book about thought and reasoning, *The Mind in the Making,* James Harvey Robinson asserts:

   > Few of us take the pains to study the origin of our cherished convictions; indeed, we have a natural repugnance to so doing. We like to continue to believe what we have been accustomed to accept as true, and the resentment aroused when doubt is cast upon any of our assumptions leads us to seek every manner of excuse for clinging to them. *The result is that most of our so-called reasoning consists in finding arguments for going on believing as we already do.*

   We tend to ignore arguments and information, however telling, that conflict with our preconceptions and prejudices. As an exercise in mental agility and the clearing out of a few cobwebs, not to mention gaining the benefits of seeing things from another person's perspective for a change, write an essay that takes a view *opposite to your own* on some controversial issue (gay rights, bilingual education, abortion, fascism, the insanity defense for murder, the banning of drug abusers from professional sports, or the sale of federal park lands, for example). Treat your assumed stance on the issue seriously; try to offer a sound argument in its support.

5. After writing an essay supporting a viewpoint that in fact you oppose, write an analysis of the difficulties you encountered in the undertaking. Did you find your own position modified in any way after considering an opposite viewpoint?

6. In the same book by James Harvey Robinson quoted above, the author argues that the "good" (that is, socially acceptable or praiseworthy) and the "real" reasons for our opinions are usually quite different from each other. A person might have a whole set of "good" reasons for attending a particular college, for instance, but her real reasons might have more to do with the accessibility of beaches, the fact that her older brother went there, or the fact that her parents refused to pay tuition at any other school. Another person might be opposed to varsity athletics really out of resentment for having no athletic ability himself or herself. A third might oppose the fraternity system as much for having been cut in rush as for the cookie-cutter conformity of the Greeks. Discuss the problem for us, as students of argument and reason, of having "real" reasons that we do not recognize or will not admit. Support your argument with examples.

7. In junior high school I became a Candy Striper at a local hospital. My "good" (socially acceptable) reasons for giving up my Saturday mornings and Monday afternoons to volunteer work you could fill in yourself: to help people in need, to free the nurses from doing minor chores, and so on. My "real" reason was that I liked the uniform. But I came to like the work as well, and I stayed with it for five years through high school and another year in college. Write an essay, illustrated and supported by experiences or observations of your own, in which you demonstrate that a laughable or lamentable motive for doing something can lead to a commendable outcome all the same.

8. Find two or more news articles about an issue or event of current interest. Examine them for instances of selection and charged language. Which seems to be most fair? Which most slanted? Discuss your findings or write an essay in which you argue for your conclusions about the relative fairness of the articles. Be specific in the examples you cite and compare.

9. Some say that nowadays no one will speak up about either major issues or minor irritations. People are unduly afraid of being thought illiberal or petty—or of being shot by someone who takes offense! Others say that we grumble, and strike, and sue all too readily. Which do you think is closer to the truth? Write an essay supporting your contention, developing your argument with narrative examples from your own experience or knowledge.

2

Creating Arguments

> *"Know thyself" was an oracle addressed to the individual, charging him to become a person; to know, as a matter of fact, almost everything other than himself, to know the world for what it is, for what it "honestly deeply means," and above all to substitute for the inquiry "What do I think?" the inquiry "What can be thought?" The emphasis is not upon his reason but upon reason; not upon himself but upon his kind. Obeying the oracle, he endeavors to rear within himself that third man who is present when two men speak, and who is happy when they understand each other.*
>
> **—Mark Van Doren**

We create arguments every time someone asks us, or we ask ourselves, "Why?" or "What difference does it make?" As Chapter 1 suggested, arguing is as natural as breathing—and nearly as inevitable. At its best, it is an organic and even creative process, by means of which we discover causes, find solutions, decide on actions and motivations, or interpret our world. It can be a way of "knowing the world for what it is," a search for truth and understanding. At its worst, it is not creation but cloning: the mindless parroting of others' assertions and reasons.

But arguments, however organic their origin, do not grow well without attention. They tend to ramble and sprawl all over the page, or the conversation, unless staked and pruned so that reasons and evidence and the conclusions drawn from both develop in clear, logical relationship to each other. For this reason, many who discuss argument consider it in architectural rather than botanical terms. We speak of "building," "constructing," or "shoring up" an argument, and even "hammering home" our points. Certainly argument lends itself to such description. With arguments we impose order; we build foundations upon which our assertions can be supported. Order does not assure a reader's understanding, but it makes understanding more likely. Happily, the two processes (if not the two metaphors) work well together. The process of invention and that of development and revision—creation and construction—are not antithetical but complementary.

THE RHETORICAL CONTEXT

An argument begins with a question, a speculation, a reaction, an inspiration—or an assignment. While many arguments are generated spontaneously, the assigned argument is anything but spontaneous. And yet the assigned argument holds just as much potential for creative development as do the others. Your boss or your committee chairperson or your professor presents you with a problem:

"I need a report on the Wight Widget ad campaign. They're not happy with their sales profile since we took over their advertising. Emphasize the positive results if you can find any."

"We need to decide which of the local nonprofit organizations runs the most efficient operation, using donated funds wisely and well. Then we can determine who should be the beneficiary of our fund-raising efforts this year."

"Write an essay advocating or opposing a standardized syllabus and final exam for English 101."

—and you are on your own. When the problem is not one that first occurred to you, you may think initially that you have nothing to say. The whole matter may seem either too thorny (the widgets *haven't* sold), too obvious, or too dull to bother with. Or it may seem wrong-headed: If you oppose the very existence of English 101, how are you supposed to argue for or against a standardized syllabus?

But in the world at large, as well as in the academic world, many—if not most—papers are written in response to just such a request or assignment. So how do you create a convincing argument with a believable persona when even the subject is not of your own choosing? Fortunately, even the narrowest assignment usually leaves you the freedom to focus the paper as you see fit, within certain parameters. Those parameters typically include:

1. **General subject matter,** whether the first law of thermodynamics or the need for mass transit in your city.
2. **A prescribed or suggested approach to the subject,** such as opposition to or support for new zoning laws, or a favorable report to your superiors at the McClintock Company on the results of your new marketing strategy. If you cannot, in all honesty and fairness and self-interest, take the prescribed approach (perhaps the new marketing strategy has failed abysmally), take what approach you can and express it with tact, or choose another subject if you have that option.
3. **A length requirement or guideline,** perhaps a certain number of pages in a college assignment, or "short enough to fit in the annual report" in a business assignment.
4. **An indication of a need for documented evidence** to support your thesis, and perhaps an indication of the extent of source materials required.

Such requirements give the writer an understanding of the limitations of the assignment, but not of the possibilities. However uninspiring the guidelines, you may have little choice but to come up with something. You can wait for the muse to speak, or for lightning to strike; or you can invite inspiration by more prosaic, but effective, means. Begin by considering the rhetorical context in which you will be working. Every written message is created out of a rhetorical context. It has a *purpose* (sometimes a complex one) and a potential *audience,* and communicates both *content* and a *persona* (the reader's sense of the writer). By carefully considering the first two, purpose and audience, you will discover what content your argument needs to develop and will create a believable persona.

Consider Your Purpose

You can save yourself any number of missteps and false starts if you consider your purpose before you write. After all, if your boss asks you for a summary of activity on the Wight Widget account during the past year, your purpose is to provide succinct chronological information, not an assessment of the current advertising campaign. If your committee chairperson wants a memo suggesting how to determine which nonprofit group should receive funds, your purpose is to argue for a set of standards for making that decision, not to leap ahead to a recommendation of a specific charity. And if your professor assigns a paper on the projected impact of plus/minus grading on grade point averages, your purpose is to estimate the consequences of such a policy on GPAs, not on the mental health of honors students. Sometimes you can broaden or narrow the scope of an argument; sometimes you can redirect it toward your own ends; but always, you must keep sight of your original purpose.

When a writing task is assigned, make sure you understand just what you have been asked to do. Just as important, make sure you understand what you have not been asked to do—and, on occasion, what you have been asked *not* to do! If your supervisor says, "Now I know you think the Wight Widget campaign was a stupid idea from the start, but please don't ride *that* hobby horse in your report," or your professor says, "Please stick to the quantitative impact of plus/minus grading and don't launch into a diatribe on 'Teachers Who Done Me Wrong'"—keep those limits in mind as you contemplate your purpose.

Consider Your Audience

As you think about the issue about which you will write, you must keep constantly in mind the image of the intended and potential readers of your paper. Those readers offer at once a curb and a spur to invention and development of argument; as you write, you must take into account both what the readers are likely to know and not to know about the subject, and what biases and misconceptions they are likely to harbor about the subject and possibly about you, the writer. Keeping the readers in mind, along with your purpose in addressing them, keeps you on the path and out of the underbrush of tangential issues and unnecessary pleas and explanations.

Who are your readers? For papers written for this course, one will generally be the instructor. But not just the instructor: Another may be your roommate or spouse or a friend to whom you will read a preliminary draft. Then, too, at some point members of your composition class are likely to read the essay or hear it read. For papers written as part of your job, one reader nearly always will be your boss. But your boss's boss may be another reader, your colleagues both in and outside the company a collective third. The potential audience for your essay is both large and uncertain—the identity, biases, knowledge, and frame of mind of all of its members impossible to know for certain as you write. And yet some consideration of just those matters—the identity, biases, knowledge, and disposition of the readers—is essential to successful writing of any kind. If you bore your readers by explaining terms they already understand, or condescend to them, or baffle them with unfamiliar terms, you probably will not convince them that you are a person whose opinions they should value.

This is the paradox of the writer's situation: To know the audience is both crucial to establishing an effective persona and apparently nearly impossible. Even if you know the identity of at least one reader positively—your rhetoric instructor, for example—what do you really know about him? He is college educated, with one or more advanced degrees from a large midwestern university (according to diplomas on the wall in his office); tall, Anglo, with sandy hair and hazel eyes; married, with a couple of children (judging from the wedding band he wears and the snapshots of children on his office desk). And even if you know these things about your instructor, what do you know about the extent of his knowledge or about his values? How much is he likely to know about the pros and cons of nuclear energy, U.S. Central American policy, the need for government subsidy of Olympic contenders or of the fine arts, or the advantages of hiking? What are his biases likely to be concerning the issue at hand?

Stereotypes, however noxious the term may be in other contexts, offer some help to you in search of your reader. **Stereotypes** are conventional characteristics of groups as perceived by outsiders or by members of the group themselves. They can be misleading and unfair, and even at best they overlook individual variations. Carefully considered, however, they can offer a starting point in reader analysis: Your instructor, for example, because of his education, is likely to have a good vocabulary and at least a basic understanding of nuclear energy. He probably knows, too, that American athletes operate at a financial disadvantage compared to Eastern European Olympic hopefuls who are supported by their governments. He is likely to be reasonably well informed about current events, though his knowledge of literature may surpass his knowledge of Latin America. These generalizations, stereotyped though they are, are probably sound. So you have some idea, by considering the stereotypical characteristics of a college instructor, of which terms you will need to explain and which you may take for granted. You also have some idea, although here we tread upon uncertain ground, of what his preconceptions about the subject might be.

However, you may pursue stereotypes too far. College instructors are a notoriously liberal bunch, so you might decide that yours probably opposes the use of nuclear power to develop weapons and perhaps even to produce energy. He may well be a pacifist, and thus may oppose American military intervention in troubled Central American countries. He is bound to be bookish and may regard hiking as a pastime suitable only for the hardy simple-minded. He probably likes symphonic music and considers country-and-western lyrics maudlin. Chances are, he is bored with football and considers fraternities a waste of time. And so on.

Stereotypes of this more particular sort differ from the preceding generalizations about education and familiarity with certain subjects. The more you pinpoint characteristics, the more likely you are to be wrong. Such stereotypes are more likely to shut off thought than to open up possibilities for developing arguments. Your instructor may very well be a fan of both football and Garth Brooks, and somewhere in his dark past he may have joined a fraternity. If you write an essay opposing scholarships for football players simply in an attempt to "write what sells," you may find the attempt self-defeating. You may also run into trouble with classmates or other readers who like football and support the concept of athletic scholarships, by your casual assumption that anyone who reads your paper is opposed to them. Besides, if your instructor is fair-minded, he will give high marks to a well-written essay on *any* side—there are often more than two sides—of an issue.

The writer is at best always a bit uncertain of the reader, even if the two are the closest of friends. If the reader is unknown, or if there are many readers, the difficulty is compounded. But one cannot type away in a vacuum as if there will be no reader, or behave as if the reader is a passive sponge that will soak up the writer's ideas, however messily she spills them out on the page. Nor can one assume that there will be but a single reader, even for a class assignment or a confidential report. Nor that any single reader has but one dimension. Rhetorician F. L. Lucas has claimed (in "What Is Style?") that a spoken or written encounter between two minds involves six identities:

1. A's real self
2. A's perception of himself
3. A's perception of B
4. B's real self
5. B's perception of himself
6. B's perception of A

And that six-way encounter is for an audience of one. If twenty members of your rhetoric class are reading copies of your essay, you may marvel that the room can hold all the operating personas. Certainly you cannot hope to hold them all in mind at once as you write. The resulting essay would be overly cautious—or confused.

The Invented Reader

What you as a writer must do, finally, is to visualize an appropriate reader for what you are writing. Rhetorician Walter Ong calls this your "invented reader." If you were writing an essay on hiking to be submitted for a composition course, for example, your invented reader might be a person with a high school education (or more) who has never tried hiking, but would at least be willing to consider the idea. For this reader a certain level of vocabulary, knowledge, and experience can be assumed: You will not need to identify the Alps, but you may need to identify the location of the less well known Davis Mountains if your discussion centers on hiking there. You will not need to define *knapsack,* but you may want to indicate desirable features in a backpack. You will not need to convince your reader that mountains are beautiful or that the country is more healthful than the city, but you may need to offer some convincing arguments that hiking offers the best way to enjoy the outdoors.

This "invented" reader helps you determine which topics to explore for her benefit and your own, and what arguments to offer in support of your conclusion; she also saves you from needlessly agonizing over whether or not your instructor (and possibly your classmates) likes hiking. Of course, if you *know* that your actual reader despises any setting more rural than Central Park or any activity more strenuous than hailing a taxi, your arguments may need to be fuller and stronger than if you know that reader to be not only a hiker but also a proficient technical climber who has scaled Mt. McKinley. Should the latter be true, on the other hand, you hardly need persuade her at all. Try an essay on racquetball.

The point at which real and invented reader meet is the moment of actual reading: a moment and place at which you may not be present to explain, interpret, or defend what you have written and why you have chosen to argue as you have. So the invented reader must be a comfortable fit for the actual one: You appeal to the reader as a reasonable, well-educated, and informed person—just the sort of individual that the actual reader likely wants to be. The reader accepts the voice that regards her so highly and is favorably disposed toward its assertions. She begins to regard the issue through the selective filter of your persona.

As you think about your subject and jot down ideas for developing it, invent an appropriate and plausible reader for a discussion of the issue at hand, and consider—treading lightly on the stereotypes—the questions in the following list.

Audience Analysis

1. How much is the reader likely to know about the subject?
2. How much, in the way of background and explanation, does the reader need to know?
3. What are the reader's biases and misconceptions about this issue likely to be?
4. How does the reader regard the writer (if at all) before reading the paper?

The fourth question in the list matters if the reader's opinion of the writer is very strong—especially if it is strongly negative. In this case, the writer must take special pains to be diplomatic, convincing, and thorough. Ideally, that care would be taken in any event. If you have considered the issue, your purpose in writing about it, and the nature and needs of your intended audience, you will discover what you need to say, and how much. In so doing, you will also create a persona that will add to the persuasiveness of your essay. You will, without being cynical or manipulative about it, write what really sells.

EXERCISE 2–1

Write down all the stereotypical characteristics (including fields of knowledge, likes and dislikes) you can deduce from your observations of your rhetoric class-mates. Limit yourself to characteristics that seem typical of a majority of the students. Also list probable characteristics and areas of knowledge for your instructor. Discuss your "audience analysis" with the rest of the class. Are most people in agreement?

WORKING TOWARD A THESIS

Having marked some boundaries by preliminary thinking about the rhetorical context of purpose and audience, you will find that the subject at hand has assumed a more manageable size. Your specific *thesis* should be your next concern if the purpose and audience or the assignment itself has not already suggested the thesis. **The thesis of any organized expository or argumentative paper is the statement of its controlling idea, the main thrust of the argument.** This thesis defines the scope and limitations of the topic you propose to address. It states what is important to you—what you will show your readers to be important—about your subject. It should anticipate and promise answers to a reader's bored or skeptical "Why?" or "So what?"

Your complete thesis statement, consisting of a conclusion and its main supporting points, may appear at the beginning of your paper, at the end of the introductory paragraph or section, or in the conclusion. It is even possible that the thesis in its complete form—that is, including its supporting points—may not appear as such in the finished essay. Instead, you may state only its main clause, the asserted claim. In that case, you will spell out the supporting points separately, as topic sentences within the essay. But no matter what the final form of the thesis, no matter where in the essay it appears, a well-formulated thesis is always limited sufficiently and precisely enough to be stated in a single sentence. It thereby helps you keep on track as you develop an essay and assures unity in your argument.

How do you develop a thesis? Once you have your purpose and audience clearly in mind, various invention strategies can help you. We will look at three kinds of invention strategies in this chapter: using topical checklists, finding and resolving contradictions, and examining influences and consequences. These strategies are not mutually exclusive; on occasion you will need all three—and perhaps the muse as well.

Invention Strategy: Using Topical Checklists

Discovering the dimensions of an issue and the possibilities it holds, and then developing a thesis that explores both, is the creative part of even the most pro-saic assignment. Paradoxically, one stimulus for creativity in argument may be found in formulaic lists of stock issues, or **topics:** not lists of essay assignments to which we sometimes apply the term *topics,* but lists of possibilities for developing different kinds of subjects.

The classical rhetoricians divided the topics into "common" and "special" categories, according to whether the subject was an ordinary one or a matter for public deliberation. As an example of the latter, a speech presenting a choice be-tween possible courses of action—perhaps whether or not to grant diplomatic recognition to Cuba—would take up the overriding topic of advantage: Which course of action would be more advantageous to us? The arguer would then con-sider whether to develop the argument according to advantages of security or those of honor, or perhaps both. (If the United States were to recognize Cuba, perhaps that closer relationship with a neighboring country would lead to strate-gic advantages worldwide. Or perhaps we should consider the humanitarian and diplomatic obligations a large and powerful country owes to one smaller and weaker.) Subcategories of the topics of security and honor then stimulate the dis-covery of further supporting arguments. These categories were set down in the anonymous *Rhetorica ad Herennium* some two thousand years ago, and yet they are still relevant. When arguing in favor of one course of action over others, we still work from the topic of advantage to discover ways in which the action we favor will serve the interests of our audience. And, as we address the interests and needs of our audience, we create a considerate and empathetic persona, in-creasing the ethical appeal of our arguments.

The topics can serve as aids to *invention* of arguments, not merely as aids to uncovering some preexisting arguments of superior merit. Rarely is there but one way to make a point; by mulling over a topical checklist, the writer can circum-vent the writer's block of having "nothing to say" and can discover a number of possibilities for developing a thesis. The important thing is to ask questions. The following list of topical questions may help you formulate a preliminary thesis or may suggest to you still other questions about your subject.

An example will illustrate the usefulness of asking questions to generate content for a paper. Suppose that you have been asked to write an argumentative essay on rock music. Specifically, you are asked to defend or attack some aspect of rock to an audience of your peers, most of whom enjoy at least some rock music. You, too, like rock music, but you draw a blank or your response seems to

---

Developing a Thesis: Questions to Consider

1. **Exactly what is my subject?** Do I need to define it more clearly? Has my subject been misunderstood or misconstrued?
2. **Do I need or want to emphasize positive or negative aspects of my subject?** What are those aspects?
3. **Can my subject be divided up into parts?** Is one aspect more important or more relevant than others? What do I need or want to stress?
4. **Just what does my subject remind me of?** What associations does it have for me? Is my subject, whether a thing, a person, or an event, similar to another thing, person, or event that is probably familiar to my readers? Are there any unexpected and enlightening similarities? Is the comparison favorable or unfavorable? Does the comparison make my subject easier to understand?
5. **What caused or created my subject, if an event or a thing?** Would understanding the cause or precedent make it easier to understand my subject?
6. **What effects has my subject had or is it likely to have?** Are the effects important or unexpected?

---

you self-evident and not in need of justification: "Well, I like it. . . . So who doesn't?" What *about* rock music? Looking at the list of questions above and adding to it further questions as they occur to you, you consider what rock music is and what associations it brings to mind. The checklist questions elicit the following responses from you:

> Beatles. Stones. Electric instruments. Repetition, heavy beat. Most effective played at full volume. Soul music influence (according to Mick Jagger). Less twangy than country; faster beat than soul or folk; lyrics less sentimental than other popular music forms—more inclined to the bizarre or even the humorous. Less associated with protest than is folk music. Does have connotative associations with youth, rebellion, desire to shock, intense sexuality. Often associated with the youth rebellion and "free love" movement of the '60s. I don't like ALL forms of rock—'70s acid rock, for instance, or the really venomous anger of some groups.

Of your responses to the questions, one may touch a chord of interest and of memory: Perhaps it is rock music's debt to soul. You remember reading an interview with Mick Jagger in which Jagger acknowledged the great influence soul music has had on his own work. That creative transformation of older forms—didn't rock owe something to country music as well?—would support a strong defense of rock, especially against the charge that "it all sounds just alike," that rock music lacks creativity. Once you have narrowed your ideas and found specific threads that tie them together, you are well on your way to a thesis, and to an essay.

Other possible essays could have been generated from your answers: You might have defended the social relevance of rock by discussing the development of its lyrics of protest. You might have contrasted "classic" rock with what you regard as inferior and transient forms evolved from it, such as acid or punk rock. The whole point of the topics, or "stock issues," as they are also known, is to break the vacuum of the writer's first response to an assigned topic: "So what?" If you can come up with an approach that you can believe in, that you find worth developing, the ethical appeal of your argument will be strong.

In breaking the vacuum, you also begin to work toward what rhetorician Sheridan Baker has called the "argumentative edge" of your thesis—giving your paper a reason for being, an answer to the "So what?" question. Your thesis will have an argumentative edge if it takes a stance toward its subject: "Rock music is a popular form of music" is no more than a statement of the obvious, but "The appeal of rock music will endure into the next century" has some meat on its rhetorical bones. You have asserted a claim in the latter sentence; you have something to prove to your reader.

Analyzing your subject through considering topical questions is especially useful in narrowing a broad subject to manageable proportions for a short paper. "Rock music" is broad enough to serve as the subject of an entire book; "the relationship of rock music concerts to hearing loss" or "logistical problems in staging outdoor rock concerts" might be developed in a research paper; and "the artistic impact of the Beatles' *Abbey Road* album" could serve as the subject for a shorter argument.

Once the subject is narrowed appropriately, it still must be focused; to do so, you will need to develop a "because" clause—a *premise*—to show your reasons for making the thesis assertion. Finding the support you need will send you back to the topical checklist and perhaps to the library. The kinds of theses likely to emerge from this process of narrowing and focusing will center on questions of *fact* and questions of *definition:* What is X? What does X mean? In both cases, the "because" clause will explain and much of the body of the paper will illustrate the thesis assertion.

EXERCISE 2–2

A. Apply questions in the topical checklist on page 40 to three or four of the following subjects. What additional questions occur to you for these subjects? Based on the answers you develop, suggest two or three tentative thesis assertions for each subject. Your audience is your rhetoric classmates, and your purpose is to persuade them to take some kind of action—you must decide what kind. You wish to project an honest, believable, and convincing persona, which you will do by looking hard at the subject and kindly at the readers.

The insanity defense for accused criminals
Jogging

The results of the next presidential (or congressional) election
Academic cheating
Keeping dogs as pets in apartments
The Motion Picture Academy's rating system for movies
Allocating research funds among AIDS and other diseases
The purpose of higher education
Volunteer work

B. For each of the thesis assertions developed in part A, answer the following questions about your audience:

1. How much are my readers likely to know about this subject? For what aspects of it will I need to provide background information, and in what detail?
2. How interested are my readers likely to be in this subject? If their interest is likely to be low, how can I generate greater interest? What kinds of appeals are they likely to respond to?
3. Are my readers likely to agree with my position on the issue(s), or disagree? If they are likely to disagree, with what kinds of arguments and illustrations might I convince them to hear me out, and perhaps even to change their minds?
4. Are the readers likely to regard me as trustworthy and knowledgeable on this subject? If not, how can I win their confidence?

C. Modify your "because" clause (or add one if you have none) for each of the assertions developed in part A after considering what arguments will most effectively reach your audience, based on your analysis in part B.

Invention Strategy: Finding and Resolving Contradictions

Sometimes, of course, narrowing a topic to a component element will not satisfy your purpose; and sometimes a topical checklist will not help you discover the most compelling and relevant aspects of a particular problem. A second invention strategy—finding and resolving contradictions in the subject—can supplement or replace the topical checklists in those cases. This strategy begins with a close and critical look at the subject with a specific objective in mind: contradictions. Look for the claims that don't quite mesh, the experiments that reach different conclusions, the experts who disagree with each other, the "facts" that are in some way incompatible with other "facts" about the subject.

Take, for example, the subject of smoking. Suppose that, as an employee of Medicare, you've been asked by your boss to prepare a report on the economic costs to American society of tobacco smoking. A preliminary thesis assertion would probably come immediately to mind: The economic costs of smoking are enormous. But you reserve judgment and do some research. You find a Surgeon

General's report that estimates the annual economic impact of smoking to be about $27 billion, including the cost of "decreased work productivity" due to cigarette breaks, absences due to smoking-induced respiratory ailments, and the like. You also skim a report from the U.S. Public Health Service that attributes to tobacco use medical costs of $23 billion each year and "another $30 billion lost to society because of illness and premature death."

So far, so good. But then you turn up a more recent study made by an esteemed group of Stanford University researchers, sponsored by the National Bureau of Economic Research. This group of researchers argues that the comparatively large number of smokers who die before reaching retirement age help fund Social Security and Medicare through the taxes they pay during their working years—while those same smokers die too soon to receive many (or any) benefits in return. Seventeen percent fewer smokers live to age 65 than do nonsmokers, thereby actually *saving* the system from $10,000 to $20,000 apiece, for a total of some $14.5 billion in benefits uncollected by smokers born in 1920 alone. *Now* you have a problem to solve, and that problem will help you define both the scope of your thesis and the content of your argument. Is smoking an economic drain on society or, in a perverse and surprising way, an economic boon? Resolving the contradiction between the studies becomes your purpose; your thesis will remain an unanswered question—but far from a directionless or unfocused one—as you suspend judgment and work out the problem.

In using this approach to the invention of argument, you look for sources (either written sources or people you have talked with) that disagree with each other. The kinds of disagreement tend to be of three basic types, from each of which you can develop a particular kind of argument. First, your sources might disagree about the **facts.** Source X makes a statement about the subject you are interested in, and Source Y says something conflicting. Your thesis question, then: Who is right? Your argument will show that X is right and Y is mistaken, or perhaps the reverse, by focusing on evidence that backs up the factually correct source. Your argument will **explain** and **offer evidence** to support the truth of X. Occasionally, as you research the question, you will decide that X and Y are *both* wrong—Z is correct. If you are working on the tobacco issue, the costs of smoking, you may decide that the sources contradict each other on the facts. You resolve it as you examine the evidence closely and determine that a number of the dollar figures reached in the various studies are essentially unknowable statistics. How, for example, can we put an accurate dollar figure on the productivity lost to smoking breaks on the job? The evidence seems to be largely estimate and guesswork, even if highly educated guesswork. You may decide that the Stanford researchers' numbers are more closely tied to real evidence than were the Surgeon General's. If Stanford has better evidence, its conclusions are more supportable: Your essay then argues that the conflict can be resolved in favor of the Stanford study's assertions.

But suppose that your analysis of the evidence points in another direction. You may decide that Source X and Source Y are describing the same thing in different terms, or that they are focusing on different aspects of the same thing. In other words, you may determine that the contradiction between Source X and

Source Y is merely a superficial one. The disagreement is only **apparent,** not real. Your own argument in such cases becomes a matter of showing how to **define** and **illustrate** the issue clearly enough to resolve the verbal disagreement. In the example we are considering, the conflict between two reports on the economic impact of smoking, you may find that the studies use the concept of *cost* in different ways. Most of the studies focus on costs demonstrably incurred (such as medical bills); some focus on costs presumably incurred (such as decreased work efficiency); and the Stanford study focuses on costs presumably avoided by the premature deaths of smokers. Therein may lie the problem: These studies reflect different senses of *cost*. Pinpointing those differences may well show that the contradictory results are only apparent, not real. The problem is a matter of definition, not substantive disagreement.

Occasionally your analysis of your sources will show that Source X and Source Y do indeed differ—and both are right. This situation we call a **paradox,** a state of conflicting but coexisting truths. Your argument will then unite the supposedly incompatible claims made by your sources. This process is known as **synthesis,** the combining of apparently disparate elements to attain fuller understanding of a subject. When you show that your sources are each right (at least in some key respect), you thereby give your reader insight into the subject. You can then draw a conclusion about the net effect of the paradoxical situation. In the case of the studies on smoking costs, for example, you may find that the Stanford study points up a paradox rather than either a factual or a merely verbal contradiction. You may conclude that smoking both costs the system and saves the system. The net result may be a negligible economic impact, and such may be the conclusion of your own argument.

Searching out and resolving contradictions in your subject has several advantages to the writer of argument. It is a strategy that compels you to postpone judgment—and premature judgment, as semanticist S. I. Hayakawa and others have noted, closes the mind and makes developing arguments more difficult. Moreover, this approach provides a focus, a goal, and a direction to pursue that goal. It gives new life to the subject, new interest for both writer and reader. We all enjoy seeing a thorny problem solved—and even more, solving it!

Finding and Resolving Contradictions: Focusing Your Argument

- When **facts** conflict, use **evidence** and **explanation.**
  Your aim is to correct error.

- When **labels** conflict, use **redefinition** and **illustration.**
  Your aim is to show that there is no real conflict.

- When **ideas** conflict, and both are right, use **synthesis.**
  Your aim is to show how the conflict can provide deeper understanding of the subject.

EXERCISE 2–3

A. Identify two or three contradictory notions that people hold about the following subjects. Decide if each contradiction you find centers on facts, labels (that is, how people or things are defined), or paradox.

> pornography (For example: Some say it is a "victimless" crime; some say it victimizes women and children.)
> euthanasia
> equal pay for women
> electing, rather than appointing, judges
> "pot luck" roommates
> television ads for beer and wine
> careers in the military
> government subsidies to tobacco farmers
> surrogate mothers' bearing children for others
> organ transplantation
> bilingual education

B. If you are part of a peer writing group, discuss with the other members how you might develop a written argument from two or three of the conflicts you find. Consider the different emphases, the different kinds of support, the likely patterns of organization that your arguments might demonstrate. Would an argument centering on a paradox tend to be longer or shorter than an argument centering on a factual contradiction? Would an argument centering on a verbal disagreement, a matter of definition, ordinarily be easier or harder to organize and support than the other two kinds?

C. Develop a thesis question for one of the contradictions you have identified. Consider possible answers to the question, and write out a tentative thesis statement: an answer to the question plus a "because" clause. How would you go about developing a written argument to support this thesis? Would library research be required? Do you need really up-to-date source material for this subject? Discuss the strategies you might employ to develop your argument.

D. Suppose that you will write a paper developed from the thesis question and tentative thesis statement you have worked out. How, if at all, might you need to modify your thesis or your support for it in order to reach and engage an audience consisting of the members of your rhetoric class? Discuss briefly.

Invention Strategy: Examining Influences and Consequences

A third strategy for developing arguments focuses on what has influenced your subject and what your subject in turn has influenced. After all, in this world nothing but a writer facing a blank sheet of paper exists in a vacuum. Considering influences and consequences can reveal important and overlooked aspects of a subject as you identify those influences and distinguish relationship from mere coincidence.

And, in fact, such an examination will help you develop an argument much more satisfactorily than will approaching your subject from two other perspectives that we associate with argument even more frequently. The first of these is the question of **policy:** "What should be done?" or "What stance should be taken?" The second is the question of **value:** "What is X worth?" Two examples will illustrate the developmental difficulties policy and value theses create for a writer. Returning to the problems posed a student writer and a fund-raiser earlier in the chapter, we might develop theses such as the following:

> A standardized syllabus and final exam should not be adopted for English 101, because standardization interferes with academic freedom and inhibits the flexibility needed to address the individual needs of classes and to reflect the individual teaching styles of professors.

> The Children's Hospital, because it has a computerized central supply and planning office, does a superb job of using funds efficiently.

Both of these proposed theses seem all right. The first one in particular sounds full of developmental possibilities—or at least of long-winded phrases. But, surprisingly, both have problems that will hinder their development into full, well-reasoned arguments.

First, the student's proposed thesis about a standardized syllabus presents a complex developmental problem. It sets up a question of policy—that is, a discussion of what *should* be done—and what kind of issue could be more suitable to argument? But the student writer can't persuade an uninformed or skeptical audience to support a policy until she has established the values on which the policy is to be based and considered the influences leading to and consequences following from that policy. Then, too, there are some slippery terms to define and illustrate: *standardization, academic freedom, flexibility.* And all of this should *precede* the writer's declaration of the thesis, unless she is addressing people who already fully agree with her assertions—and if so, what need is there for persuasion?

Next, the fund-raiser's argument centers on evaluation: The Children's Hospital does a great job. The problem again will lie in development. Just what constitutes a "great job"? Theses centering on questions of value tend to get sidetracked into clarification and defense of the writer's chosen criteria of value rather than the specific issue at hand. For instance, *does* computerization alone automatically make an organization efficient?

It is the matter of audience that makes policy and value questions risky choices for theses if we truly wish to persuade. Both of these sample arguments are headed for trouble once the writers recall their rhetorical context and consider their audience—each with its probable questions, preconceptions, and doubts—and attempt to develop a convincing paper. If the audience does not share the writer's hierarchy of values, the paper is doomed to rhetorical failure; if it does share those values, the argument may be unnecessary and therefore seem trivial.

All the same, the point is *not* that you should avoid all questions of policy or value; they are important to argument. Value and policy arguments may develop naturally in conclusions to papers. And in appropriate contexts (when you are addressing an audience already predisposed to agree with you) either can serve as theses. Rather, the point is that such statements can lead to a dead end; they provide little help in generating and developing the basic structure of a written argument. So, unless your assignment specifies a policy or value thesis, **avoid creating theses centering on questions of policy or questions of value.**

But theses centering on questions of influence can lead to well-developed arguments on the same subjects. And because they have greater persuasive possibilities, they can even enable you to steer the reader toward policy and value conclusions that follow from the influences and consequences you demonstrate. If, for example, you believe that athletes should be tested regularly for drug use, what kinds of reasons could you offer in support of that policy? Some possibilities: "Drugs are bad" (value statement); "Public health is more important than privacy" (value statement); "People in public life should be compelled to set a good example for the rest of us" (policy statement). But each of these claims would immediately and unproductively alienate part of your audience, and each would be difficult to "prove." Instead, you might try a different approach to both subject and audience:

> Testing athletes for drug use leads to improvement in the overall quality of athletics because precautionary procedures of this kind encourage athletes to maintain their health and fitness.

This thesis focuses on influences and consequences rather than values or policy. If you can demonstrate that the relationships you claim here do indeed exist, you can persuade your reader of the validity of your conclusion: "Testing athletes for drug use leads to improvement in the overall quality of athletics." It then becomes much easier to further assert, by way of conclusion to your essay, that if we grant that drug abuse is undesirable (an easily accepted value claim) and if you have demonstrated that testing athletes really does lead to greater health and fitness among athletes (the main thrust of your argument), we cannot deny the reasonableness of the policy claim that athletes *should* be so tested.

THE ENTHYMEME AS THESIS

As we have seen, every written argument makes a claim and offers support for it: "X because Y." It also makes assumptions about the subject and the audience: "X because Y (and of course Z, but we all know that!)." When you write out a tentative thesis statement, or **working thesis,** you identify Y but usually not Z—or L, M, N, or the host of other operative assumptions. Even though you do not write those assumptions, you need to think about them all the same. If your assumptions are mistaken, your argument falls on deaf ears—or falls apart.

Assumptions in argument begin, then, with assumptions about the potential audience. In addition, a major assumption underlies any thesis statement. It constitutes the primary shared ground between the elements of the argument, the starting point that makes the argument possible. This shared ground is called the **major premise** or **warrant**. We can use the earlier argument about drug testing for athletes to illustrate the importance of the unstated major premise to the success or failure of an argument. Suppose the thesis argument is phrased in this way:

> Testing athletes for drug use leads to quality athletic performance because precautionary measures of this kind promote health and fitness.

This statement makes a claim: "Testing athletes for drug use leads to quality athletic performance." And it gives a reason for making the claim: "Precautionary measures of this kind promote health and fitness." What is left *unsaid,* however, is that *health and fitness are related to quality athletic performance.* If you are the writer, you may justifiably feel that readers will both understand and accept that implicit premise. If you were wrong in that major assumption, however, the thesis argument would fall apart, for it would fail to connect drug testing and quality athletic performance.

How can you be sure that you have made logical connections between the elements of your thesis argument? You can do so by expressing your thesis as an **enthymeme.** The enthymeme is a rhetorical model, developed centuries ago by Aristotle, that can help you develop sound arguments. **An enthymeme is a core argument consisting of a claim, a "because" clause giving reason(s) for that claim, and a major, unstated assumption linking the claim to the reasons offered to support it.** The rules for constructing enthymemes are fairly simple:

1. **An enthymeme links three entities.** The significance of three, rather than two or four, is shown below. These three entities may be Scuba divers, people who vote Libertarian, Siamese cats, or Ming vases. It doesn't matter. What matters, rather, is the next rule:

2. **The three linked entities must be different things, rather than different names for the same thing.** Otherwise, you will reason in a circle, begging the question. (To beg the question is to assume what you ought to be proving.) For example, if you work out a thesis that

> The U.S. presidential primary system is outmoded because it no longer fits the needs of late-twentieth-century voters,

you have nowhere to go in your argument. Your "thesis" reduces to "the primary system is outmoded because it is outmoded." Compare that question-begging thesis to this one:

> The U.S. presidential primary system fails as a democratic institution because it removes the selection of a president from the hands of the populace.

This is an arguable thesis. The three entities linked are "the U.S. presidential primary system," "democratic institutions," and "things that remove the selection of a president from the hands of the populace." The writer in this case has a point to make and work to do.

3. **No more than three entities may be linked in a single enthymeme.** Otherwise, you conflate multiple arguments into what appears to be just one, one that then fails to prove its claim. This most often happens when you use two terms that appear to be synonymous but are not. For instance, *drug* can mean any pharmaceutical product, even aspirin, but in some contexts the term means specifically illegal drugs. If you argue that

> Drugs harm athletes,
> and aspirin is a drug;
> therefore, aspirin harms athletes.

you have used four terms rather than three—and the conclusion is not warranted.

Any of the three entities linked in an enthymeme may have multiple characteristics and components, *as long as they are treated as a unit throughout the argument*. You can argue about drugs, illicit drugs, or legal but harmful drugs. You can argue about people, people in China, or people who enjoy dangerous hobbies. Each of these would be a different unit in an argument.

Enthymemes typically take this form:

	— A —	———————— B ————————	
(CONCLUSION)	Subject	Active, Transitive Verb	Object
		BECAUSE	
	— A′ —	———————— C ————————	
(PREMISE)	Subject	Active, Transitive Verb	Object

In an argument based on an enthymeme, you want to show a relationship between A and B. You begin by assuming a relationship between B and C—a relationship that will be accepted without challenge by your potential audience. This major assumption underlies the relationship you then demonstrate between A and C, and the two—the assumed relationship and the demonstrated relationship—logically permit you to make your claim about the relationship between A and B. Naturally, *the assumed relationship (C ↔ B) should express an idea that the audience can reasonably be expected to grant without argument*.

To develop a workable enthymeme of this kind for a written argument, pay particular attention to your verbs:

4. **Use active transitive verbs in both clauses of your "X because Y" enthymeme.** * Why? Use active verbs because passive verbs obscure the true agent of an action, and you want your argument to be clear. Use specific verbs

---

*By contrast, in testing the logical structure of an argument by restating it according to a formal model (called a syllogism), you *remove* the transitive verbs and recast the core argument with "to be" verbs. We can analyze arguments with the syllogism; we can create arguments with the enthymeme.

rather than "to be" verbs for two reasons: first, because "to be" verbs obscure the precise *action* on which your argument may focus; and second, because "to be" verbs tend to lead to redundant arguments with only two terms. This is suitable only for an argument with the sole purpose of defining a term.

5. **Avoid verbs of policy in your thesis enthymeme.** "Verbs of policy" means verbs that state or imply "should," "must," "ought to," or the like. Many arguments advance policy claims, of course, but "should" statements work best in conclusions, rather than core arguments, unless your readers are predisposed to agree with you.

6. **Avoid thesis enthymemes that express only evaluation.** These sentences convey little more than the writer's approval or disapproval of the subject. Typically they rely on some form of "to be" as the verb. For example: "Cartoon violence is harmful to children," or "The presidential primary system is inherently undemocratic." Such assertions all too often lead to vague claims or arguments that defend the chosen values more than they discuss the intended subject. Where possible (for there will be exceptions), defer major judgments until the concluding paragraphs of your written arguments. By that point they will be justified.

Bear in mind that the complete enthymeme may not appear as a single sentence in the essay, though its conclusion (the thesis claim) and its stated reason will be written out at the points where they are demonstrated. The shared assumption may or may not be stated explicitly. If it is stated, it usually appears in the introduction.

Looking again at the argument about drug abuse, you can see that it fits the enthymematic model for an arguable thesis:

(A)   Testing athletes for drug abuse
(B)   leads to quality athletic performance
                    BECAUSE
(A restated)   precautionary measures of this kind
(C)   promote health and fitness.

It makes a claim—"Testing athletes for drug use leads to quality athletic performance"—based on a supporting claim about the influence of fear on athletes' behavior: "Precautionary measures of this kind promote health and fitness." The major assumption that links the conclusion with the supporting claim can be expressed as

(C)   What promotes health and fitness
(B)   leads to quality athletic performance.

This is reasonable enough. In thinking about your potential audience, you may accept this idea as likely to be a major shared ground between writer and readers.

The enthymeme's stated reason, on the other hand, needs to express an idea that will not be granted quite so readily, or else no argument is needed. Here, "Precautionary measures of this kind promote health and fitness" expresses an idea with which not everyone will agree. Some say that such measures lead to paranoia among athletes, a state hardly likely to promote health and fitness. Others might assert that no positive correlation can be shown between the absence of drugs in the system and good physical condition. Still others might question just what we mean by *health* or *fitness*. So you have some defining and explaining to do, some evidence and examples to muster in support of the premise.

If the major assumption is widely accepted and you have demonstrated the stated premise persuasively, the final business of an argument is to declare its conclusion, your thesis claim. And if you have done your job well, that thesis will appear inevitable and incontrovertible to a reasonable reader.

Guidelines for Developing a Thesis Enthymeme

1. Link exactly three distinct entities.
2. Express the enthymeme as a main clause and a dependent ("because") clause.
3. Where possible, argue influences and consequences rather than policy or evaluation. Leave policy and evaluation claims to the end of the essay, once you have proven a substantive claim.
4. Use precise, active verbs.

SHAPING THE ARGUMENT

Now let's see how a strong enthymeme can help you develop a written argument. First you may want to write it as a question, or a series of questions, as we discussed earlier in the chapter. Once you have done some brainstorming, reading, discussing, and reflecting, you will be ready to write out a tentative thesis enthymeme. We'll call this the **working thesis,** as a reminder that you may need to modify it as you develop your argument and think further about all its implications. A good suggestion is to write out the thesis on a separate piece of paper and keep it before you as you develop your argument. Write out the major shared assumption, too, that links your claim with the stated reason for it.

An example will illustrate how this process works. As an intern for a U.S. Senator from a northeastern state, you have been asked to prepare a paper on the subject of farm subsidies. The Senator is undecided whether or not to vote in favor of an upcoming bill eliminating most of those subsidies in an effort to balance the federal budget. You do some research and decide, to your surprise, that farm subsidies actually hurt farmers in the long run. But, although from a heavily industrialized state, the Senator has a number of farmers in his constituency; he will need some persuading to see the issue as you now understand it. So you work on a core enthymeme that will help you find the strategy you need. It develops along these lines:

Farm subsidies should be eliminated.

> No—only two terms and a policy assertion. The Senator would never accept that right off the bat. Besides, this is in passive voice and obscures the agent: The Senate has to act, though I don't want to dwell on that unpleasant fact until I've made my case.

Farm subsidies are harmful in the long run.

> Not enough—only two terms and a value assertion. "To be" verb doesn't point toward any specific action.

Farm subsidies are harmful in the long run and therefore should be eliminated.

> No—still nothing specific to work with; just combines value and policy claims.

> OK: Time out. Just what *is* so bad about farm subsidies? They hurt farmers. *How?* Well, all the data I've found suggests a kind of rebound effect from the huge imbalances subsidies create in supply and demand. But how can I convince the Senator that's so? He would probably grant that imbalances in supply and demand are bad for farmers. Perhaps he would accept the notion that artificial manipulation of the marketplace leads to imbalances—I could show a lot of evidence for that. And aren't farm subsidies artificial manipulation of the marketplace? So:

(A) Farm subsidies ultimately (B) hurt farmers because (A') this artificial manipulation of the farm economy (C) creates huge imbalances between production and demand.

> This should work. I'll first discuss the general point that farmers are important contributors to this country's economy, so the last thing we want to do is lessen farmers' ability to make a livelihood (B). No; better leave that point out. The Senator already is convinced of it, and I'll just annoy him by spelling it out for him. I'll begin with the idea that imbalances in production and demand hurt the farm economy and thereby tend to hurt farmers (C → B).
> Next I should argue that artificial manipulation of the farm economy—better define and illustrate this term (A')—leads to such undesirable imbalances (A' → C). I'll need some strong statistics here and authoritative statements from a couple of leading economists. Some illustration of manipulation creating problems would help here, too.
> Then my conclusion: First, show that farm subsidies constitute artificial manipulation of the agricultural economy (A = A'); then, my thesis: Farm subsidies really hurt farmers in the long run (A → B).

The enthymeme, by compelling you to keep the rhetorical context of purpose and audience in mind, helps you to discover what your argument needs to accomplish and even how to go about developing it. An essay begins to take shape. You have considered your subject and your stance toward it, you have considered your audience and its needs and interests, and you have generated a rough framework of ideas that is solid and honest—and therefore likely to be convincing. Additional research may be necessary, depending on the topic, the potential readers, and your purpose in addressing them, but you are ready to write.

Evaluating a Working Thesis Enthymeme

1. Reconstruct and evaluate the implied premise (C ↔ B).
   - It should be believable, likely to be readily accepted by the reader.
   - It should not be trivial.
2. Evaluate the expressed premise (A′ → C).
   - It should sum up the major thrust of your argument, including the major point(s) you intend to develop.
3. Evaluate the conclusion (A → B).
   - It should be a statement that the intended audience either does not yet know, does not yet understand, or does not yet accept.
4. Be prepared to modify the thesis enthymeme as you work through the process of writing the paper.

EXERCISE 2–4

A. Each of the following statements concerns a question of influence, value, or policy. Identify each accordingly, then comment on the problems and/or possibilities it presents as a thesis for an article that you, as a summer intern for the National Park Service, might write for the Park Service employees' newsletter at Rocky Mountain National Park in Estes Park, Colorado. Which seems to hold the greatest potential for development? Briefly discuss why. Modify that statement into a thesis enthymeme appropriate to your own beliefs, purpose, and audience.

B. What definitions and relationships will your article need to discuss or prove, based on the thesis enthymeme you have developed?

Injured hikers should bear the cost of their rescue because they undertook hiking with full awareness that it entailed risks.

Hiking permit fees to enable the Park Service to fund the rescue of injured hikers will lead to fewer hiking injuries because the act of paying into a rescue fund impresses on hikers the dangers of back country trekking and the need to take precautions.

The lives of injured hikers are less valuable than those of people who attempt to rescue them because the hikers were probably careless.

Requiring injured hikers to bear the cost of their rescue will maintain national park operating funds because making people assume responsibility for their own actions decreases unnecessary risk-taking.

Hikers get injured because they take unnecessary risks.

Other ways of generating an essay are possible; there may be as many strategies for invention as there are writers. Some writers begin by creating a formal outline—and stick to it. Some simply sit down and write everything that comes to mind regarding the topic, and later rework what they have written into a coherent whole. Some wait for inspiration to strike—but many who wait for the muse to speak wait in vain. Katherine Anne Porter claimed, "I always write my last line, my last paragraphs, my last page first." Many writers of arguments (notably those developing enthymemes) write their conclusion first, then look for evidence to support that conclusion. Do what works for you. But when you find yourself up against that wall with no opening, writer's block, *begin by asking questions, by looking for gaps and contradictions, by considering your subject in its context with its attendant influences and consequences.* And always consider your purpose and your audience. You will find that you can go over the wall, or around it. Or knock it down.

As you write a rough draft developing the thesis you have worked out, you will need to define key terms and concepts, and you will need to offer examples and other evidence to support your claims. The next two chapters provide some specific advice about those elements of argument. If you are willing to spend a little extra time both planning and shaping your arguments, you will find that out of the rubble of that wall of writer's block you can construct a strong and persuasive essay.

READINGS

GROUP DISCUSSIONS ARE BENEFICIAL

(Student Draft)

1   A study entitled *The American Freshman—National Norms* shows that first-year college students aren't studying as much as in the past. The study asked 204,000 freshmen numerous questions, including how much time they spend studying each week. The startling response is that almost half of the freshmen, 48.2 percent, study less than five hours each week. That's less than one hour per week per class, folks. Only about 20 percent said they study more than 10 hours each week.

2   It's only natural to question whether our future leaders will treat major problems with the same energy as they do their studies. Is the "Ward Cleaver effect" taking its toll?

3   Our generation has been raised on television. Studies show that, by the time they graduate from high school, young adults have spent more time watching television than they have spent in the classroom. For most, TV is the perpetual teacher. Witness the problem of Ward Cleaver.

4   In the first few minutes of any *Leave it to Beaver* episode, Theodore or

Wally does something reprehensible (like calling someone a "stinker" or blowing up the Dairy Queen). Twenty minutes into the show, Ward finds out about the mischief and resolves the crisis within the half hour. After removing the commercials, Beave's crisis is presented, discovered and resolved in 22 minutes of show time.

5   Unfortunately, many Americans come to expect their answers quickly— whether it be answers to the quiz on *Silas Marner* or answers to the *Contra* funds diversion. It is apparent that current college students think one scant hour a night of studying is more than enough. One hour a day of thinking, however, is not going to solve the problems of this nation, present or future.

6   Therein lies the problem: College has become too much memorization and not enough thinking.

7   I want to sharpen my critical thinking skills, not merely learn a trade. Had I wanted just a "job license," I would have gone to one of those technical schools that advertise on late night TV. Instead, I came to college to get a diploma—to learn how to reason, how to interpret and how to think.

8   Unfortunately, too many professors teach as if college is an extension of high school. They lecture for three hours and assign hundreds of pages of reading each week. At the end of six weeks, they give tests that include so many questions that there is no time to both think about the answers and finish the test. The only way for a student to maximize his or her grade is to memorize facts and spit them back out just as they are offered in the teachers' lectures. The student who takes the time to think about the questions will never finish.

9   What challenge is there in rote?

10   Of course, this does not apply to all professors, but in my experience at this university, it includes more than half.

11   Students are also to blame. Very few are willing to participate in discussion groups outside of classtime. They attend the lectures, take the tests and stop thinking once the bell rings.

12   Discussion groups are the best way to learn. Most of the facts needed to answer test questions today can easily be relearned years from now at any library. The opinions of my peers, however, cannot be learned from any text or reference book.

13   Remember, I am here to sharpen my critical thinking skills as well as to learn how to operate a TV camera. There is no better way to learn about my own thought processes than to hear how others reach decisions. I wish I had more of an opportunity to exchange ideas with other students, both inside and outside the classroom.

QUESTIONS AND IDEAS FOR DISCUSSION

1. The author of this material, a member of a campus newspaper writing staff, was told he needed to write a column of about 1,000 words. The intended

audience is composed of college students and faculty. Does the author have a clear sense of his purpose in addressing them? Comment.

2. What is the author's main point? Does he have a thesis? If so, what is it? Does it cover the argument's actual content? Could you suggest an improved version? If you find no apparent thesis, suggest one that might give a firmer shape to the essay.

3. What idea(s) in this draft would have to be eliminated in an essay developed from your suggested thesis statement?

4. What idea(s) in this draft would need to be developed more fully in a well-thought-out essay developed from your suggested thesis statement?

5. Do you find any gaps in the reasoning in this argument? If so, how might they be remedied?

6. Comment on the appropriateness of the title.

PAY EQUITY IS UNFAIR TO WOMEN

Linda Chavez

1 Striking secretaries at Yale recently threatened to bring the 284-year-old university to a standstill over what they saw as discrimination in wages favoring men over women. Female workers in Washington State won a discrimination suit in a federal district court that may cost the state government nearly $1 billion in back pay and increased wages. The U.S. House of Representatives passed a bill in the last session of Congress that required all federal jobs to be reevaluated, with the aim of raising the pay for jobs held mainly by women.

2 All these actions were taken in the name of comparable worth, a controversial theory that jobs have an intrinsic, measurable value that should dictate the wages paid. Sounds like a great deal for women trapped in underpaid occupations, doesn't it? In the short run it may be: women in jobs directly affected by the strikes, suits, and legislation could get higher wages. But in the long run all women will lose. If the proponents of comparable worth succeed in their quest, they will bring about the most radical alteration of our economy in the nation's history, replacing the market system with a system of administered wages. Why, then, have so many otherwise sensible people endorsed comparable worth?

3 The answer lies partly in the ability of comparable worth advocates to cloak themselves in the rhetoric of fairness. They have even coined a phrase to describe their goal: pay equity. Mimicking the strategy of the civil rights movement, they point to the statistical disparity between the average earnings of men and women and conclude that discrimination must exist. They note the high concentration of women in certain occupations and claim job segregation. But equal pay for equal work is the law of the land, as is the

guarantee that any woman has the right to any job for which she is qualified. What pay equity requires is not the fairness of equal opportunity, but something disturbingly different.

4   In recent years the courts have held that government ought to remedy any disparities in the success achieved by various groups in society. Courts routinely find, for example, that discrimination exists when an employer's work force has fewer blacks in it than their proportion in the local labor market. With people conditioned to think this way, comparable worth advocates have only to prove that women earn less than men to convince many that discrimination is the cause. The fact that women earn 72 cents for every dollar that men earn, based on their average hourly wages, leads few people to ask why. Instead, they ask what we can do about it.

5   The wage gap between men and women is a complex phenomenon. No single explanation suffices. Women continue to work at different jobs than men, with fully half of all women concentrated in three occupations despite strides in opening up positions that have been male enclaves. These female occupations—sales, clerical, and professional—command salaries in the market commensurate with the supply and demand of people able and willing to perform the work.

6   Earnings clearly play only a partial role in women's decision to work in a limited number of jobs. Of far greater importance is the need that most women have to balance the demands of a job with the responsibilities of family life. Working mothers may be willing to take less pay to get other benefits—a job that doesn't penalize the woman who intermittently interrupts her career for childbearing, or a job that provides regular working hours and proximity to a telephone in case of a child-related emergency.

7   Comparable worth advocates want no part of such complexities. It is as if they cannot conceive that women are capable of acting in their self-interest. Instead, they depict working women as victims of conspiracy and oppression, incapable of making rational decisions about their needs and desires. The fact that women continue to seek employment primarily in low-paying, female-dominated jobs despite expanded opportunity in higher-paying, traditionally male occupations does not suggest to comparable worth advocates that the non-monetary benefits of certain jobs may have appeal. Rather, it suggests to them that women need protection from the consequences of their choices.

8   While espousing feminist ideology, the comparable worth advocates offer up protectionist legislation to insulate women from the demands of the market. But like so much of what passes for protection, comparable worth may make victims of its intended beneficiaries. Women will ultimately be the biggest losers.

9   If comparable worth becomes the law of the land, higher salaries almost certainly will mean fewer jobs in traditionally female occupations. Employers forced to pay higher wages with no concomitant rise in productivity have to raise prices or reduce the number of jobs. What manager, faced with a deci-

sion between losing his competitive edge by hiking prices or making do with
fewer secretaries, will choose the former, particularly in the age of computers
and word processors?

10   Australia has had a variation of comparable worth in both the public
and private sectors since 1972. Within five years of enactment of its law, female unemployment in Australia rose, the number of women working part
time increased, and the growth of female participation in the labor force
slowed.

11   What the comparable worth advocates always ignore is who will bear
the costs of the pay increases their system would mandate. The costs will not
be borne by some elite band of larcenous employers. They will be borne
mainly by women.

QUESTIONS AND IDEAS FOR DISCUSSION

1. What is the main point—the thesis conclusion—of this essay? Where is it
   stated? Why do you think Chavez expresses it at the point at which she does?

2. What are the major supporting points for the thesis? Is each supporting point
   itself supported by adequate and persuasive explanation, examples, and/or
   definition? Identify any points that seem to warrant further development or
   modification to be convincing.

3. Discuss your response to this essay. Did you agree with Chavez's basic position before reading? If so, how did that affect the closeness with which you
   considered her actual argument? Whether or not you disagreed with the
   author's basic position before reading, were you put off by any unsupported
   value statements or assumptions? If so, identify them.

4. Chavez centers much of her argument on contradictions she finds in the
   movement toward "comparable worth" pay in the job market. Describe the
   contradictions she finds. Are they, in her judgment, real or only apparent? Do
   you agree? Comment.

5. Chavez also offers an enthymeme in her essay. We might restate that enthymeme (found in paragraph 9) as follows:

   A comparable worth policy leads to higher salaries in traditionally female jobs.
   Higher salaries, however, lead to fewer traditionally female jobs.
   So, a comparable worth policy leads to fewer traditionally female jobs.

   Does Chavez fully develop and convincingly prove this argument? Comment.

6. Is Chavez trying to do too much in this essay? Should she have focused more
   specifically on either persuading us of the contradiction she finds in the
   whole notion of comparable worth, or persuading us of the argument expressed in the enthymeme in paragraph 9? Whether or not you agree with
   her position, create a thesis that would limit her argument clearly and that
   would be "provable" in a short essay such as this one.

Suggestions for Writing and Further Discussion

1. Develop a thesis, using any of the methods discussed in this chapter, on the subject of grading. Assume that your purpose is to convince the faculty senate (to change/not to change) the grading system at your school. Evaluate the thesis, perhaps in a small group discussion with members of your writing class. After making whatever changes are needed in the thesis, write an essay developing its argument through explanation, examples, and other detail.

2. Develop a thesis and, from it, an essay arguing that all this talk about considering readers is just so much insincere hot air (we won't worry just now about the improbability of that metaphor): No writing is worth reading—indeed, no writing is *possible*—that is not written for oneself first and foremost.

3. What underrated musical artists of the twentieth century will people listen to in the twenty-first century? Convince your readers (members of your writing class) to take seriously a particular composer/performer/group you admire.

4. Write an essay from one of the theses you developed in Exercise 2–2. Suggestions for purpose and audience are given in the exercise, but you may stipulate others instead.

5. What do you think about the expanding movement to ban smoking in public places? Write a letter to your city or town council putting forward your views in hopes of affecting local policy. (Then, mail it!)

6. Write an essay from the thesis you developed in Exercise 2–3.

7. Colleges and universities have recurring problems with two kinds of abuses within athletic programs: play-for-pay and drug use among athletes. Given the readers of your alumni magazine as an audience, decide on a purpose for addressing them about some aspect of one of these problems and develop a thesis and then an essay suitable for the magazine to print.

8. If you are from a farming region or are otherwise knowledgeable about farming, write an essay that will enlighten your classmates about a particular aspect of the farm economy and its problems in this country.

9. Writing an essay from the thesis you developed in Exercise 2–4. Suggestions regarding purpose and audience are given in the exercise.

10. Write the argument that the student writer of "Group Discussions Are Beneficial" may have intended to write. Express your own viewpoint in doing so, and support your thesis with examples of your own. Your aim is to convince your campus community to recognize a problem—and perhaps thereby to stimulate its members, both students and faculty, to do something about the problem.

11. Whether or not you are currently employed, you undoubtedly intend to be employed following your academic studies—so what Linda Chavez is concerned about in "Pay Equity Is Unfair to Women" concerns you as well. Write an essay (one that would be even more suitable for publication in *Fortune* than Chavez's) that argues either the thesis you developed in response to the questions following the essay or a contrary or otherwise modified position on the same issue.

3

Developing Arguments: Defining Terms

> *"When I use a word," Humpty Dumpty said, in rather a scornful tone, "it means just what I choose it to mean—neither more nor less."*
>
> *"The question is," said Alice, "whether you can make words mean so many different things."*
>
> *"The question is," said Humpty Dumpty, "which is to be master— that's all."*
>
> **—Lewis Carroll, *Through the Looking-Glass***

To be master or not to be master of the words you use in any communication (but especially argument) is all the choice you have; you have no alternative as to whether you will or will not use language. Wordless communication and wordless persuasion are possible, of course: One photograph of a starving child may move people to contribute their money or their time to a refugee cause more quickly than an hour's cajoling would do, or a well-placed fist to the jaw may dissuade one person from continuing to argue politics with another. But nonverbal persuasion is particularly vulnerable to misinterpretation, and it is difficult to sustain for long. Nonverbal persuasion speaks directly to the emotions; argument at least purports to address the intellect.

So if you are to construct arguments, you must use words. And, lest you be misunderstood, you are obliged to use those words carefully and precisely, aware not only of their denotations—literal meaning—but also of their connotations and possible ambiguities. Through the careful selection of words and the definition of key terms, you assure your readers' comprehension and affect your readers' reception of your arguments.

With language we make sense of the world as we see it and dwell in it. To a larger extent than we may think, words define our reality. With words we can give form to the concept of Spain for someone who has never traveled there, give meaning to the idea of tact for someone who hasn't any, or make a suggestion for producing better widgets believable in an employer's imagination. And in using language to share meaning, we rely on definition. Definition is essential to any use of language, but especially to written argument. If you express the issue fuzzily, very often your thoughts are also fuzzier than they should be. Defining the issue and the pertinent terms will help to ensure that you have a clear idea of your subject and your stance toward it, and that the reader will have a clear understanding of both subject and stance.

HOW TO DEFINE

Reportive Definitions

Just as definitions have several uses in argument—whether to clarify a term or to control the scope of a discussion—they are of several kinds, according to various purposes. Definition may be *reportive* or *stipulative*. The first, as rhetorician Gerald Runkle succinctly puts it, states "how society uses the term"; the second, "how I use the term." Reportive definitions may indicate meanings that are historical or current, general or technical, and they may do so in a number of ways. First is the formal, or analytical, definition of a term. In a formal definition we place a word or term into the general class of things into which it fits, then we analyze what makes it both part of that class and distinct from other members of that class. An accurate formal definition is *reversible:* that is, both "X is Y" and "Y is X" are true statements. (Or to put it another way, *all* X is Y and *only* X is Y.) And to be truly helpful to a reader, any definition should define a term in words that are *more familiar* to likely readers than the term being defined.

Developing a clear, reversible definition for a key term can be harder than it sounds. Sometimes even dictionaries, with their need for brevity, will offer up what seem like endless loops of unfamiliar synonyms rather than formal and comprehensible definitions. For example, we do not better understand what a double bassoon is after reading that it is a "contrabassoon." That definition by synonym is reversible, but hardly clear. To define double bassoon as a wind instrument, on the other hand, is clear but not reversible. A trumpet or even a harmonica is also a wind instrument. *The Harper's Dictionary of Music,* however, gives a clear and reversible definition: A *"double bassoon* or *contrabassoon* [is] the lowest member of the oboe family, . . . pitched an octave lower than the bassoon [with] a tube almost eighteen feet long, which is doubled back on itself four times."

Reportive definitions are not always formal. They can include:

Synonyms: Other words or phrases that mean the same thing as the term you wish to define. Dictionaries often define by synonym, and not always very helpfully. In order to help your own readers, make sure that your synonyms are clearer and plainer than the term you are defining. And even though it is often said that there are no exact synonyms, make sure that yours are as precise·

as humanly possible. Example: "An impeachment is an accusation, charge, or indictment."

Example: A particular instance, an illustration. Examples should be typical of what you are defining. Example: "Andrew Jackson was the subject of an impeachment."

Conditions for Use: Contextual setting. If you use a term only in particular contexts, describing those contexts helps readers better understand the term. Example: "We normally use the term *impeachment* only in reference to public officials."

Comparison: Analogy. A comparison shows similarities between what we wish to define and other things more familiar to the reader. Example: "An impeachment of a public official is much like an indictment of an ordinary citizen in a court of law. In both cases a hearing or trial follows."

Contrast: Distinctions between things the reader may have confused with each other, things that may have superficial similarities. Sometimes we need to know what uses of a term are *not* appropriate. Example: "An impeachment is not a conviction."

Etymology: The historical and linguistic derivation of a term. The sources of a term, its root meanings, often clarify it and make it easier to remember. Example: "The term *impeachment* comes from the Latin word for *trap*."

We can, and often do, combine these methods when we want to make a difficult concept completely clear to our readers.

Stipulative Definitions

A stipulative definition may assign meaning arbitrarily to a new term (*wabe*, as Alice correctly guesses in her conversation with Humpty Dumpty, means "the little grass-plot round a sundial"); restrict narrowly the meaning of an extant term; or even assign a new meaning to an old term—though the latter should be done for some good reason and not, as Humpty Dumpty claims, simply to show "which is to be master." Stipulative definitions may be expressed in the same ways reportive definitions are expressed. For example, one might stipulate by synonym a secondary meaning of *impeachment* for a given context: "a discrediting of someone." A cynic might stipulate a harsher synonym: "the modern equivalent of a lynching." Or the same observer might use an example: "Richard Nixon was the subject of impeachment—by the press, which seems to have designated itself the appropriate tribunal for such action." Another stipulative definition (from a different viewpoint) might give an unusual condition for the use of the term: "In an impeachment no bail is required of the individual impeached, however dangerous to the public weal that person may be."

As these examples show, how you as a writer define your terms makes apparent your attitude toward your subject and even toward your audience. Many people forget that *impeachment* does not mean *conviction*, and they may need to be reminded of that fact for purposes of clarity. Even if your readers can be expected to understand the term, you may need to define it in order to control their attitudes toward what the word represents. In any case, one caution is in order: Definitions should not be used in desperation as a starting point for an essay, or as filler. Dictionaries are available to readers as well as to writers; you risk seeming condescending to your readers if you define common words, just as you risk alienating them if you offer only cryptic quotations from dictionaries to define rare or difficult terms.

HOW TO JUDGE DEFINITIONS

A definition, whether reportive or stipulative, should adhere to certain standards of clarity and completeness:

1. **It should not be circular.** The tautology "Business is business" enlightens us not at all; "A good movie is one you like" is little better.
2. **It should not employ ambiguous or metaphorical language, or terms more difficult or obscure than the term to be defined.** Dr. Johnson is notorious for his definition of *net:* "anything reticulated or decussated, at equal distances, with interstices between the intersections."
3. **It should be exact, neither too broad nor too narrow.** The problem with saying that "a president of the United States must be a citizen of the United States" is that the statement, while true, is too broad; more than two hundred million people are U.S. citizens. "A president of the United States must be a man who is a native-born citizen of that country, and at least thirty-five years old," on the other hand, is too narrow, for a woman is also entitled to hold that position. A really thorough and exact definition is reversible, so that both "x is y" and "y is x" are true statements.
4. **It should indicate connotative values if they are significant.** *Rhetoric,* for example, is often used in a pejorative sense: We may speak of "empty rhetoric" or "mere rhetoric" in dismissing the argument of one with whom we disagree. Writers who intend to use the term in a neutral or favorable way would do well to define the term, perhaps in the classical sense: "the art of persuasion." They should indicate that the negative connotations do not apply to the term as they use it. *[handwritten: pejorative: saying it's bad]*

[handwritten margin note: rhetoric: reasoned attempt to persuade]

You will notice the warning, above, against using metaphorical language in a definition. The reason is that here we are concerned primarily with how a term is used or how the writer wishes to use it in a particular written or oral discussion. A metaphorical definition—as, for instance, Marx's famous definition of religion as "the opium of the people"—focuses less on such practical concerns than on the reader's imagination, by specifically linking the term in question to something quite unlike it in any literal sense. Metaphor can be a powerful persuasive tool, and even an illuminating one—helping readers to visualize a concept that in more pedestrian prose might elude them. Chapter 9 will have more to say about the uses of metaphor in argument.

EXERCISE 3–1

A. Decide whether each of the following definitions is primarily reportive or stipulative. Which method or methods of defining does the writer of each use to explain or to affect our attitudes toward the term defined? (Refer to the list on pages 60–61. Which definitions, if any, are at least partly metaphorical?

B. Judge the definitions according to the standards identified on page 62. Then pick two that you find incomplete or confusing and write a more exact and clearer definition for the term in question. (To do so, you will probably need to look up some words in a good dictionary and possibly need to talk to a class member who knows more about, say, quantum mechanics than you do.)

C. Which of these definitions could serve as the focus of a written argument? Why? How might the arguments be expanded from the definitions here? Discuss.

1. Crampons are metal soleplates bearing a number of sharp teeth and designed to be strapped to the soles of hiking shoes and to grip the ice as the hiker traverses glaciers.

2. Young scientists learn about Ockham's razor before they're old enough to shave. The idea, attributed to the 14th century philosopher William of Ockham, is simple: the simplest explanation that works is the best one. It's a "razor" because it helps cut away extraneous complication from scientific theorizing.

   —Tom Siegfried, "Bayes' Math, Ockham's Razor
   Could Cut Misuse of Numbers," *Dallas Morning News*, 2 Mar. 1992

3. Let Rhetoric be defined, then, as the faculty of discerning in every case the available means of persuasion.

   —Aristotle, *Rhetoric*

4. To be accepted as a paradigm, a theory must seem better than its competitors, but it need not, and in fact never does, explain all the facts with which it can be confronted.

   —Thomas Kuhn, *The Structure of Scientific Revolutions*

5. We are gorged with papers, reports, memos, the random and miscellaneous ingredients of information. Knowledge, says Boorstin, is "orderly and cumulative," the province of books that disperse the "enduring treasure of our whole human past."

   —Hugh Sidey, quoting Daniel Boorstin, in *Time*,
   3 Aug. 1987

6. Guilt is the feeling of having done something wrong, [and] because it involves *doing*, it is redeemable. . . . Shame, on the other hand, is an experience

of *being* bad, wrong, or disgusting. . . . It cannot go away with reparation because it is not the behavior but the self that is perceived as being at fault.

—Helen Resneck-Sannes, in *Women & Therapy*,
vol. 11.2, 1991

7. In the same way that the income-tax system does not exist simply to collect money, but also to provide incentives for various sorts of economic activities, so grading is not simply an evaluation process; it is a way of providing incentives for various sorts of intellectual behavior.

—Miles Pickering, "Are Lab Courses a Waste of Time?"

8. Secularization is the wonderful mechanism by which religion becomes non-religion. Marxism is secularized Christianity; so is democracy; so is utopianism; so are human rights.

—Allan Bloom, *The Closing of the American Mind*

9. The Census defines as "urban" any city or town or village having at least 2,500 residents.

—Andrew Hacker, ed., *U/S: A Statistical Portrait of the American People*

10. Wrestling: a sport in which each of two opponents struggles hand in hand in an attempt to force the other down.

—*Random House Dictionary*

11. Wrestling is not a sport, it is a spectacle. . . .

—Roland Barthes, "Wrestling," *Mythologies*

12. Biosynthesis is the production of complex substances from simple ones by or with living organisms.

—*The American Heritage Dictionary*

13. Crime control means gun control.

—Sen. Edward Kennedy

14. We shall call the absolute square of a wave function that cannot be normalized its *intensity*.

—Siegmund Brandt and Hans Dieter Dahmen,
The Picture Book of Quantum Mechanics

15. "Liberal" is, of course, one of those fine English words, like "lady," "gay," and "welfare," which has been spoiled by special pleading. When I say *liberals* I certainly don't mean openhanded individuals or tolerant persons or even Big Government Democrats. I mean people who are excited that one percent of the profits of Ben & Jerry's ice cream goes to promote world peace.

—P. J. O'Rourke, *Give War a Chance*

16. What distinguishes the sports fan from the mere spectator is that the fan believes he's part of the team. Permanently sidelined at the TV, he imagines a curious mutual dependence exists between himself and these muscular heroes, a mysterious kinship that goes far beyond worship or vicarious calisthenics. The sports fan believes, deep down, that in a mystical way his rooting can influence events on the field: correct the course of a wayward puck, say, or help introduce a stick of ash to a 0–2 fastball. He can't just sit and watch with quiet detachment; he *feels* the sting of the uppercut, the satisfying crunch of quarterback bones.

—Keith Blanchard, "Coach Potatoes," *Details*, Jan. 1992

17. The American press is diligent about covering new treatments for dreaded diseases. But if you read the stories closely you will always find a disclaimer: What looks so great in the lab may not work at all in the field. New cures often do not.

    A similar warning may apply to a new panacea being touted for the country's social ills: communitarianism, a growing movement to reawaken the average American's sense of duty to the common good. Led by several academics, the communitarian movement portrays itself as a take-charge re- action to the decline of American culture. Crime is up, test scores are down, and marriages are often nasty, brutish, and short. Meanwhile, in Washington, the politicians can't seem to do anything, let alone anything right.

    —Jeremiah Creedon, "Communitarian Manifesto,"
    Utne Reader, July/Aug. 1992

18. If you recognize a scientist as anyone claiming "above-average powers of in- sight," then you miss the whole concept of science. Insight is secondary to the discipline of stating results along with assumptions and probabilities of error. A true scientist, unlike a true advocate, will always point out that every result was observed under specific circumstances, and is subject to the chance it was a fluke (Type I statistical error), or that the failure to observe a result was an oversight (Type II error).

    For us scientists to retain (in some cases, rebuild) our credibility, we need the help of the media to reinforce the distinction between a scientist and a spin doctor. As Voltaire said, "If you would converse with me, define your terms." Scientists qualify statements with the assumptions of the studies that generated them, and include the probability of a mistake. Advocates predict outcomes and argue simple causes and effects.

    —Gregory T. M. Schildwachter, letter
    to *Wall Street Journal,* 27 Jan. 1992

19. Faith is the substance of things hoped for, the evidence of things not seen.

    —Hebrews 11.1

20. Definition always consists, as being a dialectical animal, of a body which is the genus, and a difference which is the soul of the thing defined.

    —Andrew Marvell

THE ROLES OF DEFINITION IN ARGUMENT

A certain agreement between writer and reader about definitions is necessary for clear communication. Where the possibility exists that definitions are not shared, meanings must be spelled out. Definitions of any sort, reportive or stipulative, have two functions in argument: They may be used informatively, to clarify the issue and the terms pertinent to it; and they may be used persuasively, to control the scope of the argument and the readers' responses. They may even fulfill both purposes at once, as we shall see.

Using Definition to Clarify

The first goal of definition is to achieve clarity. One benefit of a clearly defined issue and clearly defined terms is that the audience may thereby determine whether its own conclusions and beliefs coincide with or differ from the writer's; or if they differ, whether the disagreement is merely a verbal misunderstanding centering on an equivocal (ambiguous) or vague term, or one that reflects a fundamental difference of opinion. For example, if I should argue that the United States was right to intervene in Somalia, much hinges upon how broadly or narrowly I use the term *intervene*. If I mean "to send civilian advisors to mediate between the government and the revolutionaries, and to send food and medical supplies," and you understand the term as meaning "to send military troops to defeat the rebels," our verbal misunderstanding could lead to your rejecting my argument. If I define my terms, you still may reject my conclusion, but at least we will understand each other. And we might even find that we agree—if civilian advisors, food, and medical supplies are a form of "intervention" that is acceptable to you. To define ambiguous or vague key terms is to clarify the substance and extent of our disagreement, and perhaps to show that we have no real disagreement at all.

About twenty years ago, two separate landmark legal cases hinged largely on the definition of the term *racial quota*. These two were the reverse discrimination suits brought by Allan Bakke and Marco DeFunis, Jr., against the University of California at Davis Medical School (UCDMS) and the University of Washington Law School (UWLS), respectively. The problem of definition in these cases is described by Allan P. Sindler:

> There were a few things about quotas on which all sides to the dispute saw eye to eye, and this helped to narrow the areas of disagreement a bit. First, they agreed that it would be unsound policy and also illegal to limit the admittance of highly qualified minorities to professional school when, if they had been nonminority persons, they would have been admitted. This would be, of course, the old-fashioned restrictive racial quota, outlawed by the courts. Second, they agreed that the intent of the preferential practices at issue was to expand, not constrict, minority admissions. The problem context was an affirmative desire to increase minority enrollment (At least X number wanted. Welcome!), in contrast to the negative purpose of the old-style discriminatory quota (No more than X number wanted. Keep out!). Finally, they also agreed that explicit race preference was the most direct and effective means to achieve, with predictability and certainty, designated levels of increased minority admissions.
>
> A fourth item of seeming agreement turned out, when probed, to be the key object of dissension. Proponents and opponents alike shared the view that a positive racial quota in selective admissions voluntarily adopted by a professional school was an unwise policy and most probably illegal as well. It would constitute "reverse discrimination," which would prejudice the opportunities of nonminority students and which a school would find difficult to justify as reasonably consistent with its educational mission. Clearly, then, the position of supporters of UWLS and of UCDMS was that the admissions policies of these two institutions were quite different from an unsound and forbidden racial quota. But those who identified with Marco DeFunis, Jr., and Allan Bakke were no less adamant in asserting that the special admis-

sions practices for minorities were variants of a racial quota, regardless of what other name they chose to go by. Both semantically and substantively, therefore, the disagreement turned on divergent conceptions of what a racial quota meant.

Here the disagreement was real enough, but only careful definition pinpointed it. It was agreed by all parties that limiting the number of minority students would be illegal and undesirable; the substantive issue hinged on whether requiring *at least* a certain number or percentage of minority students constituted a racial quota of an equally undesirable sort—one that limited the numbers of white students illegally. All were opposed to any condition that might be labeled a racial quota; the question was, just what *is* a racial quota?

Using Definition to Control

The second goal of definition is to control the scope of the argument by defining its limits. In the argument about military intervention in Somalia, if I define what I mean by intervention, I narrow the limits of my thesis to what I am willing and able to support. If I am opposed to using military force, definition enables me to establish the limits within which I am prepared to argue my case. In the legal argument concerning reverse discrimination, Bakke's and DeFunis's lawyers defined *racial quota* in a way that the courts accepted as applying to their cases. They were able, through skillful definition, not only to clarify the question at hand but also to control its scope. This use of definition is of central importance to successful argument. It is no mere formality that the first (affirmative) speaker in a debate is responsible for defining the terms of the proposition.

Controlling the scope of the argument can also enable a writer to control the audience's responses. If you are the one to establish the issue and to make the issue clear, you can disarm a hostile audience by compelling it to deal with the issue on terms you have established. As psychiatrist Thomas Szasz has observed, definition is power:

> The struggle for definition is veritably the struggle for life itself. In the typical Western two men fight desperately for the possession of a gun that has been thrown to the ground; whoever reaches the weapon first, shoots and lives; his adversary is shot and dies. In ordinary life, the struggle is not for guns but for words: whoever first defines the situation is the victor; his adversary, the victim. For example, in the family, husband and wife, mother and child do not get along; who defines whom as troublesome or mentally sick? Or, in the apocryphal story about Emerson visiting Thoreau in jail, Emerson asks: "Henry, what are you doing over there?" Thoreau replies: "Ralph, what are *you* doing over there?" In short, he who first seizes the word imposes reality on the other: he who defines thus dominates and lives; and he who is defined is subjugated and may be killed.

Has Szasz overstated the power and importance of definition? Even if he has, we know that definitions have power. The question then arises, how do we employ this power? How ethical is it to use definition to manipulate a reader's response, to "impose reality on the other"? Consider your own experience: Surely, at some time, you have been placed at a disadvantage in a dispute because the other party first defined the issue in terms favorable to his or her own position. If your parents proclaimed, as you filled out college applications, "You're free to go to any college you choose. Of course, if you go to our alma mater, we'll pay your expenses," you may have sensed some damage done to the usual meaning of *free choice*. If a person you were dating declared, "If you go to that party without me, you don't love me. You don't know what it means to love!", you no doubt found yourself at a disadvantage in the discussion. With *love* defined as "not going to a party without me," that lovers' quarrel became a problem of definition. And just as surely, on other occasions you have been the one to define a situation to your own advantage: "Sure, I said I'd work out last weekend, Coach, and I did. Dancing *is* a workout." Whether right or wrong, the use of definition to control (handicap?) audience response is frequent, and one of which you should be aware—and wary.

Persuasive Definitions

Usually a definition is intended to be informative, but to the extent that it is designed to control the scope of the argument and the responses of the audience, its purpose is also to be persuasive, whether it is reportive or stipulative. Persuasive definitions, as Irving Copi explains in *Introduction to Logic* (8th ed.), are "phrased in emotive language and . . . intended to influence attitudes as well as to instruct." Take the everyday term *writer*, for instance. We might define it reportively as "a person who produces literary, journalistic, or technical compositions." A cynic, however, might attempt to influence our attitude toward what the term represents by defining *writer* as "a person possessed of a typewriter and an independent income." An obviously persuasive definition of *writer* is Cornelius Register's: "The writer has taken unto himself the former function of the priest or prophet. He presumes to order and legislate the people's life. There is no person more arrogant than the writer." In the same vein, Professor Copi cites a parody of letters from members of Congress to constituents that illustrates the diverse ends that persuasive definitions can be made to serve.

> Dear Sir:
>
> You ask me how I stand on abortion. Let me answer forthrightly and without equivocation.
> If by abortion you mean the murdering of defenseless human beings; the denial of rights to the youngest of our citizens; the promotion of promiscuity among our shiftless and valueless youth and the rejection of Life, Liberty, and the Pursuit of Happiness—then, Sir, be assured that I shall never waver in my opposition, so help me God.
> But, Sir, if by abortion you mean the granting of equal rights to all our citizens regardless of race, color or sex; the elimination of evil and vile institutions preying upon desperate and hopeless women; a chance for all our youth to be wanted and loved; and, above all, that God-given right for all citizens to act in accordance with their own conscience—then, Sir, let me promise you as a patriot and a humanist that I shall never be persuaded to forgo my pursuit of these most basic human rights.

Thank you for asking my position on this most crucial issue and let me again as-sure you of the steadfastness of my stand.

As you can see, it is all in how you define your terms!

READINGS

IF IT ISN'T CENSORSHIP, WHAT IS IT?

Linda Waddle

1 I wish to thank the Association and SIRS* for presenting me with the Intellec-tual Freedom Award. It's a very gratifying feeling to be honored for some-thing that is so important to me, personally and professionally.

2 Upholding the principles of intellectual freedom involves, among other things, monitoring censorship attacks in school and public libraries. As I've done my monitoring this past year, I've come to believe there is some confu-sion about what censorship is.

3 I offer these three examples as evidence of that confusion:

4 When the parents of a fourth-grader at Orchard Hill Elementary School, in my hometown, Cedar Falls, Iowa, asked the school board to remove *On My Honor* by Marion Dane Bauer from the assignment list in a reading class because it contains "two swear words and one vulgarity," they stated, "We're not seeking that the book be censored, but that it no longer be part of reading assignments." If this isn't censorship, what is it?

5 Also, in Cedar Falls, this time at Lincoln Elementary School, the princi-pal stated, in defense of removing *Walking up a Rainbow* by Theodore Taylor from the library, that this "was not a matter of censorship, but rather that the book should be removed from this library and be made available only in the secondary schools." If this isn't censorship, what is it?

6 When the Algona (Iowa) Public Library Board removed all 350 videos from the library shelves, board member Chuck Boom said, "There was some discussion of pulling the seven R-rated titles, but removing only a few movies would have been censorship. Removing the entire collection was not censor-ship." If it isn't censorship, what is it?

7 In my opinion, it's the denial of the First Amendment rights of youth, the abridgment of their right to intellectual freedom, and an insult to their integrity and intelligence.

---

*The American Library Association and SIRS (Social Issues Resources Series), a company that indexes journals on sociological issues, co-sponsored the award for which Waddle thanks them in this speech.

8   I think censors are realizing that "censorship" is a dirty word these days. As soon as the "C-word" is used, users get their names in the paper, libraries and schools put policies into motion, and the Civil Liberties Union jumps in with both feet.

9   It's not surprising, then, that censors have started to use a tactic that librarians have been using for years. Librarians will say, rather primly, "It's not censorship, it's selection." The three people quoted above are just copying librarians; they're saying, "It's not censorship, it's removal." (Ours sounds better—it's more poetic.)

10   The parents, the principal, and the library board member are all fine, upstanding citizens, I'm sure, who "want to do the right thing." They are what Frances MacDonald calls "protectors of youth." They assume that they know what is best for youth, what will harm them, what needs they have, and how those needs can be met. They wish to protect youth from themselves, from others, and from ideas. Not such a wild notion in today's crazy world, is it? These kids they want to protect are our country's future—and, don't forget, they'll be supporting us in our old age, as well.

11   As a parent and an educator, I realize there's some sense to their arguments; there are dangers in the world today that can harm young people. But, when it comes to "removal," or whatever euphemism censors use for the "C-word," they have gone too far. These people are "removing" the basic rights of young people. They are denying them access to information and ideas. That is censorship.

12   If educators and librarians wish to be protectors of youth, their interpretation of the phrase must be different. They must allow children and young adults their rights, so that they will have the freedom to read, view, or listen without their protectors passing judgment or restricting them unnecessarily. They must provide resources that present them with alternatives and choices, so that they can make intelligent, informed decisions on their own and can sustain this democratic system that people in other parts of the world are struggling to achieve.

13   This is the message that we need to pass on at every opportunity to our colleagues, to educators, and to parents as we continue to combat censorship . . . , and changing what it's called will not change what it is.

QUESTIONS AND IDEAS FOR DISCUSSION

1. This argument centers on definition—presumably, the definition of censorship. But the author, librarian Linda Waddle, does not specifically define *censorship* until paragraph 11, almost at the end of her speech. Why does Waddle define this key term so late in her argument? Discuss.

2. Waddle uses definition-by-example in paragraphs 4–6. Are her examples well chosen? Are they examples of censorship? Could you offer any similar examples from your own community or any examples that would counter Waddle's?

3. Waddle addressed an audience composed primarily of librarians when she first gave this speech at a meeting of the American Library Association. Yet in paragraph 9 she criticizes librarians. Has she failed to consider her audience? Comment.

4. Does the existence of "alternatives and choices" (paragraph 12) in itself enable children and young adults to "make intelligent, informed decisions on their own"? Does Waddle imply that it does? Evaluate Waddle's argument in this paragraph. Suggest ways of strengthening the argument if you believe doing so would prove helpful.

WHAT LASTS

Amy Taylor Haun
(Student Essay)

1 In *Gone With the Wind*, Scarlett O'Hara's father tells his daughter, "Land is the only thing in the world that amounts to anything. For 'tis the only thing in the world worth working for, worth fighting for—worth dying for." Now, at nineteen, I can understand this emphasis on the importance of land much more than I could even a few years ago. I have learned to appreciate our family farm because the land itself is such a constant in my memories of childhood. Other memories are of a world I cannot return to: friends long since moved away; pets that have died; my grade school, now torn down. But the family farm remains.

2   In recent years, our visits to the farm have often been on Sunday afternoons. My mother casually says, "I was thinking about going to the farm today. Would you like to go?" Usually I agree; so my sister Polly and I hastily gather all the dogs in the van and lock up the house. During the forty-five minute drive, on a new, smooth highway, we enjoy the scenery without conversation. When we arrive in Lone Jack, Missouri, we head for the farm house. After we enter the long, narrow driveway that bisects a hilly green lawn, we pull up next to the pink house. (Yes, a pink, compact, modern house—not the white, sprawling, ancient farmhouse people might expect.) As the dogs jump out of the car onto the lawn, my grandparents come out to greet us. It is pleasant and predictable. It is easy to take for granted.

3   Ten, or even five years ago, Polly and I felt much greater excitement in driving to the farm. Even the dogs barked excitedly in anticipation of the rare privilege of running without a leash. We would head toward the south end of the farm, stop to open the gate, and carefully drive over the bumpy trail, through the ditch, until we reached the two great hedgeapple trees that shelter the picnic area. Polly and I would scramble out of the car and run about, sometimes swinging on the swings hanging from the limbs of the trees.

4   In those days there was no house at the farm. Our meals were restricted to whatever we could cook over an open fire in the picnic area—hotdogs, hamburgers, or marshmallows. Using the tailgate of our stationwagon as a counter, my mother also prepared potato salad and baked beans. Now, we dine in style at my grandmother's big kitchen table, carved of some kind of light-colored wood from Montana. We have fresh vegetables from the garden, roasted chicken, homemade rolls, and pie. Our meals are grander these days, but we can find the old picnic area still, and the swings swaying in the breeze.

5   These days we are more likely to visit the barn where my mother stores the leftover antiques from her antique shop. When I walk past the old pie-chests and trunks, the musty odor does not bother me. I wonder sometimes where the pieces of furniture originated and how they were used. The contents of the barn change as my mother takes pieces away to be sold, or brings new finds to be stored. There are always new treasures to discover and mull over. But the elm trees in the little hollow where the barn sits are always the same, changing only with the season.

6   Sometimes we also go for walks in the woods or the garden. Through the years of growing up in the city, Polly and I have learned to appreciate the quiet beauty of this place. When we were younger, we could not tolerate the garden; we did not share the grownups' admiration for our grandfather's tomatoes, corn, and green beans. We weren't much drawn to the dark woods, either, unless accompanied by Grandpa on a "jungle hunt." We liked noisy, messy fun like splashing in the muddy pond. Nowadays, you couldn't get me into the pond on a bet—but I'm glad it is still there.

7   When it is time to go home after an afternoon's visit, and a good meal, and an evening's conversation about news, politics, or the weather, we call the dogs and head home. Polly and I often doze off in the car. The dogs always do.

8   I feel as if I have been to the farm only a week or two ago, but in reality it has been many months. When I return, though, I know what awaits me. However much my life changes, however many friends I part from as they move away, or I do, the farm—the land itself—is a constant. It may seem that Scarlett O'Hara's father was giving short shrift to other important things, but I think he was being realistic. People may die, or move away; buildings may crumble; but the land remains. And that is a good thing.

QUESTIONS AND IDEAS FOR DISCUSSION

1. Identify Haun's thesis. How can it be argued that definition is central to this essay? Is Haun primarily interested in clarifying a concept or in shaping our attitudes?

2. This essay appears to be largely a description of Haun's family farm. In what ways is it also an argument? Identify the elements of argument that you find

in the essay. If you find none, support your viewpoint with reference to the text.

3. Is Haun's essay logically convincing, emotionally persuasive, neither, or both? Why? How, if at all, could she have strengthened her argument? What points or illustrations would you develop more fully if you were writing from Haun's perspective? What would you condense or omit? Give reasons for your choices.

4. Do you agree with Mr. O'Hara's declaration about the importance of land, quoted in paragraph 1? Comment.

BORN TO BE MILD

Paul Rudnick

1   Are you a rebel? Do you own a black leather motorcycle jacket even though you always take cabs? Do you swoon over any light-beer ad featuring a mysterious loner in mirrored sunglasses and battered cowboy boots, or any movie campaign pushing an anti-hero who's "not your ordinary cop/private eye/fighter pilot"? Do your pheromones sizzle from compact cars or heavy-metal albums or after-shaves whose names include the words *outlaw, renegade, maverick, bad boy, savage, sauvage, streetwise,* or any verb with the *g* dropped off?

2   If you have answered "Yes" or "Damn straight" or even "Yo" to any of these questions, then you certainly do march to a different drummer. You make your own rules. You push the envelope, rather than just licking it. You're a rebel—just like Cher.

3   In the distant past, rebels were often individuals of both defiance and accomplishment. Examples might include the rakish Lord Byron, the pioneering Galileo or, for instance, Jesus. Behavior that was merely aberrant or anti-social, while it might assure someone a shiver in history, was condemned: Caligula, Rasputin, and Vlad the Impaler, however charismatic, were emulated in their own times only by fellow psychopaths. Only in modern America has the rebel been exalted regardless of personal achievement: Attitude is everything, and attitude can be easily purchased. Americans have grown so complacent and so bored by their own docility that they ache for the forbidden, and being Americans, they are satisfied with sunglasses, industrial zippers, and the occasional middle finger flashed at the driver of a car that is already out of sight.

4   Lately, whenever someone claims to be a rebel, it is fairly certain that he's a corporate attorney with a second mortgage and a couple of kids in prep school or therapy or both. What baby boomers fear most is becoming as safe and stolid as their parents, and this is causing a near-epidemic of faked rebellion. Today's rebel sports a tepid three-inch ponytail as his shocking pro-

test against (and apology for) his VP status at Saatchi & Saatchi*; the ponytail may even be a detachable polymer model for weekend and after-six swagger. Intentionally inefficient razors are sold that allow even a suburban pediatrician to retain a dusting of back-roads stubble. Sideburns and bad-girl black eyeliner are other popular emblems of rebellion, especially among wild and crazy M.B.A.s.

5   The more humdrum rebel might daringly leap the subway turnstile on his journey to Wall Street, his Mark Cross attaché case grazing the token slot as his lower back gives out. His female counterpart might conceal a naughty Victoria's Secret garter belt beneath her tenured gabardine, or she and her husband might toke up, after the kids are safely stowed, as they dial in their TV-infomercial order for the TimeLife *Rock 'n' Roll Era* CDs. Latterday rebels respond to "Born to Be Wild" and "Wild Thing" on the soundtracks of peanut-butter ads. They consider attending a Spike Lee or Gus Van Sant Jr. film to be the equivalent of making one; to them, even nibbling organically grown cracked-wheat muffins can become a gauntlet hurled before the Big Food Establishment.

6   The words "What can I say? I'm a rebel," usually spoken to an interviewer, are an all-purpose face-saver for any number of itchy and potentially embarrassing scenarios. You got canned? It must be because you're the office rebel, certainly not because profits plummeted in your division. Your auteur effort got slammed by the critics? Clearly they're just too numbingly conventional to appreciate the raging Oliver Stone-style insight of a maverick like yourself. Everyone in your car pool despises you? Well, they're all a bunch of button-down, line-toeing fascists, while you've got your eye on a distant horizon, you think for yourself, you're a . . . *you know.*

7   The more cozily bourgeois a culture becomes, the more its citizenry admires the iconoclast, the individual with an "attitude problem," the bad boy. (The poor can never really be rebels, at least not in any fashionable sense; only the upper classes can elevate indecency into style, into rebel chic.) In the 1950s there was a surfeit of well-fed, restless teens willing to enjoy their parents' largess while spurning their aprons and cardigans. These suburban young people, precursors of today's mall rats, were ripe for Marlon Brando in 1954's *The Wild One,* and for the brief oeuvre of James Dean. Dreamily doodling in their notebook margins, they yearned for a new place to shop, for outfits and anger.

8   Brando's Wild One led a motorcycle gang that terrorized a small town (with heinous acts such as stealing soda pop). The film is remembered almost entirely for Brando's leather cap and jacket, his Triumph, and his response to the question, "What are you rebelling against?" Brando smirked winningly and replied, "What have you got?" and a merchandizing bonanza was born. To this day, the biker remains an unflagging symbol of sultry heedlessness, of

---

*Saatchi & Saatchi is a large advertising and marketing firm based in New York.

up-yours panache. Today, Chanel sells $4,800 biker jackets to wear with evening gowns, and teensy leathers are available for newborns to raise hell. There is a Harley-Davidson boutique in Bloomingdale's, and celebrities as disparate as Liz Taylor and Claus von Bulow have posed for magazines in the classic Wild One snaps and buckles.

9   James Dean embodied a more suburb-bound version of the rebel—the too-sensitive, misunderstood kid. This was the sweet, inarticulate adolescent of *Rebel Without a Cause* and *East of Eden,* a well-intentioned, soulful lad abused by corrupt society and a dysfunctional family. Dean's legacy as a rebel is not particularly potent for a simple reason: He wore windbreakers. While appealing, he lacked the sexual threat and nihilistic self-confidence of Brando.

10   Elvis combined the trademark facial expression of the rebel (insolent sneer) with the harmlessness of James Dean; he was the first manufactured rebel, a nice boy in leather, wholly nontoxic. Elvis loved his mom and served his country and his president. In the early days, his swiveling pelvis did direct a low-down rebuke to the fatherly ilk of Bing Crosby, but his outlaw status was short-lived. In the hands of canny managers, Elvis became denatured, wholesome and mainstream, and America required a new spokesperson for rebellion. Peter Fonda got the job.

11   Fonda, in *Easy Rider* and *The Wild Angels,* restored the outsider allure to black leather by adding a layer of frayed denim and an Old Glory-painted helmet. He epitomized the hippie biker, with shaggy locks and a stash.

12   Both Brando and the hippie biker were outcasts, but they were still imperfect rebels, as they couldn't really make a decent living at it. This obvious flaw was corrected with the appearance of the rock star, allowing the rebel finally to claim his tasty chunk of the American Dream. The rock star is simply the rebel as entrepreneur.

13   Heavy metal and arena rock provide today's rock star rebel format: expensively split-ended hair, condom-tight leather pants, and daggered-skull death-row tattoos acquired while bunking at the Beverly Hills Hotel. Almost all modern rock bands promote themselves as mike-stand-swinging rebels: Axl Rose of Guns N' Roses sings out boldly against immigrants, gays, and rock journalists, while Skid Row and Mötley Crüe bravely blast women who won't sleep with them. Zillionaire third-generation headbangers are hard-pressed for targets. Then there are the movie stars. Mickey Rourke, Sean Penn, even De Niro—these are the bad boys of Bel-Air, the guys "who don't buy into the system," the so-called new breed. Their rebellion consists primarily of giving monosyllabic interviews and playing nearly identical roles in all their films.

14   Everyone is a rebel today, from Brian De Palma to Mario Cuomo to Slash to Carl Icahn. *Rebel* is a buzzword meaning "I'm sexy and unreliable, and I want your money." Is true rebellion even possible, after decades of permissiveness, ultragratification, and hair extensions? Is there anything left to nobly reject? Rappers made a tidy stab at it; the freshman efforts of NWA and

Public Enemy took on racism, policy brutality, and the drug craze rebels once applauded. Lately, however, many rappers, eager to retain their multi-platinum clout, seek only to shock and whine, reviling those hardy perennials, Jews, gays, and gals. Once a rebel succeeds, once he owns the well-surveillanced house and the Jeep-size speakers, hasn't he just maybe become the establishment, the enemy, that-which-is-rebelled-against?

15   Is there rebellion outside of marketing? A positive rebellion, a crusade that might renew the concept? Or even a concept of chic beyond the weary cycle of pasty skin and stonetumbled cowhide? A handful of candidates come to mind: ACT UP, for example, an organization founded to explode government and public indifference to the AIDS crisis. Queen Latifah may be a genuine rebel among rappers, battling the music's generic sexism. Betty Ford remains a rare White House rebel, sleekly using her position to confound her husband and her husband's party rather than as a stepping stone to becoming, say, a hack novelist of the Patti Davis literary guild.

16   True rebellion entails risk and offers little hope of personal remuneration. True rebellion also involves scant glamour and few opportunities for trademarking. No one wants to dress like Salman Rushdie (even if we knew what he was wearing). Rushdie is perhaps not an intentional rebel, but he managed to outrage a well-armed world-class religion. The students who marched and died at Tiananmen Square recall the true American rebels of the Revolutionary War, who also did not demand a cut of T-shirt sales. Bona fide rebels are often nearly anonymous. They are the men and women who file safety complaints against powerful corporations or bring discrimination, rape, or sexual-harassment charges without the questionable benefit of national TV coverage. America was founded by rebels, as are most nations. America has also led the planet in neutering and huckstering any act of defiance. So perhaps we now possess a more appropriate response to the question *What are you rebelling against?* The only defensible answer may well be "Rebels."

QUESTIONS AND IDEAS FOR DISCUSSION

1. Identify Rudnick's thesis in this essay. If it is not explicitly stated, put it into your own words. Is the thesis convincingly developed and supported? Comment, with specific reference to the text.

2. Why does Rudnick give just two paragraphs—and the last two, at that—to his definition of *rebel?* Discuss.

3. To say one thing while implying the opposite is a classic form of irony. Give several examples of ironic phrases and passages intended to discredit what Rudnick regards as fake rebels. Does Rudnick use irony persuasively, or does he overdo it? Discuss.

4. Identify as to approximate age, education, and political leanings the intended audience for this essay. Are you part of the audience Rudnick addresses? If you are not, how—if at all—does your "outsider" status affect your response to the argument here? What would you change about the essay if you wished to direct it to an audience of college undergraduates?

Suggestions for Writing and Further Discussion

1. Why do many anti-abortionists prefer to be called pro-life advocates while those in favor of abortion rights prefer to be called pro-choice advocates? Why do many handicapped people prefer to be called "physically challenged"? Why do those who oppose environmentalists call theirs the "wise use" movement? Write an essay in which you support Thomas Szasz's assertion that "he who first seizes the word imposes reality on the other: he who defines . . . dominates." Support your argument with vivid and appropriate examples. You may choose to modify or qualify Szasz's thesis.

2. Write a paper, addressed to an audience of white, black, Hispanic, and Asian college students, in which you argue in favor of or in opposition to affirmative action programs designed to ensure that a certain percentage of minority students are included in graduate programs. Bear in mind that both you and the members of your audience have a stake in the question.

3. If you are dissatisfied with Paul Rudnick's definition(s) of *rebel*, argue for a different understanding of the word. Assume that your audience is composed of people of your own generation.

4. If you had to choose a single concept that best defines your interests, what would it be? Environmentalism? Economics? Sports? Art? Just as likely, something else entirely. Write an essay aimed at those who may not share your enthusiasm, defining the concept in compelling and concrete terms.

5. Write an essay in which you redefine in a favorable light some quality or condition that is normally viewed unfavorably, such as *laziness, quarrelsomeness, evasiveness, obesity,* or *hypochondria*. Assume that your readers regard the state or condition in the usual way; attempt to win them over with a careful and persuasive redefinition.

6. In recent decades many words and phrases have been abused as well as used—words like *democracy, multiculturalism, ecology,* and many more. Think of a word or phrase that you object to or regard as misused or fuzzily abstract. Then write an essay in which you show your readers what is wrong with the usual meaning or use of the word, and what, in more concrete terms, it means or ought to mean. You might try one of the words that both ordinary people and courts of law have a lot of trouble defining, such as *decency*.

7. Suppose you were compelled to give up—to forget all the words you know except seven—what are the words you would keep?

—Kahlil Gibran

Write an essay in which you argue the reasons for your seven choices.

8. Write an essay—directed toward your classmates who, you believe, may not understand the term as they should—in which you argue a definition for one of the following terms. Use illustrations as well as explanations, and be sure to distinguish what the term accurately represents from what it does not.

myth	mental health	harassment
genius	tolerance	charity

4

Developing Arguments: Finding and Evaluating Evidence

> *Learn, compare, collect the facts!*
> *In your work and in your research there must always be*
> *passion.*
>
> **—Ivan Petrovich Pavlov**

CREATIVITY IN RESEARCH

Once you have written a preliminary thesis, have worked out the main supporting points you want to make, and have defined the key terms and issues of your argument, you will need some solid support for the reasons you offer. For some arguments you will need only to draw upon your personal knowledge, experience, or expertise. Others will require additional support—which means you will need to do some research. Unfortunately, the very word *research* puts many students off, bringing to mind visions of notecards, outlines, and what often seems the pointless rehashing of ideas and information that other people already have stated sufficiently well. But the same students may be people who enjoy puzzles, mysteries, or controversy; and true research, as opposed to cut-and-paste work, addresses those interests admirably. Effective, creative research involves solving puzzles: historical, political, scientific, economic, technical, or literary. Creative research does not come with conclusions and solutions ready-made; the researcher must be not only a worker of puzzles but also a sleuth—finding the evidence, distinguishing the valuable source or witness from the unreliable one, using imagination to reach a sound but not foregone conclusion. Creative research involves as well the awareness that sources of evidence often disagree with each other, sometimes radically. The researcher must sort through conflicting dates, theories, interpretations, and predictions in order to determine where the truth lies.

As you research and write documented essays, then, you will find that a large part of what makes research enjoyable and creative stems from your willingness to go beyond the obvious and superficial elements of your subject. In the words of G. K. Chesterton, "There is no such thing on earth as an uninteresting subject; the only thing that can exist is an uninterested person." You must take an interest in finding out what is interesting in your subject.

An important first step is to find an aspect of your subject with potential for development and with potential for more than one possible solution or interpretation. The invention strategies discussed in Chapter 2 should help you here. And if you have been assigned a subject or a limited number of options, choose the road less traveled. For a paper in medieval English history, for example, opt for the Coronation Charter of Henry I rather than the Magna Charta if your purpose is to show the influence some significant English document had on the development of the common law. A quick check in the card catalog and in an encyclopedia will show you whether or not enough material is likely to be available for developing a paper on the Coronation Charter. When you are working on a subject about which you have little prior knowledge, *make your preliminary thesis a question to be explored.* By doing so, you will keep your mind and your options open. And make it a question worth exploring. Of "Just what was the Coronation Charter of Henry I?" and "Did the Coronation Charter have any lasting effect on the government or the history of England?" the latter is more likely to offer a variety of possible responses and interpretations and, therefore, is more likely to stimulate creative analytical thinking.

Once you have a preliminary thesis question in mind, begin your search for evidence that will provide both answers and support for those answers. After some preliminary investigation (a number of possible sources are listed on pages 85–86), you will acquire enough basic material and evidence to begin to work your research question into a preliminary thesis. As we discussed in Chapter 2, be sure that your thesis, or controlling concept, is specific and limited and that it has, in rhetorician Sheridan Baker's words, an "argumentative edge." It should take a stand on the issue under investigation. And, as always, you must be willing to modify your stand if further research reveals flaws in it.

With your investigation initiated and your preliminary thesis formulated, determine key terms and define them if necessary (as discussed in Chapter 3). Then work out an outline or bare-bones draft of your proposed argument. Even if you have outline-phobia and usually write assigned outlines *after* writing essays, I urge you to write at least a list of major supporting points for your thesis, jotting down beneath each point any evidence you already have found to support that point. Doing so will give you a sense of direction: clarifying which points need support and further research, revealing imbalances in development (too many points developing the causes, not enough on the results, perhaps) or inconsistencies in organization, exposing tangential points not strictly tied to your thesis. This step will make your writing a less complicated task, particularly if the paper is to be lengthy, and will help you to be more efficient in your further research. You will spend your time looking for evidence that is needed rather than overworking points for which you already have adequate support.

Except for the length of the paper and the use of outside sources, the actual writing and revision of the documented essay is much the same process involved in any essay or report. Properly and effectively using evidence to reach and support conclusions about your subject is likely to be your greatest challenge as researcher. For evidence presents some difficulties: First, you must locate it; second, you must evaluate it, for if the facts are unreliable, they are of little use; and third, you must cite it accurately, incorporate it into your own text smoothly, and credit its source. Discussing ways to meet these challenges will be our primary concern in this chapter.

FINDING EVIDENCE FOR ARGUMENTS

Evidence used to develop an argument can be of many kinds. Facts—examples, statistics, personal and authoritative testimony, and an assortment of bits of information—are used to provide supporting evidence for conclusions. In appropriate contexts, evidence can include everything from scientific data to personal anecdotes. Some of the major kinds of evidence you will need to support your theses include examples (including even personal experiences and analogies), authoritative testimony, and statistics. We will consider these in turn.

Kinds of Evidence

Examples   These are the specific instances of a phenomenon or members of a class that lead us to hypotheses or to generalizations about the entire class. The beautiful sunset today is in part an example of the effects of atmospheric pollutants. The Granny Smith apple I hold in my hand is an example of the class of apples. Examples are concrete and illustrative; they can be very persuasive in support of arguments. But examples should be representative of their class, and even then they do not *prove*. I cannot conclude from my examples here that the effects of atmospheric pollution are attractive, or that all apples are green and tart. More representative examples might be soot-covered buildings or people suffering from respiratory illnesses, and some red variety of apple, such as Red Delicious.

However, we should never underestimate the value of examples to argument, despite their limitations. With an example we cease to tell our readers about our idea and begin to *show* it to them so that it can become theirs. Furthermore, examples create images that are far more likely to be retained by a reader than are long loops of abstract reasoning. Finally, examples help to make complex theories plainer.

Authoritative Testimony   Arguments are frequently supported by the assertions of authorities. Such support enables the writer to make a persuasive case without having to enumerate all the data supporting the claim. You will recall arguments from authority from your childhood: "Why must I?" "Because I said so!" And you may recall resenting arguments of that sort. To be acceptable, testimony first must be specific and limited—no vague and hollow verbal flourishes such as "Disarmament is a splendid idea." Second, it must be given by reputable authorities speaking within their areas of expertise. Margaret Mead may be cited in anthropological arguments; any comments she may have made about physics, on the other hand, do not carry the weight of authority. Linus Pauling was an accepted authority in chemistry, but a controversial one in nutrition and medicine. And third, the statements should be cited fairly and not out of context. Supreme Court Chief Justice Roger Brooke Taney has been unfairly condemned as a racist for having written in the Dred Scott decision in 1857 that the Negro has "no rights which a white man [is] bound to respect." Chief Justice Taney did use those words, but in a context that showed how much he deplored the idea and how wrong he considered it to be.

If authoritative testimony fulfills these three criteria, it is no fallacy to offer it as support for a relevant conclusion. To refuse to use such testimony imposes an unnecessary burden on the arguer, as columnist Ann Landers points out in her reply to a do-it-yourself reasoner:

> Dear Ann Landers:
>
> Regarding the person who wanted to know if cold water boils faster than hot water and if hot water freezes faster than cold, you said you believe in going to the top and [that you had] contacted Dr. Jerome Weisner, Chancellor of [the] Massachusetts Institute of Technology.
>
> Dr. Weisner said a problem of such extraordinary dimensions should be handled by an expert, so he turned the letter over to the dean of science, John W. Deutch. Deutch said neither statement was true.
>
> Even though Dr. Deutch gave the correct answer, that procedure is called argument by authority and has absolutely no place in science. I was able to come to the same conclusion by using a pan of hot water, a thermometer, a stove, a refrigerator, and a watch with a second hand.
>
> You, Ann Landers, exemplify what is wrong with our society. Too many bozos are too lazy to find the answers for themselves. It is easier to call on an "authority." How much more satisfying to rely on one's intelligence.
>
> Self-Reliant in Riverside
>
> Dear Self-Reliant:
>
> When a reader asks such a question, I am not about to tell him to do a home experiment, nor would I do one myself. I assure you that Dr. Deutch didn't boil any water, either. He *knew* the answer—which is the beauty of having a battery of top consultants.

In fairness to "Self-Reliant," we cannot discount the value of observation in reaching conclusions. But many questions do not lend themselves to such inductive tests and observation: How far away is the sun? Do cigarettes really cause lung cancer? What might Napoleon have done differently at Waterloo?

Expert testimony can provide valuable information to support claims in argument as long as it is **specific, relevant,** and **accurate.** Indeed, testimony supports some kinds of claims better than almost any other evidence. For example, if I want to convince you that the English major provides excellent preparation for certain careers, I would do well to quote executives from major companies in those fields on the subject. Such testimony can be more memorable and more persuasive than dry statistics.

Statistics   We often say we distrust statistics—but we love to cite them. And for all our sophistication, we tend to believe statistics unless they strike us as outrageous or unpleasant. Only when the conclusions suggested by statistical information surprise or offend us do we ask for more evidence. However, in all cases it is well to be wary of statistics. Few forms of evidence are more susceptible to manipulation and distortion.

First, we cannot judge statistics adequately unless we know how the data were collected and by what process the results were reached. A professional statistician can best assess the data and conclusions, but we nonstatisticians can follow a few guidelines to help us evaluate statistics. If a sample (such as a poll) is used to compile the statistics, we need to know something about the sample in order to determine whether it is representative and sufficient. If, for example, we know how a question in a poll was worded and how the respondents were selected, we can judge the probable fairness of the results. If we know who compiled the statistics and for what objective, we can further assess their value. If we know that a poll has been paid for by a political candidate, we examine its findings more critically than we do if the poll was undertaken by the nonpartisan League of Women Voters, for instance.

In a thorough study of the uses of evidence, Robert Newman and Dale Newman offer basic criteria for evaluating statistics:

1. Who wants to prove what?
2. What do the figures really represent?
3. What conclusion do the figures support?

We can see the usefulness of these questions by considering two examples of statistics. Read both, then consider the likely answers to Newman and Newman's three questions. Do both passages use statistics fairly, as far as you can judge?

The first passage summarizes some findings made by Robert Lichter and Linda Lichter, codirectors of the Center for Media & Public Affairs, and Stanley Rothman, director of the Center for the Study of Social & Political Change at Smith College. The Lichters and Rothman analyzed 620 television entertainment shows from Library of Congress video archives, a cross-section of those aired between 1955 and 1986. According to *Forbes* writer Peter Brimelow, they found that

> whereas FBI statistics indicate that about half of America's murders are committed by blacks, in TV-land the proportion is around 3%. Instead, 90% of TV murderers are white, with seven out of ten from "a generic northern European background." But why does one out of every four TV Hispanics commit a crime, including twice as many murders as any other identified ethnicity?
>
> Which is still better than businessmen. Although they make up only about 8% of TV characters, businessmen are responsible for about a fifth of all TV crimes and a third of the murders—considerably more murders, in fact, than TV's professional

criminals. And an extraordinary one in three of the crimes committed by TV businessmen is violent.

—"TV's Killer Businessmen," *Forbes* 23 Dec. 1991

Consider not only the source of the statistics, but also the secondary source who has summarized (and thereby interpreted) them for us. Notice what the writer emphasizes, and how, and what he plays down.

The next passage comprises part of an argument by Princeton economics professor Alan S. Blinder. He relies on research by a Princeton colleague, Sanders D. Korenman, and University of Michigan professor Arline T. Geronimus to support the claim that teenage motherhood does *not* cause poverty. The researchers used a data source of 51 teenage mothers whose sisters were not teenage mothers. According to Blinder,

> [E]conomic failure might be a cause, rather than an effect, of teen childbearing. Teenage mothers are not selected for motherhood at random; they tend to come from the ranks of the disadvantaged. Compared with other women, teenage mothers are more likely to have come from single-parent families and to have had poor, uneducated parents. Since these attributes are leading indicators of economic failure, some teenage girls may look at their poor prospects in life and opt for early motherhood. . . . Among all the young women in the main sample that Geronimus and Korenman analyze, average family income is 33% lower among those who were teenage mothers. . . . But remember that teenage mothers often come from disadvantageous circumstances to begin with, so many were destined for failure anyway. If you control for socioeconomic background by looking only at the 51 families in which at least one sister was a teenage mother and at least one was not, the income gap narrows to just 16%. . . .
>
> The suggestion, then, is that much of the economic failure commonly associated with teenage motherhood really stems from disadvantaged social backgrounds. Having a baby per se may not be much of an economic handicap after all. This conclusion is so contrary to popular belief that Geronimus and Korenman tested it on a second source of data. Doing so yielded similar results. . . .
>
> —*Business Week*, 27 May 1991

Again, think about the credentials of the source of the statistics and those of the writer. Evaluate the sample to the extent that you can. Consider what the researchers found, and what they may have failed to consider.

The value of carefully determined statistics—and of evidence generally—is dramatically underscored by a significant event in twentieth-century history, the disastrous 1962 Bay of Pigs invasion of Cuba by American-backed forces. As Charles W. Roll and Albert H. Cantril explain in *Polls: Their Use and Misuse in Politics*, a missing piece of evidence might have averted the whole fiasco:

> During April and May 1960, Lloyd A. Free conducted an opinion survey in Cuba for the Institute for International Social Research. . . . A report was prepared based upon 1,000 carefully executed interviews in Havana and other urban areas throughout Cuba—where about 60 percent of the Cuban people live. The report showed that far from despair, the Cuban people backed Castro overwhelmingly, were enthused [sic] about the revolution Castro had brought to Cuba, were relieved that the days of Batista were over, and were optimistic about the future of the country. . . . Nonetheless, in the transitional days between the Eisenhower and Kennedy Administrations the

report got buried and forgotten. It surfaced only after the ill-fated invasion attempt. When it was later learned that the report's findings directly contradicted the assumption of the invasion—that the Cuban populace would join the handful of invaders in an overthrow of the Castro regime—Arthur Schlesinger wrote poignantly that he only wished a copy had come to his attention earlier.

Accurate information and valid statistics can do more than support arguments; they can save face—and lives.

Locating Background and Historical Evidence

Where do you locate the examples, statements from authorities, statistics, and other facts your writing assignment requires? In the preliminary stages of researching a topic that may well be new and unfamiliar to you, you probably will turn to encyclopedias and bibliographies of books that provide an overview of your subject. The general information available in encyclopedias will help you formulate questions to pursue in arriving at a working thesis and then developing your arguments. If your assignment is historical in nature—that is, having to do with an event, a work, or an issue not recently in the news—you may well find all the material you need in books and back issues of periodicals and newspapers. An annotated list of some of the best sources of background and historical data follows. Under each category the most general works are listed first, followed by specialized works in alphabetical order.

Encyclopedias   In addition to the following, you can find specialized encyclopedias by identifying the subject heading for your research topic in the *Library of Congress Subject Headings* (two volumes; the reference librarian can direct you to it) and then looking in the card catalog under "[Subject]: ENCYCLOPEDIAS."

New Encyclopedia Britannica. 15th ed. 30 vols. Chicago: Encyclopedia Britannica, 1980. General encyclopedia. Signed articles with bibliographies. Use the "Micropaedia" index to locate your subject in the 19-volume "Macropaedia."

Encyclopedia Americana. 30 vols. with annual supplements. New York: American Corporation, 1992. General encyclopedia. Use the index volume to locate your subject.

Britannica Encyclopedia of American Art. Chicago: Encyclopedia Britannica, 1973. Includes short articles on all fields of art with bibliographies, glossary, and information on museums.

Cassell's Encyclopedia of World Literature. John Buchanan-Brown, ed. 3 vols. Rev. ed. New York: William Morrow & Co., 1973.

Daniel, Howard. *Encyclopedia of Themes and Subjects in Painting: Mythological, Biblical, Historical, Literary, Allegorical and Topical.* New York: Harry N. Abrams, 1971.

Encyclopedia of Philosophy. 8 vols. New York: Macmillan Publishing Co., 2nd ed., 1973. Articles covering Eastern and Western philosophy from ancient times to the present.

Encyclopedia of Sociology. Guilford, Conn.: Dushkin Publishing Group, 1991. Covers terms, theories, and important theorists in the field.

Harper Encyclopedia of the Modern World. New York: Harper & Row, Publishers, 1970. Covers historical events from 1760 to late 1960s.

International Encyclopedia of the Social Sciences. D. L. Sills, ed. 17 vols. New York: Macmillan Publishing Co., 1968. Articles in anthropology, economics, history, law, political science, psychology, and sociology. Biographical Supplement, 1979.

McGraw-Hill Encyclopedia of Science and Technology. 7th ed. 15 vols. with supplementary yearbooks. New York: McGraw-Hill Book Co., 1992. Written for the nonspecialist.

The New Illustrated Encyclopedia of World History. William L. Langer, ed. 2 vols. New York: Harry N. Abrams, 1975.

Bibliographies   Bibliographies list books and periodical articles covering a particular field or, as in the *Bibliographic Index* below, a number of fields of study. For additional bibliographies in these and other fields, consult the library card catalog for "[Subject]: BIBLIOGRAPHIES" listings.

The Bibliographic Index. New York: Wilson, 1938 to present. Issued twice a year and cumulated annually. A bibliography of bibliographies. Indexes bibliographies in both books and periodicals.

Ballou, Patricia K. *Women: A Bibliography of Bibliographies.* 2nd ed. Boston: G. K. Hall, 1986. Women's studies issues.

Bibliographic Guide to Business and Economics. Boston: G. K. Hall, 1975 to present.

Day, Alan E. *History: A Reference Handbook.* Hamden, CT: Linnet Books, 1977. A guide to bibliographies, handbooks, dictionaries, and other sources.

Dyment, Alan R. *The Literature of the Film: A Bibliographic Guide to the Film as Art and Entertainment, 1936–1970.* London: White Lion, 1975.

Ehresmann, Donald L. *Fine Arts: A Bibliographic Guide to Basic Reference Works, Histories & Handbooks.* 3rd ed. Littleton, CO: Libraries Unlimited, 1992.

Guerry, Herbert. *A Bibliography of Philosophical Bibliographies.* Westport, CT: Greenwood Press, 1977. Includes entries on subjects and on particular philosophers.

Harmon, Robert B. *Political Science Bibliographies.* 2 vols. Metuchen, NJ: Scarecrow, 1973, 1976. A bibliography of bibliographies.

MLA International Bibliography of Books and Articles on Modern Language and Literature. New York: Modern Language Association of America, 1921 to present.

Van Fleet, David D. *An Historical Bibliography of Administration, Business & Management.* Monticello, Ill.: Vance Bibliographies, 1978.

Woodbury, Marda. *A Guide to Sources of Educational Information.* 2nd ed. Washington, D.C.: Information Resources Press, 1982. Annotated.

Locating Current Evidence

Encyclopedias and books listed in specialized bibliographies or gathered directly from the card catalog are an excellent source of information for subjects that are not recent or are given to changes over time, and of background information for almost any subject. But all too often beginning writers *end* their quest for evidence at just this point, with encyclopedias and a stack of dusty books. The advantage books offer the researcher is considerable, for books often provide comprehensive, in-depth treatment of important issues in the subject of your research. In addition, books often include bibliographies that refer you to still more sources of information and ideas. But the time required for writing and publishing books makes much of the information available in them at least five years old. This limitation may be of little or no consequence if your subject is literary or historical (including past scientific and technical issues), but it is a drawback if you need current, up-to-the-minute data—as is the case with all arguments about current events and controversies and most professional research done for employers.

If you need updated or recent information on your subject, turn to the periodical indexes. The most well-known of these is the *Reader's Guide to Periodical Literature,* which is reasonably up-to-date (supplements are issued biweekly) and can provide adequate resources for many subjects and occasions for writing. However, the *Reader's Guide* suffers a limitation as well. The more than 160 periodicals referenced therein are largely "general interest" magazines and journals that may not offer the specialized information you require for some projects and papers.

Writers of argument sometimes need just what the card catalog and the *Reader's Guide* cannot always offer us: current or specialized information. Fortunately, some resources are available that can provide recent and even up-to-the-moment bibliographic and reference material, while others can offer information as specialized as *Nineteenth-Century Literature Criticism* and *Bibliography of North American Geology.* Recent material may be gathered from a number of sources, as the following samples indicate:

Indexes, Abstracts, and Almanacs Updated Annually

Statistical Abstracts of the United States. Washington, D.C.: Bureau of the Census, 1878 to present. Summarizes social, political, economic, and cultural statistics, with sources identified. Some regional, state, and metropolitan information included.

World Almanac & Book of Facts. New York: Newspaper Enterprise Assn. (now, Pharos Books), 1868 to present. Useful detailed index of wide range of subjects.

Indexes Updated Quarterly or Monthly

Art Index. New York: Wilson, 1929 to present. Issued quarterly. Indexes art periodicals, museum bulletins, and related materials; covers both European and English-language publications.

Biological and Agricultural Index. New York: Wilson, 1964 to present. Issued monthly. Notes the inclusion of bibliographies, charts, illustrations, and the like for each item indexed.

Book Review Digest. New York: Wilson, 1905 to present. Issued monthly. Includes excerpts from reviews.

Business Periodicals Index. New York: Wilson, 1958 to present. Issued monthly. Covers (by subject) periodicals in accounting, advertising, banking, finance, insurance, labor, and taxation.

Current Biography. New York: Wilson, 1940 to present. Issued monthly. Useful articles about people recently in the news. Monthly issues and annual yearbook are both indexed.

Editorials on File. New York: Facts on File, 1970 to present. Issued monthly and cumulated bimonthly. Covers U.S. and Canadian newspapers. Reprints editorials, arranged by subject.

Education Index. New York: Wilson, 1929 to present. Issued monthly. Covers all subjects related to education.

Film Literature Index. Albany, NY: SUNY-Albany, 1973 to present. Issued quarterly. Indexed by author and subject. Includes television.

Humanities Index. New York: Wilson, 1965 to present. (Before 1974 entitled *Social Sciences and Humanities Index.*) Issued quarterly. Covers archaeology and classical studies, area studies, folklore, history, language and literature, literary and political criticism, performing arts, philosophy, religion and theology, and related subjects.

Music Index. Detroit: Detroit Information Service, 1949 to present. Issued monthly. Lists articles by author, subject, composer, and famous performers.

New York Times Index. New York: New York Times, 1913 to present. Issued bimonthly. Alphabetically cross-referenced by subjects, persons, and organizations. Helpful in locating articles in unindexed newspapers in that it provides researcher with dates under which to look.

Reader's Guide to Periodical Literature. New York: Wilson, 1900 to present. Issued monthly. Indexes about 160 general, nontechnical magazines. Articles are cross-referenced by author and subject.

Social Sciences Index. New York: Wilson, 1965 to present. (Before 1974 entitled *Social Sciences and Humanities Index.*) Issued quarterly. Covers anthropology, economics, environmental sciences, geography, law and criminology, public administration, political science, psychology, social aspects of medicine, sociology, and related subjects. Includes separate author listing of book reviews.

Indexes and Bulletins Updated Biweekly and Weekly

Congressional Quarterly Weekly Report. Washington, DC: Government Printing Office, 1945 to present. Issued weekly with quarterly index. Describes congressional actions of the preceding week and reprints important texts and speeches. Provides charts showing the progress of major legislation through committee and floor sessions.

Facts on File. New York: Facts on File, 1941 to present. Issued weekly, indexed annually. Digest of world news organized by subject.

Public Affairs Information Service Bulletin. New York: PAIS, 1915 to present. Updated biweekly with quarterly cumulations and an annual. Covers books, government publications, pamphlets, and periodical articles relating to economic and social conditions, public administration, and international relations.

Vital Speeches of the Day. Stronghold, NY: City News Publishing Co., 1934 to present. Issued biweekly and indexed in *Reader's Guide.* Full texts of recent addresses by prominent individuals, mostly American.

Weekly Compilation of Presidential Documents. Washington, DC: Government Printing Office. Updated weekly. Texts of presidential speeches, press conferences, and other presidential materials.

Still, if you are interested in a current issue not having to do with American national politics and policy, even these sources may not provide facts and opinions appropriate to or recent enough for your purposes. A raging controversy about last month's state elections, the newest treatment for cancer, an innovative soil additive for drought-stricken regions, or a just-released, best-selling exposé of the plastics industry—subjects like these require information that has not yet reached the compilers of indexes, let alone the writers of books. Fortunately, you can query computer database networks for almost any imaginable current data.

Computerized information services are widely available in university and college libraries. Access to them may be available to undergraduates, usually for a fee. You can also do a great deal of research from your desk if you have a personal computer and subscribe to an online service. Three widely used online services are BRS Information Technologies, CompuServe Information Services, Inc., and Dialog Information Services, Inc. These services include databases in the list below as noted in parentheses.

Some databases are based on bibliographic indexes also available in print. However, the database versions can locate the exact information you need in a fraction of the time you might spend thumbing through the printed volumes. Some offer information not available through print resources. All offer the most up-to-date information and references available.

The following alphabetical list covers broadly useful databases in several disciplines. For additional databases, consult your reference librarian, **Database of Databases** (CompuServe, DIALOG), or **Data Informer** (CompuServe). One valuable feature of Data Informer is that it emphasizes free and low-cost databases. Data Informer also advises you on ways to make your searches efficient and cost-effective.

Selected Database Sources

Academic Index (BRS, DIALOG). Indexes journals held in most large university libraries. Updated monthly.

Accountants Index (CompuServe). 1974 to present. Indexes worldwide English-language journals in accounting, data processing, financial reporting, and taxation. Updated quarterly.

Art Index (CompuServe). Indexes worldwide literature in the arts (including photography and city planning). Covers November 1984 to present. Updated twice weekly.

Books in Print (CompuServe, BRS, DIALOG). Lists forthcoming, current, and recently out of print books according to author, subject, and title. Updated monthly (print editions are available annually.)

Business Dateline (BRS, CompuServe, DIALOG). Gives *full text* of more than 100 U.S. and Canadian business publications and nine newspapers. Covers 1985 to present. Updated weekly.

Business Periodicals Index (CompuServe). Duplicates the print version of the index but is updated twice a week. Covers June 1982 to present.

Econbase (CompuServe, DIALOG). Lists statistics in all areas of economics, business conditions, finance, manufacturing, household income distribution, and demographics. Updated monthly.

Enviroline (CompuServe, DIALOG). Indexes more than 300 periodicals concerned with all aspects of environmental issues.

Facts on File (CompuServe, DIALOG). News summaries divided into four categories: international affairs, U.S. affairs, world news, and miscellaneous. Covers 1982 to present. Updated weekly.

Georef (CompuServe, DIALOG). Indexes geology, geochemistry, geophysics, mineralogy, paleontology, petrology, and seismology. Worldwide in scope, but 40% of the material indexed is U.S.-published.

Historical Abstracts (CompuServe, DIALOG). Covers more than 2,000 worldwide periodicals from 1973 to present. Updated quarterly.

Lexis/Nexis: Lexis indexes and provides *full text* and abstracts of federal and state appellate court decisions. Nexis provides both *full text* and abstracts of articles from more than 100 newspapers, magazines, trade publications, newsletters, and wire services. It also provides congressional information and access to *Medline*, which indexes journals in medicine, psychology, and sociology. Updated daily.

Magazine ASAP (BRS, CompuServe, DIALOG). Gives *full text* for more than 100 magazines indexed in Magazine Index. Covers 1983 to present. Updated monthly.

Magazine Index (BRS, CompuServe, DIALOG). Indexes more than 400 popular magazines in wide-ranging fields of interest. Covers 1959 to present (except for 1971 and 1972). Updated monthly.

National Newspaper Index (BRS, CompuServe, DIALOG). Indexes *Christian Science Monitor, New York Times,* and *Wall Street Journal.* Covers 1979 to present. Updated weekly.

Newsearch (BRS, CompuServe, DIALOG). Indexes key items from more than 1,700 newspapers, magazines, and other periodicals. Covers current month only. *Updated daily.*

Readers' Guide to Periodical Literature (CompuServe). Duplicates the print version but is updated biweekly.

Zoological Record (BRS, CompuServe, DIALOG). Indexes more than 6,000 worldwide journals in zoology. Covers 1978 to present. Updated monthly.

Personal Knowledge and Research

Not all the data-gathering you will do to create and support written arguments will begin and end in the library, or at your computer. Occasionally you will be lucky enough to have the opportunity to write about subjects of which you have first-hand knowledge. If you have worked at a camp for chronically ill children, you can write with authority about the value of camping experiences for children with physical limitations. You will be able to call on specific, vivid examples of children who found new strength, new enthusiasm for living. You will be able to quote the medical staff on therapeutic camping. You will cite your own observations and experiences. In another context, you may be able to call upon your memory of having your leg in a cast to pinpoint some of the problems people confined to wheelchairs face in a world still not wholly attuned to their needs. Your personal knowledge will supplement your research in crucial ways. Similarly, if you have ever started or worked for a small business, you can write about the hurdles such businesses face with a degree of specificity and conviction that other classmates cannot match.

Personal knowledge does present a few hurdles of its own if you are to use it successfully in your written arguments. First, you must continue to focus on your subject and your audience. Don't be self-indulgent or egoistical; rather, use your own knowledge and experience as concisely and objectively as possible. Remember that people enjoy the high points, but they don't want a blow-by-blow replay. Second, be absolutely specific. Avoid adjectives and adverbs. As many writing teachers before me have said, don't *tell* your readers, *show* them. Don't say, "The children really enjoyed the many activities at camp"; rather, describe their faces as they finished the ropes course. And don't forget to say just what the ropes course consisted of. Third, don't present yourself as an authority unless you are one. Modesty is the best policy. In the same vein, be careful not to assume that your experience, if limited, was typical. If you bear these cautions in mind, you will find that your personal experience can enliven many written arguments and enhance their persuasiveness.

You can also supplement library research with personal research, drawing not from your own knowledge and experience but from others'. Among the avenues available to you are letter and telephone inquiries, interviews, and polling. This kind of research can open up exciting possibilities for your written arguments. Your research—and your argument—will be on the cutting edge. You will have up-to-date data that may be nowhere else available.

You will have all this dazzling array of firsthand, unpublished support *if*, that is, you have the time and tenacity to find it, and if you can approach potential sources with both persistence and courtesy. What may surprise you is that people other than film and television celebrities often will be both flattered by and receptive to your interest in their subject. Sources in the reference libraries will help you find out how to contact authors, editors, researchers, and professors. You will get the best—and quickest—results from the experts if you try to follow these guidelines:

1. **When time permits, write a letter.** It should be brief and to the point. Be specific in identifying the information you seek. Be sure to include your return address and telephone number. Your correspondents will appreciate even more a stamped return envelope and an invitation to call collect.

2. **If time is quite short, consider telephoning if a number is available for your potential source.** If you do telephone, clearly identify yourself and your reason for calling, and ask if a call at another time would be more convenient for the person you have called. Write out in advance the exact questions you would like to ask. Keep them focused and few in number.

3. **If you need and are granted a personal interview, ask permission before tape recording the interview.** (Permission may not be given; be prepared to take careful notes.) If the subject matter is complicated or controversial, your source will appreciate it if you offer to let him or her review your quotations and summary comments for accuracy. Quote directly only when you have recorded the comments exactly, whether on tape or on paper.

4. **Follow up written correspondence, telephone conversations, or personal interviews with a prompt letter of thanks.** Most sources will appreciate, and some will require, a copy of your essay as well.

You are likely to be pleasantly surprised by the "kindness of strangers." I have been. Of the dozens of writers—some quite renowned—whom I have contacted over the years, only one was less than cordial. My husband and my father are both given to calling up writers of articles that interest them, to discuss the subjects further; both have had fascinating and informative conversations with authorities on subjects ranging from Texas history to theories in physics. If you respect the workloads of busy researchers and writers, and do not impose on their time unduly, you will meet with success much more often than not. Even when the sources you first contact cannot help you, they may suggest other avenues to pursue.

Polling   A statistics course is a good idea if you anticipate having to sound out public opinion frequently. If formal study is not possible, try to read one of the books for laypeople on the subject, such as Darrell Huff's classic *How to Lie with Statistics* (1954) or Gregory A. Kimble's *How to Use (and Misuse) Statistics* (1978). These should be available in your campus library. But perhaps neither of those options is possible—at least, not by Friday when your essay is due. As long as you resist any temptation to make more of them than warranted by your level of expertise, informal polls still can back up your argument on subjects of local interest.

Your aim in polling must be to generate data about local public opinion that is fair and typical of the population from which you draw your sample. You make an informal poll fair by giving attention to how you phrase your questions and how you pick your pollees. Some suggestions for both:

Developing Questions for Polls

1. **Avoid complex questions**—that is, two or more questions masquerading as one. The classic example is "Have you stopped beating your wife?" Properly broken down into two parts, most complex questions can be salvaged: "(1) Have you ever beaten your wife? If so, (2) have you stopped?"
2. **Phrase your questions as briefly and directly as possible.**
3. **Limit the number of questions.** People lose interest, and their attention wanders.

Picking a Sample Population to Poll

1. **Choose a group to sample that is directly concerned with the questions you propose to ask.** For instance, ask apartment-dwellers in your campus neighborhood about crime in the neighborhood, if you like, but not about the moribund downtown shopping district. If your concern is the latter, you must range farther afield to find appropriate people to question.
2. **Choose people to question who are representative of their group.** Someone who is subletting an apartment only for a couple of weeks while his house is painted, or someone who spends most of her time out-of-town on business, would not accurately represent apartment-dwellers in the neighborhood.

3. **Limit your claims to statements about the population surveyed.** Typically this group will be drawn from students at your college or perhaps residents of your community. You may choose to limit the population further: apartment-dwellers in your campus neighborhood, for instance, or people who shop downtown on weekends. Given the limited group you will sample, refrain from drawing conclusions about *all* apartment dwellers or *all* local shoppers.

Even in the hands of expert statisticians, polls cannot offer sure support for your claims. Remember that polls center on *perception* and *opinion*. Be careful not to transform that opinion into certainties. Even if a hundred people think that Herman Ross will be elected mayor, he may not be. Even if most people you speak to favor installing light-rail public transportation in your city, you still do not know if they will vote to increase the sales tax to pay for such a system.

Gathering first-hand and up-to-the-minute facts and testimony through letter and telephone queries, interviews, and polls has two drawbacks: It takes time and tenacity, and it can be expensive. It can also be fruitless: You may receive no reply to your letter, and the polls may not turn up anything you can use. To decide whether or not to pursue such sources of information, consider the importance to your argument of the evidence you hope to get and the importance of your argument itself. For a short, informal essay, such an investment of time and money may not be worthwhile or even necessary. Your own knowledge and experiences may suffice. For a term paper or a major presentation, however, the investment may be essential.

EXERCISE 4–1

Decide which of the following questions would be suitable for informal polls of students on your campus. Why would they be appropriate questions to ask that particular group? Which questions would be unlikely to give useful results on campus? For each of the latter, suggest what groups might more appropriately be polled on the subject.

1. Is it healthy for children to be raised in day-care centers?
2. Should the SAT be used as an admissions standard at this college? If so, what should be the minimum acceptable score, and why? If not, why not?
3. Have you voted in a local or state election? If not, why not?
4. Should funding for the National Endowment for the Humanities be reduced?
5. How often have you eaten fast food in the past week? What food items did you eat?
6. Should universities and colleges eliminate investments in companies that do not recycle? Why or why not?
7. Should abortion be illegal? If so, under what circumstances?
8. Altogether, how many Amendments have been made to the United States Constitution? Please paraphrase or summarize three of them.

9. What are three major issues that you believe this country will have to confront in the next decade? Please comment.

10. Should some system of nationalized health care be implemented? If yes, how? If no, why not?

EXERCISE 4–2

1. Suppose that you want to find out more about the issue of hazardous waste disposal. You read that John Doe, an environmental biologist at the state university, has argued against a proposed dump site near the town where you attend college. How do you contact Professor Doe to learn more?

2. You want to find out what students at the state college you attend think about a Bible study session being held each Wednesday in a meeting room at the student center. Design a list of questions and write out your specifications for whom to poll and where and when to poll. Defend your questions and your sampling on the basis of fairness and accuracy.

3. You have read an essay in a national monthly magazine that raises points germane to your research in a current writing project. How do you contact the author? Suggest at least three options to pursue in case others do not work out.

4. You have been reading about inaccuracies in high school history textbooks, and you plan to argue that such inaccuracies are (1) inexcusable or (2) usually trivial and unlikely to harm young scholars. Regardless of your bent, suggest three paths of personal research, and explain how you would contact the sources you need to reach for more details or expert opinion.

EVALUATING EVIDENCE

> Facts are stubborn things; and whatever may be our wishes, our inclinations, or the dictates of our passions, they cannot alter the state of facts and evidence.
>
> —John Adams

> But one must not be misled by the evidence.
>
> —Sigmund Freud

John Adams was quite right: Facts are stubborn things, and it requires tremendous mental agility to avoid dealing with them or to escape the conclusions they point toward. But Freud was right as well, for facts are also slippery and elusive things; they can be misleading, so that we sometimes hardly know whether to accept them or to denounce them as frauds. Not long ago our ancestors accepted as fact the notions that the earth was flat and that witches could not drown. And more recently it was settled fact that the atom could not be split nor could human beings be conceived in a petri dish. What is presented as fact—and believed—is sometimes conceived in error or ignorance or falsehood. Some people hesitate to use the word *fact,* so slippery is it. But whether we use the word or not, much reasoning relies on data we call, from preference or habit, **facts**—that is, beliefs we hold about our world based on evidence we have chosen to attend to.

Evidence cannot be gathered indiscriminately; in deciding what sources to use and in assessing the material gathered from them, we must make judgments about the quality and appropriateness for our purposes of the evidence we are searching for and the evidence we find. Pertinent evidence provides premises that support conclusions. Since the conclusions to such arguments are never more than probable, their persuasiveness depends on evidence that is

1. **recent** (or contemporaneous, in historical arguments);
2. **primary,** if possible ("eyewitness" evidence);
3. **unbiased** (as far as humanly possible);
4. **representative** of its class;
5. **sufficient** in quantity to carry conviction.

Recent Evidence

Always note the dates of evidence offered in support of a writer's thesis. Recent evidence is often desirable—as the emphasis in the previous section on ways of gathering current material reflects. If you are writing about the sciences (natural, social, or political), business, or technology—all fields in which new developments and discoveries occur almost daily, often invalidating or modifying previous thought—you must use the most recent evidence available on your subject, if your argument is to be credible. For this reason periodicals, newsletters, news reports, and computer databases will provide valuable evidence. Because of the time required for publishing, books in these fields may be somewhat dated by the time they appear in print. They provide useful background information, however, and their bibliographies may lead you to further sources.

On the other hand, if you are writing about history, philosophy, the fine arts, or literature—all fields in which a little distance from the subject can add context and perspective to your evaluation of it—books and periodicals can be equally useful. Even if your topic is, say, the recent work of Jasper Johns, books dealing with his earlier works or with twentieth-century artists in general can provide a context for comparison and evaluation, while contemporary art journals such as *Artforum* or *Art in America* can offer a counterpoint to your own judgments of Johns's recent paintings.

Primary Evidence

Evidence is *primary* if it comes from the original source. It is *secondary* if it comes from someone else's report on or evaluation of the original source. For example,

Jasper Johns's actual paintings (or, less satisfactorily, prints of them) are a primary source; Meyer Shapiro's discussion of them is a secondary source. Marx's *Communist Manifesto* is a primary source; Edmund Wilson's discussion of the impact of Marxist socialism in *To the Finland Station* is a secondary source. Jean Froissart's account of the Hundred Years' War is an interesting case, for he was not on hand for many of the events he reports in the *Chronicles*. In relative terms, however, the *Chronicles* offer primary information, while Geoffrey Brereton's assessment of them and their author (in Brereton's introduction to the Penguin edition, 1968) is secondary material.

The advantage of primary evidence is obvious: Using primary evidence, you make your own assessment without having to judge through the filter of someone else's vision—a filter that might be inaccurate or otherwise distorted. Herein lies the advantage, too, of reading foreign-language material in the original tongue, for inaccuracies can occur and biases creep into translations. It is ideal to know German if you are reading Freud or Marx, French if you are reading Froissart, classical Greek if you are reading Aristotle. If you cannot read German or French or classical Greek, it is well to know the relative merits and demerits of the translators. Consult your instructor or reference librarian for help in choosing the most accurate translations. Also note which translations your secondary sources seem to favor.

Secondary source material should always be reviewed and assessed in light of whatever primary evidence is available. Unfortunately (but life—and research—would be dull otherwise), you will find that the authors of secondary sources frequently disagree with each other, sometimes in minor details and sometimes in major conclusions. However, the more secondary material you accumulate, the better you will be able to assess the reliability of each source, balancing one claim against a contradictory one in order to identify and eliminate as many inaccuracies and biases as possible.

This is not to suggest that all primary evidence is superior to all secondary evidence. Even the eyewitnesses to events or the developers of new processes and products or the discoverers of previously uncharted geographical and astronomical bodies are human and subject to all kinds of prejudices, biases, and misperceptions—particularly about themselves and their own observations, discoveries, inventions, or pet subjects. You must evaluate written primary evidence as you would any other. In doing so, recall the discussion of emotional appeals and slanting in Chapter 1. As with secondary sources, try to find more than one primary source in order to weigh their relative merits.

Unbiased Evidence

First principle: Nothing that is written is totally without bias—even recipes. (For years I was intimidated by a pound cake recipe that sternly instructed, "Use butter *only*." Margarine, it turns out, works fine.) So in evaluating evidence in others' arguments for use in your own, consider first what the biases must be and then whether they are strong enough to affect the value of the evidence. Sometimes the writer's bias is as obvious as it is unconscious, as one reader of *Scientific American* notes:

> In her otherwise admirable article on the life of Sophie Germain [*Scientific American*, December 1991], Amy Dahan Dalmédico repeats the worn-out stereotype that "her charm [was] appreciated by all." Why is charm never ascribed to male mathematicians?
>
> —Morton Nadler, letter to *Scientific American*, April 1992

When you read, consider: Has the writer a reputation for fairness, or, if she is unknown to you, has she created a trustworthy persona in what she has written? A careful reading and comparison with other material written on the same subject will help you to determine what biases are reflected in the material at hand.

Just as you consider your own rhetorical stance in preparing to write an argumentative paper, you need to consider the rhetorical stance of the authors of both primary and secondary source material in order to assess the material's merit as evidence. In evaluating evidence and arguments, consider the writers' points of view about the subject matter and their purpose in writing about it. For instance, an author who is interested in how Henry James's work is connected with his life will approach *The Portrait of a Lady* differently from one who is interested in the development of the American novel. One point of view is no more valid than the other, but each affects the scope and emphasis of the respective work. A writer's purpose—the thesis, or whole aim in writing—also affects the content of the argument and reflects the author's biases about the particular subject. Read the preface or "author's note" of a book to get an immediate idea of both the writer's point of view and purpose in writing. In his concluding note to *The Best and the Brightest*, for example, author David Halberstam states both:

> At that point I was looking for a new assignment, and my colleague at *Harper's*, Midge Decter, suggested that I do a piece on McGeorge Bundy, who was after all the most glistening of the Kennedy-Johnson intellectuals. It would be a way not only of looking at him—very little was known about what he really did and stood for—but also of looking at that entire era. . . . When the article was finished I had a feeling of having just started. . . . I wanted to find out the full reasons why it [the escalation of the war in Vietnam] had all happened, I wanted to know the full context of the decisions, as well as how they were made. Why had they crossed the Rubicon? . . . The question that intrigued me most was *why*, why had it happened. So it became very quickly not a book about Vietnam, but a book about America, and in particular about power and success in America, what the country was, who the leadership was, how they got ahead, what their perceptions were about themselves, about the country and about their mission.

Halberstam spells out, more fully than this excerpt can suggest, just what his subject is and what his purpose in writing about it is. Not incidentally, he shows us the excitement creative research—research that is discovery and not just recapitulation—can generate. He is frank about his own biases, his belief that the men in power at the time were intelligent people who made some incredibly irrational decisions. Of his own position regarding the war, Halberstam writes, "[I]n the fall of 1963 I came to the conclusion that it was doomed and that we were on the wrong side of history." Such frankness is helpful to us as we evaluate the evidence any writer offers. When frankness is not forthcoming or the book or article includes no note, the prose itself almost always provides clues. What, for example, are the apparent biases of the *Wall Street Journal* staff reporters who penned the following paragraphs during the 1992 presidential race?

> Despite a month-long pummeling by Republicans and in the press, Ross Perot looks as strong as ever—and that's likely to be a shadow over next week's Democratic national convention.
>
> For Mr. Perot, the billionaire undeclared presidential candidate, the past month could have been brutal. First, there was a Wall Street Journal story detailing his use of private investigators in business and political disputes. Other articles followed, ranging from a Washington Post story that he investigated then-Vice President Bush to allegations in Time magazine that he destroyed a coral reef in Bermuda in order to dock his yacht more conveniently. Meanwhile, he was coming under heavy fire from White House surrogates.
>
> In the convention that opens [in New York] next week, Democrats plan to target George Bush's weaknesses and largely ignore Mr. Perot. . . .
>
> But a new Wall Street Journal/NBC News poll suggests the Democrats' confidence about Mr. Perot's fading may be at best premature—and at worst badly misplaced. The poll conducted earlier this week finds that Mr. Perot, even after all the bad news of recent weeks, nonetheless is favored by 33% of the 1,105 registered voters surveyed, compared to 31% for President Bush and 28% for Gov. Clinton.
>
> —*Wall Street Journal* 9 July 1992

What the reporter could not know, of course, was that Mr. Perot—who had never officially announced his candidacy—would withdraw from the presidential race the very week of the Democratic convention. Nor could the reporter have guessed that Mr. Perot would reenter the race several months later. (He won no electoral votes, but about 20% of the popular vote.)

Representative Evidence

If you want to argue that blue jays are the most obnoxious of creatures, you cannot observe and catalogue every blue jay. A handful of examples and anecdotes will suffice. But the blue jays you describe should be typical of their class; that is, they should not be blue jays raised by hand and kept in cages. The same is true of weightier matters: Any evidence you cite should be typical of the class about which the conclusion is drawn. If you question eighty students at a wealthy, church-related university about their political preferences in order to support a generalization that college students in the United States are politically conservative, you may draw conclusions that are unreliable—your sampling (besides being relatively small and limited to a single campus) is not representative of American college students in general. Since the constraints of time, good sense, and space usually preclude using all the available examples of a class, those you cite should be typical.

Sufficient Evidence

What constitutes "sufficient" evidence to carry conviction will vary. As a rule, one example can illustrate, but not convince. A thousand examples can convince, but readers are likely to doze off long before they reach the end of the litany. Readers really do not want to hear about every flamingo in captivity or about every single play in a soccer match, however brilliantly played. Generally, the greater the controversy or the more unexpected the conclusion drawn, the more evidence needed. Regardless of the audience, more evidence would be required to make a convincing case on either side of the gun control issue or the insanity defense for murder than would be required to support an argument on the educational and ecological value of zoos. Or flamingos.

Evaluate Evidence with Regard to:

Your Source	Your Subject	Your Audience
Primary or second-ary?	Representative? Specific?	Sufficient to convince this audience?
Up-to-date?	Relevant to this subject?	Relevant to this audience?
Unbiased?		Comprehensible to this audience?
Relevant point of view?		
Expert in this field?		

EXERCISE 4–3

For each of the following topics, indicate whether current information and evidence (no more than three to four months old) would be essential, important, useful, or not necessary.

1. Race relations in South Africa since 1990
2. The justness of the insanity defense for murder
3. The rise and fall (and rise and fall) of OPEC (Organization of Petroleum Exporting Countries)
4. The difficulties of living with a roommate
5. Women in science: trends over the last decade
6. Possible cures for AIDS
7. The viability of NATO
8. The claim that Austrian President Kurt Waldheim was guilty of Nazi war crimes in World War II
9. The health of the Social Security system

10. The relationship, if any, between legal drinking age and the number of serious traffic accidents in this state

---

EXERCISE 4–4

First, identify the type of evidence offered in each item below: example, testimony, statistic, or other kind of "fact." If the evidence is not common knowledge, a source will be mentioned; indicate your assessment of the source as likely to be accurate and fair, not likely to be accurate and fair, or unknown to you and impossible to evaluate. Then evaluate the evidence according to the first four standards described earlier: Does it appear to be recent (or contemporaneous) or outdated, primary or secondary, unbiased or biased, and representative or unrepresentative of its class?

1. One of the first black American businesswomen to become a millionaire was Sarah Breedlove Walker, who lived from 1867 to 1919.
   —*Notable American Women,*
   The Belknap Press of Harvard University Press, 1971

2. Debussy's *Pelléas et Mélisande* is "the only significant opera that impressionism has produced."
   —*Harvard Dictionary of Music,* 2nd ed., 1969

3. As someone who has spent six months in Spain (in 1972), I can state from experience that relations between the Guardia Civil (state police) and the university students are anything but cordial.
   —Sally De Witt Spurgin

4. Philomel is the name poets give to nightingales, but in the myth it was Procne who became a nightingale; Philomel was transformed into a lark.

5. A seven-year study by the National Institute for Occupational Safety and Health found that 14.8 percent of pregnant women who worked at VDTs [video display terminals] reported miscarriages. However, 15.9 percent of pregnant women in identical professions with similar lifestyles who did not work at VDTs also reported miscarriages. Both figures fall within the population-wide 11 percent to 20 percent miscarriage rate.
   —*Reason,* Aug./Sept. 1991

6. Table salt is not a salt at all, but sodium chloride.

7. One sector of the [airline] industry—commuter airlines—has historically had a worse accident record than that of major airlines. Commuter airlines fly short routes between hubs and small airports, often using planes with 30 or fewer seats. Between 1980 and 1990, fatal commuter-airline crashes were about four times more frequent than those of large carriers (2.2 crashes per million flights versus 0.58 crashes per million flights).
   —*Information Please Almanac,* 1992

8. More people in the West than in any other region of the United States approve of abortion during the first trimester of pregnancy.
   —*Gallup Poll of Public Opinion,* 1981

9. *Albion* is the poetic name for England.

10. Both men and women agree that a woman's life is more difficult than a man's.

> —*Gallup Poll of Public Opinion, 1935–1971*
> This statement is based on a
> poll taken in April 1946.

11. Among John Updike's poetic works are "Ex-Basketball Player," "Insomnia the Gem of the Ocean," and "Tao in the Yankee Stadium Bleachers."

> —*Granger's Index to Poetry*, Columbia University Press, 1982

12. Burundi and Cameroon are two African countries.

13. No other symptom . . . is as specific to schizophrenia: 75 percent of all patients hear voices—voices that command you to kill yourself, voices from outer space, two voices carrying on a conversation, even the voice of God.

> —Dr. Fuller Torrey, schizophrenia researcher and
> senior psychiatrist at St. Elizabeth's Hospital,
> Washington, D.C., as qtd. in *Discover*, Sept. 1992

14. More than a hundred distinct ethnic groups inhabit the former Soviet Union.

15. In the late 1400s, the African kingdom of Songhay was larger than western Europe. It had a public-school system and was particularly proud of its savants. Timbuktu's university was famous throughout Africa and Europe, and its medical center near the Niger attracted the ill from all over.

> —*Isaac Asimov's Book of Facts*, 1979

EXERCISE 4–5

Revise each of the following generalizations (or one of the variations suggested in parentheses) to a statement precise and limited enough to be supported in a short essay (three to five pages). Write out your revised generalization, and then discuss briefly the kinds of support—examples, testimony (including your own knowledge and experiences), statistics, and other kinds of "facts" that would be effective in an argument addressed to the other members of your rhetoric class.

1. Fraternities are inherently a bad (good) idea.
2. Politicians should (should not) be independently wealthy.
3. Math (any other major) is a useful college major.
4. Video games are interesting.
5. Soccer (any other sport) is superior to football.
6. The number of law school graduates should be restricted; there are too many lawyers.
7. Motorcycles (speedboats, snowmobiles) are a public hazard and should be outlawed.
8. Travel to foreign countries is fun and educational.
9. Cheating in college can sometimes (never) be justified.

10. The income tax amounts to creeping socialism (keeps needy people from dying for lack of food, shelter, or medical care).

USING EVIDENCE IN DOCUMENTED ESSAYS AND RESEARCH PAPERS

Summarizing, Paraphrasing, Quoting

Once you return from the library, armed with all sorts of ammunition with which to demolish the opposition in your written argument, two temptations and two difficulties arise. The first temptation is to use every bit of the material you have worked so hard to find, even if some of the evidence is tangential to your thesis, or even if you have so much material that to summarize or quote from all of it will leave you no room or energy to develop your own ideas in response to it. The second temptation occurs when the source material is written so concisely and clearly that you cannot imagine expressing the information in any other way. This usually unwarranted humility can result in an unattractive patchwork of a paper largely made up of lengthy quotations seamed together with transitional remarks—or in plagiarism, whether unconscious or deliberate.

Therefore, your first task must be to test your working outline and your evidence against each other. Your research may have turned up additional points to support your thesis, or it may have exposed flaws in your thesis that require you to modify your stance. Some fascinating material may not fit anywhere in your outlined argument, and you must let that material wait for another day and another essay. Then, too, what you have learned may suggest a more logical way of ordering the points you propose to make. And inadequacies in the support you have gathered will become apparent as you briefly identify the evidence you have found under each entry in your outline or bare-bones draft (if you use notecards, simply arrange them according to the major points they support). Where support appears inadequate, you must decide whether to modify or eliminate that particular point, or return to the library.

Now, how do you record the supporting material in such a way that you avoid that second temptation? Summarize most of it; paraphrase what is important but difficult to grasp in the original; and quote what is crucial, brief, and clear. If you are using a general or research handbook, these three ways of recording your research are explained in some detail therein. Briefly, to **summarize** is to express another's ideas *in your own words* and to do so in many fewer words than the original. To **paraphrase** is to express another's ideas *in your own words* and to do so in about the same number of words or even more words than the original. To **quote** is to express another's ideas *in that person's own words* and to indicate clearly that you have done so. In each case, you credit the source in your paper.

Even after you have put temptation behind you and have summarized most of your source material and have put aside all of it that is not directly relevant to your argument, the two difficulties remain to be dealt with. The first difficulty is that fitting source material into your own prose may be difficult to manage without ending up with something that reads as if it had been cut and pasted; the second, that the punctuation, pronouns, and verb tenses in the source material may not mesh well with your own writing. When the latter is the case, the quotations seem obtrusive even if they are introduced properly.

In order to overcome or avoid these difficulties, keep in mind a few points:

1. **Direct quotations should be few and significant.** The paper is to be your essay and your argument, after all. Too many other voices overpower your own. Instead, rely on restatement, summary, and evaluation of much of the source material in your own words.

2. **Quotations (and paraphrases and summaries) must be accurate.** An inaccurate quotation is careless and can be misleading, and a quotation taken out of context can be distorted.

3. **Quotations ordinarily should be preceded or followed by comment or analysis.** If a passage does not merit comment or analysis, it usually does not merit direct quotation. (In which case, summarize instead.)

4. **Quotations must be grammatically and logically incorporated into the paragraph in which you use them.** They should fit into, not just be appliquéd on, your own argument.

5. **All sources, whether quoted, paraphrased, or summarized, must be properly cited.**

To accomplish these aims, first, take most of your notes in your own words. This bit of advice is time-worn but still valuable. Taking notes in your own words has the initial advantage of requiring that you read closely and truly understand what you are reading, a requirement not exacted by a photocopier. In addition, understanding the material will facilitate your use of it in your own argument; and because it will be recounted in your own words, you will avoid the patchwork effect of excessive quotations. (Of course, citations still will be required.) Save direct quotations for brief, brilliant comments, controversial statements, statistics, and personal testimony that you believe will strengthen your argument. Always indicate directly quoted material with quotation marks and page references in your notes so that you will avoid confusion later as you write and revise.

Incorporating Quotations

Second, as you write the essay, incorporate quoted material grammatically and logically into your own paragraphs. Quotations should not crop up unannounced, without evident context. Those running longer than three lines of typescript should be indented ten spaces (and instructors may prefer that you also single-space them) and should be introduced by an entire sentence or by a clause and a colon. Shorter quotations also must be given a context that fits them grammatically and logically into your argument and your words. Brief quotations may be incorporated in an almost limitless number of ways, as the following examples indicate:

(1)

Mark Antony uses irony in his funeral oration for Caesar. "I come to bury Caesar, not to praise him" (3.2.79–80) asserts just the opposite of Mark Antony's intentions. He uses the oration to praise Caesar backhandedly and to attack Caesar's murderers while pretending to applaud them.

(2)

Mark Antony's funeral oration for Caesar uses irony effectively, for after declaring, "I come to bury Caesar, not to praise him" (3.2.79–80), Mark Antony goes on to attack Caesar's murderers through the irony of his repeated reference to "the noble Brutus." As the whole context of his speech makes clear, Caesar's ally means the opposite of what he says here.

(3)

Never was a funeral oration used to better political effect than that of Mark Antony over the body of the dead Caesar. He begins with a disclaimer: "I come to bury Caesar, not to praise him" (3.2.79–80). Having lulled Caesar's enemies, Mark Antony then turns the crowd against them through the heavy irony of his repeated praise of them, "all honorable men."

In the first example the quotation serves as the subject of a sentence explaining its meaning. In the second the same quotation is grammatically imbedded within a sentence that gives it a context in the play and in the student writer's argument. The quoted phrase, "the noble Brutus," is incorporated without punctuation because it functions as the object of a preposition. And in the third selection the quotation is introduced by a clause and a colon as is typical of longer quotations, and the quoted phrase "all honorable men" serves as an appositive describing the murderers.

But suppose that the quotation is written in the past tense, and your paragraph is written in the present; or that the quotation begins with a capital letter, but a capital letter is not needed at the point in your own sentence at which you quote; or that you want to omit words or sentences preceding, following, or in the middle of what you plan to quote—what then? The following pointers should help you resolve most dilemmas of this sort.

Changes   Generally, avoid changes in the quoted material. If you must have them, put brackets around the altered letter or word. Do not alter punctuation except as noted below.

1. If the quoted material begins with a capital letter and its placement in your own sentence requires a lower-case letter, change the initial letter to lower case. Conservative usage dictates brackets around the altered letter, but brackets can be distracting. Try to rephrase your own sentence so that the quotation can be incorporated without such changes. (If your typewriter has no bracket keys, you must ink in any brackets required, for parentheses do not indicate added or altered words). Make the same kind of change if the original quotation begins with a lowercase letter and your grammatical context for it requires a capital.

Original Statement: The one function that TV news performs very well is that when there is no news, we give it to you with the same emphasis as if there were news.

—David Brinkley

As Quoted: David Brinkley has observed that "[t]he one function that TV news performs very well is that when there is no news, [newscasters] give it to you with the same emphasis as if there were news."

2. **If the quoted material uses present tense and you would prefer to have it in past tense, avoid making a change in the quoted material by wording your introduction in such a way that the shift in tense is accounted for without changing the original.** In brief quotations involving only a single verb, you may change the tense and bracket the altered word, but try to avoid the need to do so by reworking your own sentence or by omitting from the quotation the part containing the troublesome verb.

Original Statement: Those who make peaceful revolution impossible will make violent revolution inevitable.

—John Kennedy

As Quoted: The United States was culpable in the Iranian revolution of 1979 to the extent that it did all in its power to keep the Shah in sole control of the government, despite the widespread opposition to many of the Shah's policies. The U.S. failed to heed John Kennedy's warning made almost two decades earlier: "Those who make peaceful revolution impossible will make violent revolution inevitable."

Original Statement: Boswell is the first of biographers.

—Thomas Macauley

As Quoted: In the nineteenth century Macauley declared Boswell to be "the first of biographers."

3. **Commas, semicolons, colons, and periods ending quotations may be changed to the punctuation mark that fits your own grammatical context (usually a period, comma, or no punctuation).** Do not end a quotation with double punctuation (the original writer's and then your own).

Original Statement: If the life of a human being is more valuable than the life of, say, a cabbage, this must be because the human being has qualities like consciousness, rationality, autonomy, and self-awareness which distinguish human beings from cabbages. How, then, can we pretend that the life of a human being with all these distinctive qualities is of no greater value than the life of a human being who, tragically, has never had and never will have these qualities?

—Peter Singer and Helga Kuhse, rev. of Robert and Peggy
Stinson, *The Long Dying of Baby Andrew*

As Quoted: As Singer and Kuhse observe, it is pointless to "pretend that the life of a human being with all these distinctive qualities [such as rationality and self-awareness] is of no greater value than the life of a human being who, tragically, has never had and never will have these qualities" (16).

4. **Change double quotation marks (" ") within quotations to single marks (' ') unless the whole passage is set off from the text.**

Original Statement: Apparently, now that he knew he was in trouble, his thoughts had turned to his God. "Have mercy!" they heard him shouting indignantly. "I say have mercy, damn it!"
                                    —Clarence Day, *Life With Father* (Knopf, 1935) 26

As Quoted: Day's father was a man not to be trifled with, even by Almighty God. On the rare occasion when the senior Day felt the need to call upon his Maker, it was as if he called upon an equal: "'Have mercy!' they heard him shouting indignantly. 'I say have mercy, damn it!' " (26).

Omissions Whenever you omit parts of a quoted passage, make sure that what you do quote still shows grammatical continuity and logical sense. For example:

Original Statement: Singer and Kuhse (above).

Unclear Abridgement: As Singer and Kuhse cogently argue, "a human being is more valuable than the life of a cabbage . . . because . . . these distinctive qualities are of . . . greater value than the life of a human being who, tragically, has never had and never will have these qualities" (16).

Effective Abridgement: As Singer and Kuhse cogently argue, "the life of a human being is more valuable than the life of a cabbage [primarily because of] . . . qualities like consciousness . . . and self-awareness" (16).

1. **If you omit words, phrases, or sentences in the middle of a quoted passage, indicate the omission with ellipses (. . .).** Use four dots if the words on either side of the ellipses are both grammatically complete sentences or if a sentence ends and another begins in the omitted section.

Original Statement: The cult of "reason," so widely applied in the course of the last three centuries, has come to seem to me in a sense a blind alley. Our thoughts and actions may be controlled by but they do not spring from what we call reason.
                        —Edmund Wilson, *The Dead Sea Scrolls, 1947–1966*
                                            (Oxford UP, 1969) 277

As Quoted: Logic is not the source of ideas, Wilson reminds us: "The cult of 'reason' . . . has come to seem to me in a sense a blind alley. Our thoughts and actions may be controlled by but they do not spring from what we call reason" (*Dead Sea Scrolls* 277).

[An abbreviated form of the title is included in a reference to one of several works written by the same author(s).]

2. **If you omit sentences before the quoted material (as you ordinarily will), do not use ellipses.** If you omit words or sentences following the quoted material, and the next words in the sentences are your own, do not use ellipses. But if you end your own sentence with quoted words that do *not* end a sentence in the original, you must use ellipsis dots following the quotation.

Original Statement: Her long, black hair, always drawn and braided in the day, lay upon her shoulders and against her breasts like a shawl. I do not speak Kiowa, and I never understood her prayers, but there was something inherently sad in the sound, some merest hesitation upon the syllables of sorrow.
                        —N. Scott Momaday, *The Way to Rainy Mountain*
                                            (New Mexico UP, 1969) 10

As Quoted: His grandmother's reverence touched him: "I do not speak Kiowa, and I never understood her prayers, but there was something inherently sad" in her quiet chanting (10).

As Quoted: His grandmother's reverence touched him: "I do not speak Kiowa, and I never understood her prayers, but there was something inherently sad in the sound . . ." (10). He would never forget it.

Additions   Always make sure that it will be clear to a reader that anything you have added is not in the original quotation. Added words are bracketed. Never confuse brackets with parentheses; if words appear in parentheses, they are assumed to be part of the original quotation.

1. **If you insert words of your own into a quoted passage for transition or explanation, put them in brackets.**

Original Statement: Wilson's, above.

As Quoted: Logic is not the source of ideas, Wilson reminds us: "The cult of 'reason' . . . [is] in a sense a blind alley. Our thoughts and actions may be controlled by but they do not spring from what we call reason" (*Dead Sea Scrolls* 277).

2. **If you put some of the quoted words in italics (indicated in a typewritten paper by underlining), follow the quotation with "(emphasis added)."**

Original Statement: And love is an impediment to marital happiness. Founded on projection, abetting the quest for indirect self-acceptance, love can contribute neither to candid intimacy nor to self-acceptance.

—Snell Putney and Gail J. Putney,
The Adjusted American (Harper, 1966) 118

As Quoted: Many psychologists have argued that what we call *love* is a destructive emotion: "Founded on projection, abetting the quest for *indirect* self-acceptance, love can contribute neither to candid intimacy nor to self-acceptance" (Putney and Putney 118; emphasis added).

3. **If the quoted material contains an error, follow the error with "[sic]" so that your readers will know the error is not yours.**

Original Statement: In reviewing its provisions, we could not determine how the bill might effect future Supreme Court rulings.

—John Q. Legislator, letter to constituents

As Quoted: Senator Legislator wrote that the committee "could not determine how the bill might effect [sic] future Supreme Court rulings."

CITING SOURCES

Avoiding Plagiarism

As you write your essay, you must cite your sources of evidence whether you are quoting directly, paraphrasing, or summarizing. You must also cite the sources of ideas that are not your own. The only statements that do not require citation are common-knowledge statements expressed in your own words, and your original ideas, interpretations, and conclusions. Failure to cite sources, and cite them accurately, constitutes plagiarism—a kind of theft that violates every aim of scholarship and integrity that academic institutions hold dear.

For the following thorough definition of plagiarism I am indebted to Nancy Hilts Deane, *Teaching with a Purpose,* 5th ed. (New York: Houghton Mifflin, 1972):

> Plagiarism is the presentation of the words, ideas, or opinions of someone else as one's own. A student is guilty of plagiarism if he submits as his own work a part or all of an assignment copied or paraphrased from a source, such as a book, magazine, or pamphlet, without crediting the source; the sequence of ideas, arrangement of material, or pattern of thought of someone else, *even though he has expressed it in his own words* [emphasis added]. Plagiarism occurs when such a sequence of words or ideas is used without having been digested, integrated, and reorganized in the writer's mind, and without acknowledgement in the paper.
>
> Similarly, a student is an accomplice in plagiarism and equally guilty if he allows his paper, in outline or finished form, to be copied and submitted as the work of another; if he prepares a written assignment for another student and allows it to be submitted as that student's work; or if he keeps or contributes to a file of papers or speeches with the clear intent that they be copied and submitted as the work of anyone other than the author.

One difficulty students encounter in avoiding plagiarism is deciding whether some statements are common-knowledge information or the intellectual property of a particular writer. Certainly it is easy to see that you need not cite a source for the dates of wars or of reigns, or the names of presidents, princes, and publishing companies. But what about the formula for making ordinary glass or the fact that *Albion* is a poetic name for England? What about the name of the first African-American professional baseball player, or his batting average? What about a brief identification of the First Law of Thermodynamics? All these bits of information are, just like the name of the first president of the United States, part of the **body of common knowledge.** Common knowledge is information common to any person informed in a given field. Any textbook on the subject, any specialized (and sometimes general) dictionary or encyclopedia is likely to contain such information.

As you begin your study of a particular field of knowledge, of course, almost everything you learn will be new to you. Initially, then, you may cite sources unnecessarily. You will begin to identify the common knowledge in the field as you read more widely. But when in doubt, cite your source. Better too many citations than too few.

Citing sources accurately and appropriately not only shows you to be an honest scholar but also adds the weight of authoritative testimony to arguments concerning subjects on which you cannot speak personally as an authority. In both ways, proper citation adds to the persuasiveness of your paper. But endless numbers of footnotes do not add to any paper's persuasiveness; they distract readers by continually sending them to the bottom of the page or the end of the paper. Parenthetical citations are preferable. The one exception occurs when you want to cite several sources simultaneously, which would require a long and obtrusive parenthetical citation. Discursive notes (notes commenting on, but not strictly part of, the text of the paper) cannot always be eliminated but should be few in number.

As you take notes for your research paper, record all the following information that is applicable for each source. All numbers (except page numbers for prefaces and other front matter in books, which are distinguished from the text proper by the use of lower-case Roman numerals) should be given in Arabic numerals.

Books

Author(s)
Editor(s) of anthologies of essays, stories, poems, and the like
Translator (if any)
Title of Chapter or Part of Book (if only part is used; also note page numbers of chapter or part used if it constitutes an identifiable unit of the book; put title in quotation marks)
Title of Book (including subtitle, if any; both italicized or underlined)
Name of Series (if work is part of a series; series name neither underlined nor put in quotation marks)
Number of Volumes with This Title (if work is in more than one volume; and number of this particular volume)
Place of Publication
Publisher
Year of Publication

Periodicals

Author(s) of Article
Title of Article (in quotation marks)
Name of Periodical (underlined)
Volume Number and Year (for scholarly journals)
Month and Year (for general circulation magazines; include day of month for weekly or biweekly magazines and for newspapers)
Page numbers for the entire article (separately record *specific* page numbers with passages to be cited within your paper)

Recording all the applicable information on a notecard for each source will help you avoid return trips to the library when you prepare your "Works Cited" list.

Citations in the Humanities

In order to meet both the goal of properly citing all source material and that of eliminating purely bibliographic footnotes, follow one general principle: *Give the least amount of information needed to send the reader to the appropriate point in the appropriate text.* Most of the identifying information about each work cited will be given in a list of works cited at the end of the paper. Citations in the text itself will direct the reader to a specific page (or line, if the reference is to a poem or play) in that work; they will not repeat the complete information given in the list of works cited.

Some additional guidelines follow.

What to Include in Parenthetical Citations

1. Do not repeat in parentheses what you have already said in the text proper.
2. Put as little as possible in parentheses to keep interruptions to a minimum. Author's* surname and page number will suffice if you have only one work by that author in your list of works cited. Page number alone will suffice if you mention the author's name in the text proper and you have used no other work by that author.

   If your paper largely concerns works by a single author, you need not repeat the author's name each time you quote or refer to what is obviously one of his or her works.
3. If you have used more than one work by the same person or persons, include an abbreviated form of the title in the citation.
4. If you have used works by different authors with the same surname, give first name or initial as well to distinguish the works from each other.
5. If a work has two authors, include both names in the citation. If it has three authors or more, you may use the first author's name and the Latin abbreviation "et al." (meaning "and others").
6. If you use an indirect reference—for example, you refer to a statement by Smith as quoted in a work by Jones—make clear that you are not using the original source with the abbreviation "qtd. in" (for "quoted in").
7. If your reference is to a poem, indicate line numbers rather than page numbers. Do not use the abbreviations *l.* or *ll.*, which could be confused with numbers. Instead, write out *line* or *lines* until the reference to lines is clearly established; thereafter, just give the numbers.
8. If your reference is to a play, indicate act, scene, and line(s) with Arabic numbers and periods: 3.2.112 directs a reader to Act 3, scene 2, line 112.
9. The abbreviations *p., pp.,* and *vol.* are no longer used when the reference is clearly to page numbers or volume number.

How to Punctuate Parenthetical Citations

1. Use no punctuation between author's name and page number: (Smith 268)
2. Use no punctuation between title and page number: (*Ideas* 268)
3. Put a comma between author's name and title (if title is needed): (Smith, *Ideas* 268)
4. Place parenthetical citations after the closing quotation mark and before the

---

*References to *author* also apply to *editor* when you are referring to entire anthologies and other compilations.

period except in the case of long, blocked quotations. Then they follow the period at the end of the quoted passage.

Basic Forms for Lists of Works Cited

Entries in the list of Works Cited are alphabetical. For each, the author's surname is given first, flush against the left margin. Subsequent lines, if any, are indented five spaces from the left margin.

Examples of Basic Forms for Entries in Works Cited List (Alphabetically)

Book

Galbraith, John Kenneth. *The Anatomy of Power*. Boston: Houghton, 1983.

Collection or Anthology

Barthelme, Donald. "Lightening." *Overnight to Many Distant Cities*. New York: Putnam's, 1983.
[reference to component part of book all by one author]

Groutz, Samuel, ed. *Moral Problems in Medicine*. Englewood Cliffs, NJ: Prentice, 1976.
[reference to entire book]

Szasz, Thomas. "The Right to Health." *Moral Problems in Medicine*. Ed. Samuel Groutz. Englewood Cliffs, NJ: Prentice, 1976.
[reference to component part of book]

Computer Data

"The Decade Ahead: Plan for the Oil Industry." Diskette 14. Marietta, NM: Petroleum Resources, Inc., 1991.

Congressional Document

United States, 101st Cong., 2nd sess. *Cong. Rec.* 14 Apr. 1988: 4315–23. Debate on savings and loan relief.

Film

It's a Wonderful Life. Dir. Frank Capra. RKO, 1946.
[RKO was the film's distributor.]

Interview

Harris, Leon. Telephone interview. 14 Oct. 1992.

Journal Article

Perrine, Laurence. "Donne's 'Confined Love.'" *Explicator* 39 (1980): 35–36.

Brooks, Roy L. "The Affirmative Action Issue: Law, Policy, and Morality." *Connecticut Law Review* 22.2 (1990): 323–357.

Legal Citation

Johnson v. Transportation Agency. 480 U.S. 616 (1987).

Letter

Brady, Judy. Letter to author. 11 March 1991.

Magazine Article

Sachs, Andrea. "Who Should Foot the AIDS Bill?" *Time* 16 Oct. 1989: 88.

Newspaper Article

Morgan, Mary Carolyn. "Ease Up, Please, on Single Women. . . . " *New York Times* 15 July 1990, sec. 12: 26.

Dombrink, Patricia. "There's No Gender in Success." *Dallas Morning News* 10 Aug. 1982: 11A.

Review

Aspen, Marvin. Rev. of *The Jury in America,* by John Guinther. *Judicature* 72.4 (1989): 254–55.

Citations in the Social Sciences

The *Publication Manual of the American Psychological Association* explains in detail the most common citation system in the social sciences. The following summary of APA documentation is reprinted with the kind permission of Lynn Quitman Troyka from the *Simon and Schuster Handbook for Writers* (Englewood Cliffs, NJ: Prentice Hall, 1987) 648–49.

What to Include in Parenthetical Citations

1. If a parenthetical citation comes at the end of your sentence, place the sentence's period after the parenthesis.
2. If you are paraphrasing or summarizing material and you do *not* mention the name of the author in your text, do this: (Jones, 1982).
3. If you are quoting, and you do *not* mention the name of the author in your text, do this: (Jones, 1982, p. 65).
4. If you are paraphrasing, summarizing, or quoting material and *do* mention the name of the author in your text, do this: (p. 65).
5. If you use more than one source written in the same year by the same author(s), assign letters (*a*, *b*, etc.) to the works in the References list and do this for a parenthetical reference: (Jones, 1983a).
6. If you refer to a work more than once, give the author's name and year only the first time; then use only the name.
7. If you cite several sources in one place, put them in alphabetical order by

authors' last names and separate the sources with a semicolon: (Bassuk, 1984; Fustero, 1984).

Guidelines for the Reference List

1. Arrange the list of sources cited alphabetically by author's last name. For two or more works by an author, arrange the works by date, most recent first.
2. Start with an author's last name, followed by initials for the author's first name and middle names. If there is more than one author, name them all (up to six authors)—again starting with the last name and using initials for first and middle names. If there are over six authors, use only the first author and the words *et al.*
3. Put the date of publication in parentheses immediately after the author's name. If you list two works by the same author published in the same year, assign letters (*a, b,* etc.) to the year: (1984a), (1984b).
4. Put the title after the year of publication. Capitalize only the first word and any proper names in a title or subtitle. Do not put articles in quotation marks. Underline (that is, italicize) titles.
5. Put the city of publication and the publisher next. Use short forms for the names of well-known publishers: New York: Harper.
6. Put page numbers next, but use *p.* or *pp.* only for page numbers of articles in newspapers or popular magazines. Do not use *p.* or *pp.* with pages numbers of articles in professional journals. In contrast, parenthetical references to specific pages always include *p.* or *pp.*—no matter what type of source.
7. Start each item at left margin, but if the item has two or more lines, indent all lines after the first line five spaces.

Citations in the Natural Sciences

The following sources will show you the correct documentation methods for various sciences.

Biology

Council of Biology Editors' Style Manual Committee. *CBE Style Manual.* 5th ed. Bethesda, MD: Council of Biology Editors, 1983.

Chemistry

American Chemical Society. *American Chemical Society Style Guide.* 2nd ed. Washington, DC: American Chemical Society, 1986.

Geology

Bates, Robert L., Rex Buchanan, and Marla Adkins-Hejlson, eds. *Geowriting: A Guide to Writing, Editing, and Printing in Earth Science.* 5th ed. Alexandria, VA: American Geological Institute, 1992.

Physics

American Institute of Physics. *Style Manual for Guidance in the Preparation of Papers.* 4th ed. New York: American Institute of Physics, 1990.

If your coursework and your interests lead you to write research papers often, you will want to invest in a good research handbook. In the meantime, this chapter gives you the information you need to support your claim in a documented essay. You have a good idea where to go when you need up-to-date information in fields ranging from art to zoology. Just as important, you know how to be selective, evaluating evidence to make sure that it is recent; primary, if possible; unbiased; representative; and sufficient to carry conviction. You are aware that you need to tailor the kind and quantity of evidence to the readers for whom you write. And you know how to smoothly incorporate other people's ideas and words into your own arguments. Finally, you have some ideas about how to make your research both more productive and more interesting.

READINGS

REPORTS, INFERENCES, JUDGMENTS

S. I. Hayakawa

1   For the purpose of the interchange of information, the basic symbolic act is the *report* of what we have seen, heard, or felt: "There is a ditch on each side of the road." "You can get those at Smith's Hardware Store for $2.75." "There aren't any fish on that side of the lake, but there are on this side." Then there are reports of reports: "The longest waterfall in the world is Victoria Falls." "The Battle of Hastings took place in 1066." "The papers say that there was a smash-up on Highway 41 near Evansville." Reports adhere to the following rules: first, they are *capable of verification;* second, they *exclude,* as far as possible, *inferences and judgments.* (These terms will be defined later.)

Verifiability

2   Reports are verifiable. We may not always be able to verify them ourselves, since we cannot track down the evidence for every piece of history we know, nor can we all go to Evansville to see the remains of the smash-up before they are cleared away. But if we are roughly agreed upon the names of things, upon what constitutes a "foot," "yard," "bushel," "kilogram," "meter," and so on, and upon how to measure time, there is relatively little danger of our misunderstanding each other. Even in a world such as we have today, in which everybody seems to be quarreling with everybody else, *we*

still to a surprising degree trust each other's reports. We ask directions of total strangers when we are traveling. We follow directions on road signs without being suspicious of the people who put them up. We read books of information about science, mathematics, automotive engineering, travel, geography, the history of costume, and other such factual matters, and we usually assume that the author is doing his best to tell us as truly as he can what he knows. And we are safe in so assuming most of the time. With the interest given today to the discussion of biased newspapers, propagandists, and the general untrustworthiness of many of the communications we receive, we are likely to forget that we still have an enormous amount of reliable information available and that deliberate misinformation, except in warfare, is still more the exception than the rule. The desire for self-preservation that compelled men to evolve means for the exchange of information also compels them to regard the giving of false information as profoundly reprehensible.

3   At its highest development, the language of reports is the language of science. By "highest development" we mean greatest general usefulness. Presbyterian and Catholic, workingman and capitalist, East German and West German *agree* on the meanings of such symbols as $2 \times 2 = 4$, $100°$ C, HNO_3, 3:35 A.M., 1940 A.D., 1,000 kilowatts, Quercus agrifolia, and so on. But how, it may be asked, can there be agreement about even this much among people who disagree about political philosophies, ethical ideas, religious beliefs, and the survival of my business versus the survival of yours? The answer is that circumstances *compel men to agree,* whether they wish to or not. If, for example, there were a dozen different religious sects in the United States, each insisting on its own way of naming the time of the day and the days of the year, the mere necessity of having a dozen different calendars, a dozen different kinds of watches, and a dozen sets of schedules for business hours, trains, and television programs, to say nothing of the effort that would be required for translating terms from one nomenclature to another, would make life as we know it impossible.

4   The language of reports, then, including the more accurate reports of science, is "map" language, and because it gives us reasonably accurate representations of the "territory," it enables us to get work done. Such language may often be dull reading: one does not usually read logarithmic tables or telephone directories for entertainment. But we could not get along without it. There are numberless occasions in the talking and writing we do in everyday life that *require that we state things in such a way that everybody will be able to understand and agree with our formulation.*

Inferences

5   Not that inferences are not important—we rely in everyday life and in science as much on *inferences* as on reports—in some areas of thought, for example, geology, paleontology, and nuclear physics, reports are the foundations; but inferences (and inferences upon inferences) are the main body of

the science. An inference, as we shall use the term, *is a statement about the unknown made on the basis of the known.* We may *infer* from the material and cut of a woman's clothes her wealth or social position; we may *infer* from the character of the ruins the origin of the fire that destroyed the building; we may *infer* from a man's calloused hands the nature of his occupation; we may *infer* from a senator's vote on an armaments bill his attitude toward Russia; we may *infer* from the structure of the land the path of a prehistoric glacier; we may *infer* from a halo on an unexposed photographic plate its past proximity to radioactive materials; we may *infer* from the sound of an engine the condition of its connecting rods. Inferences may be carefully or carelessly made. They may be made on the basis of a broad background of previous experience with the subject matter or with no experience at all. For example, the inferences a good mechanic can make about the internal condition of a motor by listening to it are often startlingly accurate, while the inferences made by an amateur (if he tries to make any) may be entirely wrong. But the common characteristic of inferences is that they are statements about matters which are not directly known, made on the basis of what has been observed.

6   The avoidance of inferences . . . requires that we make no guesses as to what is going on in other people's minds. When we say, "He was angry," we are not reporting; we are making an inference from such observable facts as the following: "He pounded his fist on the table; he swore; he threw the telephone directory at his stenographer." In this particular example, the inference appears to be safe; nevertheless, it is important to remember, especially for the purposes of training oneself, that it is an inference. Such expressions as "He thought a lot of himself," "He was scared of girls," "He has an inferiority complex," made on the basis of casual observation, and "What Russia really wants to do is to establish a communist world dictatorship," made on the basis of casual reading, are highly inferential. We should keep in mind their inferential character and . . . should substitute for them such statements as "He rarely spoke to subordinates in the plant," "I saw him at a party, and he never danced except when one of the girls asked him to," "He wouldn't apply for the scholarship, although I believe he could have won it easily," and "The Russian delegation to the United Nations has asked for *A, B,* and *C.* Last year they voted against *M* and *N* and voted for *X* and *Y.* On the basis of facts such as these, the newspaper I read makes the inference that what Russia really wants is to establish a communist world dictatorship. I agree."

7   Even when we exercise every caution to avoid inferences and to report only what we see and experience, we all remain prone to error, since the making of inferences is a quick, almost automatic process. We may watch a car weaving as it goes down the road and say, "Look at that *drunken driver,*" although what we *see* is only *the irregular motion of the car.* I once saw a man leave a dollar at a lunch counter and hurry out. Just as I was wondering why anyone should leave so generous a tip in so modest an establishment, the waitress came, picked up the dollar, put it in the cash register as she punched

up ninety cents, and put a dime in her pocket. In other words, my description to myself of the event, "a dollar tip," turned out to be not a report but an inference.

8   All this is not to say that we should never make inferences. The inability to make inferences is itself a sign of mental disorder. For example, the speech therapist Laura L. Lee writes, "The aphasic [brain-damaged] adult with whom I worked had great difficulty in making inferences about a picture I showed her. She could tell me what was happening at the moment in the picture, but could not tell me what might have happened just before the picture or just afterward." Hence the question is not whether or not we make inferences; the question is whether or not we are aware of the inferences we make. . . .

Judgments

9   . . . By judgments, we shall mean *all expressions of the writer's approval or disapproval of the occurrences, persons, or objects he is describing.* For example, a report cannot say, "It was a wonderful car," but must say something like this: "It has been driven 50,000 miles and has never required any repairs." Again, statements such as "Jack lied to us" must be avoided in favor of the more verifiable statement, "Jack told us he didn't have the keys to his car with him. However, when he pulled a handkerchief out of his pocket a few minutes later, a bunch of keys fell out." Also a report may not say, "The senator was stubborn, defiant, and uncooperative," or "The senator courageously stood by his principles"; it must say instead, "The senator's vote was the only one against the bill."

10   Many people regard statements such as the following as statements of "fact": "Jack *lied* to us," "Jerry is a *thief*," "Tommy is *clever*." As ordinarily employed, however, the word "lied" involves first an inference (that Jack knew otherwise and deliberately misstated the facts) and second a judgment (that the speaker disapproves of what he has inferred that Jack did). In the other two instances, we may substitute such expressions as, "Jerry was convicted of theft and served two years at Waupun," and "Tommy plays the violin, leads his class in school, and is captain of the debating team." After all, to say of a man that he is a "thief" is to say in effect, "He has stolen *and will steal again*"—which is more of a prediction than a report. Even to say, "He has stolen," is to make an inference (and simultaneously to pass a judgment) on an act about which there may be difference of opinion among those who have examined the evidence upon which the conviction was obtained. But to say that he was "convicted of theft" is to make a statement capable of being agreed upon through verification in court and prison records.

11   Scientific verifiability rests upon the external observation of facts, not upon the heaping up of judgments. If one person says, "Peter is a dead-beat," and another says, "I think so too," the statement has not been verified. In

court cases, considerable trouble is sometimes caused by witnesses who cannot distinguish their judgments from the facts upon which those judgments are based. Cross-examinations under these circumstances go something like this:

> *Witness:* That dirty double-crosser ratted on me.
> *Defense Attorney:* Your honor, I object.
> *Judge:* Objection sustained. (Witness's remark is stricken from the record.) Now, try to tell the court exactly what happened.
> *Witness:* He double-crossed me, the dirty, lying rat!
> *Defense Attorney:* Your honor, I object!
> *Judge:* Objection sustained. (Witness's remark is again stricken from the record.) Will the witness try to stick to the facts.
> *Witness:* But I'm telling you the facts, your honor. He did double-cross me.

This can continue indefinitely unless the cross-examiner exercises some ingenuity in order to get at the facts behind the judgment. To the witness it is a "fact" that he was "double-crossed." Often patient questioning is required before the factual bases of the judgment are revealed.

12 Many words, of course, simultaneously convey a report and a judgment on the fact reported, as will be discussed more fully in a later chapter. For the purposes of a report as here defined, these should be avoided. Instead of "sneaked in," one might say "entered quietly"; instead of "politician," "congressman" or "alderman," or "candidate for office"; instead of "bureaucrat," "public official"; instead of "tramp," "homeless unemployed"; instead of "dictatorial set-up," "centralized authority"; instead of "crackpot," "holder of nonconformist views." A newspaper reporter, for example, is not permitted to write, "A crowd of suckers came to listen to Senator Smith last evening in that rickety fire-trap and ex-dive that disfigures the south edge of town." Instead he says, "Between 75 and 100 people heard an address last evening by Senator Smith at the Evergreen Gardens near the South Side city limits." ...

How Judgments Stop Thought

13 A judgment ("He is a fine boy," "It was a beautiful service," "Baseball is a healthful sport," "She is an awful bore") is a conclusion, summing up a large number of previously observed facts. The reader is probably familiar with the fact that students almost always have difficulty in writing themes of the required length because their ideas give out after a paragraph or two. The reason for this is that those early paragraphs contain so many judgments that there is little left to be said. When the conclusions are carefully excluded, however, and observed facts are given instead, there is never any trouble about the length of papers; in fact, they tend to become too long, since inexperienced writers, when told to give facts, often give far more than are necessary, because they lack discrimination between the important and the trivial.

14 Still another consequence of judgments early into the course of a written

exercise—and this applies also to hasty judgments in everyday thought—is the temporary blindness they induce. When, for example, a description starts with the words, "He was a real Madison Avenue executive" or "She was a typical hippie," if we continue writing at all, we must make all our later statements consistent with those judgments. The result is that all the individual characteristics of this particular "executive" or this particular "hippie" are lost sight of; and the rest of the account is likely to deal not with observed facts but the stereotypes and the writer's particular notion (based on previously read stories, movies, pictures, and so forth) of what "Madison Avenue executives" or "typical hippies" are like. The premature judgment, that is, often prevents us from seeing what is directly in front of us, so that clichés take the place of fresh description. Therefore, even if the writer feels sure at the beginning of a written account that the man he is describing is a "real leatherneck" or that the scene he is describing is a "beautiful residential suburb," he will conscientiously keep such notions out of his head, lest his vision be obstructed.

QUESTIONS AND IDEAS FOR DISCUSSION

1. Is it possible to write an argument using only reports? Explain.
2. Is Hayakawa correct in the statement, "Reports are verifiable" (paragraph 2)? Can you think of a nonverifiable report? Discuss.
3. Consider the map analogy Hayakawa uses in paragraph 4 and elsewhere. Map is to territory as the language of reports is to what?
4. Discuss the points at which it becomes more difficult to distinguish among reports, inferences, and judgments than this excerpt suggests. Do inferences ever underlie judgments? Do judgments ever underlie reports? If you believe so, give examples.
5. How do judgments stop thought? What is the implication of this problem for writers?

Dequa Thompson

Professor Cross

English 1302

February 17, 1993

                    The Problems with Television News

Thanks to satellites and databases, television network
news can take viewers to more places, more quickly, and provide more information, more quickly, than anyone would have
thought possible only a few years ago. When riots broke
out in Los Angeles in April 1992, reporters with minicams
hovered overhead, recording everything as it happened.
Television reporters actually greeted the Marines landing
on the beaches in Somalia in December 1992.

Television news reporting is also powerful. More than
two-thirds of Americans rely on television to provide them
with all the information they will receive about current
events (Westin 267). Through their presentation of the
news, television reporters and anchors control what is
"news."

This power would be not be a problem if varied points
of view were always presented. However, television newspeo-
ple tend to share similar outlooks. According to a study
made by Smith College government professor Stanley Rothman
and S. Robert Lichter and Linda Lichter of the Center for
Media and Public Affairs in Washington,

Rothman and company found the media elite to be,
broadly speaking, liberal. Fifty-six percent of
the 238 surveyed identified their colleagues as
being mostly on the left, while only 8 percent
placed their fellow journalists on the right.
Eighty percent or more of those questioned said
they voted Democratic in the presidential elections between 1964 and 1976. (Bernstein, "Press"
14)

Even if eighty percent of the "media elite" vote Democratic, that would not be a problem if they carefully kept
their own biases out of their presentation of the news.
But Terry Eastland of the Ethics and Public Policy Center
in Washington, D.C., claims that they do no such thing:

Confronted with information showing that the
three major networks gave George Bush a tougher
time than Bill Clinton, NBC's political director,
Bill Wheatley, told the Washington Post that
there hadn't been any "active bias at work." At
least he agrees there was bias.... (72)

Eastland identifies a couple of stories that he claims the
media failed to pursue in the 1992 presidential race:
tapes in which candidate Bill Clinton asks a woman, Genni-

fer Flowers, to lie about their alleged affair and the state job he had arranged for her; and a link between Iran-contra independent counsel Lawrence Walsh and the Clinton campaign (74-75). Eastland maintains that the pro-Democratic television news people would not pursue the stories because "their" candidate might have been harmed by them.

Whether or not Eastland is right, the people who present the network news have more in common than political affiliations. In the same study by Rothman and the Lichters cited earlier, the researchers found that news executives, anchors, and correspondents are mostly white males brought up by upper-middle-class, nonreligious families in the northeast (Bernstein, "Press" 14). Almost all have college degrees, and many have graduate degrees as well. The people who bring the news to America have a lot in common with each other, but they do not have a lot in common with most of their viewers.

Similarities among the news broadcasts are becoming more pronounced, and not just because of shared political viewpoints or backgrounds. Due partly to shrinking budgets, the networks now work together surprisingly often. For example, they cooperated to cover the 1992 political conventions, allotting only 14.5 hours altogether, while in 1988 they had given 34 hours coverage and had competed more

directly (Frank 383). None of the networks assigned a reporter to cover each major candidate fulltime in the 1992
election (Katz 81). Also, according to Rolling Stone reporter Jon Katz, "[t]he networks' Washington, D.C., bureaus
and CNN have begun pooling coverage of the White House
daily briefings" (81). Between the budget-cutting and the
pooled coverage, Katz predicts that it is "unlikely three
evening newscasts will remain on the air, especially three
whose editorial formats are so indistinct" (82).

Cost-cutting also may have led to one feature of television news that results not just in sameness among the networks but in outright misrepresentation of facts. That feature is "fake news"--video press releases that have been
put together by public-relations firms but are shown on
news programs (often by all the networks) as if they were
actual news reports. One example described by reporter
David Lieberman shows how "fake news" works. A personal-in-
jury lawyers' lobby group produced a video piece on dangers
of automatic safety belts. This piece was shown on the CBS
Evening News on June 13, 1991, carrying the CBS "eye" logo
and nothing to indicate it was not CBS's own report. The
piece, looking like legitimate news reporting, could then
be shown in court during trials. Lieberman notes that "ju-
ries find reports aired by CBS more credible than, say,
some taped test by a group with an obvious ax to grind"

(11). People watching television news have no way at present to know whether they are watching real news or video press releases.

One incident of "fake news" did receive a lot of publicity. Both ABC's 20/20 and CBS's 60 Minutes had segments in January 1992 about a Congressional caucus hearing in 1990 during which a girl who was identified as a Kuwaiti refugee told about atrocities committed by the Iraqis against her people. The testimony was broadcast by all of the networks and had a strong effect on American viewers. However, it turned out that the "refugee" was in fact the daughter of the Kuwaiti ambassador to the United States, and her emotional testimony was fabricated (Strong 11). What is even more alarming is that "[w]hen Kuwait was invaded, it was a public-relations firm and its camera crews--not news organizations--that distributed much of the news and film about atrocities in the occupied country and whipped up war fever" (Lieberman 14). Once the war began, news was carefully orchestrated by the military. The American public did not see the war in Kuwait "live," but we thought we did (Frank 413-15).

Just as the network news programs tend to cover the same stories and broadcast the same "fake news," there are plenty of perfectly real stories none of them covers. Print reporters Joanmarie Kalter and Jane Marion have identified several. These are not trivial issues. They in-

clude issues about race, class, foreign events, the economy, and labor. On the first issue, Kalter and Marion
quote Roger Wilkins of the Institute for Policy Studies:
"'There's a big group of blacks,' says Wilkins, 'who have
never escaped the long tentacles of slavery.... Some are
hopelessly dependent, and some are viciously destructive,
and our inattention to this problem is costing us
enormously'" (3). The Los Angeles race riots in 1992 were
covered in horrifying detail by the networks, but the social problems and racism that gave rise to them are not
"news."

In the same way, most foreign events are ignored by
network news. ABC <u>Nightline</u> senior producer Deborah Leff
said, after a year spent in London,

> "One of the things that was most striking to me
> while I was in London ... is how much more time
> the British press spends reporting foreign news
> than the American [media do]. For example, the
> flooding in Bangladesh was the lead story day
> after day after day, and so was the famine in the
> Sudan." (Kalter and Marion 4)

But in the United States viewers see coverage of such foreign catastrophes and political events only briefly. This
is especially true of events in Asian and African coun-

tries. The senior vice-president of ABC News, Richard
Wald, admits there is an information gap: "We should, in
general, do a better job on the Pacific nations.... I
think we could cover black Africa a bit better" (qtd. in
Kalter and Marion 3). For example, it took absolute devastation in Somalia before Americans began to take a real interest. Cursory news coverage before late 1992 was partly
responsible.

Television newscasting on the three major networks
pleases almost no one. Educated people lament the "tab-
loid" tendencies toward sensational stories about murders
(which are considered sensational only when white people
are the victims and perpetrators) and sex scandals. People
who are not themselves wealthy white males do not see their
concerns addressed by the anchors (and the big corporations
who employ them) very convincingly. Conservatives complain
about the liberal agenda.

The list of complaints is long. Some people complain
that TV news is concerned only with "pictures": "Anyone who
has worked in TV news will tell you the executive producer
always asks, 'What are the pictures?'" (Edwin Diamond;
qtd. in Kalter and Marion 4). Others complain that TV news
is no longer concerned with pictures of news as it happens.
Reuven Frank writes, "I found a third fundamental change
when I came back to management: There was no photojournal-

ism in television news. The word people had won" (405).
Frank explains this paradox:

> All news reports, even on arcane subjects, became
> all-picture, yet rarely using pictures of the
> event reported. Even the smallest news organiza-
> tion has its "archive" of videotapes of events,
> scenes, and things. After words are written, pic-
> tures are matched to them, relevant or irrele-
> vant, that day's or last year's, but pictures....
> As Congress debates price supports, script will
> be spoken against farms being auctioned five
> years ago, corn pouring into a freighter--any old
> freighter will do--tractors, seamed faces. The
> viewer has not seen anything happen. He does not
> learn from the pictures; only from the words.
> (406)

There is some truth in all the many complaints, even
the conflicting ones, about television news. The best hope
for viewers is probably to read as well as to watch, and to
watch CNN as well as the original three networks. CNN offers at least part of the answer to the problem with television news. But as of 1991, forty percent of American homes
did not have cable (World Almanac and Book of Facts, 1992).

Also, CNN's approach does have some weaknesses, because broadcasting all day every day inevitably means that much time is devoted to "filler." Not every day brings a hurricane or an invasion to fill CNN's hours with fast-breaking news.

But all these hours of news can mean that viewers become "editors" of the news (Rosen 60). Woody West, associate editor of conservative news magazine Insight, describes what might be called the "CNN effect" this way: "What we have had, then, is a blizzard of informational odds and ends from the tube.... It is as if a newspaper reporter simply were to transcribe his entire notebook, dumping scuttlebutt, speculation, and conjecture onto the printed page with no editing and no mediating thoughtfulness" (64). West is complaining, but what he is complaining about may be a promising trend in TV news, at least the CNN variety.

The very fact that CNN shows news all day means that it will broadcast

important news conferences and announcements in their entirety, avoiding the tyranny of the soundbite and the TV reporter's breezy, overly facile wrap-up. Granted, what CNN considers "important" is likely to involve government officials, but there's still a net gain for viewers,

who can watch, listen, and decide for themselves
what they think.   (Rosen 624)

For decades Dan Rather, Peter Jennings, Tom Brokaw, Ted
Koppel and others have patiently explained things to the
American public.   The American public is not especially
grateful: At the height of the Persian Gulf war, 83 percent
did not think the media was doing a "fair and responsible
job" of reporting events (Bernstein, "CNN" 10).   If people
are ready to draw their own conclusions, and to watch entire congressional hearings rather than sound bites at
6:30, CNN may provide the best option for television news
viewing.

CNN is no longer a minor player in the news game.   People watch it worldwide (Bernstein, "CNN" 8).   When Kuwait
City was liberated during the Persian Gulf war, an old Kuwaiti man said on camera: " 'We give special thanks to Mr.
Bush and all the allies....   The British, the French, the
Egyptians, CNN ...' " (Diamond 26).   But if the networks
let CNN take over news broadcasting, the problems related
to "sameness" that afflict ABC, CBS, and NBC news programming will automatically become CNN's problems. One news network cannot be better than three for a country that values
diversity and values real news.

Works Cited

Bernstein, Jonas. "CNN at the Front Line of News."   <u>Insight</u>
18 Feb. 1991: 8-11.

---. "Press Showing Its Stripes."   <u>Insight</u> 28 Jan. 1991:
14-15.

Diamond, Edwin.   "Who Won the Media War."   <u>New York</u> 18 Mar.
1991: 26-29.

Eastland, Terry.   "Crossing the Line."   <u>The American Specta-
tor</u> Jan. 1993: 72-75.

Frank, Reuven.   <u>Out of Thin Air: The Brief Wonderful Life
of Network News</u>.   New York: Simon, 1991.

Kalter, Joanmarie, and Jane Marion. "The Big Stories TV
News Is Missing--and Why." <u>TV Guide</u> 22 July 1989: 3-5.

Katz, Jon.   "Say Good Night, Dan . . ."   <u>Rolling Stone</u> 27
June 1991: 81-84.

Lieberman, David.   "Fake News."   <u>TV Guide</u> 22 Feb. 1992:
10-26.

Rosen, Jay.   "The Whole World Is Watching CNN."   <u>The Nation</u>
13 May 1991: 622-25.

Strong, Morgan.   "Portions of the Gulf War were brought to
you by . . .   the folks at Hill and Knowlton."   <u>TV
Guide</u> 22 Feb. 1992: 11-13.

West, Woody.   "TV War Coverage Run Amok."   <u>Insight</u> 11 Feb.
1991: 64.

Westin, Av. <u>Newswatch: How TV Decides the News</u>.   New York:
Simon, 1982.

Thompson 12

"When to Beat Up on Political TV." <u>New York Times</u> 13 July

    1992: A14.

<u>The World Almanac and Book of Facts, 1992.</u> New York:

    Pharos Books, 1991.

QUESTIONS AND IDEAS FOR DISCUSSION

1. Evaluate Thompson's sources according to the standards described in this chapter.

2. How well does Thompson incorporate evidence from outside sources into her essay? Pick two or three instances where she might have incorporated a quotation more effectively or more smoothly, or where she failed to comment on a quotation that needs to be discussed. Write out the passages as you would have written them, skillfully incorporating the quotations.

3. What is Thompson's thesis, and how well does she organize and develop her argument in support of it? Comment, with specific reference to the text. Suggest any changes you would have advised her to make.

4. Did you find this documented essay interesting to read? Explain why or why not. Did you learn anything new from it? Discuss.

Suggestions for Writing and Further Discussion

1. Even in a world such as we have today, in which everybody seems to be quarreling with everybody else, we still to a surprising degree trust each other's reports.

—S. I. Hayakawa

Write a documented essay in which you demonstrate the truth of the above statement by offering examples from what you have read and from what you have experienced personally. In working for an argumentative edge, consider whether we are wise or unwise to be so trusting, and whether our trust is symptomatic of health or of an apathy that makes us unwilling to investigate things for ourselves.

2. The one function that TV news performs very well is that when there is no news, we give it to you with the same emphasis as if there were news.

—David Brinkley

David Brinkley's wry comment on the news industry—in which thirty minutes must be filled daily whether or not anything has happened in the world that day—pinpoints one of the problems inherent in the rigid structure of televisions news: a half-hour every day devoted to international and national news, weather reports, and sports. Watch national and local news programs for a week and take notes on the content, length, and presentation of "non-news" human interest and idle-curiosity stories. Are such stories treated "with the same emphasis" as elections, coups, and natural disasters? Based on your observations and accumulated data, write one of the following: an essay addressed to one of the national networks or your local television station in which you argue the dangers or the benefits of such indiscriminate treatment; an essay addressed to David Brinkley in which you argue that emphasis on the unimportant is no longer commonplace in television news reporting; or an essay addressed to the national networks in which you argue in favor of a variable-length news broadcast, perhaps supplemented (to even out the time-slots) with educational programming when needed.

3. Use one of the following questions to generate a working thesis and ultimately a documented essay.

Who decides what's news?

Does our help hurt the homeless?

Is technology out of control?

Are black males an endangered species?

Is reading extinct? Are we better off without it?

Should *you* have kids? Should anyone?

Can you manage without a car? In a medium-sized city?

What was the significance of the Boxer Rebellion?

What effect do pets have on their owners' health?

Should the United States send economic aid to the countries of the former Soviet Union? All of them?

Should all adoptions be open adoptions?

Why was Churchill defeated in his bid to become prime minister after World War II?

How well has the BART public transportation system worked in California?

How should the Social Security system be modified to meet the needs future decades will bring?

Should the tenure system in American colleges be changed?

How can public school education be improved?

How did Thomas Jefferson treat the Native Americans?

Are the benefits of liver transplants worth the costs?

How should money for medical research be allocated among the major diseases such as AIDS, heart disease, and cancer?

Are labor unions still needed in the United States?

What new applications for computers will we see in the next ten years?

What were Alfred Hitchcock's contributions to the art of filmmaking?

Is sexual harassment in the workplace a major or a minor problem? Can it be reduced or eliminated?

Is it possible to support animal rights *and* medical research?

Should intercollegiate sports programs be required to be self-supporting?

5

Testing Arguments:
Inductive Reasoning

The shrewd guess, the fertile hypothesis, the courageous leap to a tentative conclusion—these are the most valuable coin of the thinker at work.
—Jerome Seymour Bruner

Now we will look carefully at the logical patterns that underlie the essays you write, not only in this course but every time you have put pen to paper (or fingers to keyboard) to make a point. Argument is the process of reasoning, and you cannot be fully confident that you have argued well if you have no idea how to judge the soundness of your reasoning. As you write arguments, you can apply basic principles of logic to make sure that your convictions have not blinded you to gaps or wrong turns in your reasoning.

All reasoning follows one of two paths (and sometimes moves back and forth between them). Either you go beyond what is known in order to conclude something about the unknown, or you draw out of what is known the implications contained within it. The former process is called **inductive reasoning,** and the latter, **deductive reasoning.** You need to be concerned with the difference simply because you judge the two processes of reasoning according to different expectations. For reasons we will discuss in this chapter and the next, sound inductive arguments can never guarantee their conclusions; sound deductive arguments can do so. Both processes are inevitable in any reasoning being; understanding how the processes work and how to redirect them when they go astray can be invaluable to the reasoning writer.

PATTERNS OF INDUCTIVE REASONING

The process of inductive reasoning leads you to discover relationships between like things (analogies), between causally related events, and between the assertions of an authority speaking in her field of expertise and a conclusion having to do with that field of knowledge. *The distinctive feature of inductive reasoning is that the conclusion always stretches beyond the premises; it is never completely assured.* You may ride the same elevator every weekday for eleven years and, based on that experience, assume that it never will become stuck between floors. But one dark day, so confident in your inductive conclusion that you are not even aware of your trust, you may get on the elevator and spend forty-five minutes with a group of strangers between the fifteenth and sixteenth floors.

Despite the lack of certainty in inductive conclusions, inductive reasoning is often called the "scientific method" of reasoning, a label likely to intimidate those of us who would do anything to avoid taking a chemistry lab class. But even when the people in the white lab coats are employing it, the so-called "scientific method," for all its usefulness, is not rigidly methodical. For example, James Watson, codiscoverer of the double helix structure of DNA, writes in his autobiographical account, *The Double Helix,* that he first became interested in DNA after reading an article written by Linus Pauling, of which he grasped little more than that "it was written with style." Watson was a graduate student at the time, but within two years he played an instrumental role in one of the greatest biochemical discoveries of the twentieth century. Watson's model for DNA resulted not so much from years of plodding labor and lab tests—"scientific induction"—as from an idea that came to him as he was riding a bus to class, an idea "so simple that it had to be right."

Inductive reasoning takes several forms. When two friends of mine, Steve and Scott, were in graduate school, they half-seriously decided to find a minor Olympic event at which they could excel and thereby earn a spot on the Olympic team. Both were in good physical condition; Scott had even been a starting member of the University of Texas football team. In their quest for the perfect Olympic sport for the weekend athlete, they reasoned inductively:

> Finding a sport with few U.S. competitors, learning to compete in it, and practicing diligently during our spare time for a year might earn us a place on the U.S. Olympic team.
>
> [CAUSAL ANALYSIS]

> Kayaking requires too much shoulder strength.
> Sculling, the same.
> Sailing requires an expensive investment in equipment.
> Bicycling requires expensive equipment and is too popular a sport.
> Handball is too popular—too much competition.
> Riflery is monotonous, and bad for the ears.
> Table tennis is a sport dominated by the Chinese.
> Evidently, all minor Olympic sports are inappropriate for our purposes.
>
> [EXAMPLES]

> For a couple of weekend athletes to contemplate trying out for the Olympics is like an amateur tennis buff's deciding to take on Boris Becker. Therefore, we would be foolish to attempt to participate in the Olympics.
>
> [LITERAL ANALOGY]

For that matter, for a couple of weekend athletes to contemplate trying out for the Olympics is a lot like a meat butcher's deciding to try a little brain surgery. Therefore, we would be foolish to attempt to participate in the Olympics.

[METAPHORICAL ANALOGY]

All these arguments are inductive, for the simple reason that their conclusions move *beyond* the scope of the premises; each requires an "inductive leap" from premises to conclusion. The conclusions of inductive arguments can be strong and plausible, but they are never certain. Just because none of the sports considered was appropriate to Steve's and Scott's purpose does not mean that another might not be (as of the 1992 Olympics they were able to consider—and quickly reject—yet another sport, tae kwon do). And just because their attempting to become part of the Olympic team was analogous to an amateur tennis player's taking on Boris Becker would not assure their failure in the attempt. Still, failure was inductively probable. But in comparing weekend athletes to butchers, Steve and Scott moved from arguments with some degree of logical acceptability to a metaphorical analogy. Here they left the realm of logical argument. Metaphor can be highly persuasive emotionally, but it can never be offered as proof.

All of us have reasoned inductively, perhaps without realizing it: Kelly has always refused dates with Blake, so she is likely to do so again if he calls her; every native Kansan I have met (and I have met hundreds) has been friendly, so I assume that most Kansans are friendly; you know twelve of the students signed up for Economics 4312, and they are all economics majors, so you assume that the other six students in the class are also economics majors. And you may have read many inductive arguments without realizing that they were inductive, or even that they were arguments. The following defense of the camel is an inductive paragraph that ends with the topic sentence, the conclusion to its argument:

The camel . . . sweats very little; its body temperature can go all the way up to 105 before it begins to sweat at all. Also the camel is very sparing in its urination. It is believed that water which in other animals would be passed off by the body is, by the camel, used over again: in effect recycled, as if the camel had an almost closed air conditioning system. In spite of the old joke that the camel looks as if it had been made by a committee, it is in fact very efficiently designed in terms of its environment.

—Tom Burnam, *Dictionary of Misinformation*

Concrete details noted in this paragraph lead to the conclusion that the camel "is in fact very efficiently designed in terms of its environment."

Induction centers on the concrete. It involves reasoning from particulars. The concrete and the specific are both attractive and satisfying in a world of shifting standards, a world where reality sometimes seems hard to pin down. Inductive reasoning includes drawing conclusions from analogy, from cause and effect, and from the examination of particulars. The common element among these forms of inductive reasoning is the observation of similar or causally related elements, and the drawing of probable conclusions based on the relationship noted. We will consider each of these three forms of induction in turn. To support inductive arguments, you will sometimes find that your personal knowledge and experience will provide you with all the examples and other evidence you need; for arguments beyond your immediate experience and expertise, refer to Chapter 4's discussion of the kinds of evidence used to support inductive conclusions and deductive premises, and how to find, evaluate, and use that evidence.

ARGUING FROM ANALOGY

Literal Analogy

In an analogy two or more things, people, events, or other phenomena are observed to be alike in several respects; and the conclusion is reached that they are also alike in a further respect that has not yet been observed. Literal analogy compares things with fundamental similarities that are often apparent even superficially; metaphorical analogy compares things that are both apparently and actually different but hold some enlightening, unexpected parallels. Literal analogy may be used—carefully—in argument; metaphorical analogy can provide only illustration, never logical proof. Even literal analogy is at most suggestive, not conclusive, but such is the nature of the inductive process. A literal argument from analogy goes like this:

> The climate of Arizona and that of Saudi Arabia are similar, as are their soils and native vegetation. Therefore, the irrigation system that has worked so well in parts of Arizona should prove successful in Saudi Arabia.

Analogical arguments have the form "X and Y share characteristics a, b, c, [and so on]; therefore, they might also share characteristic m." Notice that the conclusion is qualified: X and Y "might" or "are likely to" share, not "will definitely" share, characteristic m. Analogies always break down at some point because the things compared are never completely identical; therefore, we must take care never to push an analogy to that breaking point. We could not, for instance, claim on the basis of climatic and soil similarities between Arizona and Saudi Arabia that the two regions are likely also to have the same number of rivers. Nor could we safely assume that they would be likely to raise identical crops.

The force of the conclusion to an argument from analogy depends on the closeness and the extent of the similarities between the things being compared. To begin with, **the similar features should be pertinent to the conclusion drawn.** In the irrigation argument a further similarity between Arizona and Saudi Arabia might be that each has at least one city with a population over 50,000, but that point of similarity has nothing to do with crop irrigation. To include it would be irrelevant. Second, **the similar characteristics should be several in number, and the greater the number of pertinent similarities, the greater the force of the argument.** Our argument about irrigation systems is reasonably convincing as it stands, since climate, soil, and native vegetation are strong points of appropriate similarity between Arizona and Saudi Arabia. But we would make the analogy even stronger if we could add that both regions contain similar underground water reserves, that both possess the technology and the trained technicians to implement a successful irrigation system, or that the Saudis hope to raise the same kind of crops grown in the irrigated Arizona farmland.

Analogical arguments such as this one can carry considerable weight with a reader, although (as in all other inductive arguments) the conclusion is never certain and should not be offered as certain. An inductive leap is required: Just because X and Y are alike in all these respects never assures us beyond all doubt that they also will be alike in any further respect, including the one we have in mind. But the greater the number of pertinent points of similarity, the greater the likelihood of the further similarity we propose. We can argue analogies between World War I and World War II, between the Korean War and the Vietnam War, between Paris fashions and New York fashions, between parents and teachers, between ditch digging and road building, between coal mining and working in a chemical factory. Where strong, pertinent, and literal correlations are known to exist, the possibility of further correlations is not far-fetched.

Metaphorical Analogy

Analogical argument requires literal analogy—the comparison of things, events, or ideas that are fundamentally similar. Metaphorical analogy, on the other hand, compares things that are fundamentally different in order to create a mental picture that furthers the reader's understanding of the more complex of the entities compared. Sometimes the line between literal and metaphorical analogies is not clearly demarcated; some analogies have both literal and metaphorical elements. But, generally, metaphor is intended to be evocative—to arouse emotional, rather than rational, responses in the reader.

That is not to say that the writer of argument should avoid metaphor—far from it. Metaphorical analogy can clarify and explain concepts (the idea of a "black hole" in space, for example) that would otherwise elude most readers. Although nonlogical—and, if offered as proof, logically fallacious—metaphor may be powerfully persuasive. But whether the comparison is explicit ("My love is like a red, red rose") or suppressed (My love is a red, red rose"), metaphorical analogy draws similarities between things that are fundamentally *unlike*. My love, even if ruddy-faced and sweet-smelling, is not really much like a rose. So I need not—and should not—conclude on the basis of the analogy that he will lose all his hair (as a rose loses its petals) or live a short life. A rose, as Gertrude Stein once observed, is a rose is a rose. A true love is something else altogether.

Evaluating Arguments from Analogy

An argument from analogy always will be fallacious if it purports to guarantee the conclusion, or if it reasons from a metaphorical comparison instead of a literal one. We find such faulty analogies frequently in letters to newspapers, such as the following:

In response to the recent letter from Marvin Crenshaw supporting the *Times Herald's* views on South Africa and apartheid, I submit both have forgotten how our forefathers created this country.

Our treatment, then and even now, of the original people of America, the Indians, was and is deplorable.

It appears to me that the *Times Herald,* the Crenshaws and the like should start condemning their own failings and butt out of those which don't concern them. Such a "pot calling the kettle black" attitude further alienates the United States in the world today. No wonder no one likes or respects Americans anymore.

—Letter to the *Dallas Times Herald*

In this argument the writer argues from a literal analogy—that the white South Africans treat the black South Africans much as the white Americans treated and continue to treat Native Americans. The analogy is an apt one, but the writer draws a conclusion from it that the premises do not support. He believes that if our government has treated the Indians unfairly, we have no right to condemn the South African government for treating blacks unfairly. In using his analogy to support this conclusion, he commits the fallacy known as **tu quoque** (Latin for "you're another")—that is, you're not entitled to argue a point because you're no better than the people you are criticizing. The pot can call the kettle black if the kettle is indeed black. The pot may be due for a polishing itself, but that is a separate issue logically.

To test the strength of your own or another's argument from analogy, consider the following:

1. **Does the argument refrain from claiming that the analogy** *guarantees* **the conclusion?**
2. **Is the analogy nonmetaphorical?**
3. **Are the points of similarity between the entities compared strong, relevant, and numerous?**
4. **Are the points of dissimilarity (for differences inevitably will exist) minor, irrelevant, and few?**
5. **Is the inductive leap from the premises to the conclusion a reasonable one, easy to make?** That is, is the scope of the conclusion limited according to the limitations of the analogy, and does the conclusion follow logically from the premises?

EXERCISE 5–1

Decide whether or not the following argument from analogy seems reasonable. Is the analogy sufficiently close and literal to support the conclusion inductively? Explain your answer.

In my ignorance, I had always thought that "fresh air" was infinitely available to us. I had imagined that the dirty air around us somehow escaped into the stratosphere, and that new air kept coming in—much as it does when we open a window after a party.

This, of course, is not true, and you would imagine that a grown man with a decent education would know this as a matter of course. What *is* true is that we live in a kind of spaceship called the earth, and only a limited amount of air is *forever* available to use.

The walls of our spaceship enclose what is called the "troposphere," which extends about seven miles up. This is all the air that is available to us. We must use it over and over again for infinity, just as if we were in a sealed room for the lifetime of the earth.

No fresh air comes in, and no polluted air escapes. Moreover, no dirt or poisons are ever "destroyed"—they remain in the air, in different forms, or settle on the earth as "particulates." And the more we burn, the more we replace good air with bad.

Once contaminated, this thin layer of air surrounding the earth cannot be cleansed again. We can clean materials, we can even clean water, but we cannot clean the air. There is nowhere else for the dirt and poisons to go—we cannot open a window in the troposphere and clear out the stale and noxious atmosphere we are creating. . . .

The United States alone is discharging *130 million tons of pollutants a year* into the atmosphere, from factories, heating systems, incinerators, automobiles and airplanes, power plants and public buildings. What is frightening is not so much the death and illness, corrosion and decay they are responsible for—as the fact that this is an *irreversible process*. The air will never be cleaner than it is now.

And this is why *prevention*—immediate, drastic and far-reaching—is our only hope for the future. We cannot undo what we have done. We cannot restore the atmosphere to the purity it had before the Industrial Revolution. But we can, and must, halt the contamination before our spaceship suffocates from its own foul discharges.

—Sydney J. Harris, *For the Time Being*

EXERCISE 5–2

Evaluate the following arguments from analogy according to the criteria on page 139. Identify each as literal or metaphorical. If the analogy is literal, does it hold up as far as the argument takes it? If it seems flawed, explain what the problem is and what might be done to strengthen the inductive value of the analogy.

1. The Student Senate recognized campus organizations for female students, foreign students, students interested in the perceived problem of reverse discrimination, and students belonging to a variety of religious groups. The Gay Students' Organization is, like all of these, a special-interest group and, like some of them, a group interested in political activism. Because of its similarity in kind and purpose to other campus organizations, the GSO deserves recognition, too.

2. According to *The American Woman 1987–1988* (released by the Congressional Caucus for Women's Issues), female college graduates have a great deal in

common with male high school dropouts: Both groups earn about the same amount of money annually.

—*Time*, 2 Aug. 1987

3. Dr. Huxley ridicules people who "still maintain that the planets are kept in their course by God and not by gravitation." He could equally ridicule those who maintained that London was lit by man and not by electricity.

—Letter to the London *Times*,
qtd. in E. R. Emmet, *Handbook of Logic*

4. The role of the textbook (or teacher) in a good lab course is like that of a guide in a foreign country. The book should point out what to look (and look out) for, not what the traveler is to see.

—Miles Pickering, "Are Lab Courses a Waste of Time?",
Chronicle of Higher Education, 19 Feb. 1980

5. Television, much like marijuana and alcohol, is a kind of addictive buffer. It allows people who have only superficialities in common to be together in a form of peace and seeming contentment.

—Jeffrey Schrank, "There Are No Mass Media—
All We Have Is Television," in *Snap, Crackle, and Popular Taste*

6. To praise a historian for his accuracy is like praising an architect for using well-seasoned timber or properly mixed concrete in his building. It is a necessary condition of his work, but not his essential function.

—Edward Hallet Carr, *What Is History?*

7. The great danger is not that Americans may make too little of history but that they will make too much of it. In politics, dubious policies have a far easier chance of winning public support when they are defended on historical grounds. Support for the decision to go into Vietnam, for instance, was considerably strengthened when it was explained that fighting communism in Asia was analogous to fighting Nazism in Europe.

—Richard Shenkman, *I Love Paul Revere,
Whether He Rode or Not*

8. Education needs to learn a lesson from baseball. First, education, like baseball, needs to celebrate multiple forms of excellence—great reading, outstanding writing, good oral composition, and so forth. Labeling a student "a good student of the English language arts" is like labeling Williams and DiMaggio "great ballplayers." Williams is known as the great hitter, and DiMaggio as the great all-around player. The distinction is important.

Second, in the scoring of performance—writing samples or whatever—education should follow baseball's example and not separate the rubrics for different levels of performance from the samples of that performance. Baseball gives us the rubric of Williams's hitting—his stance, his eye, the flow in his swing—and at the same time shows us samples of his performance. This approach invites us, the public, to participate in the discussion among the pros about the qualities of Williams's performance.

In education, we, too, should not separate the rubrics or features of good writing or reading from the samples of the performance. In this way, we invite the public to participate.

—Miles Myers, "The Ambiguity of Performance,"
The Council Chronicle, Sept. 1991

9. Tom Ehrenfeld asks why AIDS-stricken children or adults infected through non-sexual contacts . . . get sympathy while infected homosexuals and drug users don't. Isn't it obvious? When people engage in high-risk behavior, they have to accept the consequences. If I play hopscotch on the freeway and get hit by a car, should I expect sympathy?

   —Pam Palmer, letter to *Newsweek*, 18 Nov. 1991

10. The Rodney King riots* gave black politicians and civil rights leaders yet another opportunity to demonstrate their rapidly disintegrating moral values. They and white liberals focus on the "rage" of the rioters. Jesse Jackson carped, "Desperate people do desperate things." Referring to the Los Angeles arsonists, looters, murderers and rioters, Rep. John Conyers, Jr., babbled, "Those weren't criminals; they were outraged citizens."

   What would we say of someone who dismissed the Nazis who looted and burned Jewish businesses as "desperate people doing desperate things"? What if we trivialized the behavior of the cops who beat Rodney King simply as men filled with "rage"? What if we're asked to understand Klan lynching and burning simply as work of "outraged citizens"? Any person who'd ask us to understand such despicable behavior or have any sympathy for the perpetrators, because they were outraged or desperate, would be seen as a moral midget.

   —Walter Williams, syndicated columnist, 26 May 1992

ARGUING FROM CAUSE OR EFFECT

A second form of inductive reasoning is used to argue that a given cause or causes lead to a given effect or effects, or that a given effect or effects result from a specific cause or causes. We can argue causally about past, present, or future events. That is, we might argue that the freak behavior of El Niño (a west-to-east Pacific wind current) and the fallout from the volcanic eruptions in the Philippines caused the unusually wet spring in the western United States in 1992; or we might argue that an unusually snowy winter this year will result in a late thaw, flooding, and enough mud to hurt the summer tourist trade in the mountain states. In such arguments, like other inductive processes, we again observe particulars and consider the relationship between them. The simplest causal arguments deal with single causes and single effects, and have the conclusion

    C is the cause of E;

or

    E is caused by C.

---

*Riots occurred in Los Angeles in 1992 following the acquittal of white police officers in the videotaped beating of African-American Rodney King following a high-speed freeway chase.

Both statements have the same core meaning, and we will treat them as two ways of expressing the same argument. "Infections cause fevers" and "Fevers are caused by infections" are logically equivalent, though grammatically the first statement emphasizes the cause and the second statement emphasizes the effect. More complex causal arguments involve multiple causes and/or multiple effects, such as the following example, in which "A, B, and C" and "E, F, and G" represent any number of causes or effects:

> A, B, and C are [or are among] the causes of E, F, and G.

The following are assertions of causal analysis involving multiple effects or causes:

> Poison ivy and wool make me itch.

> Imploding the hotel is likely to create a lot of dust and break glass in buildings across the street.

> Unemployment, lack of political freedom, and hunger can give rise to despair and revolt.

Our wording of a causal assertion or argument reflects the degree of our certainty about the completeness and sufficiency of the causes or effects we have argued for the phenomena we have noted. "C is the cause of E" indicates certainty that C alone is the necessary and sufficient cause of E; "C is the primary cause of E" acknowledges other contributory causes of E; "C is one of the causes of E" makes a much smaller claim than either of the preceding statements. (In this last case other causes may be equal to or more important than the cause examined.) The same considerations apply when the argument moves backward, from effects to causes.

The first of the three kinds of conclusions to causal arguments, that "C is *the* cause of E," will require more supporting evidence than will "C is *one* of the causes of E" or "C can cause E." But the first conclusion, if it can be supported adequately, is inherently more interesting than the second or third. A strong causal argument supporting the assertion that "U.S. policy in Iran in 1978–79 made the Shah's downfall inevitable" will be read with attention; an argument claiming only that "U.S. policy in Iran may have contributed to the Shah's downfall in 1979," on the other hand, will attract less notice. The extra work involved and the extra evidence required in making a strong claim are often worth the trouble.

In any causal argument, however complex or simple, the writer must demonstrate one of three things:

1. **The cause is *necessary* to the effect.** That is, without this cause the effect will not occur. For example, cold weather is necessary for snow to fall. Oxygen is necessary for a gas explosion. If event E has occurred, we know that condition C has occurred.

2. **The cause is *sufficient* for the effect.** If the cause occurs, then the effect occurs. If the IRS computer program picks a taxpayer's identification number at

random for an audit, an audit will take place. If a car runs out of gas, it will soon stop. Notice the difference from a necessary cause: If event E has occurred, we do not know on that basis alone that condition C has occurred. Different causes can lead to a given effect. An income tax return may be audited for any one (or several) of a number of reasons, each of which is sufficient in itself to trigger an audit. A car may come to a stop because the driver applies the brakes, or even because it crashes in a wall.

3. **The cause is both *necessary* to *and* *sufficient* for the effect.** If condition C occurs, effect E will follow. Moreover, effect E will not occur in the absence of condition C. If gas and oxygen in certain concentration meet with ignition, a gas explosion follows. The three causes create a condition both necessary to and sufficient for the effect.

Understanding the differences among the three kinds of causal relationships will help you avoid drawing untenable conclusions in your own arguments. If your argument demonstrates that a cause is necessary to a given effect, you may claim that "C is an important factor in causing E," for instance. If you can substantiate that C always leads to E, and C has occurred, then you can claim that "E will occur" or "E will be found to have occurred." If you are sure that only C leads to E, and always leads to E, you can assert with confidence that "because C has occurred, E will occur (or will be found to have occurred)," or "because E has occurred, C has occurred."

The soundness of causal arguments can be tested by applying Mill's Methods. These principles were first articulated in the nineteenth century by philosopher John Stuart Mill and are relied on by scientists to test their hypotheses. You will find them a useful test of your own working theses when those involve causal analysis. The Method of Agreement tests for necessary conditions; the Method of Difference tests for sufficient conditions; and the Joint Method of Agreement and Difference tests for conditions both necessary and sufficient. These three of Mill's Methods are described below.

The Method of Agreement. If several sets of circumstances give rise to a similar result, but the circumstances differ in all respects except one, the shared element must have caused the effect. For example, if a number of people experience food poisoning after eating together, and the only food eaten by all of them was potato salad, we can conclude that a toxin in the potato salad caused the food poisoning. We have found the point at which the data agree: We have found the necessary condition that caused the food poisoning.

The Method of Difference. Just as the Method of Agreement helps us establish links, the Method of Difference helps us sort out disparities. If we have similar circumstances that should all give rise to similar results, and one leads to a different result, we look for what might have given rise to the unexpected effect. If only one difference can be found, it has most probably caused the effect that interests us. For instance, if real estate developers find that their new residential development is a failure, although they have planned it to be just like their several previous successes, they search for the overlooked difference. Perhaps it is that the new development has poor access to major thoroughfares and public transportation, while the others did not. If poor access is the only discernible difference, they have found the probable culprit. They have found the point at which the circumstances *disagree*, and thus a sufficient condition for the effect.

The Joint Method of Agreement and Difference. Using the tests of Agreement and Difference together will show if we have found a cause, or set of causes, that is both necessary to and sufficient for a given effect. This is the line of reasoning by which the famed South Seas explorer, Captain James Cook, determined how to prevent scurvy decades before the discovery of Vitamin C. Captain Cook noted that, regardless of other living conditions, seamen who ate sauerkraut and onions did not develop scurvy, while seamen who ate primarily dried meat did tend to develop scurvy. The Method of Agreement showed that the healthy sailors were alike in their sauerkraut and onion consumption, even when their circumstances were otherwise different. The Method of Difference showed that even when circumstances were quite similar—for example, those of sailors in similar health embarking on the same ship—the difference between the sick and well sailors lay in whether or not they ate sauerkraut and onions on the voyage.

The Post Hoc Fallacy

The relationship in a causal argument is always chronological (causes must precede effects), but it must be logical as well. If it always rains after I wash my car, I cannot assume that it rains *because* I have washed my car. Along slightly different lines, if my car's finish appears duller after two years of regular washing at the neighborhood automatic carwash, I cannot argue that the abrasive brushes at the carwash have ruined my car's finish, and then sue the owner. Environmental pollution and an inferior finish—in fact, many things over two years—could also contribute to a dull finish. The arguer of causal relationships should eliminate mere coincidence and try to account for all the possible causes or effects of the phenomenon in question.

Despite these twin hazards of coincidence and unaccounted-for multiple causes, causal analysis can produce reasonable inductive conclusions, but only if the arguer bears in mind its limitations and resists the temptation to think that chronology assures a causal relationship. Superstitions arise from this kind of thinking: Two events occur in sequence, and the first is assumed to be the cause of the second. No doubt, somebody once met with misfortune after walking under a ladder, opening an umbrella indoors, or breaking a mirror. And now millions more are apprehensive each time they do the same. Even when we do not rationally believe in a causal relationship, we may act as if we did. If Jim Roberts wears an orange shirt once and finally breaks par, he may wear the shirt every time he plays golf, long after it is faded and frayed.

Then, too, we sometimes oversimplify causal relationships that do exist. If we treat a partial cause or a partial effect as if it were the entire cause or the entire effect, our argument will be unsound. Food and technology embargoes do not assure changes of policy in unfriendly countries, even those that import most of what they consume. The assassination of Archduke Ferdinand was not the only cause of World War I. Practice alone will not make Alicia Pérez the best sprinter on the track team. Sam Elliot's knack for tying complicated knots and whittling will not get him a job as a camp counselor unless those talents are accompanied by other desirable qualifications.

Either of these errors—assuming that chronology implies causal relation or assuming that a partial cause or effect is the entire cause or effect—results in fallacious argument. If every U.S. president elected in years ending with a zero has been the victim of an assassination attempt, I still cannot conclude that years ending with a zero cause bad fortune for presidents. If you reason that, because you have studied more hours than anyone else in your anthropology class, you will make the highest grade in the class on the upcoming exam, you may be disappointed. In both instances we are guilty of the fallacy of reasoning known as **post hoc ergo propter hoc** ("after this, therefore because of this"). The term is frequently called *post hoc* or "false cause." In this case the Latin term is preferable to the English, for the latter can be misleading. The cause ascribed is not always false; it may be, as in the last instance above, merely partial.

Evaluating Causal Arguments

1. Does the argument refrain from claiming that the conclusion is certain?
2. Does the argument demonstrate that the causal relationship is more than coincidental or chronological?
3. Is the cause (or are the causes) both necessary and sufficient for the effect (or effects)? If necessary but not sufficient, is the partiality of the cause or effect acknowledged? If sufficient but not also necessary, has the argument recognized that other sufficient causes may lead to the same effect?

EXERCISE 5–3

Are the following causal arguments acceptable? Why or why not? Evaluate them using the questions in the chart above.

#3 NO

1. John bought a new sports car and shortly thereafter was involved in three auto accidents, all of which were technically his fault. Since he had a clean driving record before, some mechanical malfunction in the car must have caused the accidents. #1

2. John bought a new sports car and shortly thereafter was involved in three auto accidents, all of which were technically his fault. Each accident involved

his rear-ending a car ahead of him. Since John had a clean driving record before buying the sports car, and since he is normally a safe and cautious driver, <u>it is possible</u> that some mechanical malfunction in the new car's braking system led to the accidents.

3. The increase in World War II–related TV shows during the Vietnam era <u>probably</u> "buttressed administration arguments linking Vietnam with World War II."

   —Erik Barnouw, *Tube of Plenty*

4. People who work all day at green phosphor VDTs (video display terminals) have begun to complain that they see pink auras around everything for several hours each weekday evening. On weekends they have no such complaints. None of the individuals had any such visual problem before beginning to work daily at a VDT. Therefore, it seems likely that the VDTs are causing the workers' visual distortions.

5. This is what explains the attraction of the beach in our society: total physical and mental inertia are highly agreeable, much more so than we allow ourselves to imagine. A beach not only permits such inertia but enforces it, thus neatly eliminating all problems of guilt.

   —John Kenneth Galbraith, preface to Gloria Steinem,
   The Beach Book

6. I know several cabinetmakers who have worked actively into their eighties. There must be something about working with wood that promotes longevity.

7. Katrina made a higher grade in German 4311 than Ellen did because Katrina studied harder.

8. After Mr. Mims eats certain brands of nacho-flavored corn chips, he becomes dizzy and breaks out in a cold sweat. After he eats Chinese food, the same thing happens. Evidently, something in the nacho-flavored corn chips and the Chinese food causes the dizziness and cold sweats. But the only thing the two have in common is the ingredient MSG (monosodium glutamate). Therefore, MSG causes the dizziness and cold sweats.

9. There is more than one reason for the lack of emphasis on foreign languages in the United States, but one word, *Americanization*, explains a major part of it. . . . This Americanization process encouraged Italian, German, Armenian, Japanese, Nigerian, and other immigrants to be "American" in their attitude, culture, and citizenship. A heavily accented English, or strange clothing, or habits that did not fit completely into this new world were "deficiencies" they wanted their children to avoid. . . . The last thing most of these parents wanted their children to learn in school was a foreign language.

   —Paul Simon, *The Tongue-Tied Americans*

10. Famed linguist and social critic Noam Chomsky has noted that the public is unable or unwilling to digest social issues unless there's a face attached. Apparently that's why we tend to drop everything and join a nation-wide media vigil for the rescue of a baby trapped in a well, but ignore the fact that America's infant mortality rate is becoming an embarrassment to our First World standing.

    —Casey McCabe, *The Nose*, Nov. 1991

ARGUING FROM EXAMPLES

A third form of inductive reasoning involves examining instances, examples, or other bits of data, finding similarities among them, and drawing conclusions about further particular cases or about the entire class of things or events to which all the particulars belong. Suppose, for instance, that it has rained in Cincinnati on each of the eight Tuesdays you have spent there during the last three months. Based on your observations, you may generalize that it nearly always rains on Tuesdays in Cincinnati; or you may conclude that it probably also rained on the four Tuesdays that you did not spend in Cincinnati during the quarter; or you may conclude that it will rain this coming Tuesday in Cincinnati. The last conclusion—that it is likely to rain this coming Tuesday in Cincinnati—concerns an additional particular case, and demonstrates the inaccuracy of the common assertion that inductive argumentation is limited to reasoning from examples to generalizations. We see that inductive reasoning from examples may lead to generalizations or to conclusions about further particular cases. The story of how former president Ronald Reagan became a Republican illustrates both kinds of conclusions. As actor Bob Cummings recalls it (as quoted in Doug McClelland, *Hollywood on Reagan*), the future Republican president said, "Well, I sat down and made a list of all the people I admired. And they were all Republicans." And on the basis of that generalization from particulars, Reagan reached a decision about a further particular—himself.

Inductive conclusions leading to generalizations are offered as applying to all or most of the members of a particular class and are based on observation of a number of members of the class. Such statements are useful to argument, for they enable us to organize data and make sense of our world, to draw broad conclusions from narrow experience. Although generalizations are based on pertinent data, we do not attempt to examine every instance or every member of a class of things before drawing conclusions about the category of event or class of things observed. We use sampling, instead. High school students visit a college campus and observe the students, then make a generalization about all the students based on those they have seen. A scientist observes the size, shape, and behavior of bacteria when exposed to a particular antibiotic and makes a generalization about the effect of the drug on all bacteria of that type.

Evaluating Arguments from Examples

If the conclusion to an argument based on the examination and enumeration of evidence concerns a further particular case or instance, the arguer has a special problem; individual cases often assert their unique characteristics inconveniently. Tell a rain-weary Scot to visit Phoenix because "it never rains," and the Scot will be drenched in the worst flash flood in ten years. Note that your brother always drops by on Sunday afternoons, and the following week he will show up on Tuesday. Write a letter to the newspaper praising the mayor's politically liberal policy decisions and the next one she makes will be, by your standards, painfully conservative. Buy a collie puppy because your previous five collies were calm, sweet-natured animals, and this one will turn out to be a wild-eyed, howling monster. The professor who never calls roll will do so the first time you miss class. We can, and must, make conclusions about particular instances, but rarely can we be certain of them.

In making conclusions about additional examples based on observed examples, improve the odds that your conclusion will be borne out by limiting it to individual instances that do not depart in any radical way from those you have observed. For instance, suppose that you have found women in politics to be supportive of women's rights, and so you have made a habit of voting for female political candidates. But in an upcoming election, the lone female candidate announces her opposition to abortion rights. You would not be wise to conclude that this woman will support women's rights once in office. And if winters were mild during your freshman, sophomore, and junior years in the state where you attend college, it would still be wise to pack a coat when you go off to school for your senior year. Weather is not certain; even Florida has an occasional freeze.

Despite the limitations of inductive reasoning about particulars, it is reasonable to expect future instances of a phenomenon to follow the pattern of past instances. If Democrats have almost always won the congressional elections in your district, you expect, inductively, that the Democratic candidate will win the next election, too. But one kind of thinker distrusts inductive regularity, expecting patterns to reverse themselves every so often. This thinker commits the **gambler's fallacy:** Luck, the gambler thinks, is bound to turn. But the laws of probability indicate no such likelihood for any given instance of a phenomenon. For example, my doctor and his wife had a seventh child, and five of the preceding six are girls. The actual probability of the seventh child's being another girl was roughly 50 percent. But the prudent inductive reasoner, observing a trend toward daughters in this family, would have expected another girl. And the gambler would have reasoned that because five out of six are girls, including the last two, the seventh child would certainly be a boy. The prudent inductive reasoner would have been right this time. The couple had a daughter.

It is somewhat safer to draw generalizations from particular cases than to speculate about further particular cases because generalizations allow room for exceptions. And because generalizations permit us to understand many things without having to experience all of them, generalizations are not only useful but necessary: We cannot observe every example of giraffes or of books in order to make statements about either class. However, like most kinds of conclusions, generalizations create problems if they are arrived at erroneously or hastily. First, they may be distorted or simply wrong; second, they fail to account for individual eccentricities; third, they can lead to the kind of misunderstandings exemplified by stereotyping. (Recall the discussion of stereotyping and audience analysis in Chapter 2.) The particulars that constitute our sampling of the entire class should be typical of the class and as numerous as possible. After observing five giraffes in the local zoo, all of whom are sullen and prone to bite, we cannot generalize that giraffes are animals who live in zoos or that giraffes are animals with un-pleasant dispositions. We cannot conclude from observing the books in a library, even a large one, that all books have rows of call numbers and letters labeled on their spines. In making generalizations in written arguments, then, we do well to avoid such faulty generalizations as much as possible by testing our samplings and our generalizations—and those of other writers—against the following con-siderations:

1. **Is the evidence *accurate?***
2. **Is the evidence *representative?*** Is it typical of the class about which the gen-eralization is made?
3. **Is the evidence *sufficient* in quantity to warrant the generalization made?** What constitutes sufficient evidence depends on the amount of variety in the evidence and in the class from which it is drawn. We could make a fair gen-eralization about the physical characteristics of the tree crab from a small sample; to make a generalization about the political values of Americans would require an enormous or meticulously executed random sampling.
4. **Finally, is the *conclusion inductively plausible*, considering the nature and amount of the evidence?** That is, does it avoid going improbably far beyond the limits of the evidence?

EXERCISE 5–4

A. In the following passage X. J. Kennedy claims that King Kong is not so much an ape-monster as he is a courtly lover. Evaluate his argument from exam-ples. Are you convinced? Comment.

> In his simian way King Kong is the hopelessly yearning lover of Petrarchan conven-tion. His forced exit from his jungle, in chains, results directly from his single-minded pursuit of Fay. He smashes a Broadway theater when the notion enters his dull brain that the flashbulbs of photographers somehow endanger the lady. His per-ilous swinging up a skyscraper to pluck Fay from her boudoir is an act of the kindli-est of hearts. He's impossible to discourage even though the love of his life can't lay eyes on him without shrieking murder.
>
> —from "Who Killed King Kong?"

B. The next passage sets out to support the claim that Barbie is not a bimbo. Are the examples used strong enough to make the claim convincing? If not, can you add further examples to make a stronger case? Try to do so.

> Barbie fan Diane Bracuk . . . claims Barbie was a "truly revolutionary doll, one that inspired, rather than oppressed, young girls' imaginations." Proof? Particularly in Barbie's pioneer years, she represented a liberating counter to the omnipresent image of woman as housewife drudge. Barbie was an astronaut years before Sally Ride, and her mid-'60s appearance as "Career Girl" Barbie predated many of her real-life counterparts' entry into the work world. Barbie was not a kept woman,

Bracuk notes: While she dates Ken, she's never married him, ostensibly paying the Barbie Dream Home mortgage herself.

—Helen Cordes, *Utne Reader*, Mar./Apr. 1992

Limiting Generalizations

The fourth test—Is the conclusion plausible?—occasionally will make clear that the conclusion you want to draw is too broad or requires too great a leap from the evidence. In such cases you must find more evidence to narrow the gap, or else you must narrow the conclusion itself. The latter, often preferable, enables you to make more accurate statements. Rather than asserting that "blind dates are always miserable experiences," you might narrow that assertion to "Blind dates arranged by relatives are always miserable experiences." Rather than claiming, "Women are discriminated against in all areas of life," you might narrow that claim to something you could support in a five-page argument: "Women are discriminated against by the life insurance industry," or "Graduates of Schoneman Law School who have child-bearing potential have been discriminated against in the hiring practices of legal firms," or "Female athletes do not receive news coverage on television comparable to that accorded male athletes." Generalizations of narrow scope can be more fully developed and supported in a short argument than can such sweeping statements as "Killing can never be justified" or "America's impact on the rest of the world is less today than ever before in the nation's history." Attempting to support inductively such sweeping generalizations in a few pages of argument will inevitably lead to fallacies such as assuming what you should be proving (begging the question) and hasty generalizations.

A final word about generalizations: Not all (perhaps not even many) are inductive in origin. We tend to *begin* with a hypothesis—like that which struck James Watson about the structure of DNA—and then test it by accumulating evidence and examples, rather than to collect all kinds of data haphazardly and then suddenly notice a common feature: "Eureka! All the blond males on this campus ride bicycles!" We consider generalizations here because they are established by examples, a means of supporting conclusions that is generally held to be inductive. But we will encounter generalizations again, and frequently, in Chapter 6—Deductive Reasoning.

EXERCISE 5–5

A. Rank the following list of generalizations from 1 (lengthiest argument and greatest amount of evidence likely to be required for support in an essay) to 10 (shortest argument, least amount of evidence likely to be required for support). Assume that your readers are your rhetoric classmates. Discuss with the rest of the class the differences you find in your rankings. Why are differences likely to occur—what preconceptions and biases do those differences reflect?

B. Reverse the meaning of each generalization (for example, you would change "Women are inferior to men" to "Women are superior to men") and repeat exercise A. What differences do you find in the rankings, and why?

C. Take five generalizations that you numbered 1 through 5 in either set of exercises, and suggest ways of narrowing their scope to a statement that could be adequately supported for the same audience in a paper of five pages or less. List three alternatives for each of the five broad generalizations.

1. The truth is always the strongest argument.

—Sophocles

2. Criminal trials should not be televised.

3. All people should provide for their organs to be donated after their death to needy recipients.

4. All religious cults in this country should be outlawed.

5. Sugar is poison.

6. If we consider democracy not just as a political system, but as a set of institutions which do aim to make everything available to everybody, *it would not be an overstatement to describe advertising as the characteristic rhetoric of democracy.* (emphasis added)

—Daniel Boorstin, *Democracy and Its Discontents*

7. Computers are bad for children.

8. The electoral college is outmoded and should be abolished.

9. Nothing is more fun than the circus.

10. It is a truth universally acknowledged, that a single man in possession of a good fortune must be in want of a wife.

—Jane Austen, *Pride and Prejudice*

READINGS

IS BUSINESS BLUFFING ETHICAL?

Albert Z. Carr

1   A respected businessman with whom I discussed the theme of this article remarked with some heat, "You mean to say you're going to encourage men to bluff? Why, bluffing is nothing more than a form of lying! You're advising them to lie!"

2   I agreed that the basis of private morality is a respect for truth and that the closer a businessman comes to the truth, the more he deserves respect. At the same time, I suggested that most bluffing in business might be regarded simply as game strategy—much like bluffing in poker, which does not reflect on the morality of the bluffer.

3   I quoted Henry Taylor, the British statesman who pointed out that "falsehood ceases to be falsehood when it is understood on all sides that the truth is not expected to be spoken"—an exact description of bluffing in poker, diplomacy, and business. I cited the analogy of the criminal court, where the criminal is not expected to tell the truth when he pleads "not guilty." Everyone from the judge down takes it for granted that the job of the defendant's attorney is to get his client off, not to reveal the truth; and this is considered ethical practice. I mentioned Representative Omar Burleson, the Democrat from Texas, who was quoted as saying, in regard to the ethics of Congress, "Ethics is a barrel of worms"—a pungent summing up of the problem of deciding who is ethical in politics.

4   I reminded my friend that millions of businessmen feel constrained every day to say *yes* to their bosses when they secretly believe *no* and that this is generally accepted as permissible strategy when the alternative might be the loss of a job. The essential point, I said, is that the ethics of business are game ethics, different from the ethics of religion.

5   We can learn a good deal about the nature of business by comparing it with poker. While both have a large element of chance, in the long run the winner is the man who plays with steady skill. In both games ultimate victory requires intimate knowledge of the rules, insight into the psychology of the other players, a bold front, a considerable amount of self-discipline, and the ability to respond swiftly and effectively to opportunities provided by chance.

6   No one expects poker to be played on the ethical principles preached in churches. In poker it is right and proper to bluff a friend out of the rewards of being dealt a good hand. A player feels no more than a slight twinge of sympathy, if that, when—with nothing better than a single ace in his hand—he strips a heavy loser, who holds a pair, of the rest of his chips. It was up to the other fellow to protect himself. In the words of an excellent poker player,

former President Harry Truman, "If you can't stand the heat, stay out of the kitchen." If one shows mercy to a loser in poker, it is a personal gesture, divorced from the rules of the game.

7   Poker has its special ethics, and here I am not referring to rules against cheating. The man who keeps an ace up his sleeve or who marks the cards is more than unethical; he is a crook, and can be punished as such—kicked out of the game or, in the Old West, shot.

8   In contrast to the cheat, the unethical poker player is one who, while abiding by the letter of the rules, finds ways to put the other players at an unfair disadvantage. Perhaps he unnerves them with loud talk. Or he tries to get them drunk. Or he plays in cahoots with someone else at the table. Ethical poker players frown on such tactics.

9   Poker's own brand of ethics is different from the ethical ideals of civilized human relationships. The game calls for distrust of the other fellow. It ignores the claim of friendship. Cunning deception and concealment of one's strength and intentions, not kindness and openheartedness, are vital in poker. No one thinks any the worse of poker on that account. And no one should think any the worse of the game of business because its standards of right and wrong differ from the prevailing traditions of morality in our society. That most businessmen are not indifferent to ethics in their private lives, everyone will agree. My point is that in their office lives they cease to be private citizens; they become game players who must be guided by a somewhat different set of ethical standards.

10   The point was forcefully made to me by a Midwestern executive who has given a good deal of thought to the question: "So long as a businessman complies with the laws of the land and avoids telling malicious lies, he's ethical. If the law as written gives a man a wide-open chance to make a killing, he'd be a fool not to take advantage of it. If he doesn't, somebody else will. There's no obligation on him to stop and consider who is going to get hurt. If the law says he can do it, that's all the justification he needs. There's nothing unethical about that. It's just plain business sense."

11   The illusion that business can afford to be guided by ethics as conceived in private life is often fostered by speeches and articles containing such phrases as, "It pays to be ethical," or "Sound ethics is good business." Actually this is not an ethical position at all; it is a self-serving calculation in disguise. The speaker is really saying that in the long run a company can make more money if it does not antagonize competitors, suppliers, employees, and customers by squeezing them too hard. He is saying that oversharp policies reduce ultimate gains. That is true, but it has nothing to do with ethics. The underlying attitude is much like that in the familiar story of the shopkeeper who finds an extra $20 bill in the cash register, debates with himself the ethical problem—should he tell his partner?—and finally decides to share the money because the gesture will give him an edge over the s.o.b. the next time they quarrel.

12   I think it is fair to sum up the prevailing attitude of businessmen on ethics as follows:

13   We live in what is probably the most competitive of the world's civilized societies. Our customs encourage a high degree of aggression in the individual's striving for success. Business is our main area of competition, and it has been ritualized into a game of strategy. The basic rules of the game have been set by the government, which attempts to detect and punish business frauds. But as long as a company does not transgress the rules of the game set by law, it has the legal right to shape its strategy without reference to anything but its profits. If it takes a long-term view of its profits, it will preserve amicable relations, so far as possible, with those with whom it deals. A wise businessman will not seek advantage to the point where he generates dangerous hostility among employees, competitors, customers, government, or the public at large. But decisions in this area are, in the final test, decisions of strategy, not of ethics.

14   If a man plans to take a seat in the business game, he owes it to himself to master the principles by which the game is played, including its special ethical outlook. He can then hardly fail to recognize that an occasional bluff may well be justified in terms of the game's ethics and warranted in terms of economic necessity. Once he clears his mind on this point, he is in a good position to match his strategy against that of the other players. He can then determine objectively whether a bluff in a given situation has a good chance of succeeding and can decide when and how to bluff, without a feeling of ethical transgression.

15   To be a winner, a man must play to win. This does not mean that he must be ruthless, cruel, harsh, or treacherous. On the contrary, the better his reputation for integrity, honesty, and decency, the better his chances of victory will be in the long run. But from time to time every businessman, like every poker player, is offered a choice between certain loss or bluffing within the legal rules of the game. If he is not resigned to losing, if he wants to rise in his company and industry, then in such a crisis he will bluff—and bluff hard.

16   Every now and then one meets a successful businessman who has conveniently forgotten the small or large deceptions that he practiced on his way to fortune. "God gave me my money," old John D. Rockefeller once piously told a Sunday school class. It would be a rare tycoon in our time who would risk the horse laugh with which such a remark would be greeted.

17   In the last third of the twentieth century even children are aware that if a man has become prosperous in business, he has sometimes departed from the strict truth in order to overcome obstacles or has practiced the more subtle deceptions of the half-truth or the misleading omission. Whatever the form of the bluff, it is an integral part of the game, and the executive who does not master its techniques is not likely to accumulate much money or power.

QUESTIONS AND IDEAS FOR DISCUSSION

1. How, according to Carr, is business like poker? How, in fact, is it *not* like poker—that is, at what point does the analogy break down?
2. What constitutes lying and cheating depends, says Carr, on the context. Discuss the ways in which he defends and supports this claim in the context of conducting business.
3. If you disagree with Carr's conclusion, how would you go about refuting his thesis to him? How would you go about refuting his thesis to your rhetoric class? Your "Introduction to Marketing" class? Would speaking to the different audiences necessitate making major or minor differences in your own argument?
4. If you agree with Carr's conclusion, what additional examples, analogies, testimony, or other inductive support can you suggest to add to Carr's argument?
5. The audience to whom this essay was initially addressed was businesspeople (business*men*, specifically), readers of the *Harvard Business Review*. Indicate specific details of examples, assumptions, and vocabulary that seem to have been chosen with that audience in mind. If you work in business now or plan to in the future, do you find yourself able to identify with Carr's stance? If you have no experience in or plans to engage in business as a career, do you find Carr's argument totally alien to your understanding and interests? Explain. Does the way in which businesses are run affect only businesspeople—or all of us?

WHY I WANT A WIFE

Judy Brady

1 I belong to that classification of people known as wives. I am A Wife. And, not altogether incidentally, I am a mother.

2 Not too long ago a male friend of mine appeared on the scene fresh from a recent divorce. He had one child, who is, of course, with his ex-wife. He is looking for another wife. As I thought about him while I was ironing one evening, it suddenly occurred to me that I, too, would like to have a wife. Why do I want a wife?

3 I would like to go back to school so that I can become economically independent, support myself, and, if need be, support those dependent upon me. I want a wife who will work and send me to school. And while I am going to school I want a wife to take care of my children. I want a wife to keep track of the children's doctor and dentist appointments. And to keep track of mine, too. I want a wife to make sure my children eat properly and are kept clean. I want a wife who will wash the children's clothes and keep

them mended. I want a wife who is a good nurturant attendant to my children, who arranges for their schooling, makes sure that they have an adequate social life with their peers, takes them to the park, the zoo, etc. I want a wife who takes care of the children when they are sick, a wife who arranges to be around when the children need special care, because, of course, I cannot miss classes at school. My wife must arrange to lose time at work and not lose the job. It may mean a small cut in my wife's income from time to time, but I guess I can tolerate that. Needless to say, my wife will arrange and pay for the care of the children while my wife is working.

4   I want a wife who will take care of *my* physical needs. I want a wife who will keep my house clean. A wife who will pick up after my children, a wife who will pick up after me. I want a wife who will keep my clothes clean, ironed, mended, replaced when need be, and who will see to it that my personal things are kept in their proper place so that I can find what I need the minute I need it. I want a wife who cooks the meals, a wife who is a *good* cook. I want a wife who will plan the menus, do the necessary grocery shopping, prepare the meals, serve them pleasantly, and then do the cleaning up while I do my studying. I want a wife who will care for me when I am sick and sympathize with my pain and loss of time from school. I want a wife to go along when our family takes a vacation so that someone can continue to care for me and my children when I need a rest and change of scene.

5   I want a wife who will not bother me with rambling complaints about a wife's duties. But I want a wife who will listen to me when I feel the need to explain a rather difficult point I have come across in my course of studies. And I want a wife who will type my papers for me when I have written them.

6   I want a wife who will take care of the details of my social life. When my wife and I are invited out by my friends, I want a wife who will take care of the babysitting arrangements. When I meet people at school that I like and want to entertain, I want a wife who will have the house clean, will prepare a special meal, serve it to me and my friends, and not interrupt when I talk about things that interest me and my friends. I want a wife who will have arranged that the children are fed and ready for bed before my guests arrive so that the children do not bother us. I want a wife who takes care of the needs of my guests so that they feel comfortable, who makes sure that they have an ashtray, that they are passed the hors d'oeuvres, that they are offered a second helping of the food, that their wine glasses are replenished when necessary, that their coffee is served to them as they like it. And I want a wife who knows that sometimes I need a night out by myself.

7   I want a wife who is sensitive to my sexual needs, a wife who makes love passionately and eagerly when I feel like it, a wife who makes sure that I am satisfied. And, of course, I want a wife who will not demand sexual attention when I am not in the mood for it. I want a wife who assumes the complete responsibility for birth control, because I do not want more children. I want a wife who will remain sexually faithful to me so that I do not have to clutter up my intellectual life with jealousies. And I want a wife who

understands that *my* sexual needs may entail more than strict adherence to monogamy. I must, after all, be able to relate to people as fully as possible.

8   If, by chance, I find another person more suitable as a wife than the wife I already have, I want the liberty to replace my present wife with another one. Naturally, I will expect a fresh, new life; my wife will take the children and be solely responsible for them so that I am left free.

9   When I am through with school and have a job, I want my wife to quit working and remain at home so that my wife can more fully and completely take care of a wife's duties.

10   My God, who *wouldn't* want a wife?

QUESTIONS AND IDEAS FOR DISCUSSION

1. This essay was written for the inaugural issue of *Ms.* magazine, Spring 1972. Describe the audience toward which it was probably aimed. Do you fit that description? If not, how does the difference between the initial audience and yourself affect your understanding of and attitude toward Brady's argument? Must a person be married or have been married in order to be able to judge the argument fairly?

2. More than two decades have passed since the essay was written. Which of Brady's inductive points now seem dated, and which still seem apt? Comment specifically.

3. How great or small is the inductive leap between the premises and the conclusion in this essay? Preconceptions and personal biases aside, are we moved to accept Brady's conclusion on the weight of her examples?

4. How does Brady analyze her subject and organize her supporting points for the conclusion that "anybody would want a wife"? Is that, by the way, all of her thesis, or is there more to it, implied but not stated?

5. Describe the persona Brady creates in this essay. How does her use of irony and humorous detail affect her persona? Are we more or less likely to give ear to her serious underlying argument because of the voice with which Brady speaks? Explain. What seems to be Brady's persuasive aim?

CONCEALED WEAPONS CAN SAVE LIVES

Suzanna Gratia

1   On Dec. 17, 1991, in Anniston, Ala., a restaurant patron defended himself and saved the lives of nearly two dozen others held hostage by two armed would-be robbers. The reluctant hero, who was legally carrying his .45 caliber firearm, stopped both assailants before they could complete their crime or injure any other innocent customers.

2   On Oct. 16, 1991, in Killeen, Texas, an armed homicidal maniac methodically killed 22 people and then himself, facing no resistance from the scores of potential victims, including me.

3   That tragedy will be forever etched in my memory. My parents were brutally murdered, and I was helpless to protect them. None of us in that restaurant could control our own destinies, for Texas politicians had seen fit to keep us disarmed.

4   State law prohibits the concealed carrying of firearms, denying me or someone else the right to have a gun that day to protect ourselves and our loved ones from the rampages of a madman. That's flat-out wrong. And I intend to do everything in my power to change that ill-gotten law to avert needless suffering by others.

5   The violent incidents in Anniston and Killeen ended far differently because of the laws governing the concealed carrying of firearms. Alabama has a fair concealed-carry law, but in Texas the government has said, in effect, that decent citizens can't be trusted to carry firearms for self-protection. The facts simply do not justify that conclusion.

6   Despite claims of gun prohibitionists, allowing law-abiding citizens like me to choose to obtain a permit to legally carry a handgun in no way increases criminal behavior. In Florida, a concealed-carry reform law was passed in 1988. Anti-gun groups and the Florida media predicted an outbreak of shootings in the Sunshine State.

7   But this fair and more uniform concealed-carry law simply hasn't shaken the foundations of the Florida legal system, as doom-sayers predicted. According to John Fuller, general counsel for the Florida Sheriff's Association, "I haven't seen where we have had any instance of persons with permits causing violent crimes, and I'm constantly on the lookout."

8   In fact, it has the opposite effect on homicide rates. After statewide concealed-carry law reforms were enacted in Florida, the homicide rate decreased 6 percent between 1987 and 1990 as the national rate climbed 13 percent. In Oregon, reformed carry laws adopted in 1990 returned a 20.8 percent drop in the homicide rate. Again, the gun prohibitionists had predicted mayhem, and again, their predictions proved false.

9   Research proves why: A government-funded survey of 1,874 felons by noted criminologists James D. Wright and Peter H. Rossi, designed to deter-

mine the experiences of convicted felons with firearms and their perceptions of gun laws, found about 40 percent of the felons sampled said they had decided not to commit a crime because they feared the victim was carrying a firearm. And 34 percent had been "scared off, shot at, wounded or captured by an armed victim."

10   Clearly, concealed-carry laws translate to saving the lives of loved ones in a manner similar to health or life insurance. If ever there arises that time when it is needed, no substitute will do, and I don't intend to be victimized again.

11   In drafting the Bill of Rights, the Founding Fathers acknowledged self-protection as a prime goal incorporated in the Second Amendment. In quoting criminologist Cesare Beccaria, still renowned for his work *On Crimes and Punishments* penned in 1764, Thomas Jefferson said: "Laws that forbid the carrying of arms . . . disarm only those who are neither inclined nor determined to commit crimes. . . . Such laws make things worse for the assaulted and better for the assailants; they serve rather to encourage than to prevent homicides, for an unarmed man may be attacked with greater confidence than an armed man."

12   The question of carrying a concealed handgun is one that is highly personal. It is a choice that should be made by the individual. And it is a choice that should not be forbidden to an honest citizen like myself by an overprotective government, particularly one which has no responsibility to provide real protection when my life is threatened.

13   Americans are expressing concerns regarding police protection when the explosion in crime literally overwhelms police departments across the nation. In a public opinion survey done by the Gallup Report for the U.S. Justice Department's Sourcebook of Criminal Statistics, citizens were asked, "How much confidence do you have in the ability of the police to protect you from violent crime?" Nationwide, 50 percent of the American public polled responded "not very much" to "none."

14   In the District of Columbia, where there has been a virtual gun ban since 1976, the local court of appeals followed the long-accepted rule that the police have no duty to protect individuals, only the community at large.

15   In states with no provision for concealed carry, legislation should be proposed, passed and enacted to allow law-abiding citizens the chance to protect themselves from criminal attack. In those states that employ discriminatory and unfair concealed-carry laws which virtually forfeit citizen opportunities for these permits, legislation must shift the burden of proof to the issuing authority to show reasons for denial and away from the honest citizen seeking a permit.

16   While organized police forces do attempt to protect the public, more and more they are unable to do so. In fact, armed private citizens encounter and thwart three times as many criminals as law enforcement. This is not to suggest a diminished role for our nation's law enforcement, but rather to emphasize the importance of armed self-defense before police can respond to a

crime in progress. Evidence indicates that the armed citizen is probably the single most effective deterrent to crime in the nation.

17   When it comes to arbitrary enforcement or prohibition on the lawful concealed carrying of firearms, what has the law-abiding American public done to warrant such a mistrust of their competency and character? Ask your elected officials. I'm asking mine.

QUESTIONS AND IDEAS FOR DISCUSSION

1. Suzanna Gratia has written an essay supporting what many of her readers may oppose: the freedom for citizens to carry concealed weapons. How does she attempt to refute the arguments of the opposition? How well does she succeed? Comment.

2. What support does Gratia offer for her thesis? Find inductive premises—analogy, examples and other evidence, causal reasoning—offered in support. Give examples of each. Is the support strong enough for the thesis claim?

3. How does Gratia organize her argument? What, if anything, would you change if this were your own draft? Why? If you find the essay to be well-organized, explain why it succeeds, with specific reference to the text.

Suggestions for Writing and Further Discussion

1. Albert Carr declares that "the major tests of every move in business, as in all games of strategy, are legality and profit." Not ethics. When Carr's essay on "bluffing" in business was published by the *Harvard Business Review*, the editors solicited additional essays supporting or refuting Carr's argument. Write such an essay, directed to the readers of the *Review*. Use an extended analogy of your own—don't just refute Carr's poker analogy—and examples to support your argument.

2. Write an essay in the spirit of Brady's "Why I want a Wife," entitled, "Why I Want an Assistant" or "Why I Want a Computer."

3. Suzanna Gratia has written a compelling argument against a specific form of gun control—"concealed-carry" prohibitions. If you disagree with her thesis, write an argument in favor of "concealed-carry" prohibitions or some other aspect of gun control. Write as if Gratia will be one of your readers, along with the members of your rhetoric class. If you agree with Gratia's thesis, write an argument on some topic about which you have strong opinions. In either case, be sure to support your claim, as Gratia does, with facts, examples, analogy, and other inductive support.

4. Our imperfect reason often leads us to false conclusions, especially about cause-and-effect relationships. Write an essay in which you speculate about the probable causes or effects of something you have little knowledge about—perhaps what makes a car run, or what makes a camera record photographs and not blank exposures, or what makes a video game work. You

may presume that your readers have little more knowledge of the process than you do. Do not treat the topic facetiously; try to construct a reasonable argument based solely on your own observations. (After you have written the essay, look up the topic in an encyclopedia or how-to book, and note the points at which your causal analysis breaks down. Write a brief comment on what sent you astray—and how far—in your original analysis.)

5. Your sister, brother, or friend is a medical student, and writes to you that the "right to die" is a hot issue right now at the medical school. In response, write a letter to the dean of the medical school in which you attack or defend euthanasia. You may choose to limit or qualify either position, perhaps defending euthanasia only when a terminal patient asks for it, or attacking deliberate euthanasia while supporting the right to withhold extraordinary life support. To support your conclusion, cite actual instances of this dilemma from the experiences of your own family and friends or from what you have heard about on the news and in the newspapers.

6. Write an argument from analogy in which you compare a thing, event, process, or person that is familiar to you—but likely to be unfamiliar to your rhetoric classmates—to something else that your classmates should understand readily. For example, "Rappelling down a cliff is not as frightening or as difficult as you might expect; it is very much like—," or "Everyone should experience deep-sea diving at least once in a lifetime. The experience is like—," or "Attending the Olympics is not like attending any other sporting event. The Olympics are more like—," or "My neighbor, Mr. Martino, looks like the retired mechanic that he is, but at heart he is more like—."

6

Testing Arguments: Deductive Reasoning

> *"I see nothing," said I....*
> *"On the contrary, Watson, you can see everything. You fail, however, to reason from what you see. You are too timid in drawing your inferences."*
> —**Arthur Conan Doyle, *The Sign of Four***

DEDUCTION IN FICTION AND FACT

When we think of deduction, we often think of something akin to the following argument:

"The identity of the murderer is perfectly obvious," announced the Famous Detective smugly. "He is a left-handed attorney from Kansas City who walks with a limp and was disguised as a ranchhand when he committed the deed."

"But how do you know all this?" gasped the minister and her brother.

"A simple matter of deduction, my friends. The villain wore these cowboy boots (we know this because they still smell of sweaty feet, and are too large for the feet of the deceased). They were intended as part of a disguise, for no real ranchhand would be caught dead—or red-handed—in cowboy boots from Saks, as the label inside indicates these are. The curious wear pattern on the right sole is indicative of a limp, and the dust on the boots is of a kind peculiar to Kansas City. Moreover, the murder weapon was this pair of blood-stained left-handed scissors. You see how obvious it all is!"

"Ah, but you haven't accounted for his being an attorney," said the minister's brother, irritated by the detective's condescension.

"That is the most certain point of all!" the detective exclaimed. "All residents of Kansas City who wear cowboy boots are attorneys."

We associate deductive reasoning with the work of detectives such as Sherlock Holmes and Hercule Poirot and their imitators, like the overconfident fellow above. In the world of fiction, of course, the detective always will be proved right:

The killer will indeed turn out to be a murderous, left-handed attorney from Kansas City, who presumably will be caught limping barefooted into his legal offices. But reasoning of this kind strikes us as contrived and unreal; we consequently dismiss deductive reasoning as the concern only of paperback detectives and formal logic textbooks, in which arguments sound nothing like the way people actually talk and write. One of the Famous Detective's arguments, were it to appear in a logic textbook, would look like this:

> No real ranchhands are persons who wear cowboy boots from Saks Fifth Avenue.
> The murderer is a person who wears cowboy boots from Saks.
> Therefore, the murderer is not a real ranchhand.

And, of course, no real person writes arguments this way, neatly and redundantly laid out on separate lines.

But all who reason do so in part deductively. Deductive reasoning is not unique to detective fiction and formal logic; it is a perfectly natural process of reasoning—so natural, in fact, that we can hardly avoid it for even five minutes of conscious thought. The following examples of deduction look more like the way people really reason than do the Famous Detective's arguments:

> "If Carl is angry with me, he won't speak to me at lunch. [Later:] He did speak to me at lunch, so evidently he isn't angry after all."

> "Mikey won't eat that cereal. He hates all nutritious food."

> "Successful actors can't be camera-shy, so Patrick is bound to fail in Hollywood."

This reasoning is broadly deductive in shape, for it draws out the implications contained within what we know (or assume) to be true. Our verbal arguments, written or spoken, may lack the inevitable certainty of formal logic, but not the shape of it. By examining the reasoning process we can more effectively revise our own arguments and more accurately evaluate the arguments of others. If you have developed thesis statements from enthymemes as discussed in Chapter 2, you are familiar with the broad outlines of deductive reasoning. This chapter will help you assess the strength of the deductive arguments that make up the core of most of your written arguments.

INDUCTION AND DEDUCTION

Induction, the subject of the previous chapter, and deduction, the subject of this chapter, are complementary processes of reasoning. Although we are examining them separately, most often we will find them used together in written and spoken argument. **The difference between them lies in the relationship between the premises and the conclusion.** In an inductive argument, the premises purport only to *offer support* for the conclusion. In a deductive argument, on the other hand, the premises purport to *guarantee* the conclusion. This difference is illustrated by two arguments, the first inductive and the second deductive:

> *Ross:* "I was paid last Friday and on the two Fridays before that. In fact, I have been paid every Friday since I came to work for the company. I know, then, that I will be paid today, since today is Friday."

> *Smith:* "Since today is Friday, and every Friday is payday, I know I will get a check today."

The conclusion reached in both arguments is that the person speaking will be paid "today." If the premises offered in support of that conclusion are all true (every Friday *is* payday) and related logically to the conclusion, then in the first argument the conclusion is probable but not inevitable. Perhaps the company is having a severe cash-flow problem and will be unable to issue checks today. Perhaps this week a decision has been reached that paychecks will be issued every Monday, or every other Friday, effective immediately. Such will always be the limitation of the inductive "leap of faith" between premises and conclusion, between examples and covering generalization. But in the second argument, if the premises are all true and related logically to the conclusion, the conclusion is assured.

Of course, you might object, the same calamity that might befall Ross's paycheck might also waylay Smith's. If so, the premise upon which the conclusion is based, "Every Friday is payday," would be shown to be untrue. In a deductive argument, if the premises are true and the argument is structured properly, the conclusion is guaranteed.

A second distinction often made between induction and deduction—that inductive arguments move from particular cases to summarizing generalizations and deductive arguments move from general categories to conclusions about particular cases—is not altogether accurate. For one thing, an inductive argument may conclude with particular cases; you may consider a number of examples and then speculate about another, similar instance, as Ross does in the argument cited above. And a deductive argument may move from generalization to further generalization:

> True patriots are those who not only support their country in its strengths but also work to eliminate its faults. Those who not only support their country in its strengths but also work to eliminate its faults may be perceived as disloyal. Paradoxically, therefore, true patriots may be perceived as disloyal.

The difference between deduction and induction lies not in the kinds of conclusions that are drawn but in the ways they are drawn—the relationship of the premises to the conclusion. Both kinds of argument are valuable. Without induction, as logician Wesley Salmon has noted, we could pose no arguments about future events. We could draw no legitimate generalizations. We could not speculate about similarities between phenomena. Without deduction, we could draw no inferences. We could never be assured of any conclusion.

VALIDITY, TRUTH, AND SOUNDNESS

The assurance deduction offers is possible only if we create sound arguments. An argument is **sound,** or fully acceptable, if its premises are true and the form of the argument is valid. To evaluate the merits of a deductive argument, you must first understand that validity and truth are entirely different qualities in logic. Valid arguments are arguments that are properly structured; **validity** has to do with the *form* of the argument. True statements are actually or theoretically verifiable; **truth** has to do with the *matter* of the argument. How to test for and locate true statements were major issues in Chapter 4; how to test for and construct valid deductive arguments will be our concern here. Both truth and validity are necessary components of sound argument, but they must be considered and evaluated separately. Otherwise, you might be tempted to call this argument invalid:

All cats are striped creatures.	(premise)
All striped creatures are mammals.	(premise)
Therefore, all cats are mammals.	(conclusion)

The conclusion is true, but both premises offered as justification for the conclusion are false. The argument, therefore, cannot be sound, but it is valid, as you will see later.

In another argument all the statements may be true, and the form invalid nevertheless:

All lupines are wildflowers.	(premise)
All bluebonnets are wildflowers.	(premise)
Therefore, all bluebonnets are lupines.	(conclusion)

As it happens, all three statements are true, but the premises do not support the conclusion, because just to say that two things are both part of a larger class does not necessarily mean that they overlap within that larger class. A diagram of the form of this invalid argument makes the issue clear:

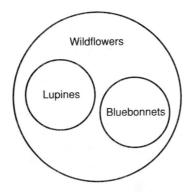

The argument is not correctly structured—it is invalid. It just happens here that bluebonnets are lupines.

Clearly, if an argument seems to fall short of being fully acceptable, we must be able to judge both its validity and its truth, for the careless workmanship may be either in the construction or in the materials used.

DISTRIBUTION OF TERMS

What makes an argument valid, its structure "correct"? To answer that question requires a thorough understanding of the words *term* and *distribution*. A **term** is a noun, phrase, or clause that constitutes a unit of meaning. Every sentence has two terms, a subject term and a predicate term. In the following sentence, "gorillas" is the subject term and "shy creatures" is the predicate term.

Gorillas are shy creatures.

Terms can be **distributed**—that is, they may refer to all the members of a particular group—or **undistributed**—that is, they may refer to only some of the members of a group. In the sentence "All gorillas named Chamba are intelligent creatures," the subject term is distributed: *all* gorillas named Chamba. The predicate term is undistributed: many intelligent creatures are *not* gorillas named Chamba. The predicate term does not include *all* intelligent creatures.

The Subject Term   In a valid argument, some of the terms have to be distributed. To test for distribution of the subject term, check for the explicitly stated or implied words "all" or "none." When a term does not include any modifiers such as *some* or *many*, *all* is implied. For example, when you say "potato chips," not "some potato chips" or "most potato chips," you imply "all potato chips." In the following sentences, all the subject terms are distributed:

May graduates will participate in the August graduation ceremony.

The seventeen German majors all got jobs quickly.

No cameras are permitted in the auditorium.

Anytime you see a modifier such as *some, many, most, not all*, and *a few*, and usually when you see a number such as *nine, one hundred*, or *two thousand*, you know that the subject term is undistributed—it does not include all the members of its class. (But notice an exception in the example above: The addition of "the" before "seventeen" tells you that there were seventeen German majors altogether.) In the following sentences, all the subject terms are undistributed:

Two hundred twelve May graduates will participate in the August graduation ceremony.

Many German majors got jobs quickly.

A few relatives of each graduate were permitted in the auditorium.

The Predicate Term   In all positive statements, such as "Unicorns are mythical creatures," the predicate term is undistributed. We do not consider all of the predicate term in a positive statement. In the example just stated, unicorns are not the whole class of mythical creatures, which also includes dragons and mermaids, among others. In all negative statements, such as "Some laws are *not* just," the predicate term is distributed. We exclude all or some of the subject term from *all* of the predicate term. Again, in the example just stated, some laws are excluded from the *entire* class of things that are just.

Recasting Sentences   To check for distribution of terms, sometimes you may need to recast the sentence so that a noun, phrase, or clause is linked to another noun, phrase, or clause by a form of the verb *to be*. For example,

All professors have graduated from college.

would be rephrased as

All professors are persons who have graduated from college.

This shift allows us to see that the meaning of the sentence is actually "All professors are *some* of the persons who have graduated from college." It is obvious that the predicate term is undistributed, because many college graduates are not college professors. The subject term, of course, is distributed ("all professors").

Persons and Proper Names   Individual things (the philosopher, the yellow cat, the skyscraper), including reference to them by proper names (Socrates, Tabby, the Empire State Building), are considered distributed by definition. When we speak of Socrates or of a building, we refer to all of him or it, not to a part.

Using Diagrams   In analyzing an argument for validity, it is often helpful to diagram it, as we did in the wildflower example. Examine the following statements and their corresponding diagrams:

All *successful politicians* are *good speakers.*

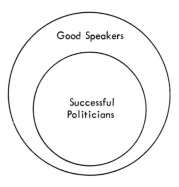

You can see from this diagram that "successful politicians" is a distributed term, but "good speakers" is an undistributed term. Some people who are good speakers—some television announcers, some preachers, some teachers, and so on—are not referred to by this sentence. The relation of the terms in this sentence can be stated as "All A (subject term) are B (predicate term)."

In the next sentence, by contrast, neither of the two terms is considered in its entirety:

Some *successful politicians* are *graduates of law school.*

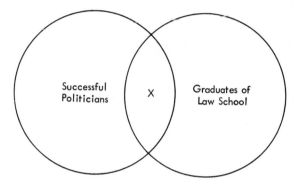

In this sentence both subject and predicate are undistributed. Only some successful politicians graduated from law school; only some graduates of law school have become successful politicians. This sentence exemplifies the relationship "Some A are B."

In yet another sentence, we find an undistributed subject term and a distributed predicate term:

Some *successful politicians* are not *people fond of kissing babies.*

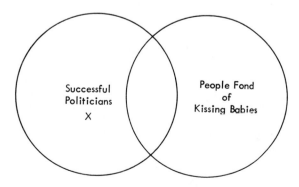

Here part of one group (successful politicians) is excluded from *all* of another group (people fond of kissing babies). Sentences of this type follow the pattern "Some A are not B."

Finally, in some sentences, the two terms do not overlap at all:

No *successful politicians* are *persons opposed to civil rights.*

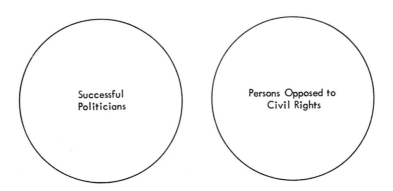

Both terms here are distributed: We have excluded *all* of the class of successful politicians from *all* of the class of persons opposed to civil rights. This kind of statement takes one of two forms: "No A are B" or "A are not B."

An argument links statements of these kinds in order to demonstrate relationships between the terms. If you can determine which terms are distributed, you can judge the validity of the relationships by testing the argument according to applicable rules, and you can thereby improve the logic of your own prose.

EXERCISE 6–1

Identify all subject terms and all predicate terms in the following statements as either distributed or undistributed. If a statement is not expressed in subject /linking verb/ predicate nominative form, rephrase it accordingly. For example, you would rephrase "Some sharks eat people" as "Some sharks are people-eaters," in order to make evident (if it was not clear already) that both subject and predicate terms in this statement are undistributed. In a more complex case, "Millions of people inhabit China" can be restated as "Millions of the living creatures inhabiting China are people" or "Millions of the people in the world are Chinese," depending on the classes you have in mind.

1. Few engineering majors believe they will enjoy English composition. ("Few engineering majors are people who believe they will enjoy English composition.")

2. Shakespeare was a great writer.
3. Some of Shakespeare's plays are not great.
4. Circumstantial evidence has merit in courts of law.
5. Tomatoes are not vegetables.

TESTING VALIDITY: THE SYLLOGISM

If a deductive argument is correctly structured, we say that it is *valid;* that is, it adheres to certain rules governing logical deduction. To determine whether the rules have been followed, it is sometimes helpful to set out the structure of the argument in explicit and simple terms. An ordinary deductive argument (called an **enthymeme**) makes explicit only part of its structure and implies the rest. "All cats are striped creatures, so they must be mammals" is an enthymeme; and even if we find the missing premise incredible, we have no great difficulty stating what it must be: "All striped creatures are mammals." In a more complex argument, the implicit premise might not be as readily apparent as it is here, or the relationships between ideas as clear. In those cases Aristotle's model for evaluating deductive reasoning, the **syllogism,** can be useful.

The syllogism offers a means of testing validity in arguments—of establishing whether or not the proper structure has been followed. In the simplest terms, the structure of a typical deductive argument is "X and Y; therefore, Z." X and Y represent the premises; Z, the conclusion. If the premises are both true and are related logically to each other, then the conclusion is true. A syllogism spells out just how statement X is related to statement Y, and how both of them are in turn related to statement Z. For example,

All A are B.	(statement X)
All B are C.	(statement Y)
Therefore,	
All A are C.	(statement Z)

This is the form of the striped-cat argument we encountered earlier, and of several others along the way.

To determine whether the syllogism is valid, we need only judge it according to six rules formulated by Aristotle:

1. There must be exactly three terms.
2. The middle (linking) term must be distributed at least once.
3. Any term distributed in the conclusion must be distributed in a premise.
4. Only one premise may be negative, or no conclusion is possible.
5. A negative premise requires a negative conclusion.
6. Only one premise may be particular, or no conclusion is possible.

The following syllogism is in standard form:

All <u>Londoners</u> are <u>residents of England</u>.   (major premise)
      middle term   major term

<u>Queen Elizabeth</u> is a <u>Londoner</u>.   (minor premise)
   minor term   middle term

<u>Queen Elizabeth</u> is a <u>resident of England</u>.   (conclusion)
   minor term   major term

The syllogism we are considering has exactly three terms: *Londoners, Queen Elizabeth,* and *residents of England.* The middle term, *Londoners,* is distributed in the major premise. No term is distributed in the conclusion that was not previously distributed in a premise, for *residents of England* is undistributed in the conclusion, and *Queen Elizabeth,* being a proper noun, is distributed by definition. The syllogism contains no negative premises and no particular premises; so the last three rules do not apply. The syllogism is valid. Its validity also can be shown by a diagram:

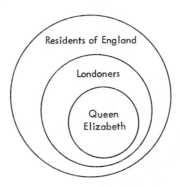

EXERCISE 6–2

Test the following syllogisms for *validity only.* Do not be distracted by nonsensical or untrue statements. Identify the three terms in each syllogism and draw diagrams to help you determine which arguments are valid.

1. Rabbits are creatures that multiply rapidly.
   Some creatures that multiply rapidly are household pests.
   Therefore, some rabbits are household pests.
2. Professor Higgins's interests are catholic.
   No Catholics are interested in walnut farming.
   Therefore, Professor Higgins's interests do not include walnut farming.

3. No sensible person does things that might endanger life.
   Skydiving might endanger life.
   Therefore, no sensible person goes skydiving.
4. Elephants are ticklish.
   Ticklish creatures are untrustworthy.
   Therefore, elephants are untrustworthy.
5. Football is like life.
   Chess is like life.
   Therefore, football is like chess.
6. All insects are arthropods, and lobsters are arthropods.
   Therefore, lobsters are insects.

EXERCISE 6–3

Determine valid conclusions for the following pairs of statements.

1. All A are B.
   No B are C.
   Therefore, ?
2. Some frogs are not handsome princes.
   Only a handsome prince can break the spell.
   (Rephrase as, "All who can break the spell are handsome princes.")
   Therefore, ?
3. All contemptible people are liars.
   Senator Smithers is not a liar.
   Therefore, ?
4. A are not B.
   C are B.
   Therefore, ?
5. All skills that can save lives are skills people should know.
   Cardiopulmonary resuscitation is a skill that can save lives.
   Therefore, ?

FORMAL FALLACIES

To violate any of the six rules of validity is to commit a **formal fallacy,** so called because of a problem in the structure (form) of the argument—that is, in the kinds of relationships drawn among the terms. Such an argument is easily refuted. We will consider the fallacies related to each of the six rules in turn.

There Must Be Exactly Three Terms.   This rule is not as mystical as it may sound; two terms or four terms in a single argument lead to the fallacies discussed below. Sometimes an argument will appear to have three terms, but will actually have two or four. If I argue that

All men are mortal beings, and	(major premise)
Margaret is not a man;	(minor premise)
therefore, Margaret is not a mortal being.	(conclusion)

I appear to be using three terms, but the first *men* refers to the entire class of human beings, and the second *man* refers to humans of the male gender. In fact, I have introduced a fourth term, and thereby have committed what is called the fallacy of **equivocation.**

Conversely, sometimes an argument will repeat the same term in different words, so that a premise offered is actually the conclusion in disguised form:

This course is a course that will appeal to you.	(minor premise)
All courses that appeal to you are courses you will like.	(major premise)
Therefore, this course is a course you will like.	(conclusion)

This is the fallacy of **circular reasoning.** The argument goes nowhere; the first premise says, in effect, the same thing as the conclusion. Circular reasoning is a way of **begging the question**—in other words, taking for granted what you should be proving, or using the conclusion as its own support. To say "You will like this course because it's great" is to beg the question of why the person addressed will like the course: Is the professor witty? Are the textbooks interesting? Does the class never meet on Fridays?

The Middle Term Must Be Distributed at Least Once.   The fallacy of the undistributed middle term is often called the *fallacy of the shared characteristic* (or **guilt by association**), a label that makes clear the fault involved. Consider the following argument:

All Methodists oppose heavy drinking.
All vegetarians oppose heavy drinking.
Therefore,
all Methodists are vegetarians.

Here, we have not considered the entire class of people who oppose heavy drinking (a class that includes such otherwise-unrelated groups as Methodists, vegetarians, and members of Alcoholics Anonymous) at any point in the argument: The middle term, or shared characteristic, is undistributed. But if we say,

All Methodists oppose heavy drinking, and
Joe Briggs is a Methodist;
therefore,
Joe Briggs must oppose heavy drinking.

we have reasoned validly.

Any Term Distributed in the Conclusion Must Be Distributed in a Premise.
Here again distribution proves crucial to establishing a valid argument. We cannot go from considering part of a class to drawing conclusions about all of it, as is done in the following argument:

> Some Central American governments are Communist-backed.
> All Communist-backed governments are governments ideologically opposed to the United States.
> Therefore, all Central American governments are ideologically opposed to the United States.

The problem with this line of reasoning is that it moves from considering some Central American governments to drawing a conclusion about all of them; a term is distributed in the conclusion that was not distributed in the premises. The argument is invalid; it contains the fallacy of **overgeneralization.**

Only One Premise May Be Negative, or No Conclusion Is Possible. Two negative premises leave the reader hanging:

> No commodities traders are afraid to take risks.
> No people who are afraid to take risks are mountain climbers.

Therefore—what? Commodities traders are likely to be mountain climbers? Not necessarily. We simply cannot draw a conclusion.

A Negative Premise Requires a Negative Conclusion. We cannot exclude a class (or part of it) in the premises and then include it in the conclusion. An affirmative conclusion from a negative premise is logically impossible:

> No goldfish are trained circus animals.
> Trained circus animals are valuable property.
> Therefore, goldfish are also valuable property.

They may be, but not on the basis of these premises. We can conclude only that some valuable property is not goldfish.

Only One Premise May Be Particular, or No Conclusion Is Possible. Attempting to draw a conclusion from two particular (subject term undistributed) premises results in a muddle like the following.

> Some mushrooms are poisonous substances.
> Some poisonous substances are man-made.
> Therefore,
> some mushrooms are man-made.

No conclusion about the relationship of mushrooms to man-made substances is possible, because neither class is considered in its entirety.

An argument can be invalid in any of these ways, and a really poor argument may include more than one fallacy at a time. But by far the most common formal fallacies are the fallacies of the *undistributed middle term* and *begging the question.* If you keep an eye out for these two in the arguments you encounter and in your own, you will recognize and avoid most fallacious argument.

EXERCISE 6–4

Identify the following arguments as valid or invalid, and indicate which formal fallacy is committed in the invalid arguments. As in the examples on pages 169–170, use diagrams of the terms and their relationship to each other to help you.

1. Freedom to make political statements is a right protected by law.
   Bumper stickers make political statements.
   Therefore, bumper stickers are protected by law.
2. All addictive substances are harmful to the body.
   Cyanide is harmful to the body.
   Therefore, cyanide is an addictive substance.
3. Some people who take flu shots develop Guillain-Barré syndrome as a consequence.
   People should not do things that make them develop Guillain-Barré syndrome as a consequence.
   Therefore, no one should take flu shots.
4. Happiness alters a person's state of mind.
   Altered states of mind make one unfit for driving.
   Therefore, happiness makes one unfit for driving.
5. Americans are uninformed about the dangers of nuclear weapons.
   People who are uninformed about the dangers of nuclear weapons are not able to make informed decisions about them.
   Americans are not able to make informed decisions about nuclear weapons.

THE LIMITATIONS OF LOGIC:
TOULMIN'S CORRECTIVE

The relationships drawn in sound deductive argument are attractive in the certainty they offer. You may have underlined or highlighted the statement in an earlier section, "If the premises are true and the argument is structured properly, the conclusion is assured." How comforting that sounds. Life offers few such guarantees: We usually look for the fine print and the limitations when we are offered one.

We must do so with argument—even deductive argument—as well. As logicians from Aristotle to Stephen Toulmin and others have pointed out, we rarely find arguments in ordinary prose neatly arranged in formal syllogisms, nor do we find the degree of certainty in ordinary propositions and assertions that we find in textbook examples. We are likely to accept arguments on their relative probability, not on their certainty.

In *The Uses of Argument*, Toulmin cites the following as an example of an argument that offers no certainty but great probability:

> Peterson is a Swede;
> Scarcely any Swedes are Roman Catholics;
> So, almost certainly, Peterson is not a Roman Catholic.

Notice the qualifiers here: *scarcely any, almost certainly*. Such qualifiers enable us to argue and to accept arguments that we could not grant in unqualified terms. However, the conclusion must not claim a greater degree of certainty than the supporting premises:

> Peterson is a Swede;
> Fewer than half of all Swedes are Roman Catholics;
> So, almost certainly, Peterson is not a Roman Catholic.

In this case we would not be likely to grant the conclusion. *Fewer than half* offers much less certainty in the argument than does *scarcely any*. In this second version, what would be an acceptable qualifier in the conclusion?

THE ENTHYMEME

The **enthymeme,** as you will recall from Chapter 2, is an elliptical argument in which a premise (or sometimes a conclusion) is left unstated. It is left unstated because it seems obvious to the arguer or is clearly implied by the context of the argument. Enthymemes can be reconstructed as syllogisms for analysis, but often such syllogistic arguments appear in disguise. An enthymeme can be a single sentence with apparently too many terms for a syllogism and too few premises:

> *Jack Snopes:* "I'm sure that Psychology 2312 will be an easy course, because Mr. Phillips, the instructor, is a great guy."

This is an argument. One indicator is the simple word *because,* which normally precedes a reason advanced to support a claim—together, all we need for a basic argument. In this case, the claim is that Psychology 2312 will be an easy course, and the premise offered to support that claim is that Mr. Phillips, the instructor, is a great guy. Moreover, this is a deductive argument. The conclusion is drawn out of, and offered as assured by, the premises. But the argument appears to be an *invalid* deductive argument. It seems to have just one premise and as many as six terms: *I, Psychology 2312, easy courses, Mr. Phillips, instructors,* and *great guys*.

To reconstruct the core argument underlying such confusing material, you must work through four steps:

1. **Identify the conclusion.** In this case, the conclusion is "I'm sure that Psychology 2312 will be an easy course." Rephrase the conclusion as a two-term statement linked by a *to be* verb. In our example, the "I'm sure" simply underscores

Jack's belief in his conclusion and is not part of the conclusion itself, leaving us with "Psychology 2312 will be an easy course."

2. **Find the linking (middle) term.** In step one, you found the major and minor terms ("easy courses" and "Psychology 2312"). The link between the two is "courses taught by great guys." Why has Mr. Phillips dropped out of the argument? He hasn't. Mr. Phillips's course is a "course taught by a great guy"; to mention Mr. Phillips by name is simply and unnecessarily to name the course twice.

3. **Reconstruct the premises as two-term statements.** In the example argument, one premise is implied but not actually stated: "All courses taught by great guys will be easy courses." The stated premise can be phrased as "Psychology 2312 will be a course taught by a great guy." For simplicity, you may change the form of the verb to present tense, and you may assign letters to designate each term. Here you will have:

All courses taught by great guys are easy courses.	All A are B.
Psychology 2312 is a course taught by a great guy [Mr. Phillips].	[All] C is A.
Therefore, Psychology 2312 is an easy course.	[All] C is B.

4. **Test the argument's validity by applying the six rules or by drawing a diagram.** Our example is valid, but Jack could be headed for trouble, because the truth of his assumption that "all courses taught by great guys will be easy courses" is questionable. When deductive argument is unsound, the fault often lies in what is taken for granted. Sometimes the assumption is factually dubious; sometimes the assumption is just what the arguer should be proving, but the question is begged. In evaluating any enthymeme, be particularly aware of the unstated parts of the argument.

The enthymeme usually centers on possibilities and probabilities rather than on certainties. We speak of "most artistic people" when we know we cannot speak of "all artistic people." We say that "usually employees are promoted on the basis of longevity" when we know that exceptions are sometimes made on the basis of merit or nepotism. Our conclusions are still acceptable and our arguments sound when our deductions are posed in terms of probabilities rather than certainties, *as long as those conclusions reflect exactly the same degree of uncertainty as the premises.* So, if Jordan is a long-term employee and promotions are forthcoming, we can conclude that *probably* she will be promoted. If most artistic people require periods of solitude, and all people who require periods of solitude are people with introspective natures, then we can safely conclude that *most* artistic people are people with introspective natures. The conclusion cannot reflect greater certainty than do the premises.

EXERCISE 6–5

A. Reconstruct valid syllogisms from the following enthymemes, following the procedure outlined above. Mark the stated premise, implied premise (or implied conclusion), stated conclusion, and the three terms. The longer arguments contain more than one enthymeme, and you will need to reconstruct more than one syllogism. In such cases, the conclusion to one syllogism is likely to be a premise in the next.

B. If an argument is weak, explain why.

1. Colleges and universities are historically lax in securing the safety of their students, and so need to be required to publish the campus crime rates in various categories. Prospective students have the right to know what they are getting into. Muggings and sexual assaults on campuses have reached epidemic proportions, and largely go unreported by campus security to local police. The schools are too unconcerned or too fearful of bad publicity to take serious action to protect students.

> —Summary of a letter to a campus newspaper,
> 8 Apr. 1992

2. By loudly denouncing all bad things—war and hunger and date rape—liberals testify to their own terrific goodness. More important, they promote themselves to membership in a self-selecting elite of those who care deeply about such things. People who care a lot are naturally superior to we who don't care any more than we have to. By virtue of this superiority the caring have a moral right to lead the nation. It's a kind of natural aristocracy, and the wonderful thing about this aristocracy is that you don't have to be brave, smart, strong, or even lucky to join it, you just have to be liberal. Kidnapping the moral high ground also serves to inflate liberal ranks. People who are, in fact, just kindhearted are told that because they care, they must be liberals, too.

> —P. J. O'Rourke, *Give War a Chance*, 1992

3. Endangered species must be protected for the long-term good of the planet. The Pacific yew tree, now raised from low esteem as a worthless weed to the eminence of being the source of a valuable cancer drug, is one such endangered species. The headlong rush to use it for medicine puts the yew in as much danger as foresters' disdain ever did. But it must be carefully conserved for the long-term good of the planet.

4. *Sports Illustrated* should produce a public outcry annually when it publishes its swimsuit issue. The portrayal of women therein amounts to blatant sexism, and sexism leads to violence. How can the public tolerate a magazine that gives rise to such evils?

> —Summary of a letter to the *Dallas Morning News*,
> 5 Apr. 1992

5. I grew up in a small coal mining town in West Virginia shortly after World War II and watched some of the miners toil under what would now be considered slave labor conditions. Mining in those days was extremely hazardous and the majority of the miners lost limbs or eyes or contracted black lung disease. As a result of these conditions, they still suffer a greater frequency of illness than does the general public. In the face of the retired miners' plight, the coal operators dusted off their 1950 agreement setting up a medical trust and promised never to use and abuse the miners again. But to avoid payment of their liabilities, many of the companies closed their unionized mines and reopened non-union operations.

Now, some people ask, "Why should coal operators who did not sign an agreement be held liable for its outcome?" Why shouldn't they, given that they assumed the benefits and profits as the unionized operators closed down? I ask, who pays for the non-union uninsured retirees' health-care costs? Surely you and I did not sign an agreement to pay for them, but just as surely we will do so.

The present mining companies may not have signed the medical trust agreement, but they ought to be held responsible for that obligation along with the benefits and profits they did assume.

—Adapted from a letter to the *Dallas Morning News*,
17 May 1992

EXERCISE 6–6

Test the degree of probability in the conclusions of the following arguments (some of which are enthymemes) against the degree of probability in the premises. Change the qualifiers in the conclusions that seem overgeneralized or unnecessarily narrow.

1. Robert is probably a graduate of Purdue, since his car has a Purdue sticker on the rear window.
2. Because several of the children asked to see the movie again, I know that at least some of them enjoyed it.
3. Studying hard makes passing the philosophy exam likely. I have studied hard, so there is a slim chance I will pass the philosophy exam.
4. People without jobs always vote against the current administration in a presidential election. Therefore, it is likely that the current administration will be defeated in the next election.
5. Because Mexico City is suffering from severe and ever-increasing pollution and overpopulation, the city is doomed to become an uninhabitable ghost town by the twenty-first century.

IF/THEN AND EITHER/OR ARGUMENTS

The syllogisms and enthymemes we have looked at so far have all been **categorical** deductive arguments, that is, arguments concerned with establishing relationships among different categories, or classes, of things. Two other common forms of deductive reasoning are **hypothetical** and **alternative** (or *disjunctive*) arguments. The former argues the outcome of hypothetical (If . . . then . . .) propositions; the latter argues for one alternative among two or more (Either . . . or . . .).

The rules for hypothetical and alternative arguments are different from those governing categorical arguments, but even fewer in number.

If/Then Arguments We will consider two common types of hypothetical arguments. These are their basic forms:

If A, then B.	If A, then B.
A.	Not B.
Therefore, B.	Therefore, not A.

In hypothetical propositions, the "if" clause is called the **antecedent,** and the "then" clause is called the **consequent.** Put into ordinary English, such arguments look something like this:

If today is Wednesday, [then] I must go to class.   (hypothesis)
Today is Wednesday.   (antecedent confirmed)
Therefore, I must go to class.   (consequent confirmed)

or

If today is Wednesday, [then] I must go to class.   (hypothesis)
I do not have to go to class.   (consequent denied)
Therefore, today is not Wednesday.   (antecedent denied)

The two other possible versions of the argument are *invalid* and take one of these forms:

If A, then B.	If A, then B.
B.	Not A.
Therefore, A.	Therefore, not B.

Using the same hypothesis, "If today is Wednesday, I must go to class," the invalidity of these forms becomes evident:

If today is Wednesday, [then] I must go to class.   (hypothesis)
I must go to class.   (consequent affirmed)
Therefore, today is Wednesday.   (antecedent affirmed)

or

If today is Wednesday, [then] I must go to class.   (hypothesis)
Today is not Wednesday.   (antecedent denied)
Therefore, I need not go to class today.   (consequent denied)

The problem in the first argument is apparent: Just because the arguer must go to class does not necessarily imply that today is Wednesday, unless Wednesday is the only day the speaker's classes meet (and the hypothesis tells us nothing on that score). It is in the second premise, which affirms the consequent, that the argument goes astray. If we grant the truth of the hypothesis and of the consequent, we still cannot grant the truth of the antecedent on the basis of this argument.

The problem with the second argument is equally evident. It offers a hypothesis, denies the antecedent, and on that basis attempts to deny the consequent. But just because the antecedent is not true or does not happen does not necessarily prevent the consequent's being true or taking place.

Evaluating hypothetical arguments is relatively simple, then: There are only two key terms to grasp (antecedent and consequent) and four ways to construct arguments from hypotheses, two valid and two invalid.

Either/Or Arguments   Alternative arguments are nearly as simple. They are "either . . . or . . . " arguments in which the arguer explores two or more alternatives and rejects all the possible alternatives but one:

Either A or B.	Either A or B.
Not A.	Not B.
Therefore, B.	Therefore, A.

Either A, B, or C.	Either A, B, C, or D.
Not A.	Not A.
Not B.	Not C.
Therefore, C.	Not D.
	Therefore, B.

All these arguments, and any number of others, are valid. They share the characteristic that every given alternative but one is denied. They share as well a necessary assumption: At least one of the alternatives must be true. But they also share an assumption that may not seem necessary at first: More then one of the alternatives may be true; in fact, all the alternatives may be true. Therefore, when a friend says, "I will either move to Boston or go to graduate school," she is saying that she will definitely do one of the two—but she also may do both, if she enrolls at a graduate school in Boston.

Bear in mind that the second logical possibility—that more than one alternative may be true—is the most difficult part of evaluating and creating either/or arguments. In ordinary conversation we tend to act as if all alternatives are mutually exclusive: Either your friend will move to Boston or she will go to graduate school, but not both. Such mutual exclusivity must be explicitly stated or the argument may prove fallacious, as these are:

Either A or B.		Either A or B.
A.	or	B.
Therefore, not B.		Therefore, not A.

You can repair the reasoning in such arguments by arguing between obviously contrary alternatives—alternatives that cannot both be true at the same time, as in "Either it is the day for the board meeting or it is not"—or by stating explicitly, "but not both": Either A or B, but not both. A. Therefore, not B. This is a valid argument. But you must be positive that the alternatives *are* mutually exclusive, as in the following cases:

> Either I will wash my car or I will let it remain dirty.
> I will wash my car.
> Therefore, I am not going to let it remain dirty.

> Either I will take my car to the carwash, or I will wash it here at home (but not both).
> I have decided not to wash it at home.
> Therefore, I will take my car to the carwash.

These examples are so simple and obvious that the conclusions need not even be stated to be clearly understood. But all too often we construct arguments that only *appear* to include mutually exclusive options. The very real difficulty is to make sure that we have considered all the possible alternatives. Either/or arguments can oversimplify situations that are not simple. Complex issues cannot always be reduced to two or three alternatives. When we do so, we commit what has been called the **black or white fallacy.** For example:

> Either we must focus on technological research and education or we will surrender our world position to the Japanese.
> We will not surrender our world position to the Japanese.
> So we must focus on technological research and education.

Are these our only options? Arguments of this sort treat issues as cut-and-dried, black and white—overlooking all the possible shades of gray, all the other possibilities. Study either/or arguments—those of others and your own—with care. Do they identify *all* the possible alternatives?

EXERCISE 6–7

A. Are the following if/then and either/or arguments valid or invalid? If they are invalid, explain why.

B. Identify from the following arguments one that you could support in a short paper (say, five pages) written for an audience of your rhetoric classmates. Identify another that would not work well in a written argument of that length for that audience. In each case, explain your reasons.

1. People who have been abused as children either abhor violence as adults or tend to repeat the pattern of abuse with their own children. We can conclude therefore that former child abuse victims who abhor violence will not repeat the pattern of abuse with their own children.

2. If young children participate intensely in competitive sports programs, they usually suffer physically and emotionally. Many children today have suffered physically and emotionally, and competitive sports programs must be held accountable for the damage.

3. If Congress continues to extend rights and privileges to senior citizens as aging Baby Boomers swell the ranks of that group, younger workers in this country will find the costs of supporting their elders through Social Security, Medicare, and other programs to be so prohibitive that they will be unable to

enjoy basic privileges themselves—such as home ownership. Congress is continuing to expand the privileges accorded to the elderly, so many people who are now in college cannot expect ever to be able to afford homes of their own.

4. The world is caught between two opposing tendencies. One, "Jihad," is the planet's growing fragmentation along tribal and sectarian lines. The other, "McWorld," is the planet's growing electronic, commercial, and cultural integration. Neither tendency is benign. If the global future is to pit Jihad's centrifugal whirlwind against McWorld's centripetal black hole, the outcome is unlikely to be democratic. Luckily for the planet, democracy has always played itself out against the odds.

—Adapted from Benjamin R. Barber,
"Jihad vs. McWorld," *Atlantic,* March 1992

5. If environmental smoke from cigarettes—so-called second-hand smoking—causes cancer, researchers should find significant amounts of smoke particles in the bodies of those exposed to others' smoking. Researchers have not found smoke particles in appreciable amounts in the bodies of people so exposed. So environmental smoke does not cause cancer.

—Adapted from Christopher Caldwell,
"Smoke Gets in Your Eyes," *American Spectator,* May 1992

I have called deduction "a perfectly natural process of reasoning," but at this point it may seem to you to be anything but natural: a process involving unfamiliar terms and rules, and too many ways to go wrong. However, by the same token, if you have been playing tennis for many years, and a tennis-pro friend suddenly comments on your serve, you may become so self-conscious for a short time that you double-fault every one. But after you get over the initial awkwardness at having something pointed out to you that you were accustomed to doing without reflection, you will return to a successful and quite possibly improved serve. Your improvement will be all the more marked if your serve was poor to begin with, and no one had ever before told you what you were doing wrong.

As with tennis, so with argument? Not in all respects, of course, but you may be surprised to find that, if you have grasped the rules and relationships set out here, you will recognize similar processes of reasoning in the reading selections that follow. Moreover, you will be able to judge in a specific and conscious way the readings and the arguments they contain, and to refute invalid arguments. Read the following selections first for enjoyment, and then you will enjoy all the more seeing how they use deductive reasoning to amuse you or to challenge your own opinions. If you agree with the arguments presented, you will now be able to say why; if you disagree, you now have the tools with which to refute invalid arguments, and to construct sound arguments of your own.

READINGS

SHOULD WE ABOLISH THE PRESIDENCY?

Barbara Tuchman

1   Owing to the steady accretion of power in the executive over the last forty years, the institution of the Presidency is not now functioning as the Constitution intended, and this malfunction has become perilous to the state. What needs to be abolished, or fundamentally modified, I believe, is not the executive power as such but the executive power as exercised by a single individual.

2   We could substitute true Cabinet government by a directorate of six, to be nominated as a slate by each party and elected as a slate for a single six-year term with a rotating chairman, each to serve for a year as in the Swiss system. The Chairman's vote would carry the weight of two to avoid a tie. (Although a five-man Cabinet originally seemed preferable when I first proposed the plan in 1968, I find that the main departments of government, one for each member of the Cabinet to administer, cannot be rationally arranged under fewer than six headings—see below.)

3   Expansion of the Presidency in the twentieth century has dangerously altered the careful tripartite balance of governing powers established by the Constitution. The office has become too complex and its reach too extended to be trusted to the fallible judgment of any one individual. In today's world no one man is adequate for the reliable disposal of power that can affect the lives of millions—which may be one reason lately for the notable non-emergence of great men. Russia no longer entrusts policy-making to one man. In China governing power resides, technically at least, in the party's central executive committee, and when Mao goes the inheritors are likely to be more collective than otherwise.

4   In the United States the problem of one-man rule has become acute for two reasons. First, Congress has failed to perform its envisioned role as safeguard against the natural tendency of an executive to become dictatorial, and equally failed to maintain or even exercise its own rights through the power of the purse.

5   It is clear, moreover, that we have not succeeded in developing in this country an organ of representative democracy that can match the Presidency in positive action or prestige. A Congress that can abdicate its right to ratify the act of war, that can obediently pass an enabling resolution on false information and remain helpless to remedy the situation afterward, is likewise not functioning as the Constitution intended. Since the failure traces to the lower house—the body most directly representing the citizenry and holding the power of the purse—responsibility must be put where it belongs: in the voter. The failure of Congress is a failure of the people.

6   The second reason, stemming perhaps from the age of television, is the growing tendency of the Chief Executive to form policy as a reflection of his personality and ego needs. Because his image can be projected before fifty or sixty or a hundred million people, the image takes over; it becomes an obsession. He must appear firm, he must appear dominant, he must never on any account appear "soft," and by some magic transformation which he has come to believe in, he *must* make history's list of "great" Presidents.

7   While I have no pretensions to being a psychohistorian, even an ordinary citizen can see the symptoms of this disease in the White House since 1960, and its latest example in the Christmas bombing of North Vietnam. That disproportionate use of lethal force becomes less puzzling if it is seen as a gesture to exhibit the Commander-in-Chief ending the war with a bang, not a whimper.

8   Personal government can get beyond control in the U.S. because the President is subject to no advisers who hold office independently of him. Cabinet ministers and agency chiefs and national-security advisers can be and are—as we have lately seen—hired and fired at whim, which means that they are without constitutional power. The result is that too much power and therefore too much risk has become subject to the idiosyncrasies of a single individual at the top, whoever he may be.

9   Spreading the executive power among six eliminates dangerous challenges to the ego. Each of the six would be designated from the time of nomination as secretary of a specific department of government affairs, viz.:

1. Foreign, including military and CIA. (Military affairs should not, as at present, have a Cabinet-level office because the military ought to be solely an instrument of policy, never a policy-making body.)
2. Financial, including Treasury, taxes, budget, and tariffs.
3. Judicial, covering much the same as at present.
4. Business (or Production and Trade), including Commerce, Transportation, and Agriculture.
5. Physical Resources, including Interior, Parks, Forests, Conservation, and Environment Protection.
6. Human Affairs, including HEW, Labor, and the cultural endowments.

10   It is imperative that the various executive agencies be incorporated under the authority of one or another of these departments.

11   Cabinet government is a perfectly feasible operation. While this column was being written, the Australian Cabinet, which governs like the British by collective responsibility, overrode its Prime Minister on the issue of exporting sheep to China, and the West German Cabinet took emergency action on foreign-exchange control.

12   The usual objection one hears in this country that a war emergency requires quick decision by one man seems to me invalid. Even in that case, no President acts without consultation. If he can summon the Joint Chiefs, so can a Chairman summon his Cabinet. Nor need the final decision be unilateral.

Any belligerent action not clearly enough in the national interest to evoke unanimous or strong majority decision by the Cabinet ought not to be undertaken.

13 How the slate would be chosen in the primaries is a complication yet to be resolved. And there is the drawback that Cabinet government could not satisfy the American craving for a father-image or hero or superstar. The only solution I can see to that problem would be to install a dynastic family in the White House for ceremonial purposes, or focus the craving entirely upon the entertainment world, or else to grow up.

Analysis of Barbara Tuchman, "Should We Abolish the Presidency?"

In this essay Barbara Tuchman argues for the replacement of the office and functions of president of the United States with a six-person cabinet in which all the former executive functions would be vested. Her thesis, carefully qualified, is stated in the first paragraph: "What needs to be abolished, or fundamentally modified, is . . . the executive power as exercised by a single individual." Her argument centers on the reasons for this proposal, reasons that are grounded first in the practicability and justness of a cabinet government in contrast to the abuses of power inevitable in an individual chief executive. Tuchman is not concerned with proving the existence of these abuses; she anticipates that her readers will agree with her basic assumptions.

  To evaluate the argument properly, we must ferret out its specific assumptions and examine them. Two enthymemes are buried in the first sentence of Tuchman's essay. Working backward from the major conclusion, the thesis, and looking for the premises, both implicit and explicit, we can reconstruct the deductive arguments that form the foundation of Tuchman's essay:

> The presidency was intended by the Constitution to function as one of three *equal* branches of government.   (Implicit Premise)
>
> The presidency is not now functioning as one of three *equal* branches of government.   (Implicit Premise)
>
> [Therefore,] the presidency is not now functioning as the Constitution intended.   (Stated Conclusion and Premise to Second Argument)
>
> What does not function as the Constitution intended is perilous to the State and should be abolished or fundamentally modified.   (Implicit Premise)
>
> [Therefore,] the presidency should be abolished or fundamentally modified.   (Stated Conclusion and Thesis of Essay)

Some of the implicit statements, as is often the case, comprise the heart of the argument. The first implicit premise, that the executive was intended to be a branch of government equal in power to the Congress and the Supreme Court, is not controversial. Tuchman accordingly offers no lengthy support for this premise; but her "first justification" for abolishing the one-person presidency loosely supports the premise by advancing the argument that one person cannot well fulfill the Constitution's aims of equality for the executive branch. The second implicit premise—that the presidency is not equal to, but rather stronger than, the Congress—is subject to debate. Tuchman supports that premise with her "second justification," showing just how the president's power has come to be so disproportionately great. She may, however, beg the question of whether or not the power *is* disproportionately great. She offers but a single specific example of excessive power: President Nixon's authorization of the Christmas 1972 bombing of North Vietnam. And the decision to drop those bombs was made collectively with members of the cabinet and the military.

We might also have some trouble with the third implicit premise, forming part of the second argument in the chain: that what does not function as the Constitution intended is perilous to the State. The framers of the Constitution would marvel at half the functions of American government as we know it today. For example, the two-party political system, which emerged after the Constitution was adopted, is now integral to our governmental structure. Governments can and must mature and evolve as the world changes. Tuchman cannot assume that we will automatically grant this implicit part of her argument, on which much of the rest of it hangs.

If we do grant Tuchman's implicit premises and her conclusions, we must grant that her argument is sound (true premises logically linked); all that remains is to ask, "But replace the president with what?" The second paragraph provides Tuchman's answer to that question, and the balance of the essay offers her reasons. Except for its lack of a formal conclusion, the essay follows the divisions of a classical argument: The first two paragraphs introduce the writer's thesis; the third gives background and preparatory information; paragraphs 4 through 11 develop the points of the main argument (divided between attention to the problem, in paragraphs 4 through 8, and the solution, in paragraphs 9 through 11); and the last two paragraphs offer a refutation of the opposing viewpoints.

Loosely related to the first premise of the thesis argument, as noted above, is Tuchman's "first justification" that one-man rule is uncommon and unwise in the world today: "No one man is adequate for the reliable disposal of power that can affect millions." Tuchman illustrates her point with an analogy comparing the government of the United States to those of other countries, using as examples the governments of Russia and China. Given that Russia was (when Tuchman wrote this argument) and China still is perceived by Americans as being more authoritarian than our own country, the analogy has an ironic force. We have more power vested in a single individual than does either of these countries, for Tuchman has been proven largely correct in her post-Mao prediction for China. Paragraphs 4 and 5 argue causally that the presidency got into trouble because the Congress became weak (no longer counterbalancing the presidency), and the Congress became weak because the citizens elected weak and unqualified representatives, and that therefore "the failure of [the presidency] is a failure of the people."

As a second justification for replacing the presidency with a six-member cabinet, Tuchman offers a second causal analysis: Television has inspired an obsession with "image" on the part of the chief executive; and the obsession with image has led in turn to policy-making based on the image that policy projects, rather than its inherent worth or usefulness. Paragraph 7 argues what Tuchman sees as a consequence of this image-consciousness and focus on the individual character of the president. This single individual has no peers to assist him, no one who may not be fired at the president's whim. Stated as syllogisms, the problem is that

> The U.S. president has no independent advisors. (Stated Premise)
>
> A president with no independent advisors is a president who has too much power. (Implicit Premise)
>
> The U.S. president has too much power.
> (Stated Conclusion of First Argument; Premise of Second)
>
> A president who has too much power presents too great a risk to the country. (Stated Premise)
>
> Therefore, the U.S. president [as the office now exists] presents too great a risk to the country. (Implicit Conclusion)

The argument is valid. If it has any weakness, it is likely to lie in the implicit premise—is a president with no independent advisors automatically a president who has too much power? Surely his power must depend more directly on what has been granted by the provisions of the Constitution, and on the strength of Congress and the Supreme Court. If we find the premises to be true, however, we must grant the conclusion. The one-person presidency is dangerous.

A specific solution to the "dangerous challenges to the ego" inherent in a one-person executive is spelled out in paragraphs 9 and 10, in which Tuchman proposes six cabinet positions and indicates their respective responsibilities. In paragraph 11 she offers analogical support for leadership-by-committee by citing the successful cabinets of Australia and West Germany, which are empowered to overrule their respective prime ministers. Then, in paragraphs 12 and 13, Tuchman anticipates key objections to her plan and defends it against those objections. She offers no formal conclusion, but ends with an enthymeme tinged with sarcasm: "The only solution I can see to that problem [the 'American craving for a father-image or hero or superstar'] would be to install a dynastic family in the White House for ceremonial purposes, or focus the craving entirely upon the entertainment world, or else to grow up." We need no prompting to see which of the three alternatives Tuchman regards as the only acceptable one.

QUESTIONS AND IDEAS FOR DISCUSSION

1. This essay was written (during the 1973–74 political upheaval that has been known almost from the beginning as "Watergate") in an attempt to offer a constructive solution to the problems created by the power vested in the presidency. How does Tuchman use definition to restrict her thesis?

2. Tuchman's solution to the problem of the presidency can be expressed as an alternative argument:

   > The presidency must be administered either by an individual or by a group. It should not be administered by an individual. Therefore, it should be administered by a group.

   Based on the argument Tuchman gives, create a categorical syllogism that supports (and concludes with) the minor premise of the argument just given: "The presidency should not be administered by an individual."

3. "The problem of one-man rule has become acute for two reasons." What are those reasons? Is this a deductive argument? Explain.

4. "The usual objection one hears in this country that a war emergency requires quick decision by one man seems to me invalid." Examine Tuchman's argument refuting that objection. How does she use the word *invalid* here?

5. Is Tuchman's argument well-written? Discuss, with specific reference to the text.

6. Propose a different solution to the problem of the presidency from that offered by Tuchman. List some of the reasons, evidence, and examples you would use to support your own argument. In what respects might your proposed argument be stronger than Tuchman's? In what respects might it be weaker? How would you deal with the weaker aspects in a written argument?

WE'LL NEVER CONQUER SPACE

Arthur C. Clarke

1 Man will never conquer space. Such a statement may sound ludicrous, now that our rockets are already 100 million miles beyond the moon and the first human travelers are preparing to leave the atmosphere. Yet it expresses a truth which our forefathers knew, one we have forgotten—and our descendants must learn again, in heartbreak and loneliness.

2 Our age is in many ways unique, full of events and phenomena which never occurred before and can never happen again. They distort our thinking, making us believe that what is true now will be true forever, though perhaps on a larger scale. Because we have annihilated distance on this planet, we imagine that we can do it once again. The facts are far otherwise, and we will see them more clearly if we forget the present and turn our minds towards the past.

3 To our ancestors, the vastness of the earth was a dominant fact controlling their thoughts and lives. In all earlier ages than ours, the world was wide indeed, and no man could ever see more than a tiny fraction of its immensity. A few hundred miles—a thousand, at the most—was infinity. Only a lifetime

ago, parents waved farewell to their emigrating children in the virtual certainty that they would never meet again.

4   And now, within one incredible generation, all this has changed. Over the seas where Odysseus wandered for a decade, the Rome-Beirut Comet whispers its way within the hour. And above that, the closer satellites span the distance between Troy and Ithaca in less than a minute.

5   Psychologically as well as physically, there are no longer any remote places on earth. When a friend leaves for what was once a far country, even if he has no intention of returning, we cannot feel that same sense of irrevocable separation that saddened our forefathers. We know that he is only hours away by jet liner, and that we have merely to reach for the telephone to hear his voice.

6   In a very few years, when the satellite communication network is established, we will be able to see friends on the far side of the earth as easily as we talk to them on the other side of the town. Then the world will shrink no more, for it will have become a dimensionless point.

7   But the new stage that is opening up for the human drama will never shrink as the old one has done. We have abolished space here on the little earth; we can never abolish the space that yawns between the stars. Once again we are face-to-face with immensity and must accept its grandeur and terror, its inspiring possibilities and its dreadful restraints. From a world that has become too small, we are moving out into one that will be forever too large, whose frontiers will recede from us always more swiftly than we can reach out towards them.

8   Consider first the fairly modest solar, or planetary, distances which we are now preparing to assault. The very first Lunik made a substantial impression upon them, traveling more than 200 million miles from the earth—six times the distance to Mars. When we have harnessed nuclear energy for spaceflight, the solar system will contract until it is little larger than the earth today. The remotest of the planets will be perhaps no more than a week's travel from the earth, while Mars and Venus will be only a few hours away.

9   This achievement, which will be witnessed within a century, might appear to make even the solar system a comfortable, homely place, with such giant planets as Saturn and Jupiter playing much the same role in our thoughts as do Africa or Asia today. (Their qualitative differences of climate, atmosphere and gravity, fundamental though they are, do not concern us at the moment.) To some extent this may be true, yet as soon as we pass beyond the orbit of the moon, a mere quarter-million miles away, we will meet the first of the barriers that will separate the earth from her scattered children.

10   The marvelous telephone and television network that will soon enmesh the whole world, making all men neighbors, cannot be extended into space. It will never be possible to converse with anyone on another planet.

11   Do not misunderstand this statement. Even with today's radio equipment, the problem of sending speech to the other planets is almost trivial. But the messages will take minutes—sometimes hours—on their journey, because

radio and light waves travel at the same limited speed of 186,000 miles a second.

12   Twenty years from now you will be able to listen to a friend on Mars, but the words you hear will have left his mouth at least three minutes earlier, and your reply will take a corresponding time to reach him. In such circumstances, an exchange of verbal messages is possible—but not a conversation.

13   Even in the case of the nearby moon, the 2-½ second time-lag will be annoying. At distances of more than a million miles, it will be intolerable.

14   To a culture which has come to take instantaneous communication for granted, as part of the very structure of civilized life, this "time barrier" may have a profound psychological impact. It will be a perpetual reminder of universal laws and limitations against which not all our technology can ever prevail. For it seems as certain as anything can be that no signal—still less any material—can ever travel faster than light.

15   The velocity of light is the ultimate speed limit, being part of the very structure of space and time. Within the narrow confines of the solar system, it will not handicap us too severely, once we have accepted the delays in communication which it involves. At the worst, these will amount to 20 hours—the time it takes a radio signal to span the orbit of Pluto, the outermost planet.

16   Between the three inner worlds of the earth, Mars, and Venus, it will never be more than 20 minutes—not enough to interfere seriously with commerce or administration, but more than sufficient to shatter those personal links of sound or vision that can give us a sense of direct contact with friends on earth, wherever they may be.

17   It is when we move out beyond the confines of the solar system that we come face to face with an altogether new order of cosmic reality. Even today, many otherwise educated men—like those savages who can count to three but lump together all numbers beyond four—cannot grasp the profound distinction between solar and stellar space. The first is the space enclosing our neighboring worlds, the planets; the second is that which embraces those distant suns, the stars, and it is literally millions of times greater.

18   There is no such abrupt change of scale in terrestrial affairs. To obtain a mental picture of the distance to the nearest star, as compared with the distance to the nearest planet, you must imagine a world in which the closest object to you is only five feet away—and then there is nothing else to see until you have traveled a thousand miles.

19   Many conservative scientists, appalled by these cosmic gulfs, have denied that they can ever be crossed. Some people never learn; those who 60 years ago scoffed at the possibility of flight, and ten (even five!) years ago laughed at the idea of travel to the planets, are now quite sure that the stars will always be beyond our reach. And again they are wrong, for they have failed to grasp the great lesson of our age—that if something is possible in theory, and no fundamental scientific laws oppose its realization, then sooner or later it will be achieved.

20   One day, it may be in this century, or it may be a thousand years from

now, we shall discover a really efficient means of propelling our space vehicles. Every technical device is always developed to its limit (unless it is superseded by something better), and the ultimate speed for spaceships is the velocity of light. They will never reach that goal, but they will get very close to it. And then the nearest star will be less than five years' voyaging from the earth.

21　　Our exploring ships will spread outwards from their home over an ever-expanding sphere of space. It is a sphere which will grow at almost—but never quite—the speed of light. Five years to the triple system of Alpha Centauri, 10 to the strangely-matched doublet Sirius A and B, 11 to the tantalizing enigma of 61 Cygni, the first star suspected to possess a planet. These journeys are long, but they are not impossible. Man has always accepted whatever price was necessary for his explorations and discoveries, *and the price of Space is Time.*

22　　Even voyages which may last for centuries or millennia will one day be attempted. Suspended animation has already been achieved in the laboratory, and may be the key to interstellar travel. Self-contained cosmic arks which will be tiny traveling worlds in their own right may be another solution, for they would make possible journeys of unlimited extent, lasting generation after generation.

23　　The famous Time Dilation effect predicted by the Theory of Relativity, whereby time appears to pass more slowly for a traveler moving at almost the speed of light, may be yet a third. And there are others.

24　　Looking far into the future, therefore, we must picture a slow (little more than half a billion miles an hour!) expansion of human activities outwards from the solar system, among the suns scattered across the region of the galaxy in which we now find ourselves. These suns are on the average five light-years apart; in other words, we can never get from one to the next in less than five years.

25　　To bring home what this means, let us use a down-to-earth analogy. Imagine a vast ocean, sprinkled with islands—some desert, others perhaps inhabited. On one of these islands an energetic race has just discovered the art of building ships. It is preparing to explore the ocean, but must face the fact that the very nearest island is five years' voyaging away, and that no possible improvement in the techniques of shipbuilding will ever reduce this time.

26　　In these circumstances (which are those in which we will soon find ourselves) what could the islanders achieve? After a few centuries, they might have established colonies on many of the nearby islands and have briefly explored many others. The daughter colonies might themselves have sent out further pioneers, and so a kind of chain reaction would spread the original culture over a steadily expanding area of the ocean.

27　　But now consider the effects of the inevitable, unavoidable time-lag. There could be only the most tenuous contact between the home island and its offspring. Returning messengers could report what had happened on the nearest colony—five years ago. They could never bring information more up to date than that, and dispatches from the more distant parts of the ocean would be from still further in the past—perhaps centuries behind the times. There would never be news from the other islands, but only history.

28   All the star-borne colonies of the future will be independent, whether they wish it or not. Their liberty will be inviolably protected by Time as well as Space. They must go their own way and achieve their own destiny, with no help or hindrance from Mother Earth.

29   At this point, we will move the discussion on to a new level and deal with an obvious objection. Can we be sure that the velocity of light is indeed a limiting factor? So many "impassible" barriers have been shattered in the past; perhaps this one may go the way of all the others.

30   We will not argue the point, or give the reasons why scientists believe that light can never be outraced by any form of radiation or any material object. Instead, let us assume the contrary and see just where it gets us. We will even take the most optimistic possible case and imagine that the speed of transportation may eventually become infinite.

31   Picture a time when, by the development of techniques as far beyond our present engineering as a transistor is beyond a stone axe, we can reach anywhere we please instantaneously, with no more effort than by dialing a number. This would indeed cut the universe down to size and reduce its physical immensity to nothingness. What would be left?

32   Everything that really matters. For the universe has two aspects—its scale, and its overwhelming, mind-numbing complexity. Having abolished the first, we are now face-to-face with the second.

33   What we must now try to visualize is not size, but quantity. Most people today are familiar with the simple notation which scientists use to describe large numbers; it consists merely of counting zeroes, so that a hundred becomes 10^2, a million, 10^6, a billion, 10^9 and so on. This useful trick enables us to work with quantities of any magnitude, and even defense budget totals look modest when expressed as $\$5.76 \times 10^9$ instead of $\$5,760,000,000$.

34   The number of other suns in our own galaxy (that is, the whirlpool of stars and cosmic dust of which our sun is an out-of-town member, lying in one of the remoter spiral arms) is estimated at about 10^{11}—or written in full, 100,000,000,000. Our present telescopes can observe something like 10^9 other galaxies, and they show no sign of thinning out even at the extreme limit of vision.

35   There are probably at least as many galaxies in the whole of creation as there are stars in our own galaxy, but let us confine ourselves to those we can see. They must contain a total of about 10^{11} times 10^9 stars, or 10^{20} stars altogether. 1 followed by 20 other digits is, of course, a number beyond all understanding.

36   Before such numbers, even spirits brave enough to face the challenge of the light-years must quail. The detailed examination of all the grains of sand on all the beaches of the world is a far smaller task than the exploration of the universe.

37   And so we return to our opening statement. Space can be mapped and crossed and occupied without definable limit; but it can never be conquered. When our race has reached its ultimate achievements, and the stars themselves are scattered no more widely than the seed of Adam, even then we shall still be like ants crawling on the face of the earth. The ants have covered the world, but have they conquered it—for what do their countless colonies know of it, or of each other?

38   So it will be with us as we spread outwards from Mother Earth, loosening the bonds of kinship and understanding, hearing faint and belated rumours at second—or third—or thousandth-hand of an ever-dwindling fraction of the entire human race.

39   Though Earth will try to keep in touch with her children, in the end all the efforts of her archivists and historians will be defeated by time and distance, and the sheer bulk of material. For the number of distinct societies or nations, when our race is twice its present age, may be far greater than the total number of all the men who have ever lived up to the present time.

40   We have left the realm of human comprehension in our vain effort to grasp the scale of the universe: so it must always be, sooner rather than later.

41   When you are next outdoors on a summer night, turn your head towards the zenith. Almost vertically above you will be shining the brightest star of the northern skies—Vega of the Lyre, 26 years away at the speed of light, near enough the point-of-no-return for us short-lived creatures. Past this blue-white beacon, 50 times as brilliant as our sun, we may send our minds and bodies, but never our hearts.

42   For no man will ever turn homewards from beyond Vega, to greet again those he knew and loved on the earth.

QUESTIONS AND IDEAS FOR DISCUSSION

1. Comment on Clarke's strategy in his introductory paragraph—beginning with a short declaration of his thesis, ending with a mysterious prediction. Is the introduction effective or alienating? Why?

2. Express Clarke's main argument as a syllogism with the conclusion, "Man will never conquer space." Is the argument sound?

3. Clarke acknowledges the probability of future space travel but paradoxically denies the possibility of conquering space. The paradox is resolved by his restricted definition of *conquer*. Much of his argument hinges on the definitions of this and other key terms. What other words does Clarke restrict in meaning in order to prove his points?

4. Do you agree with Clarke's assertion that "if something is possible in theory, and no fundamental scientific laws oppose its realization, then sooner or later it will be achieved"? Evaluate his reasoning.

5. Do you ordinarily read with interest essays and articles about space and other scientific subjects? If so, how well does Clarke's writing measure up—in ease of reading, interesting detail, careful descriptions—to other essays

written for lay readers on scientific subjects? Give illustrations from the text. If, on the other hand, you usually have no great interest in subjects like these, how successfully does Clarke overcome your bias against his subject matter? Again, give illustrations from the text.

A FEW KIND WORDS FOR AFFIRMATIVE ACTION

Hosea L. Martin

1   What with all the debate about the current versions of the Civil Rights bill, I feel it's time for me to raise my voice. I'm for affirmative action. I can make the argument on economic grounds—the disproportionate number of blacks out of work in this country should be enough evidence that the policy isn't taking jobs away from whites.

2   But there's a second reason for my bias. Except for a sweaty warehousing job that I was forced to take when laid off in 1984, all the jobs I've had since graduating from college in 1960 were because of affirmative action. In most cases, I was one of only a handful of black managers or professionals in an organization, and a few times I found myself to be the only one in a department. I never got around to feeling lonely, because I was too busy being grateful for being on the payroll.

3   Nor did I have gnawing doubts about my qualifications for the jobs I held. I know that it's currently popular to believe that I always sat silently in the darkest corner of the conference room, ashamed that I was hired for "political reasons," but that wasn't the way it was for me.

4   The truth is, I sat as close to the boss as possible and pontificated as much as anyone else at the table. I realized that somewhere there was someone who could do my job better than I could, but I also knew that every person in the room would have to say the same thing if he or she were strictly honest. Every single one of us—black and white, male and female—had been hired for reasons beyond our being able to do the job.

5   That's the case with just about every job in this country. There's a lot of hoopla about the U.S. being a meritocracy, but even a casual examination of performances tells us that this is a myth.

6   I know that this is hard to accept. Quite often the reaction to hearing it is similar to that of a swaggering gunfighter of the Old West. "Somebody's faster 'n me? You're loco!" But somewhere there was someone quicker on the draw. Ask any ghost from Boot Hill.

7   It's the same in today's job market. Every person wants to believe that he or she was selected over hundreds of other applicants because he or she was the "fastest gun." 'Tain't so. There probably were dozens of faster guns in that stack of resumes on the personnel director's desk, but you, if you were the lucky person who got the job, were judged to be the "best fit."

8   Being the best fit for a job entails more than having the best set of credentials (e.g., good grades, high test scores, impressive record). Usually, the people who apply for a particular job have met all the criteria—education, experience, career expectations, etc.—that the ad asked for, and you can be sure that a low-level clerk has been instructed to screen out those applications that fail to clear this initial barrier. What winds up on the personnel director's desk is a stack of resumes that are astonishingly uniform. A black Stanford MBA may have survived the cut, but you can bet that a black high-school dropout didn't.

9   The task of the personnel director (or whoever does the hiring) would be easy if all he or she had to do was pick the person who could "do the job"—chances are, anyone in the stack could—but there are other considerations that have to be made, and these considerations aren't always limited to race and sex. Satisfying these considerations means responding to pressures outside as well as inside the organization.

10   If that Stanford MBA is selected, and finds himself the only black person in his department, he shouldn't feel deflated when he learns that he owes his good fortune to affirmative action. Eventually he'll find out that just about everybody he's working with got special consideration for one reason or another. Some had connections who were able to get them interviewed and hired; others had attended the "right" schools; still others had been hired because they were from a particular part of the country, or were members of a particular class, religion, nationality or fraternity. (I'll never forget when, as an Army clerk, I had to type dozens of application letters for a white officer who was being discharged; he never brought up his college academic record—which I knew was horrible—but in every single letter he mentioned that he was a member of Phi-something fraternity. He got a great job.)

11   Seldom will you find a person who got a job because he was the very best at doing it. No? Come on, are you trying to tell me that Dan Quayle was the best that George Bush could find?

12   Sure, there are some exceptionally capable people, and I've observed that they don't gripe about affirmative action; they know that, sooner or later, talent will out. The run-of-the-mill plodders are the ones who complain that affirmative action is blocking their career path; take away this excuse and they'd probably blame their lack of progress on sunspots. For them, it's always something.

13   Affirmative action is needed in education as well as in the workplace. Those who criticize affirmative action in their campaign against "political correctness" are wrong. Without the policy there would be a sharp drop in the already-small number of black professionals that colleges produce to serve inner-city communities and small towns. The affirmative action programs that raised the share of minorities in medical school to 10% in 1980 from about 5% in the 1960s produced tremendous benefits to society.

14   As for me, each morning I go to work with pride and confidence. I know I can do the job. I also know that I'm a beneficiary of a law—good ol' affirmative action—that does not require an organization to hire a person

who clearly doesn't have the education, credentials or skills that a job demands. Any organization that has done this is guilty of ignoring qualified minority people, and of cynically setting someone up for failure. Such an organization began with the premise that no minority person could do the job, and set out to prove it.

15   One final question: If it's true that affirmative action is cramming the offices and board rooms of corporate America with blacks, why do I see so few of them when I'm walking around San Francisco's financial district on my lunch hour?

QUESTIONS AND IDEAS FOR DISCUSSION

1. What is Martin's thesis? Can it and its main supporting points be expressed as a valid syllogism? Try to do so. Is the argument convincing?
2. Discuss Martin's inductive support for his premises—his use of example, analogy, and causal reasoning. Which does he use most effectively?
3. Is Martin's persona—your sense of him when you read his words—a strong and effective one? How does he make it so, or why does he fail to?
4. How well does Martin organize his essay? What, if anything, would you change if this were your own work? If you were told that you had to cut its length to fit a magazine or newspaper column length restriction, what would you cut out? How would doing so affect the strength of the writing? How would it affect the strength of the argument?

Suggestions for Writing and Further Discussion

1. "On the contrary, Watson, you can see everything. You fail, however, to reason from what you see. You are too timid in drawing your inferences."
                                                                    —Sherlock Holmes

   Write an essay in which you describe something or someone you have seen (perhaps an old man who sits on a bench at your bus stop every day, or a package abandoned under a tree near the library, or a letter left unopened on your roommate's dresser) and "reason from what you see."
2. Listen to the generalizations you and the people around you use in a day. Write an essay, addressed to an audience of your peers, in which you oppose the use or defend the necessity of broad generalizations. Consider this the question: Can we function without generalization? You may find it helpful to review the discussion of stereotyping in Chapter 2 and the discussion of generalizing from particulars in Chapter 5.
3. Write an essay, addressed to Barbara Tuchman, in which you refute her argument in "Should We Abolish the Presidency?" or offer a solution to the problems of the presidency that is different from hers.

4. ... the great lesson of our age [is] that if something is possible in theory, and no fundamental scientific laws oppose its realization, then sooner or later it will be achieved.

    —Arthur Clarke

    Construct an essay with a conditional deductive framework in which Arthur Clarke's hypothesis, above, is the major premise. The "something" that he argues eventually will be achieved is travel to the stars. Your "something" might be the cloning of human life, a worldwide international government, robot housekeepers, the elimination of cancer, the three-minute mile, or some other theoretical possibility. Any source material you use to support your case must be documented appropriately.

5. If you have held a paying job, use your own experiences and those of people you know to support or refute one of the claims voiced by Hosea L. Martin. You might choose among the following:

    Every single one of us—black and white, male and female—had been hired for reasons beyond our being able to do the job. (paragraph 4)

    There's a lot of hoopla about the U.S. being a meritocracy, but even a casual examination of performances tells us this is a myth. (5)

    [S]ooner or later, talent will out. (12)

    Affirmative action is needed in education as well as in the workplace. (13)

    Such an organization began with the premise that no minority person could do the job, and set out to prove it. (14)

7

Testing Arguments: Fallacies

"Will you walk into my parlor?" said the spider to the fly;
"'Tis the prettiest little parlor that ever you did spy."
—Mary Howitt, "The Spider and the Fly"

WHY STUDY FALLACIES?

Fallacies are arguments gone awry. Most of the time we think of fallacious arguments as intentionally deceptive, but that view is oversimplified. Not every user of fallacies intends to ensnare the unwary in a sticky web of lies. Many fallacious arguments result from the arguer's carelessness or mistakes; so to say that fallacies are "lies" is not always fair. On the other hand, to call fallacies "errors in reasoning" connotes lack of intention, and fallacies can be deliberate, as the fly in the poem learns to her sorrow.

After you have reviewed the fallacies described in this chapter, you can check your own essays to make sure that you have avoided fallacious arguments. If your argument seems to have broken down at some point, very likely you will find some inadvertent fallacy in the reasoning or evidence. You can also test the arguments you read: When something "seems wrong" in others' arguments, a close look often will reveal a fallacy.

All the same, won't identifying and studying fallacies permit the unscrupulous to use them more effectively, or tempt the scrupulous to do likewise? Perhaps, but if enough people become aware of fallacies and how they persuade, fewer people will be able to get away with using fallacies to deceive. We will never be completely invulnerable to fallacious appeals, of course; we are susceptible on an emotional level even to appeals that we regard skeptically. Jeffrey

Schrank's essay "The Language of Advertising Claims" (included in the readings for this chapter) has this caution for the overconfident:

> Although few people admit to being greatly influenced by ads, surveys and sales figures show that a well-designed advertising campaign . . . works below the level of conscious awareness and it works even on those who claim immunity to its message. Ads are designed to have an effect while being laughed at, belittled, and all but ignored.

In examining the fallacies and their role in persuasion, we will look particularly at fallacies in advertising and in political rhetoric, for those two arenas provide many examples of fallacious argument. But we will examine, too, the role of fallacies in everyday life and everyday conversation. Max Shulman's "Love Is a Fallacy" offers a tongue-in-cheek look at the fallacy of trying to apply logic to love. And magazine advertisements illustrate the use of fallacious emotional appeals in place of reason to sell products.

KINDS OF FALLACIES

In this chapter we will consider some of the more common ways that arguments go astray. You can commit fallacies both in arguments and in counterarguments (attempts to refute an argument). The chart on page 202 summarizes the fallacies alphabetically.

FALLACIES IN ARGUMENTS

Fallacies in arguments occur in two basic ways: Something goes wrong either with what the premises state or with the way they are logically connected to the conclusion. Thus, we may say that a fallacy occurs when a conclusion "does not follow" from the premises offered in its support. People often use the Latin term for this general problem, saying that an argument commits a **non sequitur** (which literally means "does not follow").

Appeal to Pity

The appeal to pity is an evasive tactic. If you appeal to your readers' pity fallaciously, you do not offer an argument so much as a hard-luck story designed to make them feel sorry for you. Of all fallacies, the appeal to pity may be the hardest to resist, particularly when the problems are indeed touching and the difficulties real. To further complicate matters, the appeal to pity has its legitimate uses. Why else but for pity would anyone become a blood donor or do volunteer work? However, an appeal to pity is unacceptable if you offer it as self-justification or as an excuse for a claim instead of a substantive reason for the claim.

Common Fallacies

Fallacies in Arguments

Appeal to Pity	Appealing to reader's compassion instead of offering substantive reasons for a claim (sometimes called by its Latin name, *ad misericordiam*)
Appeal to Popular Sentiments	Appealing to generally favored ideas, values, or symbols as a means of winning assent to a claim without confronting substantive issues (sometimes called, in Latin, *ad populum*)
Begging the Question	Offering support for a claim that is really the claim itself restated (also known as circular reasoning)
False Dilemma	Assuming that only certain options exist when more options are available
Faulty Analogy	Offering similarities between examples as proof of a claim
Guilt by Association	Failing to consider a linking category in its entirety (more formally known as undistributed middle term)
Hasty Generalization	Generalizing from an inadequate sampling
Post Hoc	Treating as a causal relationship what may be only part of a cause or may be merely a coincidence (short for *post hoc ergo propter hoc*, meaning "after this, therefore because of this")

Fallacies in Counterarguments

Lack of Contrary Evidence	Offering the lack of proof for an opposing viewpoint as "proof" of one's own claim
Oversimplification	Omitting crucial points or qualifications to make an argument appear insubstantial or even silly
Personal Attack	Disparaging an arguer rather than his or her argument (also called by its Latin name, *ad hominem*)
Shifting Ground	Shifting, often subtly, from arguing the point in question to arguing another point
Straw Man	Exaggerating premises and conclusions to make another's argument seem ridiculous
Trivial Objections	Assuming that a quibble with minor points or poorly chosen examples in itself disproves a contention

Perhaps you know a student who has relied on the following fallacy: "I couldn't concentrate on the test because my dog died yesterday and my girlfriend just walked out on me." Or, "If I don't pass this course, I'll lose my scholarship and have to dig ditches for the rest of my life." Of course, the fallacious appeal to pity is hardly restricted to the academic sphere. Here are some examples from other fields:

> I have spent all my adult life working for you in the State Senate. I have not gotten rich at the taxpayers' expense. Be loyal to one who has been loyal to you; vote for me once again.

> Don't yell at me for not getting the report out on time. My cat ran away last week and I've been too brokenhearted to concentrate on my work.

> Give me the job—I need it more than do the other applicants.

Appeal to Popular Sentiments

The appeal to popular sentiments is just the sort of "flag-waving, apple pie, and motherhood" fallacy that seems all too obvious to mislead anyone. Observe one political campaign, however, and you may be surprised how often the appeal occurs. Flag-waving is not fallacious in itself, of course, but it becomes fallacious if you use it as a decoy: "Patriotism and pride are what make our country great. Vote for Matt Edwards and continue that great tradition." Matt Edwards has given us no substantive reasons to vote for him.

And what about that apple pie? Odds are that it will be advertised as "natural," another popular favorite, but just what does "natural" mean, when the list of ingredients includes chemical preservatives? The range of popular sentiments goes far beyond politics and labeling; it includes a host of emotional appeals, including those associations with dear old Mom. A quick look through a few political and charitable solicitations will reveal many appeals to popular sentiments, such as the following (here, often to specifically *American* sentiments and values):

> Making decent, affordable health care available to all Americans is the Gray Panthers' highest priority.
> —Gray Panthers Project Fund solicitation

> The people at HALT (Help Abolish Legal Tyranny] ... have served notice on the legal profession. It is time to bring the legal system closer to the people, HALT members say.
> —California lawyer quoted in HALT solicitation

> If you have any doubts about becoming a member, just remember that every day that passes means 4,400 more American babies are killed by abortion.
> — National Right to Life Committee, Inc., solicitation

> Your immediate tax-deductible contribution will help us defend and preserve reproductive freedoms on *many fronts* while continuing our national programs of service and education.
> —Planned Parenthood Federation of America, Inc., solicitation

Begging the Question

An argument that begs the question essentially goes nowhere; it uses the conclusion as support for the conclusion. "I can't lose weight because I'm too fat to exercise" begs the question. It claims, "I'm too fat because I'm too fat." Another example of this argument is the following: "We can't justify higher salaries for public school teaching positions because we can't get good teachers." Higher pay might *attract* better teachers and enable the school systems to keep their good teachers. Spelled out more explicitly, the argument says, "We can't pay public school teachers more [in order to attract good teachers] because we can't attract good teachers [without more pay]." Another common name for this fallacy is **circular reasoning.**

False Dilemma

This is the "either/or" fallacy, sometimes called the "black or white" fallacy. If you set up an argument proposing alternatives, you must be sure that you have considered *all* the possibilities. Typically this fallacy occurs when you think only a couple of options exist when in fact more do. Review the section on "Alternative Reasoning" in Chapter 6, pages 182–183, for a fuller discussion of reasonable and unreasonable either/or arguments.

> Either we will maintain a military presence in famine-stricken African countries or we will abandon millions of starving people. [But what about a civilian presence? What if stable governments resume control? What if the drought ends?]

> I have to go to Dad's alma mater or else pay my own way through school. [What about possible scholarships? What about Mom's alma mater?]

> Given the tight job market in your field, either take this low-salaried, entry-level position or find yourself with no job at all. [But what about interviewing in another state? Or taking a job less directly in your field?]

Faulty Analogy

Like the appeal to pity or the appeal to popular sentiments, analogy has important nonfallacious uses. Figurative analogies, or metaphors, create mental images that can illuminate an unfamiliar subject. Literal analogies compare something complex or new to something else that is more familiar, as an aid to comprehension. A is like B in many significant ways, so we should treat A as we treat B. Judges reason this way in applying precedent (previously decided cases) in their written opinions: *Smith v. Doe* resembles *Jones v. Roe* in most significant respects; therefore, we can correctly hold in *Smith* as we held in *Jones*.

Analogies become fallacious, however, when they are overextended or offered as conclusive proof:

> The modern United States shares many traits with the ancient empire of Rome. No doubt the United States will come to the same sorry end.

To give the student senate any real power would be a terrible mistake, because to do so would be like letting the inmates run the asylum.

Guilt by Association

If your argument includes a linking category, you must at some point include *all* of that linking category in your reasoning. Otherwise, you cannot justify the connection you wish to make. You commit the fallacy of the shared characteristic, guilt (or virtue) by association—the undistributed middle term. The following arguments share this shortcoming:

> Fattening foods can make you gain weight, and nutritious foods can also make you gain weight. It therefore follows that fattening foods are nutritious.

> Of course Mark is a friend of Jean's. Mark is a friend of Ellen's, isn't he? Well, so is Jean.

Hasty Generalization

This fallacy occurs when we leap to conclusions from an inadequate sampling. Such a sampling is invariably small and unrepresentative. All of us are guilty of hasty generalizations, but we can at least be aware of them and try to keep them out of our own arguments.

> George Bush ran for president, and he is lefthanded. Bill Clinton ran for president, and he is lefthanded. Ross Perot ran for president, and he is lefthanded. Clearly, presidential candidates are lefthanded.

> All the best math students in my high school were boys. Boys are better at math than girls are.

> See the man across the aisle? He has on a tweed jacket and jeans. My history professor and my English professor always dress that way. The man across the aisle must be a professor.

Post Hoc Fallacy

This fallacy is often called by its Latin name, *post hoc ergo propter hoc* ("after this, therefore because of this") or simply *post hoc*. The English "false cause" doesn't describe the fallacy quite accurately, because argued causal relationships are fallacious not only if they are false but also if they are merely partial. For example, hard study alone will not insure your admission to medical school. Nor can you justifiably argue that your friend Jane got into the state university medical school because her mother is a state legislator. Hard study and having a parent in the legislature may *help* a person be admitted to medical school, but assuming that either can be the sole cause is unwarranted and therefore fallacious.

As you may recall from the discussion in Chapter 5, post hoc reasoning accounts for many superstitions. After I broke that mirror, I had a year of bad luck. Therefore . . . ?

FALLACIES IN COUNTERARGUMENTS

Although the preceding fallacies occur in both arguments and counterarguments, the following fallacies more often occur in counterarguments—attempts to refute an argument. These fallacies share a common trait: They fail to deal with the real issue. They shift responsibility for logical refutation and proof away from the writer. Some of these fallacies also distort others' arguments; they do to arguments what those wavy mirrors at carnivals do to your appearance.

Lack of Contrary Evidence

Logically, flawed or inadequate evidence set forth to support one conclusion is not bolstered by the inadequacy or absence of evidence to the contrary. Examples of fallacious reasoning that overlook this simple truth abound:

> Of course we should go ahead with the McClusky Project; nobody has voiced any objections to it.

> It is going to rain tomorrow, because the sky is overcast and none of the television weather forecasters has said it will not rain.

> Much research has demonstrated the relationship between cigarette smoking and lung cancer. Moreover, no one has proven that sidestream, environmental smoke does not cause lung cancer as well. Indeed, children have been found to be sensitive to tobacco smoke, and some nonsmoking spouses of smokers have developed lung cancer. Undoubtedly, environmental smoke causes cancer just as smoking does.

Oversimplification

Instead of building up an exaggerated man of straw, oversimplification reduces an argument or issue to a limp skeletal structure that can be leveled with a puff. Oversimplifying an argument can make it appear silly or unsubstantial. Typically, crucial premises or crucial qualifications are omitted. Instead of identifying all the reasons why many people advocate generating nuclear energy for fuel, an oversimplified argument ignores all but one or two reasons: "Those who favor nuclear energy development just want to save money. That's all that interests them." Another such argument might run along these lines: "Organizations that enable dying children to fulfill their last wish, perhaps to go to Disneyland or to meet Michael Jackson, can help only a handful of the terminally ill children in this country. Since they reach so few, they should not be supported." True, these organizations can help only a small proportion of children directly, but this argument oversimplifies the good achieved through creating public awareness of serious health problems (and the need to fund research into cures) and through the hope they offer for many more families than just those few who go to Disney World. Knowing that people care is powerful medicine.

Personal Attack

If you can't think of a good response to an argument, you may be tempted to undermine the credible persona of the arguer with a personal attack. Reasonable people try to attack the argument instead of the arguer, of course, but we all have our weak moments. Luckily for those with a sense of fair play, intelligent audiences are rarely sidetracked for long by an attack on the opposing team, and most find such attacks offensive even when they are not themselves the targets. Unfortunately, however, the more emotional the subject, the less likely it is that reason will figure in the discussion. Abortion is such an issue, one about which both sides are prone to attack the character of those on the other side, rather than to attempt to offer reasoned arguments. Gun control is another issue on which personal attacks often replace reason. Politicians who are caught in close races or who are trailing in the polls also tend to shift from a discussion of issues to a discussion of the opponent's bad character and dubious friends. Rhetoricians still call the fallacy by its Latin name, *ad hominem* ("against the man"), and the personal counterattack by its Latin name, *tu quoque* ("you're another").

Some examples of personal attacks and counterattacks:

> The chief executive officer of the largest company with which we compete was thrown out of college for cheating on a Spanish exam. I wouldn't buy his product if I were you.

> How can you speak so smugly in favor of gun control? I know for a fact that you didn't report some of your income last year. You should clean up your own affairs before you involve yourself in other people's.

> Dr. Cohen's family counseling can't be worth much. He's been divorced.

Attacking the source of an argument instead of challenging the argument itself does not logically refute it. But unless you take care, you may find yourself committing this fallacy unthinkingly—as a colleague of mine did when she argued against adopting a particular (nonpolitical) textbook because she found the author's political views unattractive. Any number of great writers, artists, musicians, scientists, and the like have been scoundrels, wastrels, or just plain jerks; their works can be great nonetheless.

Shifting Ground

Shifting ground is an evasive tactic to which some writers and speakers resort when they realize their argument has been successfully challenged or even refuted. They simply declare that they never made quite the claim that has been challenged, and then modify their position to something less shaky: "I never actually claimed X; I meant Y." "I didn't say I couldn't help you on the project; I just can't help you *at this time*."

This fallacy is not committed only in response to challenges, for occasionally writers who are either careless or unsure of the strength of their position will shift ground in the middle of their argument. This kind of shift occurs most often when writers have not thought through what they intend to advocate. In this way a writer might begin to argue in favor of adding a plus or minus designation (with corresponding numerical values) to each letter grade at Alta College, and then decide in midargument that such a system might well lower most students' grade point averages. It would be tempting to alter the essay's controlling idea at that point, shifting ground to the position that "really, plusses and minuses should appear on the transcript but should not be figured into the numerical grade point equivalents." If compelled to make such a change, the writer is also compelled to revise the thesis stated earlier and any inconsistencies in the argument that develops the thesis.

Straw Man

The straw man fallacy occurs when a person exaggerates another person's premises or conclusions to the point that even a sound and sensible argument appears ridiculous. The metaphor of the straw man is apt: A man of straw, however big, is much easier to knock down than is a real flesh-and-blood human being. But some will dress up the man of straw to masquerade as a real person, then knock him down and finally declare the real man—not the straw surrogate—to be vanquished. For example, consider this argument against the free trade agreement between the United States and Mexico:

> A free trade agreement with Mexico will flood the United States market with large quantities of goods far cheaper than those made in the United States with American labor. The impact will devastate everything from the auto industry to the clothing industry. Countless plants and businesses will shut down, and the slow economic recovery will reverse into a full-scale depression.

The writer of this argument has exaggerated the possible effects of a free trade agreement beyond what was either intended or likely to happen as a result of the agreement. By making the agreement appear ridiculous through exaggeration, the writer makes the straw version of the free trade agreement easy to refute.

Trivial Objections

Fallacious counterarguments may single out poorly chosen examples or minor points, challenge them, and then claim to have refuted the entire argument. Consider the following trivial objections:

> This textbook can't be any good. It has a chartreuse cover, and what student is going to take seriously a book with a chartreuse cover?

> I have decided not to marry Vince. I just don't like that beard.

> We are canceling the subscription to your magazine that our nephew gave us for Christmas. For a science-oriented magazine to send out gift cards illustrated with eight-pointed snowflakes (when real snowflakes are hexagonal) is a sure sign that it cannot be relied upon for accuracy.

A cover does not make a textbook, a beard does not make a man, and an eight-pointed snowflake on a Christmas card does not prove that a magazine is not to be trusted for scientific accuracy!

DETECTING FALLACIES

Fallacious arguments often bother us even before we know exactly why or what label to assign them. When asked, "Have you stopped trying to annoy Professor Wiggins?," we respond huffily, "Who ever said I *was* trying to annoy her?" The reply goes right to the heart of the fallacy, a complex question. We are not taken in by the argument, "Don't take Professor Slocum's class; he's gay. Or Mr. Schneider's; he's Jewish." Sometimes, however, the fallacy is so subtle or complex that we accept it, perhaps reluctantly, not quite sure that the reasoning makes sense, yet not quite sure that it is wrong. It is in this dusky area that the study of fallacies proves most enlightening, in order that we need not puzzle too long over the arguments by a master of fallacy as well as of logic:

> "In boxing and other kinds of fighting, skill in attack goes with skill in defense, does it not?"
> "Of course."
> "So, too, the ability to save from disease implies the ability to produce it undetected, while ability to bring an army safely through a campaign goes with ability to rob the enemy of his secrets and steal a march on him in action."
> "I certainly think so."
> "So a man who's good at keeping a thing will be good at stealing it."
> "I suppose so."
> "So if the just man is good at keeping money safe, he will be good at stealing it too."
> "That at any rate is the conclusion the argument leads to."
> "So the just man turns out to be a kind of thief."
>
> —Plato, *The Republic*, trans. H. D. P. Lee

This line of reasoning might leave some people scratching their heads, aware that the argument goes awry but not quite sure how or where. But having studied valid and fallacious reasoning gives you both a clearer understanding and a means to answer Socrates. The ability to do anything does not in itself imply the ability to do an opposite thing. Analogies among medicine, war, and thievery do not *prove* any conclusion. Nor is "a man who is good at keeping a thing" synonymous with "a just man." And a person who is able to steal is not always a person who *will* steal. Socrates's argument may *sound* logical, but it is completely fallacious.

Stalking fallacies can be challenging and even entertaining. Many fallacies, once you are able to recognize them confidently, will strike you as absurdly funny. The hunt can even become an armchair sport; you can fill a bulletin board with your trophies without the taxidermy expense big game hunters face. Here are a few specimens from my own collection:

In civilized society, personal merit will not serve you so much as money will. Sir, you may make the experiment. Go into the street and give one man a lecture on morality, and another a shilling, and see which will respect you most.

—Samuel Johnson

We evolved because of change.

—Student essay

I have given my answer; if it is wrong, it is your job to refute it.

—Socrates

Discussion in class . . . means letting twenty young blockheads and two cocky neurotics discuss something that neither their teacher nor they know.

—Vladimir Nabokov

For if life has no meaning, then we would have no vision of life and life would have no purpose, because life would be void.

—Student essay

Even if you do not know the names of the fallacies demonstrated by these statements, you should now recognize their logical shortcomings. What problems do you see?

EXERCISE 7–1

Explain what is wrong with the reasoning in the items below. If possible, identify the particular fallacy or fallacies committed (but only after first explaining the problem).

1. The insurance industry wants your money—and your rights [through getting legislatures to limit the amount of jury awards in lawsuits]. . . . These are the choices our legislators face: protect insurance profits—or protect our jury system and the rights of victims to be compensated for the harm done them.
   —"Hands Up!" brochure from the Texas Trial Lawyers Association

2. Final examinations should be eliminated because they are not worth taking.

3. Parents who allow others to care for their children do so in order to be free of their responsibility.
   —Student essay

4. If truth is on our side, the task should not be too formidable. If truth is not on our side, then our critics are right and we are wrong, advertising is wrong, business is wrong, and America is wrong. I, for one, am convinced that America is right.
   —Roy E. Larson, of Time, Inc., in a speech to the Association of National Advertisers, 1961; in *Speaking of Advertising*, ed. John S. Wright and Daniel S. Warner

5. I see no difference between a man killing a chicken and a man killing a human being, by overwork and forcing ghetto conditions upon him, both so

that he can eat a little better. If you can justify killing to eat meat, you can justify the conditions of the ghetto. I cannot justify either one.

—Dick Gregory, *The Shadow That Scares Me*

6. Manuel Mendoza's review of the Eric Clapton concert came out of the Twilight Zone! Being a pop music critic, I believe he was completely unprepared to review any performance that doesn't make the Teeny Bopper Top 40.

—Letter to *Dallas Morning News*, 26 April 1992

7. The new generation of water weapons, with their bulbous tanks and high-pressure air pumps, splash so hard, squirt so far and are so wildly popular . . . that some public officials fear the summer may be not just long and hot, but dangerously wet as well, if angry soakees shoot back with live ammunition. The mayor of Boston, reacting to a soaking and shooting that left a 15-year-old boy dead last month, asked city stores to take the water guns off their shelves. A Michigan state senator last week called for an outright ban.

—"Squirt, Squirt, You're Dead," *Time*, 22 June 1992

8. In the name of fairness, the U.S. military is being asked to abandon the last significant distinction between the sexes by sending women into combat—not as support troops but as members of units whose mission and reason for being is to kill the enemy through direct fire. Before we allow feminist ideology to prevail over human nature and common sense, we must open our eyes to the falsehoods of that ideology.

The fundamental error of feminism is its assumption that there are no significant differences between men and women other than their gross physical characteristics. Ironically, many feminists spend unlimited time and effort bemoaning male characteristics that, in another context, they deny exist. The case in point is male aggressiveness, a psychological trait that sometimes detracts from personal relationships but is vital to success in combat.

Most of what we commonly call human nature is genetically imprinted on our brains, not by some societal plot to oppress women but by generations of natural selection. The struggle to survive and procreate has given the female a superior ability to nurture her young, and the male a superior ability to protect his mate and their offspring. . . .

Letter to *Dallas Morning News*, 7 July 1991

9. Though I . . . have little use for Pat Buchanan, I confess to experiencing much pleasure watching Mr. Buchanan make an issue of the National Endowment for the Arts and of its grants to "artists" (or even artists) whose work, by common judgment, is obscene, pornographic, and blasphemous. So effective have these criticisms been that John Frohnmayer has been ousted as chairman of the NEA. . . . Mr. Frohnmayer, who was President Bush's choice to head the Endowment, quickly revealed himself to be a passive captive of his constituency—or at least of the articulate, militant elements in this constituency. His basic rejoinder to his critics took two forms:

(1) The budget of the NEA is $180 million. The grants that provoke so much controversy are small-to-modest in size and probably don't approach a million dollars. Having made this point, Mr. Frohnmayer is then amazed to discover that people are not placated to learn that less than $1 million of taxpayers' money is spent to subsidize obscenity, pornography, and blasphemy.

(2) "What," he also demands to know, "is obscenity, pornography, and blasphemy, anyhow? Who's to say?" When it is then suggested that, as chairman of the National Endowment for the Arts, he might be supposed to be able to say, he is shocked at the prospect of such presumption on his part. He has even been dismissive of the notion that his presidentially appointed (and Senate-confirmed) council should exercise such judgment. Only the artists themselves, he seemed to be arguing, had the authority to pass judgment on their work—and the peculiar "peer review" process that the NEA operates has resulted in exactly such a situation. On the whole, the "peers" who pass on grants—artists, art critics, museum directors, and museum trustees—look upon their friends' or clients' work and find it to be good.

Why on earth did George Bush put up with such nonsense for so long?

—Irving Kristol, "What Shall We Do with the NEA?"
Wall Street Journal, 16 March 1992

10. In regard to Irving Kristol's March 16 editorial-page essay, "What Shall We Do With the NEA?": What shall we do with Irving Kristol, and the conservative viewpoint that contemporary art has anything to do with obscenity, pornography, and blasphemy? (As church and state are separate in the U.S., "blasphemy" is not even a legal term.) Because art can be (and significant 20th-century art has been) made of such unlikely materials as a urinal, a Campbell's Soup can or a plastic crucifix, the panels of the National Endowment for the Arts are "conflict-free"—no individual on the panel will benefit through a grant or an exhibition from the decisions made. I wonder how Mr. Kristol's American Enterprise Institute is funded—do taxpayers ultimately foot the bill for Mr. Kristol's time to ponder?

However, I agree that the most widespread attitude toward the NEA is a "negligent, deferential" one that in my opinion does not recognize the value of controversial art. We need more controversial art, not less, to allow the troubling thoughts in our collective unconscious to bubble to the surface nonviolently, to become part of public debate, and, it is hoped, to be resolved. Instead of artists, would Mr. Kristol prefer a country of murderers? If so, I should like to be the one to murder him.

—Letter to *Wall Street Journal*, 20 April 1992

EXERCISE 7–2

About a decade ago, Miss America pageant officials took the Miss America title from Vanessa Williams upon learning that she had previously appeared nude in *Penthouse* magazine. Both Williams and the Miss America pageant carried on: Williams now pursues a successful singing and acting career, and the Miss America pageant continues to crown a young woman each September. But the incident generated a spate of arguments both for and against the whole concept of beauty pageants. Below are two of the arguments. Read them, looking for reasonable arguments and fallacies in both. Identify the fallacies you find. Then, in a paragraph or two, discuss ways to make one of the two positions more reasonable: What would you take out or rephrase? What points would you add?

In 1968, I was an organizer of the first protest against the Miss America Pageant. We were angry that women were being judged for how they looked, not who they were—and that their bodies were being commercialized.

Nothing has changed. This pageant, like all the others, is still exploiting women as much as ever. It is a silly, irrelevant, destructive anachronism.

What do women walking down a runway in bathing suits have to do with the real way women are living their lives? Bloody little.

Most people know that. When I travel around the country, I don't find any huge sentimental attachment to the pageant. It's like the hoop skirt—people don't take it seriously. Among younger women, it's an incredibly corny joke.

But in a sense, we'd be better off if people did take it seriously. Other pageants are more blatant, but they all send the same message: Men are judged by who they are and what they do; women are judged by what they look like. Women are sexual objects; their bodies are all that's of interest.

That is the message of pornography, and beauty pageants are simply the flip side of the pornographic coin.

The Miss America Pageant and *Penthouse* are the same in their basic sexism. And they need each other to survive: The pornographic sensibility needs a virginal image to violate. The pageant needs pornographers to sell the fresh-cheeked, wholesome image of American womanhood as a sexual fantasy.

It is also a fundamentally conservative fantasy. As a myth of sexual purity and prudery, of wholesome family values, the pageant becomes a kind of super-patriotism. Winners travel around the world to visit the troops and give pep talks to American boys to fight and die for the fatherland.

That's why some people got so upset about Vanessa Williams: She violated the American Legion fantasy of purity.

But these fantasies have no relevance to the lives of ordinary women, who are concerned with child care, equal opportunity, economic survival, and not being raped in the streets. Discrimination in education, jobs, and income is still rampant. That's why some young women enter beauty pageants in the first place; they tend to come from lower-middle-class backgrounds and need the scholarship money.

We'd all be better off if these pageants didn't exist. Creating the plastic woman and then selling her on television is a ridiculous waste of time.

But I have to admit mild amusement at the latest Miss America-*Penthouse* "scandal." Pageant officials are wringing their hands in public, but they're probably delighted at the publicity. *Penthouse* and the pageant—they're a marriage made in heaven, and they deserve each other.

—Robin Morgan, "Pageants are Sexist, Silly and Destructive,"
USA Today, 14 Sept. 1984

The Miss America Pageant exploits women? That's a ridiculous statement on the face of it.

Any organization that provides $4.25 million annually in scholarship money, the largest source of scholarship money for women in the world—and that provides opportunity for some 80,000 young women a year—can hardly be called exploitive.

It's been said by some that if one were to use the word "exploit," the shoe would be on the other foot. It is the young women who exploit the Miss America Pageant, and we solicit that.

Is the swimsuit competition sexist? No. If young women in swimsuits are sexist, then thousands of women on America's beaches are sexist. If the critics had their way, we'd have to close every beach in America.

Physical fitness, poise under trying conditions—I would hardly regard those things as sexist. Sexism, just as in pornography, is just in the eye of the beholder.

And to say that we judge only on beauty shows gross ignorance of what actually happens at the Miss America Pageant. The judges are fully instructed that what we seek is not an ideal—not the girl next door or even a role model.

The judges, all of whom are experts in a variety of fields, are asked to judge a young woman not only in beauty, which is only one facet of a human being, but in intelligence, articulation [sic], poise, and grace.

Our contestants are no different from other young women. We carefully explain that we're not trying to present Miss America as someone unattainable, on top of Mt. Olympus, but as someone within the reach of anyone—a goal anyone can aspire to.

And we don't, as some critics charge, insist on outdated standards of virtue. In fact, we don't insist on any whatsoever, except some very obvious things. For example, you must never have been married, and you must never have been convicted of a crime. In any job interview, you'd be asked questions like that and far worse.

People sometimes misunderstand us because they see only the two-hour telecast. That is merely the climax showcase, and you can't convey our philosophical message fully in such a short time.

We provide opportunities for tens of thousands of young women. In my 33 years of experience, I've found that when you have been Miss Whatever, the doors open for you. There's not a job, a profession, or an occupation that is not ably filled by young women who have competed at some time.

Other pageants do exploit young women—through entrance fees, charges for franchises, and so forth. If people understand this, they wouldn't lump us together under one generic term: beauty pageants.

> —Albert Marks, Jr., "Our Pageant Sexist? Don't Be Ridiculous,"
> *USA Today*, 14 Sept. 1984

EXERCISE 7–3

Read the letters to the editor of your local or campus newspaper for several days. Analyze the frequency of different patterns of reasoning: analogy, considering examples, enthymemes, and so on. Which kinds of reasoning occur most often? Give examples. Then look for fallacies. Which kinds occur most often? Again, give examples.

EXERCISE 7–4

Rewrite one logically flawed letter to the editor of your local or campus newspaper, attempting to eliminate the fallacies while preserving the point of view and conclusion reached by the original letter writer. Comment on any special problems you encounter in making the improvements.

READINGS

THE CHECKERS SPEECH

Richard M. Nixon

1   My Fellow Americans: I come before you tonight as a candidate for the Vice Presidency and as a man whose honesty and integrity have been questioned.

2   The usual political thing to do when charges are made against you is to either ignore them or to deny them without giving details.

3   I believe we've had enough of that in the United States, particularly with the present Administration in Washington, D.C. To me the office of the Vice Presidency of the United States is a great office, and I feel that the people have got to have confidence in the integrity of the men who run for that office and who might obtain it.

4   I have a theory, too, that the best and only answer to a smear or to an honest misunderstanding of the facts is to tell the truth. And that's why I'm here tonight. I want to tell you my side of the case.

5   I am sure that you have read the charge and you've heard that I, Senator Nixon, took $18,000 from a group of my supporters.

6   Now, was that wrong? And let me say that it was wrong—I'm saying, incidentally, that it was wrong and not just illegal. Because it isn't a question of whether it was legal or illegal, that isn't enough. The question is, was it morally wrong?

7   I say that it was morally wrong if any of that $18,000 went to Senator Nixon for my personal use. I say that it was morally wrong if it was secretly given and secretly handled. And I say that it was morally wrong if any of the contributors got special favors for the contributions that they made.

8   And now to answer those questions let me say this:

9   Not one cent of the $18,000 or any other money of that type ever went to me for my personal use. Every penny of it was used to pay for political expenses that I did not think should be charged to the taxpayers of the United States.

10   It was not a secret fund. As a matter of fact, when I was on "Meet the Press," some of you may have seen it last Sunday—Peter Edson came up to me after the program and he said, "Dick, what about this fund we hear about?" And I said, Well, there's no secret about it. Go out and see Dana Smith, who was the administrator of the fund. And I gave him his address, and I said that you will find that the purpose of the fund simply was to defray political expenses that I did not feel should be charged to the Government.

11   And third, let me point out, and I want to make this particularly clear, that no contributor to this fund, no contributor to any of my campaigns, has ever received any consideration that he would not have received as an ordinary constituent.

12   I just don't believe in that and I can say that never, while I have been in the Senate of the United States, as far as the people that contributed to this fund are concerned, have I made a telephone call for them to an agency, or have I gone down to an agency in their behalf. And the record will show that, the records which are in the hands of the Administration. . . .

13   And so now what I am going to do—and incidentally this is unprecedented in the history of American politics—I am going at this time to give to this television and radio audience a complete financial history; everything I've earned; everything I've spent; everything I owe. And I want you to know the facts. I'll have to start early.

14   I was born in 1913. Our family was one of modest circumstances and most of my early life was spent in a store out in East Whittier. It was a grocery store—one of those family enterprises. The only reason we were able to make it go was because my mother and dad had five boys and we all worked in the store.

15   I worked my way through college and to a great extent through law school. And then, in 1940, probably the best thing that ever happened to me happened, I married Pat—sitting over here. We had a rather difficult time after we were married, like so many of the young couples who may be listening to us. I practiced law; she continued to teach school. I went into the service.

16   Let me say that my service record was not a particularly unusual one. I went to the South Pacific. I guess I'm entitled to a couple of battle stars. I got a couple of letters of commendation but I was just there when the bombs were falling and then I returned. I returned to the United States and in 1946 I ran for the Congress.

17   When we came out of the war, Pat and I—Pat during the war had worked as a stenographer and in a bank and as an economist for a Government agency—and when we came out the total of our savings from both my law practice, her teaching and all the time that I was in the war—the total for that entire period was just a little less than $10,000. Every cent of that, incidentally, was in Government bonds.

18   Well, that's where we start when I go into politics. Now what have I earned since I went into politics? Well, here it is—I jotted it down, let me read the notes. First of all I've had my salary as a Congressman and as a Senator. Second, I have received a total in this past six years of $1,600 from estates which were in my law firm at the time that I severed my connection with it.

19   And, incidentally, as I said before, I have not engaged in any legal practice and have not accepted any fees from business that came into the firm after I went into politics. I have made an average of approximately $1,500 a year from nonpolitical speaking engagements and lectures. And then, fortunately, we've inherited a little money. Pat sold her interest in her father's estate for $3,000 and I inherited $1,500 from my grandfather.

20   We live rather modestly. For four years we lived in an apartment in Park Fairfax, in Alexandria, Virginia. The rent was $80 a month. And we saved for the time that we could buy a house.

21   Now, that was what we took in. What did we do with this money? What do we have today to show for it? This will surprise you, because it is so little, I suppose, as standards generally go, of people in public life. First of all, we've got a house in Washington which cost $41,000 and on which we owe $20,000.

22   We have a house in Whittier, California, which cost $13,000 and on which we owe $10,000. My folks are living there at the present time.

23   I have just $4,000 in life insurance, plus my G. I. policy, which I've never been able to convert and which will run out in two years. I have no life insurance whatever on Pat. I have no life insurance on our two youngsters, Patricia and Julie. I own a 1950 Oldsmobile car. We have our furniture. We have no stocks and bonds of any type. We have no interest of any kind, direct or indirect, in any business.

24   Now, that's what we have. What do we owe? Well, in addition to the mortgage, the $20,000 mortgage on the house in Washington, the $10,000 one on the house in Whittier, I owe $4,500 to the Riggs Bank in Washington, D.C. with interest $4^1/_2$ percent.

25   I owe $3,500 to my parents and the interest on that loan, which I pay regularly, because it's part of the savings they made through the years they were working so hard, I pay regularly 4 percent interest. And then I have a $500 loan which I have on my life insurance.

26   Well, that's about it. That's what we have and that's what we owe. It isn't very much but Pat and I have the satisfaction that every dime we've got is honestly ours. I should say this—that Pat doesn't have a mink coat. But she does have a respectable Republican cloth coat. And I always tell her that she'd look good in anything.

27   One other thing I probably should tell you because if I don't they'll probably be saying this about me too, we did get something—a gift—after the election. A man down in Texas heard Pat on the radio mention the fact that our two youngsters would like to have a dog. And, believe it or not, the day before we left on this campaign trip we got a message from Union Station in Baltimore saying they had a package for us. We went down to get it. You know what it was?

28   It was a little cocker spaniel dog in a crate that he sent all the way from Texas. Black and white spotted. And our little girl—Trisha, the 6-year-old—named it Checkers. And you know, the kids love the dog and I just want to say this right now, that regardless of what they say about it, we're gonna keep it. . . .

29   Now, let me say this: I know that this is not the last of the smears. In spite of my explanation tonight other smears will be made; others have been made in the past. And the purpose of the smears, I know, is this—to silence me, to make me let up.

30   Well, they just don't know who they're dealing with. . . . I intend to continue the fight. . . .

31   And I want to tell you why. Because, you see, I love my country. And I think my country is in danger. And I think that the only man that can save

America at this time is the man that's running for President on my ticket—
Dwight Eisenhower. . . .

32   And I say that the only man who can lead us in this fight to rid the
Government of both those who are Communists and those who have corrupted this Government is Eisenhower, because Eisenhower, you can be sure,
recognizes the problem and he knows how to deal with it. . . .

33   And just let me say this. We hear a lot about prosperity these days but I
say, why can't we have prosperity built on peace rather than prosperity built
on war? Why can't we have prosperity and an honest government in Washington, D.C., at the same time? Believe me, we can. And Eisenhower is the
man that can lead this crusade to bring us that kind of prosperity.

34   And, now, finally, I know that you wonder whether or not I am going
to stay on the Republican ticket or resign.

35   Let me say this: I don't believe that I ought to quit because I'm not a
quitter. And, incidentally, Pat's not a quitter. After all, her name was Patricia
Ryan and she was born on St. Patrick's Day, and you know the Irish never
quit.

36   But the decision, my friends, is not mine. I would do nothing that
would harm the possibilities of Dwight Eisenhower to become President of
the United States. And for that reason I am submitting to the Republican National Committee tonight through this television broadcast the decision
which it is theirs to make.

37   Let them decide whether my position on the ticket will help or hurt.
And I am going to ask you to help them decide. Wire and write the Republican National Committee whether you think I should stay on or whether I
should get off. And whatever their decision is, I will abide by it.

38   But just let me say this last word. Regardless of what happens I'm going
to continue this fight. I'm going to campaign up and down America until we
drive the crooks and the Communists and those that defend them out of
Washington. And remember, folks, Eisenhower is a great man. Believe me.
He's a great man. And a vote for Eisenhower is a vote for what's good in
America.

QUESTIONS AND IDEAS FOR DISCUSSION

1. Under similar circumstances today, would a speech like this one, now known
    as the "Checkers" speech, prove equally successful? Explain the reasons for
    your answer. Then, by consulting *The New York Times Index* or *Vital Speeches
    of the Day*, locate a recent speech in which a public figure offers a defense of a
    statement, position, or action. Assuming that Nixon's appeals are typical of a
    1950s defensive political speech, comment on the similarities and the differ-
    ences between defensive political speeches of the 1950s and those today.
    Which seem greater, the points of resemblance or the differences?

2. Pat Nixon later did acquire a mink coat. According to Nixon's line of reasoning in paragraph 26, what conclusions may we draw?

3. In a short passage of the "Checkers" speech, not excerpted above, Nixon says the following:

> Mr. Mitchell, the chairman of the Democratic National Committee, made the statement that if a man couldn't afford to be in the United States Senate he shouldn't run for the Senate. . . . I don't agree with Mr. Mitchell when he says that only a rich man should serve his Government in the United States Senate or in the Congress.

What fallacy does Nixon commit here?

4. The latter part of Nixon's speech centers on the theme "Regardless of what happens I'm going to continue this fight." What fight does he mean? Has he shifted ground? Comment.

LIES, FALLACIES, AND SANTA CLAUS

T. J. Stone
(Student Essay)

1 As a child approaches her second or third Christmas, her parents may begin telling her about the wonderful old elf, Santa Claus, who brings presents to good little girls and boys on the night of December 24 in the United States, but as late as January 6 in some countries, and not at all in others. In Spain, for instance, the Magi take over the gift-giving responsibilities. After all, the logistics involved for a single old man in a sleigh to deliver so many gifts in a single night are nearly overwhelming. But the child is not burdened with all these complications: She is assured categorically that Santa Claus is coming to her house on Christmas Eve after she falls asleep, and she may leave milk and cookies for him if she likes.

2 The whole thing is a terrific deal for the child who early learns not to question too closely. For the inquisitive child, however, the troubles begin early:

3 "Well, Mom, but what about Todd? He gets presents, too, but he doesn't have a chimney like us."

4 "And you say this man is fat? How does he fit down the chimney without getting stuck?"

5 "How does Santa Claus keep track of which kids get which presents?"

6 "What about Sally? She's so nice, but she gets hardly any presents. Does Santa just not like some kids?"

7 Never let it be said that a child cannot reason. She wants to believe (and is afraid that if she doesn't believe, the presents will stop coming!), but she can't help but see the gaping holes in the story Mom and Dad present. And

Mom and Dad staunchly insist on the sleigh and the eight reindeer and, generally, the whole program. Oh, if there is no chimney, they are willing to admit that Santa will use a window, but nothing so prosaic as the front door. And they cough and mumble something indistinct when pressed about the little children who get no presents, or very few. So the child, knowing what is good for her, either keeps her questions to herself or suspends her disbelief.

8   Is either of these alternatives really a healthy one? What is the virtue of telling lies to a small child, assuring her all the while that they are the gospel truth? The Santa Claus lie may be small, and relatively harmless in the long run, but it requires, for the sake of tradition, that parents tell their children things that are not true, and that children suppress their developing powers of reasoning. Some tradition!

9   A more sensible alternative is possible. Do not do away with Santa Claus or presents or Christmas trees—simply do away with the lies and evasions. Like little Virginia, many years ago, children today will find the truth just as enchanting as the fibs and fallacies. The spirit of sharing and giving at Christmastime is represented by a "pretend" figure known as Santa Claus. Real people do the giving, and children can be part of that giving: Those with more toys than they need can select one or more that they might have received to take to the Salvation Army or another charitable organization so that little Sally can have some toys at Christmas, too. No enjoyment is lost to the child who learns about Santa as a symbol and who reads "The Night Before Christmas" for what it is—a delightful fairy tale. And no loss of innocence occurs at age seven or eight in children who have known the truth all along. Santa is just too wonderful a part of Christmas to be put in the position of being exposed as a lie.

QUESTIONS AND IDEAS FOR DISCUSSION

1. What assumptions has Stone made about her audience? Are they accurate in your case? What effect do her assumptions have on your receptiveness to her argument?
2. Characterize Stone's writing style. If this essay were your own, what additions, deletions, or changes would you make? Discuss as specifically as possible.
3. Does Stone's last sentence contradict the rest of her essay? Explain.
4. What defense can you offer for the usual presentation of Santa Claus to children? Is there any virtue in telling children lies, however well-intentioned?
5. Think of other Western traditions that are based on "lies," such as the tooth fairy, the stork that brings babies, or the Easter bunny. Are these deceptions justified? Comment.

THE LANGUAGE OF ADVERTISING CLAIMS

Jeffrey Schrank

1   High school students, and many teachers, are notorious believers in their immunity to advertising. These naive inhabitants of consumerland believe that advertising is childish, dumb, a bunch of lies, and influences only the vast hordes of the less sophisticated. Their own purchases are made purely on the basis of value and desire, with advertising playing only a minor supporting role. They know about Vance Packard and his "hidden persuaders" and the adwriter's psychosell and bag of persuasive magic. They are not impressed.

2   Advertisers know better. Although few people admit to being greatly influenced by ads, surveys and sales figures show that a well-designed advertising campaign has dramatic effects. A logical conclusion is that advertising works below the level of conscious awareness and it works even on those who claim immunity to its message. Ads are designed to have an effect while being laughed at, belittled, and all but ignored.

3   A person unaware of advertising's claim on him or her is precisely the one most defenseless against the adwriter's attack. Advertisers delight in an audience which believes ads to be harmless nonsense, for such an audience is rendered defenseless by its belief that there is no attack taking place. The purpose of a classroom study of advertising is to raise the level of awareness about the persuasive techniques used in ads. One way to do this is to analyze ads in microscopic detail. Ads can be studied to detect their psychological hooks, they can be used to gauge values and hidden desires of the common person, they can be studied for their use of symbols, color, and imagery. But perhaps the simplest and most direct way to study ads is through an analysis of the language of the advertising claim. The "claim" is the verbal or print part of an ad that makes some claim of superiority for the product being advertised. After studying claims, students should be able to recognize those that are misleading and accept as useful information those that are true. A few of these claims are downright lies, some are honest statements about a truly superior product, but most fit into the category of neither bold lies nor helpful consumer information. They balance on the narrow line between truth and falsehood by a careful choice of words.

4   The reason so many ad claims fall into this category of pseudo-information is that they are applied to parity products, products in which all or most of the brands available are nearly identical. Since no one superior product exists, advertising is used to create the illusion of superiority. The largest advertising budgets are devoted to parity products such as gasoline, cigarettes, beer and soft drinks, soaps, and various headache and cold remedies.

5   The first rule of parity involves the Alice in Wonderlandish use of the words "better" and "best." In parity claims, "better" means "best" and "best"

means "equal to." If all the brands are identical, they must all be equally good, the legal minds have decided. So "best" means that the product is as good as the other superior products in its category. When Bing Crosby declares Minute Maid Orange Juice "the best there is" he means it is as good as the other orange juices you can buy.

6   The word "better" has been legally interpreted to be a comparative and therefore becomes a clear claim of superiority. Bing could not have said that Minute Maid is "better than any other orange juice." "Better" is a claim of superiority. The only time "better" can be used is when a product does indeed have superiority over other products in its category or when the better is used to compare the product with something other than competing brands. An orange juice could therefore claim to be "better than a vitamin pill," or even "the better breakfast drink."

7   The second rule of advertising claim analysis is simply that if any product is truly superior, the ad will say so very clearly and will offer some kind of convincing evidence of the superiority. If an ad hedges the least bit about a product's advantage over the competition you can strongly suspect it is not superior—maybe equal to but not better. You will never hear a gasoline company say "we will give you four miles per gallon more in your car than any other brand." They would love to make such a claim, but it would not be true. Gasoline is a parity product, and, in spite of some very clever and deceptive ads of a few years ago, no one has yet claimed one brand of gasoline better than any other brand.

8   To create the necessary illusion of superiority, advertisers usually resort to one or more of the following ten basic techniques. Each is common and easy to identify.

1 The Weasel Claim

9 A weasel word is a modifier that practically negates the claim that follows. The expression "weasel word" is aptly named after the egg-eating habits of weasels. A weasel will suck out the inside of an egg, leaving it to appear intact to the casual observer. Upon examination, the egg is discovered to be hollow. Words or claims that appear substantial upon first look but disintegrate into hollow meaninglessness on analysis are weasels. Commonly used weasel words include "helps" (the champion weasel); "like" (used in a comparative sense); "virtual" or "virtually"; "acts" or "works"; "can be"; "up to"; "as much as"; "refreshes"; "comforts"; "tackles"; "fights"; "come on"; "the feel of"; "the look of"; "looks like"; "fortified"; "enriched"; and "strengthened."

Samples of Weasel Claims

"*Helps control* dandruff *symptoms* with *regular use*." The weasels include "helps control," and possibly even "symptoms" and "regular use." The claim is not "stops dandruff."

"Leaves dishes *virtually* spotless." We have seen so many ad claims that we have learned to tune out weasels. You are supposed to think "spotless," rather than "virtually" spotless.

"Only half the price of *many* color sets." "Many" is the weasel. The claim is suppose to give the impression that the set is inexpensive.

"Tests confirm one mouthwash *best* against mouth odor."

"Hot Nestlés' cocoa is the very *best*." Remember the "best" and "better" routine.

"Listerine *fights* bad breath." "Fights," not "stops."

"Lots of things have changed, but Hershey's *goodness* hasn't." This claim does not say that Hershey's chocolate hasn't changed.

"Bacos, the crispy garnish that tastes just *like* its name."

2 The Unfinished Claim
10 The unfinished claim is one in which the ad claims the product is better, or has more of something, but does not finish the comparison.

Samples of Unfinished Claims
"Magnavox gives you more." More what?

"Anacin: Twice as much of the pain reliever doctors recommend most." This claim fits in a number of categories but it does not say twice as much of what pain reliever.

"Supergloss does it with more color, more shine, more sizzle, more!"

"Coffee-Mate give coffee more body, more flavor." Also note that "body" and "flavor" are weasels.

"You can be sure if it's Westinghouse." Sure of what?

"Scott makes it better for you."

"Ford LTD—700% quieter." When the FTC asked Ford to substantiate this claim, Ford revealed that they meant the inside of the Ford was 700% quieter than the outside.

3 The "We're Different and Unique" Claim
11 This kind of claim states that there is nothing else quite like the product advertised. For example, if Schlitz would add pink food coloring to its beer they could say, "There's nothing like new pink Schlitz." The uniqueness claim is supposed to be interpreted by readers as a claim to superiority.

Samples of "We're Different and Unique" Claims

"There's no other mascara like it."

"Only Doral has this unique filter system."

"Cougar is like nobody else's car."

"Either way, liquid or spray, there's nothing else like it."

"If it doesn't say Goodyear, it can't be polyglas." "Polyglas" is a trade name copyrighted by Goodyear. Goodrich or Firestone could make a tire exactly identical to the Goodyear one and yet couldn't call it "polyglas"—a name for fiberglass belts.

"Only Zenith has chromacolor." Same as the "polyglas" gambit. Admiral has solarcolor and RCA has accucolor.

4 The "Water Is Wet" Claim

12   "Water is wet" claims say something about the product that is true for any brand in that product category (e.g., "Schrank's water is really wet"). The claim is usually a statement of fact, but not a real advantage over the competition.

Samples of "Water is Wet" Claim

"Mobil: the Detergent Gasoline." Any gasoline acts as a cleaning agent.

"Great Lash greatly increases the diameter of every lash."

"Rheingold, the natural beer." Made from grains and water as are other beers.

"SKIN smells different on everyone." As do many perfumes.

5 The "So What" Claim

13   This is the kind of claim to which the careful reader will react by saying, "So what?" A claim is made which is true but which gives no real advantage to the product. This is similar to the "water is wet" claim except that it claims an advantage which is not shared by most of the other brands in the product category.

Samples of the "So What" Claim

"Geritol has more than twice the iron of ordinary supplements." But is twice as much beneficial to the body?

"Campbell's gives you tasty pieces of chicken and not one but two chicken stocks." Does the presence of two stocks improve the taste?

"Strong enough for a man but made for a woman." This deodorant claim says only that the product is aimed at the female market.

6 The Vague Claim

14 The vague claim is simply not clear. This category often overlaps with others. The key to the vague claim is the use of words that are colorful but meaningless, as well as the use of subjective and emotional opinions that defy verification. Most contain weasels.

Samples of the Vague Claim

"Lips have never looked so luscious." Can you imagine trying to either prove or disprove such a claim?

"Lipsavers are fun—they taste good, smell good and feel good."

"Its deep rich lather makes hair feel good again."

"For skin like peaches and cream."

"The end of meatloaf boredom."

"Take a bite and you'll think you're eating on the Champs Elysées."

"Winston tastes good like a cigarette should."

"The perfect little portable for all-around viewing with all the features of higher priced sets."

"Fleishman's makes sensible eating delicious."

7 The Endorsement or Testimonial

15 A celebrity or authority appears in an ad to lend his or her stellar qualities to the product. Sometimes the people will actually claim to use the product, but very often they don't. There are agencies surviving on providing products with testimonials.

Samples of Endorsements or Testimonials

"Joan Fontaine throws a shot-in-the-dark party and her friends learn a thing or two."

"Darling, have you discovered Masterpiece? The most exciting men I know are smoking it." (Eva Gabor)

"Vega is the best handling car in the U.S." This claim was challenged by the FTC, but GM answered that the claim is only a direct quote from *Road and Track* magazine.

8 The Scientific or Statistical Claim

16 This kind of ad uses some sort of scientific proof or experiment, very specific numbers, or an impressive sounding mystery ingredient.

Samples of Scientific or Statistical Claims

"Wonder Bread helps build strong bodies 12 ways." Even the weasel "helps" did not prevent the FTC from demanding this ad be withdrawn. But note that the use of the number 12 makes the claim far more believable than if it were taken out.

"Easy-Off has 33% more cleaning power than another popular brand." "Another popular brand" often translates as some other kind of oven cleaner sold somewhere. Also the claim does not say Easy-Off works 33% better.

"Special Morning—33% more nutrition." Also an unfinished claim.

"Certs contains a sparkling drop of Retsyn."

"ESSO with HTA."

"Sinarest. Created by a research scientist who actually gets sinus headaches."

9 The "Compliment the Consumer" Claim
17 This kind of claim butters up the consumer by some form of flattery.

Samples of "Compliment the Consumer" Claim
"We think a cigar smoker is someone special."

"If what you do is right for you, no matter what others do, then RC Cola is right for you."

"You pride yourself on your good home cooking. . . . "

"The lady has taste."

"You've come a long way, baby."

10 The Rhetorical Question
18 This technique demands a response from the audience. A question is asked and the viewer or listener is supposed to answer in such a way as to affirm the product's goodness.

Samples of the Rhetorical Question
"Plymouth—isn't that the kind of car America wants?"

"Shouldn't your family be drinking Hawaiian Punch?"

"What do you want most from coffee? That's what you get most from Hills."

"Touch of Sweden: could your hands use a small miracle?"

QUESTIONS AND IDEAS FOR DISCUSSION

1. Schrank claims that "a logical conclusion is that advertising works below the level of conscious awareness and it works even on those who claim immunity to its message." Does Schrank convince you of his claim? With what reasons and evidence does he support it?

2. Why, according to Schrank, are advertising claims so often empty or fallacious? Give an example of a specific parity product being advertised today for which superiority is claimed. Analyze the claims made for the product according to Schrank's criteria.

3. Some of the fallacious claims Schrank identifies are discussed elsewhere in this chapter. One is the question-begging rhetorical question, in which the consumer's answer is already implied. What are others? What kinds of fallacious claims does Schrank identify that we have not discussed up to this point?

4. Give additional examples from current print and television advertising for each of Schrank's ten fallacies. Do you find any fallacies he has not discussed? Comment.

5. Have you ever been guilty of unfinished comparisons or of "weasels" in your own writing? When your own aim is to persuade, how can you avoid committing the fallacies Schrank has identified?

QUESTIONS AND IDEAS FOR DISCUSSION

1. Discuss the kinds of appeals, fallacious or otherwise, in the following advertisements. (Bear in mind that not all advertising appeals are fallacious.) Describe the audience to which each appears to be addressed. Which advertisement do you find most appealing personally? Which least appealing? Why? Do you believe you are part of the intended audience for each of the advertisements?

2. Read the advertisements in a current magazine for either general or specialized audiences. What kinds of products predominate? What kinds of appeals are made? What fallacies do you find? (Give examples.) Try to find at least one advertisement that contains no fallacies. Bring examples to class for comment and discussion.

3. If you have recently received requests for donations from nonprofit agencies, political action groups, or politicians, examine them for appropriate and fallacious emotional appeals. What kinds of appeals do you find yourself responding to favorably? What elements of the written text—imagery, word choices, clever puns, and so on—appeal to you or help persuade you? What kinds of appeals put you off? What elements of the written text bother or offend you? Why? Bring an example of a solicitation to class for comment and discussion.

4. Read the classified ads in your local newspapers that describe houses or condominiums for sale. Pick out one that you find persuasive, in which the property sounds like a particularly good buy and for which an open house is advertised. Go to the open house, and comment in a paragraph on any differences you find between the rhetoric and the reality. Note any factual errors or misleading emotional appeals.

True Cracks Taste Barrier!

New True Laser-Cut "Flavor Chamber" Filter Improves Flavor...*Without Increasing Tar!*

Laser technology breakthrough challenges taste of higher tar brands.

True Exclusive. A unique filtration system that delivers a flavor-rich tobacco experience at a mere 5 mg. tar. A taste satisfaction we believe challenges cigarettes containing up to twice the tar.

TASTEFUL ULTRA LOW TAR

More Good News!
New True is packed with extra tobacco so you can enjoy it longer.
Noticeably longer.

New Breakthrough True.
Why not test it against the only taste that counts? Yours!

It tastes too good to be True.

New BREAKTHROUGH True

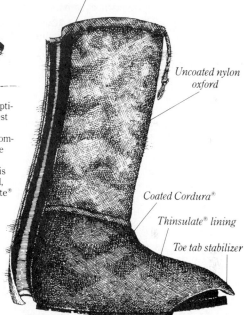

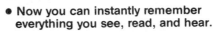

NEW PRODUCT NEWS . . .

Ohio Chemist's New Golf Ball Draws Hole-in-One Letters from All over U.S.

"After 26 years of golf during my first round I made a hole-in-one."

Company Guarantees Ball's New Gyro-Core Will Cut Strokes

64 Times More Accurate

By Mike Henson

AKRON, OH — A chemist with a small company in Ohio has developed what might be the most hook-free, slice-free ball in golf. Unsolicited hole-in-one letters from men and women all over the U.S. suggest it is 64 times more accurate than a well-known distance ball. Some report holes-in-one the first time they use it.

The ball is called Guidestar and its unusual accuracy comes from a new, oversized core that helps control it like a gyroscope. Because the core maintains near-perfect balance, it reduces the chance of an abnormal spin caused by an imperfect stroke. Abnormal spins are what cause a ball to hook or slice.

The company has conducted many tests on the ball, but the best proof of its accuracy comes from a file-full of letters like these: "Shot my first hole-in-one the first time I used Guidestar on my home course. Great balls! . . ." "After 26 years of golf during my first round with Guidestar I made a hole-in-one!"

There is even a letter from New Zealand where a minister scored a hole-in-one with the ball.

The ball is extremely lively and high compression. Bounce it on a concrete floor and it comes back at you like a rifle shot.

According to a spokesman, "The Guidestar will equal any pro-line ball on distance, but on accuracy they are no match for it, and accuracy is what counts. It's not fun hacking through bushes looking for a ball that suddenly went left or right.

These hole-in-one letters are the best proof we could have that Guidestar's unique, gyro-core helps keep shots down the middle."

In light of tests and that file-full of hole-in-one letters, the company guarantees Guidestar will cut a golfer's score dramatically. If it doesn't they will take back the balls within 30 days used, and refund their price promptly.

They also guarantee Guidestar's rugged construction will save a golfer money. If he ever cuts one, he can get *three new ones free*, if he returns the damaged ball with 50¢ for postage.

If you want to save money on lost and damaged balls, cut strokes and (who knows?) watch breathlessly on a par 3 as Guidestar's new, gyro-core carries your tee-shot toward the cup! — then try this new ball. You can't lose. A refund is guaranteed if you don't cut strokes.

To order Guidestar send your name and address to the National Golf Center (Dept. G-413), 500 S. Broad St., Meriden, CT 06450. Include $21.95 (plus $1.75 shipping) for one dozen; $19 each for two dozen or more. Six dozen cost only $99. *Free* shipping on two or more dozen. You can split your order between white and Hi-Vision yellow on a dozen basis.

To charge it include your card's name, account number and expiration date. No P.O. Boxes, please; all shipments are UPS. CT and NY must add sales tax.

You can also call 203-238-2712, 8-8 Eastern Time.

Guidestar conforms to U.S.G.A. Rules and can be used in tournament play.

Mike Hensen is a free-lance sports writer who covers golf extensively.

LOVE IS A FALLACY

Max Shulman

Cool was I and logical. Keen, calculating, perspicacious, acute and astute—I was all of these. My brain was as powerful as a dynamo, as precise as a chemist's scales, as penetrating as a scalpel. And—think of it!—I was only eighteen.

It is not often that one so young has such a giant intellect. Take, for example, Petey Bellows, my roommate at the university. Same age, same background, but dumb as an ox. A nice enough fellow, you understand, but nothing upstairs. Emotional type. Unstable. Impressionable. Worst of all, a faddist. Fads, I submit, are the very negation of reason. To be swept up in every new craze that comes along, to surrender yourself to idiocy just because everybody else is doing it—this, to me, is the acme of mindlessness. Not, however, to Petey.

One afternoon I found Petey lying on his bed with an expression of such distress on his face that I immediately diagnosed appendicitis. "Don't move," I said. "Don't take a laxative. I'll get a doctor."

"Raccoon," he mumbled thickly.

"Raccoon?" I said, pausing in my flight.

"I want a raccoon coat," he wailed.

I perceived that his trouble was not physical, but mental. "Why do you want a raccoon coat?"

"I should have known it," he cried, pounding his temples. "I should have known they'd come back when the Charleston came back. Like a fool I spent all my money for textbooks, and now I can't get a raccoon coat."

"Can you mean," I said incredulously, "that people are actually wearing raccoon coats again?"

"All the Big Men on Campus are wearing them. Where've you been?"

"In the library," I said, naming a place not frequented by Big Men on Campus.

He leaped from the bed and paced the room. "I've got to have a raccoon coat," he said passionately. "I've got to!"

"Petey, why? Look at it rationally. Raccoon coats are unsanitary. They shed. They smell bad. They weigh too much. They're unsightly. They—"

"You don't understand," he interrupted impatiently. "It's the thing to do. Don't you want to be in the swim?"

"No," I said truthfully.

"Well, I do," he declared. "I'd give anything for a raccoon coat. Anything!"

My brain, that precision instrument, slipped into high gear. "Anything?" I asked, looking at him narrowly.

"Anything," he affirmed in ringing tones.

I stroked my chin thoughtfully. It so happened that I knew where to get my hands on a raccoon coat. My father had had one in his undergraduate days; it lay now in a trunk in the attic back home. It also happened that Petey had something I wanted. He didn't *have* it exactly, but at least he had first rights on it. I refer to his girl, Polly Espy.

I had long coveted Polly Espy. Let me emphasize that my desire for this young woman was not emotional in nature. She was, to be sure, a girl who excited the emotions, but I was not one to let my heart rule my head. I wanted Polly for a shrewdly calculated, entirely cerebral reason.

I was a freshman in law school. In a few years I would be out in practice. I was well aware of the importance of the right kind of wife in furthering a lawyer's career. The successful lawyers I had observed were, almost without exception, married to beautiful, gracious, intelligent women. With one omission, Polly fitted these specifications perfectly.

Beautiful she was. She was not yet of pin-up proportions, but I felt sure that time would supply the lack. She already had the makings.

Gracious she was. By gracious I mean full of graces. She had an erectness of carriage, an ease of bearing, a poise that clearly indicated the best of breeding. At table her manners were exquisite. I had seen her at the Kozy Kampus Korner eating the specialty of the house—a sandwich that contained scraps of pot roast, gravy, chopped nuts, and a dipper of sauerkraut—without even getting her fingers moist.

Intelligent she was not. In fact, she veered in the opposite direction. But I believed that under my guidance she would smarten up. At any rate, it was worth a try. It is, after all, easier to make a beautiful dumb girl smart than to make an ugly smart girl beautiful.

"Petey," I said, "are you in love with Polly Espy?"

"I think she's a keen kid," he replied, "but I don't know if you'd call it love. Why?"

"Do you," I asked, "have any kind of formal arrangement with her? I mean are you going steady or anything like that?"

"No. We see each other quite a bit, but we both have other dates. Why?"

"Is there," I asked, "any other man for whom she has a particular fondness?"

"Not that I know of. Why?"

I nodded with satisfaction. "In other words, if you were out of the picture, the field would be open. Is that right?"

"I guess so. What are you getting at?"

"Nothing, nothing," I said innocently, and took my suitcase out of the closet.

"Where you going?" asked Petey.

"Home for the weekend." I threw a few things into the bag.

"Listen," he said, clutching my arm eagerly, "while you're home, you couldn't get some money from your old man, could you, and lend it to me so I can buy a raccoon coat?"

"I may do better than that," I said with a mysterious wink and closed my bag and left.

"Look," I said to Petey when I got back Monday morning. I threw open the suitcase and revealed the huge, hairy, gamy object that my father had worn in his Stutz Bearcat in 1925.

"Holy Toledo!" said Petey reverently. He plunged his hands into the raccoon coat and then his face. "Holy Toledo!" he repeated fifteen or twenty times.

"Would you like it?" I asked.

"Oh yes!" he cried, clutching the greasy pelt to him. Then a canny look came into his eyes. "What do you want for it?"

"Your girl," I said, mincing no words.

"Polly?" he said in a horrified whisper. "You want Polly?"

"That's right."

He flung the coat from him. "Never," he said stoutly.

I shrugged. "Okay. If you don't want to be in the swim, I guess it's your business."

I sat down in a chair and pretended to read a book, but out of the corner of my eye I kept watching Petey. He was a torn man. First he looked at the coat with the expression of a waif at a bakery window. Then he turned away and set his jaw resolutely. Then he looked back at the coat, with even more longing in his face. Then he turned away, but with not so much resolution this time. Back and forth his head swiveled, desire waxing, resolution waning. Finally he didn't turn away at all; he just stood and stared with mad lust at the coat.

"It isn't as though I was in love with Polly," he said thickly. "Or going steady or anything like that."

"That's right," I murmured.

"What's Polly to me, or me to Polly?"

"Not a thing," said I.

"It's just been a casual kick—just a few laughs, that's all."

"Try on the coat," said I.

He complied. The coat bunched high over his ears and dropped all the way down to his shoe tops. He looked like a mound of dead raccoons. "Fits fine," he said happily.

I rose from my chair. "Is it a deal?" I asked, extending my hand.

He swallowed. "It's a deal," he said and shook my hand.

I had my first date with Polly the following evening. This was in the nature of a survey; I wanted to find out just how much work I had to do to get her mind up to the standard I required. I took her first to dinner. "Gee, that was a delish dinner," she said as we left the restaurant. Then I took her to a movie. "Gee, that was a marvy movie," she said as we left the theater. And then I took her home. "Gee, I had a sensaysh time," she said as she bade me good night.

I went back to my room with a heavy heart. I had gravely underestimated the size of my task. This girl's lack of information was terrifying. Nor would it be enough merely to supply her with information. First she had to be taught to *think*. This loomed as a project of no small dimensions, and at first I was tempted to give her back to Petey. But then I got to thinking about her abundant physical charms and about the way she entered a room and the way she handled a knife and fork, and I decided to make an effort.

I went about it, as in all things, systematically. I gave her a course in logic. It happened that I, as a law student, was taking a course in logic myself, so I had all the facts at my finger tips. "Polly," I said to her when I picked her up on our next date, "tonight we are going over to the Knoll and talk."

"Oo, terrif," she replied. One thing I will say for this girl: you would go far to find another so agreeable.

We went to the Knoll, the campus trysting place, and we sat down under an old oak, and she looked at me expectantly. "What are we going to talk about?" she asked.

"Logic."

She thought this over for a minute and decided she liked it. "Magnif," she said.

"Logic," I said, clearing my throat, "is the science of thinking. Before we can think correctly, we must first learn to recognize the common fallacies of logic. These we will take up tonight."

"Wow-dow!" she cried, clapping her hands delightedly.

I winced, but went bravely on. "First let us examine the fallacy called Dicto Simpliciter."

"By all means," she urged, batting her lashes eagerly.

"Dicto Simpliciter means an argument based on an unqualified generalization. For example: Exercise is good. Therefore everybody should exercise."

"I agree," said Polly earnestly. "I mean exercise is wonderful. I mean it builds the body and everything."

"Polly," I said gently, "the argument is a fallacy. *Exercise is good* is an unqualified generalization. For instance, if you have heart disease, exercise is bad, not good. Many people are ordered by their doctors *not* to exercise. You must *qualify* the generalization. You must say exercise is *usually* good, or exercise is good *for most people*. Otherwise you have committed a Dicto Simpliciter. Do you see?"

"No," she confessed. "But this is marvy. Do more! Do more!"

"It will be better if you stop tugging at my sleeve," I told her, and when she desisted, I continued. "Next we take up a fallacy called Hasty Generalization. Listen carefully: You can't speak French. I can't speak French. Petey Bellows can't speak French. I must therefore conclude that nobody at the University of Minnesota can speak French."

"Really?" said Polly, amazed. *"Nobody?"*

I hid my exasperation. "Polly, it's a fallacy. The generalization is reached too hastily. There are too few instances to support such a conclusion."

"Know any more fallacies?" she asked breathlessly. "This is more fun than dancing even."

I fought off a wave of despair. I was getting nowhere with this girl, absolutely nowhere. Still, I am nothing if not persistent. I continued. "Next comes Post Hoc. Listen to this: Let's not take Bill on our picnic. Every time we taken him out with us, it rains."

"I know somebody just like that," she exclaimed. "A girl back home—Eula Becker, her name is. It never fails. Every single time we take her on a picnic—"

"Polly," I said sharply, "it's a fallacy. Eula Becker doesn't *cause* the rain. She has no connection with the rain. You are guilty of Post Hoc if you blame Eula Becker."

"I'll never do it again," she promised contritely. "Are you mad at me?"

I sighed. "No, Polly, I'm not mad."

"Then tell me some more fallacies."

"All right. Let's try Contradictory Premises."

"Yes, lets," she chirped, blinking her eyes happily.

I frowned, but plunged ahead. "Here's an example of Contradictory Premises: If God can do anything, can He make a stone so heavy that He won't be able to lift it?"

"Of course," she replied promptly.

"But if He can do anything, He can lift the stone," I pointed out.

"Yeah," she said thoughtfully. "Well, then I guess He can't make the stone."

"But He can do anything," I reminded her.

She scratched her pretty, empty head. "I'm all confused," she admitted.

"Of course you are. Because when the premises of an argument contradict each other, there can be no argument. If there is an irresistible force, there can be no immovable object. If there is an immovable object, there can be no irresistible force. Get it?"

"Tell me some more of this keen stuff," she said eagerly.

I consulted my watch. "I think we'd better call it a night. I'll take you home now, and you go over all the things you've learned. We'll have another session tomorrow night."

I deposited her at the girls' dormitory, where she assured me that she had had a perfectly terrif evening, and I went glumly home to my room. Petey lay snoring in his bed, the raccoon coat huddled like a great hairy beast at his feet. For a moment I considered waking him and telling him that he could have his girl back. It seemed clear that my project was doomed to failure. The girl simply had a logic-proof head.

But then I reconsidered. I had wasted one evening; I might as well waste another. Who knew? Maybe somewhere in the extinct crater of her mind a few embers still smoldered. Maybe somehow I could fan them into flame. Admittedly it was not a prospect fraught with hope, but I decided to give it one more try.

Seated under the oak the next evening I say, "Our first fallacy tonight is called Ad Misericordiam."

She quivered with delight.

"Listen closely," I said. "A man applies for a job. When the boss asks him what his qualifications are, he replies that he has a wife and six children at home, the wife is a helpless cripple, the children have nothing to eat, no clothes to wear, no shoes on their feet, there are no beds in the house, no coal in the cellar, and winter is coming."

A tear rolled down each of Polly's pink cheeks. "Oh, this is awful, awful," she sobbed.

"Yes, it's awful," I agreed, "but it's no argument. The man never answered the boss's question about his qualifications. Instead he appealed to the boss's sympathy. He committed the fallacy of Ad Misericordiam. Do you understand?"

"Have you got a handkerchief?" she blubbered.

I handed her a handkerchief and tried to keep from screaming while she wiped her eyes. "Next," I said in a carefully controlled tone, "we will discuss False Analogy. Here is an example: Students should be allowed to look at their textbooks during examinations. After all, surgeons have X rays to guide them during an operation, lawyers have briefs to guide them during a trial, carpenters have blueprints to guide them when they are building a house. Why, then, shouldn't students be allowed to look at their textbooks during an examination?"

"There now," she said enthusiastically, "is the most marvy idea I've heard in years."

"Polly," I said testily, "the argument is all wrong. Doctors, lawyers, and carpenters aren't taking a test to see how much they have learned, but students are. The situations are altogether different, and you can't make an analogy between them."

"I still think it's a good idea," said Polly.

"Nuts," I muttered. Doggedly I pressed on. "Next we'll try Hypothesis Contrary to Fact."

"Sounds yummy," was Polly's reaction.

"Listen: If Madame Curie had not happened to leave a photographic plate in a drawer with a chunk of pitchblende, the world today would not know about radium."

"True, true," said Polly, nodding her head. "Did you see the movie? Oh, it just knocked me out. That Walter Pidgeon is so dreamy. I mean he fractures me."

"If you can forget Mr. Pidgeon for a moment," I said coldly, "I would like to point out that the statement is a fallacy. Maybe Madame Curie would have discovered radium at some later date. Maybe somebody else would have discovered it. Maybe any number of things would have happened. You can't start with a hypothesis that is not true and then draw any supportable conclusions from it."

"They ought to put Walter Pidgeon in more pictures," said Polly. "I hardly ever see him any more."

One more chance, I decided. But just one more. There is a limit to what flesh and blood can bear. "The next fallacy is called Poisoning the Well."

"How cute!" she gurgled.

"Two men are having a debate. The first one gets up and says, 'My opponent is a notorious liar. You can't believe a word that he is going to say.' ... Now, Polly, think. Think hard. What's wrong?"

I watched her closely as she knit her creamy brow in concentration. Suddenly a glimmer of intelligence—the first I had seen—came into her eyes. "It's not fair," she said with indignation. "It's not a bit fair. What chance has the second man got if the first man calls him a liar before he even begins talking?"

"Right!" I cried exultantly. "One hundred per cent right. It's not fair. The first man has *poisoned the well* before anybody could drink from it. He has hamstrung his opponent before he could even start. . . . Polly, I'm proud of you."

"Pshaw," she murmured, blushing with pleasure.

"You see, my dear, these things aren't so hard. All you have to do is concentrate. Think—examine—evaluate. Come now, let's review everything we have learned."

"Fire away," she said with an airy wave of her hand.

Heartened by the knowledge that Polly was not altogether a cretin, I began a long, patient review of all I had told her. Over and over and over again I cited instances, pointed out flaws, kept hammering away without letup. It was like digging a tunnel. At first everything was work, sweat, and darkness. I had no idea when I would reach the light, or even *if* I would. But I persisted. I pounded and clawed and scraped, and finally I was rewarded. I saw a chink of light. And then the chink got bigger and the sun came pouring in and all was bright.

Five grueling nights this took, but it was worth it. I had made a logician out of Polly; I had taught her to think. My job was done. She was worthy of me at last. She was a fit wife for me, a proper hostess for my many mansions, a suitable mother for my well-heeled children.

It must not be thought that I was without love for this girl. Quite the contrary. Just as Pygmalion loved the perfect woman he had fashioned, so I loved mine. I decided to acquaint her with my feelings at our very next meeting. The time had come to change our relationship from academic to romantic.

"Polly," I said when we next sat beneath our oak, "tonight we will not discuss fallacies."

"Aw, gee," she said, disappointed.

"My dear," I said, favoring her with a smile, "we have now spent five evenings together. We have gotten along splendidly. It is clear that we are well matched."

"Hasty Generalization," said Polly brightly.

"I beg your pardon," said I.

"Hasty Generalization," she repeated. "How can you say that we are well matched on the basis of only five dates?"

I chuckled with amusement. The dear child had learned her lessons well. "My dear," I said, patting her hand in a tolerant manner, "five dates is plenty. After all, you don't have to eat a whole cake to know that it's good."

"False Analogy," said Polly promptly. "I'm not a cake. I'm a girl."

I chuckled with somewhat less amusement. The dear child had learned her lessons perhaps too well. I decided to change tactics. Obviously the best approach was a simple, strong, direct declaration of love. I paused for a moment while my massive brain chose the proper words. Then I began:

"Polly, I love you. You are the whole world to me, and the moon and the stars and the constellations of outer space. Please, my darling, say that you will go steady with me, for if you will not, life will be meaningless. I will languish. I will refuse my meals. I will wander the face of the earth, a shambling, hollow-eyed hulk."

There, I thought, folding my arms, that ought to do it.

"Ad Misericordiam," said Polly.

I ground my teeth. I was not Pygmalion; I was Frankenstein, and my monster had me by the throat. Frantically I fought back the tide of panic surging through me. At all costs I had to keep cool.

"Well, Polly," I said, forcing a smile, "you certainly have learned your fallacies."

"You're darn right," she said with a vigorous nod.

"And who taught them to you, Polly?"

"You did."

"That's right. So you do owe me something, don't you, my dear? If I hadn't come along you never would have learned about fallacies."

"Hypothesis Contrary to Fact," she said instantly.

I dashed perspiration from my brow. "Polly," I croaked, "you mustn't take all these things so literally. I mean this is just classroom stuff. You know that the things you learn in school don't have anything to do with life."

"Dicto Simpliciter," she said, wagging her finger at me playfully.

That did it. I leaped to my feet, bellowing like a bull. "Will you or will you not go steady with me?"

"I will not," she replied.

"Why not?" I demanded.

"Because this afternoon I promised Petey Bellows that I would go steady with him."

I reeled back, overcome with the infamy of it. After he promised, after he made a deal, after he shook my hand! "The rat!" I shrieked, kicking up great chunks of turf. "You can't go with him, Polly. He's a liar. He's a cheat. He's a rat."

"Poisoning the Well," said Polly, "and stop shouting. I think shouting must be a fallacy, too."

With an immense effort of will, I modulated my voice. "All right," I said. "You're a logician. Let's look at this thing logically. How could you choose Petey Bellows over me? Look at me—a brilliant student, a tremendous intellectual, a man with an assured future. Look at Petey—a knothead, a jitterbug, a guy who'll never know where his next meal is coming from. Can you give me one logical reason why you should go steady with Petey Bellows?"

"I certainly can," declared Polly. "He's got a raccoon coat."

QUESTIONS AND IDEAS FOR DISCUSSION

1. In a prefatory note to "Love Is a Fallacy," Max Shulman shares with us the following tidbit:

   > Charles Lamb, as merry and enterprising a fellow as you will meet in a month of Sundays, unfettered the informal essay with his memorable *Old China* and *Dream Children*. There follows an informal essay that ventures even beyond Lamb's frontier. Indeed, "informal" may not be quite the right word to describe this essay; "limp" or "flaccid" or possibly "spongy" are perhaps more appropriate.
   >
   > Vague though its category, it is without doubt an essay. It develops an argument; it cites instances; it reaches a conclusion. Could Carlyle do more? Could Ruskin?
   >
   > Read, then, the following essay which undertakes to demonstrate that logic, far from being a dry, pedantic discipline, is a living, breathing thing, full of beauty, passion, and trauma.

   Describe Shulman's tone in this introduction. Is "Love Is a Fallacy" an essay? Put Shulman's claim that it is into the form of a categorical syllogism and evaluate it.

2. Is love a fallacy? Why or why not? Why does Shulman indicate that it is a fallacy?

3. Dobie Gillis (the narrator) teaches Polly Espy some fallacies we have discussed, occasionally under different names. What, for example, is "poisoning the well"? Dobie also lectures Polly on some fallacies we have not discussed. Name these and give your own examples of them to back up Dobie's.

4. Polly asserts that "shouting must be a fallacy, too." Do you agree? Explain.

5. Many of my students have told me that they remember the fallacies described in "Love Is a Fallacy" more vividly than any others. How does Shulman make his "lesson" memorable? Point to specific features of the text to support your judgment.

Suggestions for Writing and Further Discussion

1. Defend advertising against its many critics. Show Jeffrey Schrank and the rest of us that advertising can be clever, illuminating, and helpful—or any other combination of qualities you believe you can support concretely. Defend, if you can, even the use of what Schrank considers to be deception in advertising messages.

2. Schrank claims that "ads are designed to have an effect while being laughed at, belittled, and all but ignored." However, his argument centers not on this claim but on the nature of the messages themselves. Write an essay for which

this claim could serve as the thesis. Use examples of current television, billboard, and print media advertising to support your conclusions about how ads achieve their effect with or without our conscious cooperation.

3. Following a suggestion of Schrank's (not reprinted here with the essay), write copy for honest advertisements to correct what you regard as distorted or misleading claims and inferences in three specific ads. Then write an essay on the problems and difficulties you encountered, if any, or on the ease of the undertaking, if that was the case. Conclude by claiming either that honest ads are not hard to create and that therefore dishonest advertisers have no excuse; or that honest ads are nearly impossible to create and that the only recourse for the consumer must be *caveat emptor*—let the buyer beware.

4.   . . . [T]he historians and archaeologists will one day discover that the ads of our time are the richest and most faithful reflections that any society ever made of its entire range of activities.

—Marshall McLuhan

    You are a historian of the mid-twenty-fourth century, researching the lives of ordinary people in the latter twentieth century. You have available to you a wealth of print advertisements. Studying the ads alone, what hypotheses can you draw about life in the 1990s? Support your claim with reference to specific ads.

5. Write an essay, based on your own and your friends' experiences, that substantiates the claim in Shulman's title, "Love Is a Fallacy."

6. Read a recent political speech by the president or another leading politician (as reprinted in *Vital Speeches* or *The New York Times*) and write an analysis of it in terms of style and logic. Does it commit any of the fallacies most prevalent in the "Checkers" speech? Any new ones? Or does it speak truth, directly and specifically? Be careful that your conclusions, based on a single speech, are not too sweeping.

7. Compare the "Checkers" speech with some of the speeches Richard Nixon made in the 1960 and 1968 presidential campaigns (consult the appropriate volumes of *Vital Speeches of the Day*), with his inaugural addresses as governor of California and as president, and with his resignation speech in 1973. What similarities and what differences do you find? Develop a thesis that argues either that the kinds of appeals Nixon used remained constant throughout his political career (and therefore that the public should have gotten the idea long before Watergate), or that his use of emotional appeals changed over the years. If the latter, show in what ways and to what extent the appeals changed. Write an argumentative essay putting forward your conclusions.

8. Since teaching people about effective means of persuasion and about fallacies may enable them to mislead others, should students be required to pass a course in ethics or to demonstrate good moral character before being allowed to enroll in a course in persuasion and argumentation? Write an essay—addressed to the dean, the president, and the provost of the university or college in which you are enrolled—arguing your answer to this question.

8

Revising Arguments: Completeness and Coherence

> *I understand a fury in your words.*
> *But not the words.*
> **—Othello, 4.2.31–32**

Once you have roughed out a thesis and have developed it into a draft, with key concepts defined, evidence mustered, and logical reasoning checked, you are likely to find that what you have before you is still far from a polished essay. Perhaps there are gaps where you've failed to make smooth transitions between points; perhaps you have no strong conclusion and the argument trails weakly off; or perhaps you see that you've failed to provide examples to illustrate a crucial point.

Fortunately, however, an essay need not begin as a unified, complete, coherent, and clear piece of writing, even though it should end up as just that. Writing is not the art of setting down fluidly what you already knew, nor is it simply a matter of justifying conclusions previously reached. As many writers and teachers of writing have reminded us, writing is often the process of discovering what you do know and learning things you may not have known before you began to write. Good writers are not afraid to modify or change their ideas. If you set your ideas in cement before you begin to write ("Lying can never be justified"; "This law is reprehensible"; "Requiring foreign language study in college is futile"), do not be surprised to find a concrete wall blocking your way at some point in the process of writing. Assertions stop thought if they are regarded as settled truths.* Besides, why write about what is obvious and irrefutable?

Thoughtful prewriting will reduce the time you spend rewriting but will not

---

*Recall S. I. Hayakawa's discussion of the dangers of judging hastily—"Reports, Inferences, Judgments"—in the readings for Chapter 4.

eliminate it. Revision is usually necessary because the first thing that comes to mind is rarely the best idea you will have; because ideas often come to mind by free association and later require rearranging in order to make sense to a reader; and because the sentence style of the first draft tends to be monotonous or convoluted. After all, you are concerned at that point with getting the ideas down on the page, not with expressing them in the clearest and most elegant prose possible.

THE AIMS OF REVISION

All writers feel a parental attachment to their words—an attachment that makes revision difficult. The thesis that you struggled to generate may need a shift in emphasis, an additional qualification, or—on occasion—a complete reversal. Some of the notes you took in researching the topic may be irrelevant to the emphasis the paper develops as it takes shape. Whole paragraphs may have to be shifted from one point in the essay to another. Writers must be willing to do a little verbal surgery.

In revising a draft, make it your goal to:

1. **Unify and complete** the argument by eliminating tangential and unrelated ideas and evidence from the essay and adding material when needed.
2. **Organize** paragraphs and sentences so that related ideas are expressed together or in sequence, and so that points are ordered and expressed logically.
3. **Improve the coherence** of the writing by checking for (and perhaps adding) subordinated sentence structures for ideas related in hierarchical or causal ways; parallel sentence structures for coordinate ideas; and appropriate transitions.
4. **Improve the clarity** of the writing by eliminating wordiness, checking the precision and appropriateness of word choices, and proofreading for grammatical and mechanical correctness.

You may have noticed that the first two points largely concern the *content* of the essay or other written message, and the last two its *style*—the way in which it has been written. In reality, style and content are nearly inseparable. If an idea is fuzzily expressed, as noted in Chapter 3, the idea itself is probably fuzzy as well. Nevertheless, we can—and do—talk about content and style as separate writing concerns, however intrinsically related they are. It *is* possible to write banal ideas in clear phrases, and it *is* possible to phrase a brilliant idea in muddy, muddled language. But in the latter case, the brilliance is usually obscured by the mud.

In this chapter we will consider just how you can revise to improve the content of your arguments and the clarity of your prose style, and, in so doing, enhance the persona—or *ethos*—created through your words. We will first look at large-scale elements of the essay (macro-revision) and then at paragraphs, sentences, and words (micro-revision). Then, in the next chapter, we will examine more sophisticated features of style, such as the use of figures of speech and the ways in which style can affect in positive ways the emotional appeal—*pathos*—of what you write.

MACRO-REVISION: THE DRAFT AS A WHOLE

Once you have worked out a rough draft from your notes, look critically at the argument you have developed to make sure that the paper is not poorly organized or sketchy in parts of its development. Just as you did in your prewriting considerations, ask questions:

- Have I discussed a single issue in my essay? Is my argument unified?
- Have I taken for granted anything that the reader might not readily understand or accept? What have I left undefined?
- Have I considered as much of the subject as my knowledge and curiosity permit and my thesis demands? What have I left undefended?
- Where have I failed to be concrete when I might have given specific examples?
- Have the logical relationships between my claim and its supporting points transferred from my head to the actual paper?
- Have I considered all the possible dimensions of this problem, or all its possible solutions?
- Have I made any necessary concessions?

Testing for Unity and Completeness

An essay is unified if it has a clearly defined thesis and if all the points and illustrations in the essay are related to and support that thesis. If you have developed your thesis with care, according to the guidelines in Chapter 2, your draft is likely to be unified in support of that thesis. But people do not always think logically, and random ideas can stray into arguments without your realizing that they are unrelated to the thesis at hand. In revising, test each supporting point, the topic of each paragraph, against the thesis. Points that do not further the argument must be dropped, however much they interest you.

For example, a student developed the following plan for an essay:

Thesis: Any minimum wage below $10 per hour compels many Americans to live in dire poverty.

1. Begin with story of the woman I talked to at the bus stop on King Street.
2. Explain Census Bureau definition of poverty line, number of people included in "poor" category. [to library for this]
3. Discuss lives of the "rich and famous" that contrast with poor people's

lives—use examples from TV show last week. Talk about the yachts, houses, and so on.

4. Identify basic living costs—housing, food, clothing, medical expenses, child care—and typical payroll deductions for poor people. [library] Try to find some more real examples, like the woman at the bus stop, to *show* how people struggle.

5. Show that about $20,000 per year ($10 per hour; 40-hour week) is minimum to be able to live "the American dream."

6. Conclusion: It is only just that all working Americans should be able to live and raise their families decently. But only a minimum hourly wage of $10 will make that possible.

After looking over this outline, a peer writing group helped this student avoid a detour to a side issue. They pointed out that his essay was not really about the rich but about the poor. He then deleted his third point, but began his essay with a description of two people at a bus stop: a prosperous-looking man with a brief-case and an expensive watch, and a woman in shabby clothes, returning to a tenement apartment and her three young children after cleaning an office building all day. At the end of his essay, he returned to that image, describing what people at a downtown bus stop might look like if the minimum hourly wage were at least $10.

But making sure that your paper is unified does not assure that you have provided all the supporting details needed to carry conviction. Effective writing provides enough support for your conclusions to be convincing; at the same time, it does not belabor the obvious or overwhelm readers with needless detail. What constitutes "completeness" in any piece of writing will vary with the rhetorical context of audience and your purpose in addressing it. A letter to college administrators arguing for smaller class sizes will be much more formal and detailed than a letter to a friend complaining that you cannot hear your psychology lecturer amidst the rustling of your three hundred classmates.

Checking Organization and Development

In working on the organization and development of your argument, you may find it helpful to test what you have written against the five parts of classical rhetorical argument: **introduction, exposition, confirmation, refutation,** and **conclusion.** How you organize your paper may well be different from the classical model, but if you have eliminated any of the parts, such as the exposition or refutation, be sure you have done so purposefully and not carelessly.

Introduction   Once you are sure that your essay covers only one issue, examine your introduction:

- Does my introduction clearly set forth my thesis? Or, if my thesis will appear near the end of the argument rather than at the outset, does my introduction carefully focus on the appropriate issue?

If the essay's focus is unclear, first consider whether changing only the thesis will make your argument sufficiently clear. An unfocused thesis often presages a foggy line of development. You may also need to revise some of your major supporting points along with the thesis.

An introduction may range in length from a single sentence to an entire chapter—depending on the length of the work and the complexity of the subject matter. Regardless of its length, every introduction has two vital functions: It must *inform* the readers about the subject of the argument, and it must *interest* them enough to make them want to read further.

Does the following draft of an introduction make you want to read further?

> The last congressional election in my district displayed many of the strengths and weaknesses of our political system. The campaign was full of mudslinging. One candidate had been in office for many years, but the other seemed more informed about the needs of our district. All in all, the system has both good and bad elements.

Odds are, you would not care to hear the rest of this student's argument. The student reached the same conclusion. She revised the introduction both to prepare readers for her actual thesis (that congressional terms should be for four years with a maximum of two consecutive terms) and to try to engage readers' interest. Compare the final version of her introduction to the one above:

> This year I worked on a political campaign for the first time, supporting a candidate for U.S. Congress. Vicky Bateson, my candidate, had years of experience in our district—as a county commissioner and later as a municipal judge. She was—and is—well acquainted with the needs of the area. She is a good speaker and a person known for her honesty and intelligence.
>
> Vicky ran against a man who has been our congressional representative for more than twenty years. He spends far more time in Washington and on "fact-finding" trips abroad than he ever does at home. He has accomplished little for our district and has a poor voting record. But he has been in office so long, and his name is so familiar to voters, that it is almost impossible to defeat him.
>
> So Vicky lost. And the next person who tries will probably lose, too. Only congressional term limits can eliminate the incredible, unfair advantage incumbents have in congressional elections.

This version is more honest, more specific, and more interesting than the first draft. It is also longer—but which paper would you prefer to read?

Introductions are important. Whether you write them first or after completing the rest of your essay, you need to give your introduction careful thought. You must find something new and important to say, or find a clearer and simpler way to discuss something often considered complex and tedious, or find a vivid example with which to pique your readers' interest.

Richard Whately, a nineteenth century theologian, identified several categories of introductions to arguments, among them the *preparatory, inquisitive, narrative, corrective,* and *paradoxical* introductions. To this list we will add the *major premise* introduction, the *concession,* and the *autobiographical* introduction. Below you will find examples of each to show you some of the possible approaches you might try in completing your own essays.

In the **preparatory** introduction the writer explains or defines the subject before discussing it in detail in the body of the essay. The preparatory introduction often culminates in the thesis statement. While it certainly has its uses, too many writers think of this kind as the *only* form introductions take.

> High school is a time for laughter and romance, parties and football games, homecoming and pep rallies—but it is also a time of conflict and distress, lost identities and bitter rivalry. My high school was structured in such a tight hierarchy of social groups that a person was labeled a misfit, a social deviant, if he chose not to belong to one. Since every adolescent longs to be accepted by his peers, almost every person belonged to some identifiable group. Each group had a unifying interest, whether drinking, surfing, toking, or dating every eligible member of the opposite sex in the school. But within each group was a secret code, a hushed understanding that every other group was to be ridiculed and its members shunned as inferior human beings. The group I belonged to was a clique-by-default, comprised of the social castoffs and so-called misfits. We should have been the most miserable of creatures, but we were not. In retrospect, I think we benefitted in some curious ways from our pariah status.
> —Kathy Taylor, "Nonconformity: The Price and the Payoff"

In this paragraph, student Kathy Taylor carefully describes the social structure of her high school to prepare readers for an unusual argument: that "we [Taylor's social group] benefitted in some curious ways from our pariah status." We have to understand just how outcast Taylor and her friends were if we are to understand and appreciate this argument fully.

The paragraph that follows this introduction details just how Taylor's group defied the social conventions of the high school. The next one, by contrast, describes the appearance and the attitudes of the more conventional students. In the fourth and fifth paragraphs, Taylor argues that in fact both groups were conformist, but that the principles to which her group conformed offered some long-lasting benefits that outweighed the shallow pleasures of high school popularity. For all of this argument the introductory paragraph has set the stage well. (The entire essay and one earlier draft appear at the end of this chapter.)

In the **inquisitive** introduction the writer asks provocative questions to stimulate the readers' interest.

> Did you know that, according to the National Science Teachers Association, the standard high school gym can accommodate about 200 science fair projects? Did you know that 199 of them are likely to be volcanoes? Did you know that out of 89 Nobel Prize and Medal of Science winners recently polled on the subject, only two had taken first place at a science fair?
>
> —Judith Stone, "Under the Volcano"

The effectiveness of this introduction is easiest to see if you consider how Judith Stone *might* have begun it:

> Nearly every high school student at some point participates in a science fair. The subjects are typically trivial and redundant, all white mice and volcanoes. Little is discovered and much is endured on the part of all the students, parents, and teachers involved. No evidence points to any lasting value in science fair projects.

While this paragraph is clear enough, it is almost as dull as the science fair projects it laments. But Stone's series of questions is both informative and entertaining—we feel assured that we will learn some interesting things in the argument that follows, and so we do. Judith Stone argues that science fairs are closer to crafts exhibitions than to demonstrations of scientific inquiry. Not content merely to complain, Stone also points the way to some solutions. (You can read the entire essay in Stone's *Light Elements: Essays on Science from Gravity to Levity,* 1991.)

In the **narrative** introduction the writer begins with an anecdote that illuminates the thesis in some way and draws the reader in. It can be a most effective introduction, for even adults enjoy a good story.

> A woman I know worked for a time in one of those prestigious sweatshops in which the imposing abodes of America's corporations are designed. A mean woman with an X-Acto knife, she was given the job of constructing the little presentation models with which her firm coaxed its clients even further into the frontiers of modern architecture. But she could stand the subsistence pay, the stiff neck, and the enforced veneration for the firm's presiding genius only long enough to complete a single model: a one-inch-to-one-foot cardboard and Mylar prototype of a huge building slated for construction somewhere in downtown Houston.
>
> A few years after she quit the firm she found herself at the Houston airport and decided to kill the two hours she had between planes by taking a cab downtown and finding the building over whose embryo she had labored so long. Though she couldn't remember what company had commissioned it, she figured she had been so intimately acquainted with its design that she could spot it without any trouble.
>
> But after an hour's search up and down the city streets, she could not for the life of her find it, and had to assume, as she boarded her plane, that the design had been changed or the project had been canceled just after she had quit. Then, suddenly, looking down at the retreating city as her plane rose in the sky, she saw her building standing right smackdab in the middle of Houston. During her search she must have passed it half a dozen times, but only now, with a bird's-eye view of it on a cardboard and Mylar scale, could she recognize it.
>
> I think my friend may have stumbled upon what's wrong with modern architecture: it is best appreciated from a couple of thousand feet off the ground. It is conceived from an aerial point of view, from the Olympian perspective of a god, an angel, a chairman of the board.
>
> —Andrew Ward, "The Trouble with Architects"

If your instructor were to invite you to read an essay on the problems inherent in contemporary architecture, you *might* not be excited at the prospect. Andrew Ward recognizes that likelihood, and so he draws you into his subject with a little story, one that epitomizes (and concludes with a direct statement of) his thesis. When you read this introduction, you know that the argument that follows will be accessible and probably interesting. (To test that assumption, look up the essay in *The Atlantic Monthly,* May 1980.)

In the **corrective** introduction the writer shows how the subject has been misunderstood and then indicates how it will be regarded in the essay at hand. Stipulative definitions often figure in corrective introductions.

> Some years ago, I clipped a cartoon out of the *New Yorker* that showed two couples seated in a living room while a giant furry beast loomed over them. The host couple

amiably explained the creature's presence to their guests this way, "We deal with it by talking about it."

I kept the cartoon as a reminder of the humor and the hubris in the idea that we can talk every problem down to size, verbally wrestle all monsters to bay. After all, I have had an abiding faith in the value of what the college course catalogues now call "communication." This belief in words has been the chicken and egg of my life as a journalist. Not to mention my life as a mother, wife and friend.

But lately I've had an urge to rewrite the caption. I sense that we are a country living with great monsters, and we are dealing with them by not talking about them. I am struck by the reticence, the unwillingness on the part of everyday people to say what they think.

—Ellen Goodman, "Celebrate Free Speech: Say What You Think"

Ellen Goodman wants to correct what she sees as the common misconception that open communication is a widespread virtue today. Goodman's thesis is that, much as we talk about "communication," we do not really communicate with each other. She puts the term in quotation marks to call our attention to the difference between how other people use the term (to mean what Goodman regards as "babbling about feelings") and how she believes we should use it (to mean "saying what you think about issues that matter"). Given the casual way we do talk about "communication," Goodman's corrective introduction works well. The image of the monsters we are not talking about will stay with you as you read the argument—which you can do by turning to page 27.

In the **paradoxical** introduction the writer shows that both parts of an apparent contradiction regarding the subject are nonetheless true. Consider, for example, the opening paragraph of Arthur C. Clarke's "We'll Never Conquer Space." (You can read the entire argument in Chapter 5.)

> Man will never conquer space. Such a statement may sound ludicrous, now that our rockets are already 100 million miles beyond the moon and the first human travelers are preparing to leave the atmosphere. Yet it expresses a truth which our forefathers knew, one we have forgotten—and our descendants must learn again, in heartbreak and loneliness.
>
> —Arthur C. Clarke, "We'll Never Conquer Space"

In this paragraph, Clarke says two things that seem opposed: (1) we'll never conquer space; and (2) "our rockets are already 100 million miles beyond the moon and the first human travelers are preparing to leave the atmosphere." Several decades after Clarke first penned these words, we could add even more accomplishments: Human travelers have visited the moon and have orbited in space for weeks and months on end. Camera- and computer-bearing rockets have sent back detailed data from the farthest planets in our solar system and beyond. In a strictly technical sense, we may well be able to conquer space. But Clarke's first statement remains true even today. In the sense he means, we never will "conquer" space, however able we may become to move through space. We will never be able to travel to Saturn as nonchalantly as we travel to Seattle, for everything will change while we are gone. Our situation, as Clarke's introductory paragraph presages, is truly paradoxical.

In the **major premise** introduction the writer establishes the ground shared between writer and reader by discussing the basic assumptions that will give rise to the thesis. This introduction is particularly effective when the thesis itself is likely to prove somewhat controversial and is best expressed at a later point in the essay.

> The AIDS epidemic may be the most serious health threat of this century. How best to deal with it has been the subject of a vigorous national debate. And out of this debate is emerging a growing and welcome consensus on a number of issues.
>
> We can all agree, for example, on the need to care for those afflicted with AIDS, by helping to ensure that families, states, localities, hospitals and others have the resources to provide adequate medical care for those suffering from this disease. We can all agree that we must prevent violations of the civil rights of those who are carriers of the AIDS virus. And we can all agree on the need to educate all of our citizens, including young people, about how the AIDS virus is transmitted and how to guard against it. Moreover, there is now nearly universal agreement on a further point: the need for more widespread AIDS testing.
>
> —William J. Bennett, "We Need Routine Testing for AIDS"

In this introduction, the former Secretary of Education under President Reagan and "drug czar" during George Bush's presidency argues a thesis that remains controversial today: We need routine testing for AIDS. Aware of the emotional aspects of the subject and of the invasion of privacy that his proposal seems to advocate, Bennett wisely begins by establishing what he believes to be the shared ground between him and most of his readers. His major premise is that nearly everyone agrees on four basic things:

- We must ensure care for AIDS patients;
- We must ensure the civil rights of HIV-positive people;
- We must educate everyone about how to guard against HIV transmission; and
- We must have more widespread AIDS testing.

If we can grant this major premise, Bennett improves the odds of convincing us that "more widespread" testing should be broadened to "universal, routine" testing. (You will find the essay reprinted in Chapter 10.)

In the **concession** the writer acknowledges whatever merit can be granted an opposing viewpoint. This kind of introduction establishes a thoughtful, reasonable persona and is well suited to arguments that are likely to elicit some opposition from the anticipated audience. The concession tends to diffuse hostilities and make readers more amenable to a differing viewpoint.

> My Dear Fellow Clergymen:
>
> While confined here in the Birmingham city jail, I came across your recent statement calling my present activities "unwise and untimely." Seldom do I pause to answer criticism of my work and ideas. If I sought to answer all the criticisms that cross my desk, my secretaries would have little time for anything other than such correspondence in the course of the day, and I would have no time for constructive work. But since I feel that you are men of genuine good will and that your criticisms are sin-

cerely set forth, I want to try to answer your statement in what I hope will be patient and reasonable terms.

—Martin Luther King, Jr., "Letter from Birmingham Jail"

Notice that King here concedes none of the points raised by the clergymen. He concedes only that their intentions are honest and well-meant. In this way he shows himself to be reasonable—knowing that if they, too, will be reasonable, they cannot help but concede in turn that his argument is just. (King's "Letter" is reprinted in Chapter 10.)

In the **autobiographical** introduction the writer tries to establish a rapport with readers through personal details or anecdotes, often identifying his or her expertise in the subject or giving particular reasons for being interested in it. A note of humor or humility is usually in order in such introductions.

> I write of nuclear power as a self-confessed coward in the face of all massive concentrations of energy. Lightning frightens me. A surge in the wind's strength makes me uneasy in an airplane. And I cannot stand at the base of a 200-foot dam without thinking of the force of gravity stored up behind it, waiting to sweep everything before it.
>
> —Roger Starr, "The Case for Nuclear Energy"

Starr calls himself a "coward," afraid of "all massive concentrations of energy." He tells us this about himself not to arouse our pity or to gain our sympathy but to show himself to be as vulnerable to fear as any one else. This personal touch is important groundwork for Starr's essay, for his purpose is to argue in favor of the most massive concentration of energy we know: nuclear power. Had he launched glibly (or stuffily) into a technical argument about the feasibility and economic profitability of nuclear energy, he would have lost many readers at the outset. The autobiographical note, however, draws us in.

As these examples show, effective introductions may take many forms. Other kinds of introductions can lead to problems, however, and should be avoided.

1. **Sweeping Declarations.** These are statements so broad you cannot hope to deal with them adequately in a short essay—or short book. "Dawn of civilization" introductions ("Since prehistoric times humankind has fought wars for economic reasons") are of this type, as are broad moral claims ("Killing is always wrong"). Such introductions are unprovable and distract readers from your specific argument.

2. **Filler.** Also known as "throat-clearing" introductions, these wordy and desperate attempts to get something—*anything*—down on paper are typified by vague statements ("Education in a heterogeneous society presents interesting problems"), obvious statements ("It is hard to understand a different culture without experiencing it firsthand"), and pointless definitions ("Propaganda is a form of persuasion").

3. **Alienating Pronouncements.** Statements that insult, offend, or otherwise alienate your readers are, for obvious reasons, deadly in introductions (and dangerous elsewhere). If you are writing about the challenge of hunting wild

turkey for an audience that includes bird watchers and gun-control advocates, for instance, there is little point in starting out with the assertion that "Nothing can match the thrill of shooting a wild turkey after a long day of stalking the wily bird."

Exposition   At some point, often after the introduction but sometimes as part of it, you may need to provide expository information about your subject, defining key terms and giving background information readers will need in order to understand the subject correctly. This part of the essay can be long or short or dispensed with altogether, depending on the audience's familiarity with the subject matter. Determine whether expository material needs to be added by asking the following questions:

- What have I left undefined?
- Have I taken for granted anything the reader might not readily understand or accept?

Here you must judge (as we discussed in Chapter 2) the extent of the audience's probable knowledge about your subject. For example, an argument favoring experimental trials of a new drug to fight multiple sclerosis will require less general background information (and more technical detail and review of previous scholarship on the subject) if it is to be published in the *Journal of the American Medical Association* for an audience of doctors than if it is to be published in *Time* for the general public. In the latter case, the writer will probably have to explain the nature of the disease itself and the fact that controversy surrounds the drug—both of which may be omitted in the argument addressed to physicians.

While the exposition is not an overtly persuasive part of an argument, it can help win readers' goodwill by reducing the potential for confusion or indifference about the subject matter. And, because all that we write is necessarily selective, the exposition can help win readers' sympathies by the information it includes.

Confirmation   "Confirmation" is the rhetorical term for the core of the argument: the reasons, examples, and evidence the writer offers in support of the thesis. If you offer no reason (for drawing your thesis conclusion) without explanation and no explanation without example, you will be unlikely to leave weak links in your argument. To check your argument for support, consider these questions:

- What have I left undefended?
- Where have I failed to be concrete when I might have given specific examples?

To see how these questions will help, read the following key passage from a student draft:

> This kind of relief [through the national flood insurance program] is essential if anyone is to dare live in many flood-prone areas. By the same token, national tornado insurance coverage could help the millions of people who live in "Tornado Alley."

> Even those who have ordinary insurance find that it cannot cover the total devastation a tornado can inflict.

This core argument draws an analogy between one kind of natural disaster, flood, and another, tornadoes. Its claim is that national insurance is as appropriate for the latter as for the former. The writer, Stacy Fikes, was initially satisfied that the paragraph made the point she wanted to make, but when she asked the two questions above, she realized that the confirmation of her thesis was incomplete. First, although she had (earlier in the essay) defined "Tornado Alley," Fikes had not defended people's choosing to live in tornado-prone areas; and second, she had not given examples to strengthen and illuminate the abstract phrase, "the total devastation a tornado can inflict."

Here is Stacy Fikes's revision of this passage:

> This kind of relief [through the national flood insurance program] is essential if anyone is to dare live in many flood-prone areas. By the same token, national tornado insurance coverage could help the millions of people who live in "Tornado Alley." Tornado Alley—stretching from Iowa to the Gulf Coast—is too vast to be evacuated, as some argue should be done in areas prone to heavy flooding. Even my own home in eastern Kansas, which has one of the highest rates of tornado frequency in the nation, is an area too important in farming, commerce, and education (it includes Kansas City and Lawrence, home of the University of Kansas) to ask people either to leave or to bear the cost of rebuilding after a tornado.
>
> Many people do have regular insurance coverage for wind damage to property. All the same, those who have ordinary insurance find that it cannot cover the total devastation a tornado can inflict. My cousins' farmhouse and barn were reduced to sticks and rubble in a tornado so fierce that it tossed their huge combine machinery into a field a quarter-mile from the barn. Their car was crushed. They even found a dinner fork with its tines driven straight into a tree trunk, and a chair, otherwise undamaged, high up in a tree far from the house. Even with the insurance, they faced additional expenses of nearly $50,000 to rebuild and replace what they had lost.

In this revision, Fikes has given her argument vitality by making it more specific and concrete. The passage is longer than before, but it is stronger, too.

Take care to organize your points clearly and logically. No magic formula for organizing points exists; just be sure you have a rationale for the ordering that makes sense and enables you to move easily and naturally from one point to the next. As new and previously unsuspected connections between ideas become apparent to you, you may decide to change the order of their presentation. While revising, keep in mind the analogy of relay race strategy: End with the strongest runner, and don't begin with the weakest.

One cardinal rule does apply: If you set up reader expectations for a particular ordering of ideas—perhaps by itemizing your main points early in the essay—you are bound to discuss those points in the same order in which you first identify them.

Refutation   You must always consider other possible ideas and viewpoints about the subject besides your own. To show that you have done so enhances your persona substantially by demonstrating that you are both well informed and reasonable. Ask questions to ensure that you have considered other viewpoints:

- Have I considered all the possible dimensions of the problem, or all its possible solutions?
- Have I made any necessary concessions to opposing arguments?

If you argue that the federal government is right to give tax credit for private school tuition, remember that many people oppose such credits, and speak to this opposition either directly or indirectly. If you claim that aliens from outer space have visited Syracuse, New York, you must bear in mind that many people do not believe that life exists elsewhere in the universe. Investigating opposing viewpoints helps you determine which points will best support your own thesis—and occasionally, if you are open-minded, will cause you to modify your own position to reflect what truth you see in the opposition.

The placement of the refutation depends on two factors: the nature of the subject matter and your sense of your audience. If the subject is controversial, put the refutation early, since the opposing viewpoint will be on the readers' minds anyway. For example, if you are writing in favor of lowering the legal drinking age in your state, and your readers include members of MADD (Mothers Against Drunk Driving), you will need to address their likely objections at the outset. If, however, the likely readers are all college freshmen, they may be more favorably disposed toward your arguments. You can defer your refutation until near the end of your essay, where it will add an extra punch to your argument.

If your subject is relatively complex, you may find it works best to alternate making your own points and refuting opposing points. Otherwise, readers may have trouble following your argument. An argument organized this way uses careful transitions to help readers follow it. The general form of a point-by-point argument looks something like this in the main body of the argument:

X says that, which is faulty because. . . .
Y, on the other hand, says this, which is correct because. . . .
X further claims that, but. . . .
Y answers this, given that. . . .
Indeed, X goes so far as to say that, not realizing that. . . .
But Y counters with this, which is right because. . . .
So, all in all, Y is right.

Typically you first describe the point you intend to refute and then argue the error in it. Next, you make your counterpoint and support it. You follow this general pattern point-by-point.

Some essays included in this book use this approach, including Clarence Darrow's "Why I Am an Agnostic." In this essay Darrow lists what he believes are the main tenets of Christianity and offers an argument opposing each in turn. Another complex point-by-point refutation and argument is Martin Luther King, Jr.'s "Letter from Birmingham Jail," in which King lists the arguments against nonviolent activism and refutes each by turn. (You will find both of these essays in Chapter 10.)

Conclusion   The conclusion can be the most difficult part of an essay to write. Questions may help you revise your conclusion:

- What idea am I trying to persuade my audience to accept?
- How can I best emphasize or reassert my original thesis?

If you don't ask questions such as these, you may be tempted just to stop, rather than to conclude. When that happens, the essay either drops off abruptly or mindlessly repeats what the readers have already been told. If your essay is long—ten to fifteen pages or more—and complex, you may need to repeat the major points you have made to support your thesis. But if your essay is less than five pages, you insult your readers' intelligence by reiterating what you have just said.

A few other pointers: the rhetorical (open-ended) question—my own favorite type of conclusion during my high school years—grows tiresome with overuse. Second, a concluding quotation can be effective, but might weaken the power of your own persona. Usually you will do best to end in your own words. And, finally, unless the essay is quite long, and the conclusion itself longer than a single paragraph, avoid all temptations to begin the conclusion with the words, "In conclusion. . . . " Readers know the end is near; don't insult their intelligence.

With all these cautions in mind, what choices do you have in writing a conclusion? Several, in fact.

You may **omit a formal conclusion,** if your essay is short. A single summing-up sentence (often your thesis) will probably suffice. For example, the following short essay reprinted in Chapter 10 ends with a single emphatic sentence:

> I'll put it bluntly: if you care for the quality of life in our American democracy, then you have to be for censorship.
> —Irving Kristol, "Pornography, Obscenity, and the Case for Censorship"

You may **end with a final illustration or anecdote** that illuminates your thesis or ties the conclusion to the introduction by completing an image or anecdote begun there. A moving essay on the significance of maps and names in the Middle East (Hebrew names replacing Arabic names, and vice versa) ends with an anecdote that sums up the writer's concerns:

> When at a certain stage I left my own immediate surroundings to seek out a more universal dimension to my experiences, I found myself in the Grand Opera House of Belfast. The first performance of Brian Friel's *Translations* was given in the Opera House—rebuilt after twenty-four bombing incidents—to an all-Catholic audience. The play dealt with the substitution of an English map of Ireland for the original, the ultimate symbolic expression of possession. When the play ended, I said to my friend, a Catholic, "You know what? We've been doing the same thing all along—translating, changing names, creating a new reality." My friend regarded me for a moment with an expression of the utmost sadness and said at last, "Well, if that's the case, may God have mercy on you all!"
> —Meron Benvenisti, "Maps of Revenge"

No one wins this kind of conflict, Benvenisti tells us. Or rather, he lets the little story he recounts do so. (You can read this story in Chapter 10.)

You also may **offer a possible solution** if your argument has identified and discussed a problem. In fact, if your argument centers on identifying a problem, you almost owe it to your readers to suggest possibilities for resolving it—if you believe it is resolvable. It is easy to point fingers, harder to find solutions. The following student essay offers a possible solution to the problem it has discussed, bias in television news reporting. It also gives a warning.

> If people are ready to draw their own conclusions, and to watch entire congressional hearings rather than sound bites at 6:30, CNN may provide the best option for television news viewing.
>
> CNN is no longer a minor player in the news game. People watch it worldwide (Bernstein, "CNN" 8). When Kuwait City was liberated during the Persian Gulf war, an old Kuwaiti man said on camera: "'We give special thanks to Mr. Bush and all the allies. . . . The British, the French, the Egyptians, CNN . . .'" (Diamond 26). But if the networks let CNN take over news broadcasting, the problems related to "sameness" that afflict ABC, CBS, and NBC news programming will automatically become CNN's problems. *One* news network cannot be better than three for a country that values diversity and values real news.
>
> —Dequa Thompson, "Problems with Network News"

Thompson has found that the problems of network news are complex; some may not be resolvable. After researching the issues, she finds the network with the fewest problems of bias or inadequacy to be CNN, and recommends watching it as a partial solution. But Thompson ends with an important warning: It is not enough to have one good news network if we have *only* one. (This essay appears in the readings for Chapter 4.)

You may **indicate a preference or final judgment** if your argument has compared two or more things. One student has elected this tactic in the following concluding paragraph to a short argument about Santa Claus. She first rejects the alternatives of requiring children either to believe all sorts of improbable things or to keep their questions to themselves. She concludes with what she feels is the most appropriate alternative. (This essay appears in the readings for Chapter 7.)

> A more sensible alternative is possible. Do not do away with Santa Claus or presents or Christmas trees—simply do away with the lies and evasions. Like little Virginia, many years ago, children today will find the truth just as enchanting as the fibs and fallacies. The spirit of sharing and giving at Christmastime is represented by a "pretend" figure known as Santa Claus. Real people do the giving, and children can be part of that giving: Those with more toys than they need can select one or more that they might have received to take to the Salvation Army or another charitable organization so that little Sally can have some toys at Christmas, too. No enjoyment is lost to the child who learns about Santa as a symbol and who reads "The Night Before Christmas" for what it is—a delightful fairy tale. And no loss of innocence occurs at age seven or eight in children who have known the truth all along. Santa is just too wonderful a part of Christmas to be put in the position of being exposed as a lie.
>
> —T. J. Stone, "Lies, Fallacies, and Santa Claus"

You may **predict an outcome** if your argument has centered on a situation as yet unresolved. In an argument against censorship, one writer talks confidently about the future:

> In a long perspective, the fear of the word is really the fear of the human. . . . [T]hose who censor and favor censorship are really saying, "I am human, but everything human is alien to me." Men and women are men and women *because* of their sexual drives, and denial of this fact by even a never-ending line of censors—liberal *or* illiberal!—will not eliminate maleness and femaleness and the male-female relationship. The censor will never outlast biology.
>
> —Eli M. Oboler, "Defending Intellectual Freedom"

Oboler here predicts that censorship cannot finally stifle what it decries, which is human sexuality. When you can ground your prediction, as Oboler does, in the probable rather than the fanciful, your conclusion can be highly persuasive. (You can read the essay that ends with this paragraph in Chapter 10.)

Finally, you may **state your thesis** (for the first time) and discuss or illustrate it. You are likely to choose this option if you have developed an enthymeme according to the model discussed in Chapter 2. In a defense of journalism, longtime *Harper's* editor Lewis Lapham first argues what journalism does and does not provide. Lapham gradually leads us to his conclusion: that the final responsibility for functional journalism rests as much with the readers as with the journalists. The first sentence of his last paragraph is the first specific declaration of Lapham's thesis:

> The newspapers yield only as much as the reader brings to his reading. If the reader doesn't also study foreign affairs, or follow the money markets, or keep up his practice of foreign languages, then what can he expect to learn from the papers?
>
> —Lewis Lapham, "Sculptures in Snow"

Like Lapham, you may choose an enthymematic organization (beginning with shared ground, substantiating a claim drawn from that shared ground, ending with the necessary conclusion) when your readers might be alienated or bored by your claim if you announced it in the first paragraph. "The newspapers yield only as much as the reader brings to his reading." If that thesis appeared in the first paragraph, you might think, "So what?" But by the final paragraph you understand the full implications and importance of Lapham's claim. (Read the essay, reprinted in Chapter 9, to see if you agree.)

EXERCISE 8–1

The following are introductory paragraphs from student essays. The essays were written after the students had read a Herman Melville story and some of the writings of philosopher Jeremy Bentham.

Evaluate these introductory paragraphs. Identify the weaknesses and strengths you find. Which of the paragraphs do you find most promising? Why? What specific suggestions would you make to each of these writers as he or she prepares to revise?

(1)

Jeremy Bentham developed a philosophical and political theory called Utilitarianism. Utilitarianism states that all decisions should be made by deciding what gives the greatest good to the greatest number. Herman Melville's short story "Bartleby the Scrivener" has characters who support and attack Utilitarianism.

(2)

The narrator in Herman Melville's short story "Bartleby the Scrivener" is confounded by the presence of his employee Bartleby. The character of Bartleby is an enigma, a man who refuses to conform to the narrator's notions of what "ought" to be done. Bartleby opposes his employer wholeheartedly, although passively, and "prefers not to" do anything the narrator asks of him. While considering the narrator's actions and his philosophies concerning Bartleby, one can also consider Jeremy Bentham's principles of utilitarianism and notice the similarities between the two men's views on Life and Human Nature. Bentham's theories are directly applicable in the case of the narrator.

(3)

There are only two characters that undergo any form of development in "Bartleby the Scrivener," a short story by Herman Melville. Of these two, Bartleby and the narrator, the latter is more complex in his action and decisions.

(4)

After reading "Bartleby the Scrivener" one would agree that Bartleby is no ordinary law clerk and that he is indeed an eccentric. But upon considering the narrator as a main character, one may also agree that he is no ordinary narrator. Not only does he report his experiences with a wayward copyist, but he acts as a moral agent. Faced with the problem of Bartleby, the narrator seeks some reasonable means through which he may understand Bartleby's resistance. In doing so, the narrator soon discovers that it is not just his curiosity that must be satisfied but his sense of moral responsibility as well.

EXERCISE 8–2

Which of the following subjects—regardless of your purpose or your specific thesis—would be likely to require extensive exposition for an audience of your rhetoric class? Which would require brief exposition? Is there any subject here for which you could dispense with the exposition entirely? Explain.

Writing letters of complaint to landlords
Deer hunting
Commodities trading
The requirements at this college for a liberal arts degree

The requirements at this college for an engineering degree

The relative merits of *WordPerfect* and Microsoft *Word*

The need for expanded mass transit in this community

The need for expanded mass transit in Miami, Florida

African photo safaris

The Russian economy

Fraternity grade requirements at this college

Ethics in argumentation

The psychological needs reflected in slang usage among high school students

The "Theory of Everything" (TOE) in physics

The enduring appeal of the game of *Monopoly*

EXERCISE 8–3

A. For one of the topics listed below, list all the supporting points you can think of for two or three different possible stances on the subject. Try to develop strong, arguable points for *each* viewpoint, not just your own.

B. Star the viewpoint you would elect to argue in an essay. Circle the two or three strongest points under the other viewpoints you have identified. Which of these would you need to address in your own argument, either by conceding them (and showing that they do not negate your own position) or by refuting them?

C. In a paragraph or two, discuss why and how you would concede or refute the particular points you have identified. For this particular topic, should the refutation come first, last, or alternate point-by-point with the arguments supporting your own position?

1. Regarding serious medical conditions, should teens have the sole right to decide what treatment they will or will not receive?
2. Should Americans buy only American cars?
3. How can we more successfully attract bright college students to teaching careers in elementary and secondary education?
4. Can racism in our society be eliminated in our lifetime? If so, how? If not, why not? In either case, what are the implications for the future?
5. Why has the Barbie doll remained a top seller for more than thirty years?
6. What are the advantages of living in a rural community?
7. Can high-risk sports (such as bungee jumping, skydiving, technical climbing) be justified because they build self-esteem in the participants?
8. Does the United States need any more lawyers?

9. Would it be a good idea to tax all personal annual income over a certain amount (perhaps $1 million) at ninety percent?

10. What role should the United States play in eastern Europe?

EXERCISE 8–4

Based on the thesis idea that obscenity laws cannot be made specific enough to serve any useful purpose, you have written a draft that includes the following points. Order them in a way that seems appropriate to your purpose of persuading your state legislators not to pass some pending legislation on obscenity. Add any additional points that would improve the argument, and take out any that do not work. Then, in a paragraph or two, explain why you made the choices you did and ordered the points as you did.

> Obscenity is an inherently nebulous concept, dependent on the viewpoint of each beholder.

> A survey of students in a mass media class showed no consensus regarding whether five slides showed indecent subjects. One of those slides was of a woman being electrocuted; another was of a scene from an X-rated movie.

> Juries that try obscenity cases are made up of ordinary citizens with no training in psychology or ethics. It is often impossible for them to reach decisions in such cases, thus wasting tax money and accomplishing nothing.

> It might be more useful to promote ethics education in schools than to pass obscenity laws.

> Many times obscenity has violent rather than sexual overtones.

> What is obscene to one person is art to another; the key question is whether either is demonstrably harmed.

EXERCISE 8–5

Suppose that you have written drafts for essays based on the following thesis conclusions. For which of them, if any, would extensive refutation be advisable? For which, if any, would a brief refutation be sufficient? Indicate for each whether you would put the refutation before, after, or alternating point-by-point with your own arguments. Assume that your audience is your rhetoric classmates, and your purpose is to persuade them to adopt your viewpoint on a subject about which they have relatively little knowledge but may have biases or preconceptions.

WordPerfect's extensive user-support system will make it the dominant word processing program for some time to come.

Fear of the AIDS epidemic in Africa will make African photo safaris by wealthy North Americans a thing of the past.

Playing *Monopoly* promotes acquisitive behavior in children.

EXERCISE 8–6

Evaluate the following concluding paragraphs from student essays as specifically as you can without having the entire essays before you. Comment on particular weaknesses and strengths.

(1)

In conclusion, this essay has demonstrated that eliminating smoking on most airline flights has increased safety and made flying more pleasant for all concerned. In the words of Homer Coombs, the frequent flyer mentioned earlier, "Let them [the smokers] eat cake—at least now I'll be able to taste mine!"

(2)

If you do all the above and you still get no response, forget about it and just don't tell any more jokes. Now you know that telling a joke well really can be hard to do. However, if you have the drive, the spirit, and the stupidity, you will probably tell a joke anyway.

(3)

Scientific evidence that contradicts certain religious beliefs shows that it is time for some of the devout to rethink their interpretation of the Bible. If the evidence of evolution conflicts with the idea that humans were instantaneously created by God, perhaps a more valid theory could encompass the significant aspects of both beliefs: God created humans in a period that, although long to finite minds, was only a day out of eternity. Is it not the Bible that says (in 2 Peter 3.8) that "a thousand years [are] as one day" with the Lord?

(4)

Thus, I find the symbol of my philosophy of life: the eternal cockroach. Although such a choice may be irreverent, it does, nevertheless, direct my path. The roach's survival throughout the ages—and throughout many people's houses—reminds me not to focus entirely on one goal. Instead, the best move is to diversify my interests and skills and thereby be prepared for whatever opportunities I encounter. In this way, I will never be forced into a small niche, like the Smilodon,* where I might face failure. Instead, I will always succeed. It is amazing that from such a small insect can come such a valuable lesson.

---

*The smilodon, this essay explains earlier, was the "sabre-toothed tiger" of the Oligocene period. It overspecialized in its hunting methods and thus died out when its prey did.

(5)

I wonder if SMU is not making a mistake in its course requirements—its devotion to the core curriculum. When we graduate, we will be competing with people who were able to decline to take an art course in preference to one in their own chosen specialty. Being well-rounded in the past meant knowing more; now, it means knowing less.*

By applying the checklists and questions up to this point in this chapter, you have reviewed and revised your argument to make it complete and unified, with a fully developed and interesting introduction; an exposition of the subject, if your readers are not likely to be familiar with it; a thorough and logically organized discussion of the support for your claim; a refutation of opposing claims, if relevant; and a conclusion that neatly and convincingly completes the argument. You have reflected, researched, reviewed, and rewritten.

You have not finished, however. The argument still may be a bit ragged around the edges. It is time to look more closely at each paragraph and each sentence.

MICRO-REVISION: PARAGRAPHS AND SENTENCES

Revising for Paragraph Unity

If every paragraph in your essay draft deals with a single topic, and every sentence in each paragraph is directly related to its topic, your writing will be unified. On a first or second draft, however, you may discover tangential ideas and observations creeping in, or you may find that you have lightly touched on a couple of different topics in a single paragraph rather than fully developing one topic. One student, Will Craig, discovered this problem in the following draft paragraph:

Many students dislike science, or at least think they do, because they think it is just lots of memorizing plus some lab experiments that usually never turn out the way they are supposed to. Actually, my junior high school did not have a real science lab at all, which added to the problem. The building had been planned for an elementary school. We met for science in a regular classroom and could do just a few experiments with scales and a bunsen burner. There was not good ventilation for any serious experiments, or any sinks to wash up in, so we could not dissect frogs or other small animals. Not surprisingly, most of us were bored stiff.

---

*I cannot resist a footnote here: The student who concluded his essay with this paragraph made a near-perfect score on the MCAT exam and went on to his "own chosen specialty" at the Johns Hopkins Medical School. Apparently he was undamaged by the core curriculum.

In revising the argument, Craig discovered that this paragraph was not unified. Its topic was meant to be "the actual reasons why many students dislike science." But it follows a long detour through Craig's junior high school science lab before getting back to the main issue. When Craig revised the paragraph, it became—not surprisingly—two paragraphs.

> Many students dislike science because they think it involves mostly memorization of dry facts and formulas. At least at my junior high and high schools, that proved to be a pretty accurate description. We memorized lists of things and took multiple choice and fill-in-the-blank tests on them. Even lab experiments did not let the students actually discover anything for themselves. The whole objective was to arrive at some result already determined.
>
> To make matters worse, my junior high school did not have a real science lab at all, which added to the problem. The building had been designed as an elementary school. We met for science in a regular classroom where we could do just a few experiments with scales and a bunsen burner. There was not good ventilation for any serious experiments, or any sinks to wash up in, so we could not dissect frogs or other small animals. There was no opportunity for discovery, to really find out for ourselves how things work.

Each of the two resulting paragraphs is unified; it deals with a single topic. The result is more fully developed and more specific than the original draft, as well as more unified.

Revising for Paragraph Completeness

Completeness within each individual paragraph involves the same considerations, on a smaller scale, as does completeness in the entire essay. A one- or two-sentence paragraph often serves well for transition or for emphasis, but for making a complex point such a length is inadequate. Even the three-sentence paragraph can be cursory. At any length, the underdeveloped paragraph leaves readers fidgeting: What does this have to do with the rest of the paper? Why does the writer draw this conclusion? How does this point fit in? What does this mean? or (worst of all), So what? Complete paragraphs may raise such questions in the reader's mind, but they also answer most of those questions. And anticipating and answering the reader's questions about the topic rarely can be accomplished in a couple of sentences.

Certainly, completeness is not determined by number of sentences or number of lines alone, but few sentences and few lines can be symptomatic of poor development. Always look closely at short paragraphs. Do they develop the topic idea thoroughly, or do they take for granted knowledge the reader may not have? Do they define key terms? Do they break down the topic idea into its component parts, if any? Do they use evidence, examples, and analogies to make clear the relationships between ideas and the reasons for the conclusions they draw? Ask these questions in evaluating any paragraph, especially the last: Does it give an example? Any paragraph benefits from an illustration.

A few examples will illustrate how each paragraph in a draft might be tested for completeness:

1. **Does the paragraph develop the topic idea thoroughly?** It is all too easy to assume that your readers understand what you are talking about, when in fact you may have left them in the dark. One student found, when he read an essay draft to his peer writing group, that they did not understand his point because they did not understand his topic.

> The idea of making something out of nothing has always been hard to describe in words. Hartle and Hawking actually describe in a pictorial way how the mathematics of creating something from nothing works. It works if we can understand that linear time is just apparent, not real.

This student was a physics major who wrote as if his readers were all physics majors, too. He had a lot of work to do before he could develop both his argument and this paragraph fully enough and plainly enough for a lay audience to follow him. Remember, when you write about subjects you know well or have studied in depth, that you cannot always assume that your readers will fully understand what you skim past.

2. **Does the paragraph define key terms?** Readers do not appreciate writers who casually introduce terms important to their argument, but pertinent only to a specialized field of knowledge, without giving the slightest hint what the words mean. Similarly, if you stipulate a particular meaning for a term other than its ordinary usage, you need to explain how you are using the term. The following paragraph defines the key term *laser:*

> The acronym "laser," coined by scientist Gordon Gould in 1957, describes in shorthand form how the device works: Light Amplification by Stimulated Emission of Radiation. In 1916 Einstein predicted that electrons in an atom could be deliberately stimulated to emit photons (light energy) of a certain wavelength. He was right. The laser must first be "pumped" with energy in a variety of ways—from Maiman's flash tube to a nuclear explosion—so that the electrons are excited into higher energy states. But these high energy electrons are unstable—and fall back to a lower energy level. On the way down, their extra energy is released as light. That light is captured inside the laser and amplified by bouncing it back and forth between mirrors. The laser beam that emerges is amplified, monochromatic, coherent light—and it shines with an unearthly power.
>
> —"The Dazzle of Lasers," *Newsweek,* 13 Jan. 1983

The term *laser* is freely used but probably little understood. In this example, the writer helps us by defining it. Of course, you do not have to define terms that should be well understood by any educated lay reader.

3. **Does the paragraph break down the topic into its component parts, if any?** All writing involves analysis—the breaking down of a subject or a problem into its component parts. The topic of almost any paragraph can be better understood if it is broken down and explained analytically, as in the following case:

> As a Wasp, the mildest thing I can say about the stereotype emerging from the current wave of anti-Wasp chic is that I don't recognize myself. As regards emotional uptightness and sexual inhibition, modesty forbids comment—though I dare say various friends and lovers of mine could testify on these points if they cared to. I will admit to enjoying work—because I am lucky enough to be able to work at what I enjoy—but not, I think, to the point of compulsiveness. And so far as ruling America,

or even New York, is concerned, I can say flatly that (a) it's a damn lie because (b) if I *did* rule them, both would be in better shape than they are. Indeed I and all my Wasp relatives, taken in a lump, have far less clout with the powers that run this country than any one of the Buckleys or Kennedys (Irish Catholic), the Sulzbergers or Guggenheims (Jewish), or the late A. P. Giannini (Italian) of the Bank of America.
—Robert Claiborne, "A Wasp Stings Back," *Newsweek,* 30 Sept. 1974

This paragraph analyzes two elements that together constitute "waspishness" in the writer's view: "emotional uptightness and sexual inhibition," on the one hand, and "ruling America," on the other.

4. **Does the paragraph provide evidence, examples, or analogies?** If it does not, add an example or two, or compare your topic to something simpler or more concrete. The example of a specific book makes the following paragraph more convincing than it would have been had it made only general assertions:

It's often the best books that draw the beadiest attention of the censors. These are the books that really have the most to offer, the news that life is rich and complicated and difficult. Where else, for example, could a young male reader see the isolation of his painful adolescence reflected the way it is in *Catcher in the Rye,* one of the *most* banned books in American letters? In the guise of fiction, books offer opportunities, choices, and plausible models. They light up the whole range of human character and emotion. Each, in its own way, tells the truth and prepares its eager readers for the unknown and unpredictable events of their own lives.
—Loudon Wainwright, "A Little Banning Is a Dangerous Thing," *Life,* 1982

Without the example of *Catcher in the Rye,* this paragraph would be composed solely of general assertions. It might have been further improved had the writer explained just how *Catcher* epitomizes all his assertions, or had he added still more examples.

Another paragraph shows how useful analogy can be in developing an idea. Suppose that you are reading an article in *Scientific American* about experiments involving microscopic ocean creatures called zooplankton. If the following paragraph had ended after the second sentence, you might not understand just what a formidable task the scientists faced:

When [biologist Cabell S.] Davis tested the equipment, he found that zooplankton easily avoided the trap. "The dexterity of these bugs was truly amazing," Davis describes. Imagine you have shrunk to one millimeter, he explains. A nozzle measuring 60 feet across comes at you at 2,000 miles an hour. When it is 60 feet away, you accelerate from a dead stop to more than 2,000 miles an hour in the opposite direction, in one-sixtieth of a second.
—Marguerite Holoway, *Scientific American,* Apr. 1992

The analogy brings the problem to life. *Now* we can grasp the enormous challenge facing the marine biologists.

Revising for Coherence

Every paragraph in a paper should be clearly related to the paper's thesis, and every sentence in a paragraph should be clearly related to the topic sentence. Each sentence must also follow logically from the sentence before it. If it does, and if the logical connections are reinforced by transitions and parallelism, your writing will be coherent.

The biggest single flaw in most writing is incoherence, and incoherence occurs largely when writers fail to justify assertions logically or when they assume that relationships between ideas are obvious or self-evident. The solution lies in thinking through and then spelling out such relationships—no easy task.

The relationships between ideas in a paragraph are made clear by **subordination, repetition** (of sentence structure, words, or pronouns), and appropriate **transitions**—but the relationships between ideas must first exist, or coherence devices create only a mockery of coherence and add to the confusion. Consider a baffling example of such mock coherence:

> Among the most liberal of educations is that received at a prep school such as the one I attended. However, prep schools offer a student the opportunity to get to know students from all over the country and from several foreign countries. This variety of students has been very interesting. For example, we had to study three foreign languages in order to graduate. Foreign languages were not difficult for me, but math certainly was hard. For that matter, the beds were hard, too. Accordingly, Sweetly Prep did not believe in coddling students. We therefore, as you can see, received a liberal and thorough education.
>
> —Student draft

What this writer has done is to freely associate ideas: liberal education → variety of students, including foreign students → study of foreign languages → hard studies and hard beds → students not coddled → students received liberal education. As he rambles, he loses sight of his real topic (what makes a prep school education "among the most liberal of educations"?) but not of the injunction to be coherent. So he ties together the argument, which he senses is getting away from him, with a string of inappropriate transitional words and repeated phrases. The attempt is no more successful than attempting to giftwrap a bicycle: The unwieldy paragraph, like the Schwinn, cannot be contained. But no paragraph is utterly beyond hope, once we recognize both its problems and its possibilities. We will return to this one.

Subordination   All ideas are not created equal, and one task of revising is to make sure that what matters most is given most prominence in your argument. This is true on the large scale, where you give most attention and greatest space to developing your strongest points. It is equally true on the sentence level, where you make sure that major points are expressed in independent clauses and minor details about those points are subordinated into dependent clauses, phrases, or even words. The importance of choices you make about what to emphasize and what to subordinate can be illustrated by the following sentences combining three bits of information: "Davis quit in disgust," "Davis flew to Tahiti," and "Stafford hired a new accountant."

1. After Stafford hired a new accountant, Davis quit in disgust and flew to Tahiti.

2. Just before Davis quit in disgust and flew to Tahiti, Stafford hired a new accountant.
3. Davis flew to Tahiti where, disgusted that Stafford had hired a new accountant, he wired the company his resignation.
4. Having quit the company in his disgust that Stafford had hired a new accountant, Davis flew to Tahiti.

In sentence 1, what seems to matter most is that Davis quit. In sentence 2, it is the fact that Stafford hired a new accountant. Sentence 3 emphasizes both Davis's flight to Tahiti and his resignation. Sentence 4 places the most emphasis on Davis's flight to Tahiti. None is "right" or "wrong," but in each sentence the emphasis is different. When you write, make sure that the information you want to emphasize is expressed in main clauses: Never bury a key point in a dependent clause.

Repetition: Key Terms, Parallel Structure, and Pronouns   Repetition of key terms, repetition of grammatical patterns (parallelism), and the use of pronouns as links back to nouns mentioned earlier also provide useful aids to coherence. Each of these three coherence devices serves to remind the reader of the relationship between the sentence he or she is reading and the ideas in previous sentences. Repeating key terms reminds readers of the topic under consideration. Repeating grammatical patterns reinforces the equivalent importance of ideas by putting them in grammatically equivalent patterns. Using and repeating pronouns helps you avoid continually renaming subjects under discussion. Any pronoun is necessarily a coherence device, for it always must refer back to some previously mentioned noun. Of course, the reference must be completely clear and unambiguous (not as in "Sam told Peter he was likely to be fired," where the intended reference might be to either man).

The following paragraph from Alfred North Whitehead's "Universities and Their Functions" illustrates the use of these three devices to reinforce the interweaving of ideas within a paragraph:

> The justification for a university is that it preserves the connection between knowledge and the zest of life, by uniting the young and the old in the imaginative consideration of learning. The university imparts information, but it imparts it imaginatively. At least, this is the function which it should perform for society. A university which fails in this respect has no reason for existence. This atmosphere of excitement, arising from imaginative consideration, transforms knowledge. A fact is no longer a bare fact: it is invested with all its possibilities. It is no longer a burden on the memory: it is energizing as the poet of our dreams, and as the architect of our purposes.

You see the repetition of the key term *university* here, which keeps our attention where Whitehead wants it. Other words are repeated, too, as the following sentences show.

The parallelism of repeated grammatical patterns can be illustrated by a single sentence and by a pair of sentences:

The University imparts information, but
     it   imparts it   imaginatively.

Here the parallel clauses are further reinforced by the repeated verb. Next, the pair of sentences:

> A fact is no longer a bare fact: It is invested with all its possibilities.

> It is no longer a burden on the memory: It is energizing as the poet of our dreams and as the architect of our purposes.

The basic grammatical structure of the second sentence echoes that of the first, with the repeated "no longer" to reinforce that parallelism. The second sentence contains an additional parallelism in the last two phrases:

> as the poet   of our dreams   and
> as the architect of our purposes

The overall effect of the parallel patterns is to make the paragraph both easy to understand and follow, and to make it memorable.

The paragraph uses and repeats pronouns to good effect, too. Rather than overuse *university*, Whitehead uses the pronoun *it* in successive parallel clauses. Never is there any doubt to what the pronouns refer.

Avoiding Repetitiousness

The careful writer, of course, uses repetition and reminder with restraint, taking care not to use the devices so much that they call attention to themselves rather than to the ideas they link. The writer of the following paragraph (written before mandatory retirement was outlawed) has failed to heed this caution.

> As we grow older, many of us begin to realize just how absurd it is to set the specific age of 65 for mandatory retirement. Why must we have mandatory retirement in the first place? Why, if we must have mandatory retirement, must retirement occur at age 65? What makes age 65 the "right" age for retirement? Why not retire at 49, or at 72? What is the significance of age 65? The truth is that during the German worker revolts of the late nineteenth century, Bismarck's advisors determined that setting mandatory retirement at age 65 would pacify most of the laborers. Why not? In the late nineteenth century, few people even lived to age 65; the new mandatory retirement law really meant that most people could work their entire adult lives. Today, the average lifespan has increased markedly, but retirement at age 65 is still the rule at most companies. Why do employers persist in following Bismarck on the issue of mandatory retirement at 65?

Such heavy-handed repetition only annoys a reader, creating a distraction rather than the intended reinforcement of ideas. The writer repeats words and phrases pointlessly where combining clauses could make such repetition unnecessary. For example, he might have combined several of the questions into one: "Why must we have mandatory retirement at all; and, if we must, why must it be at age 65?" Instead, he repeats rhetorical questions so often that they lose their rhetorical force and begin to sound merely querulous. And surely the phrases "mandatory retirement" and "age 65" could be reduced in number for the sake of the reader. Problem repetition may be avoided in these ways:

1. **Combine related sentences, subordinating less important ideas to more important ideas, and putting equally important ideas into parallel structure.** For example, certain points in the following sentences could be subordinated to others:

> The city council will vote on the proposed commercial development north of the Loop. The vote will take place next week, by which time the city council must resolve the question of conflict of interest. The possible conflict of interest stems from the fact that five of the seven city council members own property north of the Loop.

As it stands, this paragraph contains pointless, rather than emphatic or coherent, repetition. The sentences could be combined:

> The city council will vote next week on the proposed commercial development north of the Loop, by which time the council members must resolve the question of conflict of interest stemming from the fact that five of the seven members own property in the area in question.

If the resulting single sentence leaves the reader a bit breathless, it could easily be made into two sentences: " . . . north of the Loop. By that time the council. . . . " In either case, some needless repetition is avoided, and the relationship between ideas is made clear by the use of grammatical subordination.

When ideas are equal in value, parallel structure can eliminate unnecessary repetition and make unity and coherence more apparent, as demonstrated by the following paragraph and its revision.

> **Original Version:** The provost has proposed several actions for the university to take in order to achieve its goal of increasing its prestige nationally. The university should raise the standards for admission. It should improve the caliber of the faculty. It should improve the physical facilities for the natural sciences. Also, new computer science equipment and refurbishing the building in which it is housed would strengthen the computer science program. All academic courses should be made more rigorous to combat grade inflation. All these actions will require the support of the board of trustees and the support of the alumni if they are to succeed. The trustees and the alumni will need to provide funds to accomplish the provost's aims for the university. They must also provide enthusiasm if the undertaking is to succeed.

> **Revised Version:** To further the university's goal of increasing its prestige nationally, the provost has recommended that the standards for admission be raised and that the courses of study be made more rigorous. To complement those aims, he has also recommended that the caliber of the entire faculty and the quality of facilities and equipment for the natural sciences and computer science be improved. And to make possible such extensive changes, he has asked for financial and moral support from the board of trustees and the alumni.

The careless repetition of words and sentence patterns in the first version has been eliminated in the second, while the real parallelism of ideas and syntax is made clearer. Notice, too, that similar ideas have been grouped together: the quality of the academic program and of those admitted to it, the quality of the instructors and of the facilities that make possible a respected academic program, and the money and the enthusiasm that make implementing all these improvements possible. Grouping together similar ideas in similar grammatical units has improved the coherence of the paragraph and made its unity more apparent. Pronouns and transitional words underscore that coherence: *those* aims, *also, and, such* . . . changes.

2. **Vary repeated words and grammatical units slightly.** Instead of repeating a term exactly, use an occasional pronoun or synonym. A thesaurus may help you to find synonyms, but remember: There are few exact synonyms. *Home* has connotations of warmth and family that *house* lacks. A *partisan* may not be a *patriot*, or vice versa. In order to decide whether you need to use a synonym for a repeated word or phrase, try reading the passage aloud. If any term seems annoyingly frequent, use a synonym in one or two places.

The parallelism of words, phrases, and clauses is not broken but is softened by adding modifiers. For example, the sentence

> Finding a need, learning about it, and acting upon what is learned are the principles of effective community service.

contains parallel structures (three gerund phrases), but the first gerund is modified by a direct object ("finding a need"), the second by a prepositional phrase ("learning about it"), and the third by a prepositional phrase in which the object of the preposition is itself a clause ("acting upon what is learned"). That variety within the same basic structure maintains parallelism while avoiding monotony.

You also may vary parallel structures by using *ellipsis*—the omission of clearly understood words, often in parallel phrases or clauses. Look at the next-to-last sentence of the preceding paragraph: "The first gerund is modified by a direct object, the second [gerund is modified] by a prepositional phrase, and the third [gerund is modified] by a prepositional phrase. . . . " The clauses would be tedious if the words in brackets had been repeated each time. Ellipsis eliminates that needless repetition while preserving the parallel structure of the sentence.

Transitions   Both subordinate and parallel relationships among ideas are strengthened by the appropriate use of transitions. *Appropriate* is the key word here. The sentences in the "prep school" paragraph you read on page 266, for example, are not clearly related to one another and certainly are not related in the ways implied by the transitions. Transitional words and phrases are not freely interchangeable; they have meanings that state different relationships. They may appear at the beginnings of sentences or as parenthetical elements within sentences (as in the sentence "The difficulty, *however*, came not so much in arranging the trip as in recruiting the passengers"). The chart on page 271 lists some common transitions and the relationships they indicate. The following paragraph, from Walter Lippmann's "The Indispensable Opposition," illustrates the uses of simple transitions in making clear the relationships among ideas.

> The opposition is indispensable. A good statesman, like any other sensible human being, always learns more from his opponents than from his fervent supporters. For his supporters will push him to disaster unless his opponents show him where the dangers are. So if he is wise he will often pray to be delivered from his friends, be-

cause they will ruin him. But, though it hurts, he ought also to pray never to be left without opponents; for they keep him on the path of reason and good sense.

—*The Atlantic,* August 1939

Transitions

Logical outcome: therefore, thus, it follows that, consequently, hence, so, as a result, then, for this reason, accordingly

Logical cause: because, to this end, with this object, given that

Time sequence: first (second, third, etc.), next, later, afterward, then, finally, at last, previously, earlier, until, when, in the meantime, meanwhile, immediately, now, formerly, subsequently, thereupon, at that time, the following day (week, month, etc.)

Spatial relationship: here, nearby, farther away, above, below, opposite, on the left (right, top, bottom), between

Additional information: and, also, in addition, moreover, furthermore, similarly

Examples: for example, in particular, specifically, for instance, to illustrate

Comparison: similarly, by the same token, likewise, in the same way, just as

Contrast or qualification: but, however, in contrast, on the other hand, for all that, nevertheless, still, yet, notwithstanding, in spite of

Concession: admittedly, it must be granted, it is true, of course, naturally, although, granted that, no doubt, even though

Emphasis or restatement: indeed, truly, of course, chiefly, principally, in other words, in short, that is, in effect

Summary or conclusion: finally, when all is considered, at last, in conclusion, to summarize, in short, in brief

---

Coherence is a basic requirement of effective writing. It is essential to persuasion. The best way to achieve coherent writing is to put yourself in the position of your own reader. After you finish the draft of an essay, put what you have written aside, for a day or two if possible, and then try to read the piece as if you have never seen it before. Try to see only the logical connections on the page, not the ones in your head. Listen for the droning sound of pointless repetition and for the satisfying balance of parallel structure. Make sure that you mean *thus* when you say it, and not *afterward.* By putting yourself in your reader's position, you will produce writing that a reader can follow and therefore can appreciate. In so doing, you help create a persona a reader can trust, and you strengthen your argument in the process.

Revising for Coherence

Is every sentence directly related to the topic of the paragraph and to the sentence before it?

Have I used accurate transitions? Have I overused any?

Have I repeated key terms? Have I overdone it?

Have I used synonyms effectively? Or do I sound like my thesaurus?

Have I subordinated less important ideas to more important ideas?

Have I used parallel sentence structure where appropriate?

EXERCISE 8–7

Revise the following paragraph, using subordination to bring the elements of the paragraph into appropriate relationship to each other. You must first decide which points are primary, which subordinate. Reorder clauses or sentences if you find a need to do so.

> Garlic gets bad press (for causing bad breath) that it does not deserve. This problem must have arisen because people do not know enough about garlic. Garlic is a member of the lily family. It is cousin to the onion. It was long grown in the Mediterranean basin. Dioscorides was a first-century Greek physician. He believed that garlic could cleanse the body of toxins, restore energy, and increase male virility. In the centuries since, it has been claimed as a cure for everything from dandruff to athlete's foot. During World War I, children wore garlic around their necks. They did so to ward off the dreaded Spanish Influenza. British soldiers in World War I used sphagnum moss soaked in garlic juice to dress wounds when hospital gauze ran out. In Mexico, garlic soup is a folk remedy for digestive problems and intestinal parasites. Garlic may not have all the powers people have attributed to it over the years. Garlic does taste good.
> —Adapted from Stuart Teacher and Lawrence Teacher,
> *The Teacher Brothers Modern-Day Almanac*, 1983

EXERCISE 8–8

Revise the student paragraph on page 268 with the aim of eliminating its repetitiousness in favor of variety, conciseness, and—where appropriate—emphatic repetition.

EXERCISE 8–9

Revise the following paragraph (a corrupted version of a paragraph in Joseph Epstein, "The Virtues of Ambition," *Harper's*, October 1981) by improving the parallel structure of phrases and clauses.

> We do not choose to be born. Also, our parents are not chosen by us. We have no say as to our historical epoch, in what country we are born, or any say about the circumstances of our upbringing. Then, too, we do not, most of us, choose to die, or select the time or conditions of our death. But within all this realm of choicelessness, we do determine how we shall live. We can live courageously or in cowardice, act honorably or dishonorably. Also, we can live with purpose or in drift. We decide what is important in life, and what is trivial in life is our decision as well. We make the decision that what makes us important either is what we do or what we refuse to do. But no matter how indifferent the universe may be to our choices and what we decide, they are ours to make. We decide. We make choices. And as we decide and things are chosen by us, so are our lives formed. In the end, forming our own destiny is what ambition is about.

EXERCISE 8–10

Improve the coherence of the following paragraphs by adding transitional words or phrases where they are needed and combining clauses where appropriate.

(1)

After fighting the mountain for another eight hours, I managed to pass the other climbers. I reached the peak of Fremont first. I took my final step to reach the top. I realized that Mount Fremont had won the battle. I did not feel the glory I had anticipated feeling. I felt uncomfortable. I had invaded a sacred place. The mammoth mountains and their ring of clouds were serenely oblivious of my accomplishment. The vastness of all I could see made me feel as inconsequential as the little pikas squeaking defiance at me from the rocks and boulders.

(2)

All students should study abroad at some point in their academic careers. The contact with a foreign culture, even one similar to our own, provides a remedy for American insularity. We tend to think that the world revolves around the United States. We are as provincial as the people of the Middle Ages who believed the sun and planets revolved around the earth. Study abroad remedies this provincialism. It makes history, geography, and political science come to life for students. It makes us appreciate our own country and the freedom and conveniences it offers. It promotes understanding among peoples of different cultures and beliefs. Study abroad offers the most efficient and memorable way to complete a liberal education.

EXERCISE 8–11

A. Look carefully at the student paragraph on "liberal education in prep school" on page 266. Explain the logical problems in the writer's choices of transitions. Comment on the contexts in which the writer uses *however, for example, accordingly,* and (that most abused of all transitions) *therefore.*

B. One topic that finds its way into this jumble of ideas and sentences is "Prep schools offer liberal educations." Another is "Sweetly Prep did not believe in coddling students." Identify two others.

C. Develop a coherent paragraph stemming from one of the topics you have identified. Use subordination to avoid purposeless repetition; use ellipsis to vary some sentence patterns.

EXERCISE 8–12

Revise an essay draft of your own in light of the elements covered in this chapter. Be sure to review the several lists of questions as you plan a revision.

In this chapter you have considered ways to strengthen an argument and make it more interesting for readers. You have examined the large elements of an argument: the introduction, the exposition, the confirmation of your points, the refutation of opposing points, the conclusion. You have also examined smaller elements of an argument: the unity, completeness, and coherence required of each paragraph. You have seen ways to strengthen sentences and the links between them. After considering the questions identified in this chapter, you should have a good idea what to do when your drafts of arguments seem skimpy, disorganized, or uninteresting.

In the next chapter we will turn to the fine-tuning of style and sentence structure that can make a good argument also a memorable one.

READINGS

CONFORMITY AND NONCONFORMITY:
THE PRICES PAID FOR EACH
(Rough Draft)

1 My high school had a tight hierarchy of social groups, and I think that was the biggest problem anyone faced who was not part of a "popular" group. If you weren't in a group, you were labeled a misfit, a social deviant. Every person longed to be accepted by his peers, so almost every person chose to belong to a group. Each group had a certain underlying interest—drinking, surfing, etc. But within each group was a secret code, an idea that every other group was an enemy to be ridiculed and pushed aside as inferior. The group I belonged to resulted from this rigid social system of jeering ridicule and ostracism. We contrasted with the other cliques in many ways, and I think, really, that we ultimately benefited from our various differences.

2 Our group was comprised of those who could not quite squeeze into the tightly knit groups. We were tired of being misfits, so we came to the decision to form our own group in defiance. Also in retaliation, we refused to acknowledge the endless social customs of school life. Because we had been cast aside, we looked down on these supposedly trivial practices and drowned ourselves in a search for "higher meaning." We went to any extreme to differentiate ourselves from the other groups.

3 These differences were, at first, looked down upon condescendingly by the others. We were considered peculiar, weird, odd. We were resented because our nonconformity magnified their own overconformity. Our supposed individualism was a cause of discomfort for them, for they had given up much of theirs in favor of conformity. But as time wore on, we were seen as creatures of interest. They wondered at our refusal to comply to their standards. They even began to see some worth in our attempts, although we didn't see it. They began to admire our uniqueness, even though we did not see ourselves as unique.

4 Our revolt was one of defense, one of comfort. We clung together for the support we had not found in the other cliques. We were not nonconformists, even though we conformed to a guise of nonconformity. We thought of ourselves as rebels without a cause, a '60's generation reborn. We gained security by throwing ourselves into a facade of superiority. We were in revolt against the school and anything else that, if adhered to, would take away our supposed individuality. We put on the mask of young intellectuals, but it was really only a mask. As time passed, we realized that our attempts to be different only had made us aware of the high school fun we had missed: the football games, the homecoming dances, and endless other social activities. But we also came to realize that, because we had refused to adhere to these social

customs, we had gained a perseverence that would enable us to stand up against any demands that would strip us of our individual character.

5   It is this individuality that must be guarded closely. In his lifetime, a person will be invited to join an immeasurable number of social groups that will inevitably have conflicting interests. Even though some comfort may be gained through acceptance into any one of them, if their underlying interest is not his, the security gained is not worth the loss of his uniqueness.

QUESTIONS AND IDEAS FOR DISCUSSION

1. What is the paper's thesis? Is it clearly defined and restricted? Does it indicate the interest and importance of the controlling idea of the essay? Rewrite the thesis, restricting it appropriately and making it clear and interesting.
2. How well do the essay's supporting points actually support the thesis? Comment on the organization and completeness of the argument.
3. Identify any fuzzy or apparently contradictory statements in the essay.
4. At what points would examples or additional detail add interest and clarity to the essay?
5. Is the working title appropriate for the essay that takes shape here? Explain.

NONCONFORMITY: THE PRICE AND THE PAYOFF

Kathy Taylor
(Student Essay)

1 High school is a time for laughter and romance, parties and football games, homecoming and pep rallies—but it is also a time of conflict and distress, lost identities and bitter rivalry. My high school was structured in such a tight hierarchy of social groups that a person was labeled a misfit, a social deviant, if he chose not to belong to one. Since every adolescent longs to be accepted by his peers, almost every person belonged to some identifiable group. Each group had a unifying interest, whether drinking, surfing, toking, or dating every eligible member of the opposite sex in the school. But within each group was a secret code, a hushed understanding that every other group was to be ridiculed and its members shunned as inferior human beings. The group I belonged to was a clique-by-default, comprised of the social castoffs and so-called misfits. We should have been the most miserable of creatures, but we were not. In retrospect, I think we benefited in some curious ways from our pariah status.

2   Our group consisted of those who could not quite squeeze into the

tightly knit cliques and those who had been tried out and quickly discarded because of some barely discernible difference, such as long hair or pimples, out-of-style clothing, or a horsey laugh. Tired of being misfits, we rallied together in defiance; we became reverse snobs who refused to participate in or even acknowledge the endless rites of high school. We neither gave nor accepted homecoming mums; we did not deign to adorn our lockers with spirit ribbons and posters; we made a point of not wearing the school colors on the days of football games. Scorning such trivial and meaningless customs, we drowned ourselves in a search for "deeper meaning." Instead of cheering at football games, we spent endless hours arguing over Carlos Castaneda's *Don Juan*, the poetry of Leonard Cohen, and the advantages of socialism. Instead of conforming to the tailored, conservative dress of our peers, we wore ragged blue jeans and t-shirts, cowboy hats and overalls. The girls wore no make-up; the boys kept their hair long and ragged. We went to any extreme that we could devise to differentiate ourselves from the other groups.

3   Naturally, the other groups at first regarded us with revulsion or, at best, condescension. They thought us peculiar and they resented the fact that our nonconformity magnified their own conformity. Our individualism made them uncomfortable, for they had surrendered their own to status knit shirts, khaki pants, A-line skirts, and deck shoes. But as time passed, they grew used to us: We became creatures of interest to them, exotic and alien. They marveled at our refusal to conform to their standards, and a number of them, unknown to us, began secretly to admire us for what they considered our uniqueness.

4   We did not see ourselves as unique, or special. The truth was that we clung together for the solace of feeling that we belonged somewhere. We were not true nonconformists—our efforts to be different were successful because we conformed as much as the other groups did, but in our case, to a guise of nonconformity. We felt secure because we appeared to be above all the petty high school customs, but I, for one, secretly would have loved to sit in the football stadium, a ridiculous beribboned mum dusting glitter all over my A-line skirt, cheering my halfback boyfriend on to victory. Denying those feelings was a defensive ruse. If we could not have popularity, we did not want it.

5   Or so we told ourselves. We revolted against the school, against all social customs, against anything that might take away our supposed individuality. We wore the mask of young intellectuals, secretly fearing all the while that we might be unmasked. I was not the only one in our group who sensed that we were missing something valuable, not so much school dances and locker decorations for their own sake, but a bridge between childhood and adulthood. But in another sense, we had made something positive out of the hurtful experience of being excluded. We had made friendships that were deep and have lasted; we had learned to persevere in the face of ridicule and to stand up for our own and others' right to be different. We were tuned in to

the world of ideas and the real world around us while our classmates saw no further than their next date. Time will tell whether our losses or our gains were greater. I believe it will be the latter, even if I never do wear a mum.

QUESTIONS AND IDEAS FOR DISCUSSION

1. Comment on the changes from the rough draft to the final draft of this essay. What change strikes you as the most important one? Why?
2. Compare the thesis of the final draft with that of the original draft and with the revision you had proposed for the latter. Which most effectively sums up the controlling idea of this essay?
3. What are the main points of this argument? Do they seem logically arranged and adequately developed?
4. Comment on the use of coherence devices such as transitions, parallel structure, and repetition of key terms in this essay. How well does Taylor use such devices? Where would you suggest changes or additional transitions?
5. Describe Taylor's persona in the final draft of the essay. Does it differ at all from the persona of the original draft? Explain. How does Taylor avoid sounding self-pitying—or does she avoid self-pity?

Suggestions for Writing and Further Discussion

Use the following sentences, some of which are taken from sample passages reprinted in this chapter, to stimulate ideas for potential essays addressed to an audience of your rhetoric classmates. The following offer possibilities for reaction or further development. Feel free to modify any thesis as you see fit; instead of maintaining that "thin people are crunchy and dull, like carrots," you might prefer to argue that "smart people are sharp and pointed, like ice picks" or that "beautiful people are boring; they all look alike."

Lying can never be justified.

Inheritance laws [or any other law] are reprehensible.

Requiring foreign language study in college is futile.

Fraternities help students balance the academic and social demands of college life.

"[Thin people] are crunchy and dull, like carrots." (Suzanne Britt Jordan)

Bilingual education prevents children from becoming fully part of their society.

"It's often the best books that draw the beadiest attention of the censors." (Wainwright)

"The university should impart information imaginatively." (Whitehead)

Professional sports have gotten out of hand largely because of television.

"[B]luffing is nothing more than a form of lying!" (Carr)

"[M]etaphor is pervasive in everyday life, not just in language but in thought and action." (Lakoff and Johnson)

"Man will never conquer space." (Clarke)

"I'll put it bluntly: if you care for the quality of life in our American democracy, then you have to be for censorship." (Kristol)

"If the [newspaper] reader doesn't also study foreign affairs, or follow the money markets, or keep up his practice of foreign languages, then what can he expect to learn from the papers?" (Lapham)

Freshmen in college probably should not attempt to declare a major.

9

Revising Arguments:
The Power of Style

He who has nothing to assert has no style and can have none: he who has something to assert will go as far in power of style as its momentousness and his conviction will carry him.

—George Bernard Shaw

After making the large-scale and small-scale revisions we discussed in Chapter 8, you may be ready to rest on your laurels, satisfied with an argument well-wrought. But this is just the point at which you can make the difference between an essay that is merely competent and one that is both persuasive and memorable. In this chapter you will find specific advice about revising individual sentences and words in light of your audience and your overall purpose. We will begin with the elements of style, then turn to individual sentences and finally to word choices.

WHAT IS STYLE?

Consider the relative persuasiveness of the following arguments:

To the Editor of the *Denver Post:* Colorado is overrun by tourists. They bring money, but they leave trash behind them. They are not concerned with ecology. Also, they are not interested in preserving the beauty of our state. The worst ones are the ones in the big campers. They are a hazard on our mountain roads, and besides, people who stay in campers don't support our hotel industry. The best way to reduce crowding and protect our natural resources would be to engender a stiff gasoline tax. This would also bring needed revenue to the state.

[Signed] Gib Murphey

To the Editor of the *Denver Post:* Despite the revenues they bring to Colorado, tourists are arriving in such numbers that our state's natural resources are endangered.

The National Parks and Forests are being polluted by trash and exhaust fumes from countless automobiles, and the mountains trampled and eroded by countless feet in lugsoled boots. While granting the importance of the tourist industry, I propose that it be contained in a way that would also provide revenue to replace that lost to reduced numbers of tourists: a new gasoline tax. We would then see fewer campers and trailers; we would see more of our mountain wildflowers again.

[Signed] Bill Lewis

The point made in these two letters is essentially the same: Reduce the glut of tourists and the problems they bring to Colorado by instituting a higher gasoline tax. Which of the two is more likely to impress the voters and legislators reading the *Post?*

The difference between the two letters is a difference in style and in the voice (persona) that speaks through the words. In characterizing the styles of the two letters, we might be struck first by the tone of the writing: The first writer sounds belligerent; the second, reasonable and sincere. We might also talk about the elements of style that create tone: diction and the length and structure of sentences.

First, the writers' diction, or choice of words. Murphey uses short, abstract or nonspecific words *(beauty, natural resources)* for the most part; when he tries to use "big" words, he uses them incorrectly *(engender),* redundantly (ecology *is* the science concerned with "preserving the beauty" of nature), or inconsistently *(engender* is a "formal" word; *stiff,* following it, is used colloquially). Murphey repeats pronouns frequently: lots of *they*'s and a vague *this.* Lewis uses formal language ("I propose that it be contained") but relieves his abstractions ("natural resources are endangered") with concrete images ("trampled by countless feet in lugsoled boots").

Second, the writers' sentence lengths and structure. Murphey uses a total of ninety words in eight sentences of 5, 9, 6, 12, 10, 20, 19, and 9 words, respectively. The sentences vary from five to twenty words in length, but twenty words is not a long sentence, and most of the sentences are closer to half that length. Here is concrete evidence that Murphey's sentence style is short and choppy. There is more evidence: Of the eight sentences, six are grammatically simple, one is compound, and one, surprisingly enough, is compound-complex. But the latter is really two sentences expressing different thoughts, haphazardly joined together: "They are a hazard on our mountain roads, and besides, people who stay in campers don't support our hotel industry." All but one of Murphey's sentences begin with the subject; the single exception begins with a transitional word, *also.*

Lewis, on the other hand, uses ten more words than Murphey in half as many sentences. His four sentences contain 20, 28, 35, and 17 words, respectively. A little more variety might be preferable, but notice that the last sentence is really two independent clauses joined by a semicolon and so has the effect of varying sentence length with two very short sentences of eight and nine words each. The short clauses following the long preceding sentences give those last words particular emphasis. Lewis's sentence patterns are complex, compound, complex, and compound. His first sentence begins with a dependent clause ("Despite the revenues they bring to Colorado"), his third with an adverbial phrase ("While granting the importance of the tourist industry"), and the second and fourth with the subjects. The variety in sentence openers relieves the second letter from the monotony of the first, as does the variety in sentence structure.

This close look at specific features of style shows how two paragraphs on the same topic can be almost totally different in the way they sound and in the way they affect a reader. The characteristics of Lewis's style that help to make his letter more persuasive than Murphey's are the use of specific words to illustrate his generalizations; the variety of his sentence patterns; the rhythm of his sentences (especially the parallel phrases and parallel clauses in the second and last sentences); and, most importantly in terms of logic, the combination of related ideas into sentences, with less important ideas grammatically subordinated to more important ideas (for example, Lewis's first sentence, the introductory clause is a concession that Lewis regards as less important than what he says in the main clause). We will consider each of these elements of style and how you may employ them to good effect in your own arguments.

THE ELEMENTS OF STYLE

In written language, style consists largely of our **grammatical choices** and **word choices,** which together set the tempo of our prose, and which stem in part from our logical choices: the kinds of relationships we draw between ideas. In responding to style, we respond in general ways to the tone, the degree of complexity, and the distinctiveness of a piece of writing. In more specific ways we describe the writer's grammatical choices in terms of

Sentence types	(simple, complex, and so on)
Sentence openers	(transitional words, dependent phrases or clauses, or the subject of the sentence)
Sentence length	(varied by joining or subordinating clauses and phrases)
Distinctive syntactical patterns	(such as parallelism or rhetorical questions)

We speak of a writer's word choices, or **diction,** as being typically

Short or long	(*list* or *enumerate*)
Concrete or abstract	(*letter* or *correspondence*)
Specific or general	(*bull terrier* or *dog*)
Metaphorical or literal	(*love is a fire* or *love is a feeling*)
Everyday or technical	(*cancer* or *carcinoma*)

Grammar in the sense of "good" and "bad" is a feature of style only when it is faulty and thereby calls attention to itself. Good grammar is invisible.

EXERCISE 9–1

A. In a few paragraphs describe the writers' verbal and grammatical stylistic choices in both of the following passages. Give specific examples from the paragraphs to support your assertions. Then summarize the key elements of each writer's style in these passages in a single declarative sentence for each.

(1)

This summer country of my childhood, this place of memory, is filled with landscapes shimmering in light and color, moving with sounds and shapes I hardly ever describe, or put in my stories in so many words; they form only the living background of what I am trying to tell, so familiar to my characters they would hardly notice them; the sound of mourning doves in the live oaks, the childish voices of parrots chattering on every back porch in the little towns, the hoverings of buzzards in the high blue air—all the life of that soft blackland farming country, full of fruits and flowers and birds, with good hunting and good fishing; with plenty of water, many little and big rivers. I shall name just a few of the rivers I remember—the San Antonio, the San Marcos, the Trinity, the Nueces, the Rio Grande, the Colorado, and the small clear branch of the Rio Blanco, full of colored pebbles, Indian Creek, the place where I was born.

—Katherine Anne Porter, " 'Noon Wine': The Sources"

(2)

All professions have their own way of justifying laziness. Harvard professors are deeply impressed by the jeweled fragility of their minds. Like the thinnest metal, these are subject terribly to fatigue. More than six hours of teaching a week is fatal—and an impairment of academic freedom. So, at any given moment, the average professor is resting his mind in preparation for the next orgiastic act of insight or revelation. Writers, by the same token, do nothing because they are waiting for inspiration.

In my own case there are days when the result is so bad that no fewer than five revisions are required. However, when I'm greatly inspired, only four are needed before, as I've often said, I put in that note of spontaneity which even my meanest critics concede.

—John Kenneth Galbraith, "Writing and Typing"

EXERCISE 9–2

Write two paragraphs each requesting a loan so that you can buy a car. Address the first paragraph to your parents, the second to a local bank. Then write a third paragraph, analyzing the differences in style, content, and persona in the two requests. Which of the two do you believe would have greater persuasive power? Why?

SENTENCE STYLE

Sentence Types

As you know, sentences take four basic forms:

Simple	"We must preserve the woodlands." *(one main clause)*
Compound	"We must preserve the woodlands, and we must protect the woodland animals at the same time." *(two or more main clauses)*
Complex	"We must preserve the woodlands if we are to save the spotted owl." *(one main clause and at least one dependent clause)*
Compound-complex	"We must preserve the woodlands, and we must take steps quickly if we are to do so." *(at least two main clauses and at least one dependent clause)*

Ideally, the types of sentences we use in written arguments will suit the meaning they convey. For example, simple and compound sentences present one or two bits of information. We expect the information in the two parts of a compound sentence to be roughly equivalent in importance. Complex sentences show hierarchical relationships between subordinate and more important points. Using subordination clarifies the relations between ideas. Compound-complex sentences suit complexly interrelated pieces of information. This last structure should appear least often in your written arguments, for its very complexity may reveal that you have failed to be as clear and direct as possible.

Varying sentence structure not only helps readers understand the different relations among the ideas you present, but also prevents the monotony of sentences that are all structurally similar. The following paragraph contains only simple sentences:

> Some polls are not really representative surveys. Call-in polls using 900 numbers cost the participants. Only relatively affluent people participate in such polls. Magazine mail-in surveys reach only the magazine's readers. Talk-show polls reach only the viewers of a given show. Viewers of a particular show may not be representative of the whole population. In such "polls" not everyone is equally likely to be questioned.

Revised in order to vary sentence structure, the paragraph becomes less monotonous and easier to read:

> Some polls are not really representative surveys. Call-in polls using 900 numbers cost the participants, so only relatively affluent people participate in such polls. Magazine mail-in surveys reach only the magazine's readers. Talk-show polls reach only the viewers of a given show, who may not be representative of the whole population. In such "polls" not everyone is equally likely to be questioned.

Now the sentence patterns are simple, compound, simple, complex, simple. A little variety shows the relationships among the ideas all the more clearly.

Sentence Length

Just as you need to vary sentence types both for meaning and for variety, you need to vary sentence length. You can alter the tone of a passage by altering the length of sentences. Writing that consists mostly of long sentences sounds formal—and may lose readers' attention. Writing that consists mostly of short sentences sounds curt—or sometimes, childish. The first passage below has mainly long sentences; the second, mainly short sentences. Read them aloud to hear the difference in tone.

> (1)
> As a health-care worker assisting AIDS patients, I see infected people ranging from homosexuals to heterosexuals, IV drug users to hemophiliacs who must have blood transfusions to live, geriatric patients to newborn babies. No matter how these people contracted the virus, no one chooses to be infected with AIDS, and no one deserves the pain, frustration, and degradation associated with it. However tragic it may be that some famous athletes and some appealing children have contracted AIDS, their plight is neither more nor less compelling than that of individuals who are less photogenic and appealing.

> (2)
> I am a health-care worker assisting AIDS patients. In my work I see infected people of all groups in our society. They range from homosexuals to heterosexuals. Some are IV drug users while others are hemophiliacs. Some are geriatric patients; some, newborn babies. These people contracted the virus in various ways. However, no one chooses to be infected with AIDS. No one deserves the pain, frustration, and degradation associated with it. It is tragic that some famous athletes and some appealing children have contracted AIDS. All the same, the plight of all AIDS patients is equally compelling.

Paragraph (1) is formal in tone; paragraph (2), much less so. But both would benefit from more variety in sentence length. Let's consider a third version:

> (3)
> As a health-care worker assisting AIDS patients, I see infected people ranging from homosexuals to heterosexuals, from IV drug users to hemophiliacs who must have blood transfusions to live, from geriatric patients to newborn babies. No matter how these people contracted the virus, no one chooses to be infected with AIDS. No one deserves the pain, frustration, and degradation associated with it. It is indeed tragic that some famous athletes and some appealing children have contracted AIDS, but their plight is neither more nor less compelling than that of individuals who are less photogenic and appealing.

This revision is closest to paragraph (1), but the two short sentences in the middle emphasize their points all the more by contrast with the longer sentences surrounding them. Sentences need to vary in length according to emphasis and meaning, as they do here, not for variety's sake alone.

Sentence Openers

If you begin a sentence with anything other than the subject, you have used a sentence opener (just as this sentence has). Sentence openers can be words, phrases, or clauses, including:

- Adjectives
  Imposing and silent, the mountain towered above the village of Zermatt.

- Adverbs
  Clearly, something had to be done for the starving people of Zambia.

- Adverb Clauses
  Despite all the efforts we made, we were unable to master chess.

- Prepositional Phrases
  In the meantime, airport security measures will remain unchanged.

- Participial Phrases
  Tossing out ideas left and right, Karcher gave the group more leads to pursue than they had hours in the day.

- Coordinating Conjunctions
  And still the opposition stood firm.

- Conjunctive Adverbs
  However, three of the judges dissented.

- Absolute Phrases
  The applause having finally subsided, the old philosopher took his seat.

As you can see, you have much more than *thus* and *therefore* available to vary your sentence openers. All kinds of words and phrases can work. And the work of a sentence opener is to make a connection between previous ideas and a new one, or to prepare us for what follows in the main clause. If we take the paragraph about polls, above, and add a sentence opener or two, we may find its connections become clearer still:

> Some polls are not really representative surveys. For example, call-in polls using 900 numbers cost the participants, so only relatively affluent people participate in such polls. Magazine mail-in surveys reach only the magazine's readers. Similarly, talk-show polls reach only the viewers of a given show, who may not be representative of the whole population. In such "polls" not everyone is equally likely to be questioned.

The second and fourth sentences now begin with sentence openers—*for example* and *similarly*—to link ideas among sentences clearly. As long as you pay attention to meaning (you would not, for instance, replace *similarly* with *however* in the paragraph above) and avoid overusing sentence openers, they can make your arguments easier to follow.

Syntactical Patterns

Parallelism

Parallelism is the arranging of equivalent images or ideas in pairs or series of grammatically identical words, phrases, or clauses. Minor variations among the elements (the addition of an adjective to one, for instance) are acceptable and sometimes even desirable—to prevent the parallelism from becoming monotonous.

> In many ways writing is the act of saying *I*, of imposing oneself upon other people, of saying *listen to me, see it my way, change your mind.*
> —Joan Didion, "Why I Write"

> It [the declaration that standards for evaluating works of art do not exist] pleases those resentful of disciplines, it flatters the empty-minded by calling them open-minded, it comforts the confused.
> —Marya Mannes, "How Do You Know It's Good?"

Anaphora   A kind of parallelism, anaphora creates emphasis through the repetition of the same word or words at the beginning of successive clauses. In the sentence above about evaluating works of art, the repetition of *it* creates anaphora.

> Let us work together toward our common goal, and let us persevere in the face of all discouragement.

> Death is fearsome; death is shadowy and unknowable; death is inescapable.

Ellipsis   In order to prevent monotony, parallelism is sometimes modified through ellipsis, the omission of clearly implied words.

> Words can be more powerful, and more treacherous, than we sometimes suspect; communication more difficult than we may think.
> —F. L. Lucas, "What Is Style?"

(In this example, *can be* has been cut from the second independent clause.)

> Reform is affirmative, conservatism negative; conservatism goes for comfort, reform for truth.
> —Ralph Waldo Emerson, "The Conservative"

(This sentence also includes antithesis.)

Antithesis   Antithesis is a form of parallelism in which contrasting ideas are expressed in parallel clauses or phrases. The grammatical parallelism calls attention to the contrast.

> How much the world asks of them [clergy and teachers], and how little they can actually deliver!
> —H. L. Mencken, "Education"

> They [people of middle age] neither trust everybody nor distrust everybody, but judge people correctly.
> —Aristotle, *Rhetoric*, Book II

> We observe today not a victory of party but a celebration of freedom—symbolizing an end as well as a beginning— signifying renewal as well as change.
> —John F. Kennedy, Inaugural Address

Climactic Order

Climactic order, or climax, is the arranging of phrases or clauses in order of increasing importance, for dramatic impact.

> And for the support of this Declaration, with a firm reliance on the protection of Divine Providence, we mutually pledge to each other our Lives, our Fortunes, and our sacred Honor.
> —Thomas Jefferson, The Declaration of Independence

> For if we ever begin to suppress our search to understand nature, to quench our own intellectual excitement in a misguided effort to present a unified front where it does not and should not exist, then we are truly lost.
> —Stephen Jay Gould, "Evolution as Fact and Theory"

Inverted Order

Ordinary word order in English sentences is Subject–Verb–Complement. Inverting the usual word order, as in Verb–Subject or Complement–Verb–Subject, calls attention to the idea a sentence expresses by virtue of the unusual syntax.

> Cool was I and logical.
> —Max Shulman, "Love Is a Fallacy"

> From this alienation of personal power comes the sense of resignation with which we accept the political dispensations of a powerful government whose hold upon us continues to increase.
> —William F. Buckley, Jr., "Why Don't We Complain?"

> Out of its [the circus's] wild disorder comes order; from its rank smell rises the good aroma of courage and daring; out of its preliminary shabbiness comes the final splendor.
> —E. B. White, "The Ring of Time"

Somebody once parodied the overuse of inverted order by mimicking it: "Backward run the sentences, till reels the mind." The clauses in the parody are arranged Verb–Subject, as are the three example sentences above. Notice the variations, such as in Shulman's sentence, "Cool was I and logical": Predicate Adjective–Verb–Subject–Adjective.

EXERCISE 9–3

A. Identify the parallelism, climactic order, or inverted order in the following sentences and passages.

B. Read aloud the sentences and passages in the list. Pick two or three that particularly appeal to your ear and write sentences of your own, with completely different subject matter, that mimic the same syntactical patterns as those in the list. For example, if you choose the first sentence as a model, you will write a sentence of your own that employs anaphora: "Friends neither ask nor expect favors; friends do not think first of what you can do for them; friends take pleasure in your company alone."

1. We neither gave nor accepted homecoming mums; we did not deign to adorn our lockers with spirit ribbons and posters; we made a point of not wearing the school colors on the days of football games.

   —Student essay

2. Foolish indeed we would be, to accept such a compromise.

3. If you would be happy for a week, take a wife; if you would be happy for a month, kill your pig: but if you would be happy all your life, plant a garden.

   —Chinese proverb

4. He arrived at college a farmboy; he departed, eight years later, a nuclear physicist.

5. But it was among the older and least "modern" works in the museum that I found most comfort, and the message I needed: that even though God and human majesty, as represented in the icons and triptychs and tedious panoramic canvases of older museums, had evaporated, beauty was still left, beauty among our ruins, a beauty curiously pure, a blank uncaused beauty that signified only itself.

   —John Updike, "What MoMA Done Tole Me"

6. To the state the proposed highway is a convenience for travelers; to the city it is an important link between the east and the west areas; to our neighborhood it is a lifeline to the rest of the community.

7. I was no longer simply a member of the proud graduating class of 1940; I was a proud member of the wonderful, beautiful Negro race.

   —Maya Angelou, "Graduation"

8. Some are born great, some achieve greatness, and some have greatness thrust upon them.

   —Shakespeare, *Twelfth Night*

9. Grave is the situation, painful the remedy.

10. In the past we have had a light which flickered, in the present we have a light which flames, and in the future there will be a light which shines over all the land and sea.

    —Winston Churchill, from a speech to the House of Commons, 8 Dec. 1941

EXERCISE 9–4

Examine one of the essays you have written to determine where it might benefit from some changes in sentence type, sentence length, or syntactical pattern. Decide what additional sentence openers, if any, would better connect some of the ideas. Then revise the essay accordingly. Bring both the original version and the revision to class for discussion.

Sentence Logic

In every sentence, the predicate says something about the subject— and the relationship must be both grammatical and logically possible. "Tom caught the flu" and "Tom was the flu" are both grammatical sentences: The first takes the form noun–transitive verb–object, and the second takes the form noun–linking verb–predicate noun. But the second sentence is nonsense; what the predicate says about the subject is not logically possible. Less obvious, but just as illogical, is the following sentence:

> My future career will be an astronaut.

A career cannot be an astronaut; only a person can be. The sentence is illogical. An acceptable, logical version would be:

> My future career will be astronautics.

Both sentences take the form Noun–Linking Verb–Predicate Noun, but only the second one makes sense. *Career and astronautics* are logically balanced. Astronautics can be a career. An astronaut can *have* a career, but not *be* one.

The elements on either side of a *to be* verb must be "equal"— either a subject noun (or pronoun) and a predicate noun, or a subject noun and a predicate adjective describing the subject noun. In the following sentences, linking verbs join elements that are neither grammatically nor logically "equal."

<u>Waiting</u> for my roommate <u>is</u> <u>when</u> I get impatient.
subject noun   *linking verb* *adverb*

His poor <u>attitude</u> <u>is</u> <u>why</u> he is failing physics.
      subject noun *linking verb* *adverb*

The <u>reason</u> we can't go now <u>is</u> <u>because</u> the car won't start.
  subject noun   *linking verb*   *adverb*

The easiest way to avoid faulty equations is to avoid noun–linking verb–adverb patterns unless the subject is a unit of time or date ("Five o'clock is when they will arrive" is correct, though wordy; "They will arrive at five o'clock" is better). The sentences above might be revised as

> Waiting for my roommate, I always get impatient.

> He is failing physics because of his poor attitude.

> We can't go now because the car won't start.

In these revisions, people *(I, he, we)*, rather than abstractions *(waiting, attitude, reason)*, are the subjects. So the sentences not only make better sense, they are more direct and concise.

Here's another example of a grammatical but illogical sentence:

> The thought of cloning higher life forms, such as primates, is impossible at this time.

The *thought* cannot be impossible, for I just stated it; the *deed* might be impossible. A revision says what the writer really intended:

> To clone higher life forms, such as primates, is impossible at this time.

Though faulty predication is most common in sentences employing linking verbs, it can occur with any verb:

> The ball, stolen from a U.Va. running back, allowed a North Carolina tackle to score a touchdown.

Balls cannot "allow" anything to happen; they are inanimate objects. But

> Stealing the ball from a U.Va. running back enabled a North Carolina tackle to score a touchdown.

makes sense. Can you spot the illogic in the next sentence?

> The science requirement in the College of Humanities urged me to change my major to business.

The dean, your advisor, or your parents might so urge you, but requirements are abstractions and cannot speak. A more sensible version:

> My fear of the science requirement in the College of Humanities prompted me to change my major to business.

How do you spot faulty predication in your own arguments? Check the subject of each sentence against the verb, and check subject and verb against the complement (if any). If any two elements don't make sense together, recast the sentence to resolve the problem, usually with a different subject.

EXERCISE 9–5

Correct the faulty predication in the following sentences.

1. My job next summer will be a lifeguard at a girls' camp.
2. His ambition was Mt. Everest.
3. Janie's idea was eager to get started.
4. Your ability is unable to get the job.
5. The cases currently before the Honor Council include Ralph Lawrence and Peter Cardin.

6. Not only did her action steal pages from a book that wasn't hers, but she denied others access to the material.

7. The reason why Edward is only a clerk is because he cannot get along with his superiors.

8. By stopping in Memphis and changing planes enables us to save fifty dollars on the airfare.

9. The most difficult thing for me to face as a senior has been when people ask me what my career plans are, but I realize they do not know how few jobs are currently available in my field.

10. The stock market's volatility told Avery to put most of his money into bonds.

WORD CHOICES

Level of Diction

As you revise, make sure that you haven't inadvertently changed the level of diction. That is, be careful not to use slang in one sentence and pompous phrases in the next, let alone both kinds of language in a single sentence. We do well to avoid such peculiar hybrids as this one: "It is imperative that the proponents of both sides of the question get their acts together and resolve this problem." Most of the sentence is unduly pompous, while "get their acts together" is ludicrously colloquial in contrast.

The level of diction in any piece of writing—whether formal, informal, or colloquial—should be appropriate to the rhetorical situation of a writer addressing a particular audience for a particular purpose. A treaty, a judicial decision, or even a letter of application for a job requires a level of formality that would be out of place in a note to a friend or an informal column in a college newspaper. Notice the difference in persona created by the different levels of diction in these examples.

> **Formal Diction:** I trust that my experience in claims analysis will prove useful in helping your company set up a risk management program. I enjoyed meeting the members of your executive committee and look forward to hearing from you as soon as you have made a decision regarding my application.

> **Informal Diction:** I believe that my work in claims management will help me get the job with Xavier Corporation, Mr. Matthews. I appreciate your letter of recommendation.

> **Colloquial Diction:** I've got the right stuff for the job at Xavier, Joel, and if they aren't completely crazy, I'm pretty sure they'll hire me. Wish me luck!

Each of these levels of diction is appropriate to its rhetorical context, and each is internally consistent in diction.

Avoiding Pseudo-Formality The stiff formality of impersonal constructions ("It appears to this writer that") and unwieldy third-person constructions when you are using personal illustrations and comments ("one sees that" in place of "we see that," or "one goes to the first classes of the semester" when you mean "I go to the first classes of the semester") does nothing for the appeal of your persona or the clarity of your argument. Some students adopt this pseudoformality in the mistaken belief that academic writing requires that the writer shun the word *I.* What those students confuse is the use of personal illustration and the personal voice of the writer—both of which are appropriate to much academic writing—and I-centered prose, the self-indulgent, self-centered writing that offers opinions in place of reasons. I-centered prose makes statements like "I feel that the Russo-Japanese War of 1904 was a disaster from start to finish." Content-centered prose, on the other hand, makes statements like "The Russo-Japanese War was a disaster for the Russians because they underestimated both the strength and the tenacity of their Japanese adversaries."

Another typical feature of pseudoformal prose is **jargon** used to impress the reader. Jargon is the vocabulary peculiar to a given profession, trade, or other group, and it has value in some applications. It allows two doctors to communicate specifically about the nature of a medical problem without going into elaborate descriptions of the case. It enables an attorney to write a contract that will stand up to legal challenges, because many of the convoluted phrases of legal jargon have been court-tested and their precise meaning established. But jargon has earned a bad name because too often it is used not by people sharing the same vocabulary but by those trying to impress or bewilder outsiders, who are not privy to the specialized vocabulary. When doctors use medical jargon to talk over the heads of their patients, and when attorneys use legal jargon in order to perpetuate a need for their services (since nobody but other lawyers can make sense of the language), then "myocardial infarction" and "whereas the aforementioned party of the first part" amount only to so much gibberish. The abuse of jargon defeats the aim of clarity.

Choosing the Right Words Careful word choices make writing clear. When joined with a pleasing style and logical, thoughtful development of ideas, they also make writing interesting. As you revise your drafts, ask yourself whether or not your word choices reflect the following priorities.

1. **Write with verbs and nouns.** Action verbs and specific nouns strengthen your prose. The rhetorical weight of your sentences needs to be carried by your verbs and nouns, not by adjectives and adverbs. Action verbs and specific nouns are rhetorically "strong" words; adjectives and adverbs are weaker. The difference is easily illustrated by a pair of sentences:

The crucially important point is to do as much as possible to get the bill passed.

We must work, with all the energy and determination we can muster, to see Senate Bill 1234 made law.

Choosing the Best Words

- Write with verbs and nouns.
- Prefer the concrete to the abstract, the specific to the general.
- Be aware of connotative as well as denotative meanings.
- Maintain a consistent, appropriate level of diction.

The first version is colorless and nearly weightless; it gives us no sense of action or of any person acting. The subject is *point* and the verb, *is.* Even the adverb and adjective modifying *point* add no real intensity to the sentence. The second version, while only slightly more specific (naming the particular bill in question), speaks with greater force and conviction: *we work, we can muster.* This sentence speaks of people, people acting. The adjectival modifiers give way to nouns: *energy* and *determination.* Even *to get* in the first version becomes *to see,* a more graphic verb, in the second.

2. **Prefer the concrete to the abstract, the specific to the general.** Although all words are abstractions, some are even further removed from concrete reality than others. *Head of government* is more abstract than *dictator,* for *heads of government* names a bigger and more vaguely defined class, including queens, pontiffs, prime ministers, and presidents. *Dictator* is in turn more abstract than *Castro, Franco,* or *Mussolini*—names that refer to specific dictators. The tendency of language is toward ever greater abstraction: It is like some great helium balloon always trying to slip away into the stratosphere as we either watch it sail away or try to pull it back down nearer earth. It is tempting just to let our language go, to say, "The movie was pretty interesting," because saying so is nearly effortless. It may take a conscious effort to pull our words down to the specific and concrete: "What I liked about the movie was the cinematography, which gave most of the scenes the appearance of paintings." And we could, of course, be still more concrete, describing in physical detail the artistic quality of particular scenes. Both specificity (identifying particular instances and features) and concreteness (creating images of tangible things) can clarify and illuminate an assertion. We cannot avoid the abstract, but we will support it with the specific and concrete if we wish to be clear.

3. **Be aware of connotative as well as denotative meanings.** A word's *denotation* is its meaning in the most neutral sense possible—its "dictionary" meaning. Its *connotation* is the emotional baggage the word carries. In the United States, for example, *democracy* carries positive connotations and *discrimination* carries both negative and positive connotations, depending on whether we are discussing the unfair treatment of minority groups or the ability to select a fine wine. Writers must be concerned with those societal connotations, selecting words that avoid unintended or undesirable connotations.

4. **Maintain a consistent level of diction.** Choose words appropriate to your audience and your purpose. For example, *technical words* are formal terms used in specialized fields, like engineering or literary criticism. When you have occasion to use such language, you need to maintain that level of formality. So, if you are writing a research paper, perhaps for your economics class, you may use some technical terms, you write in the third person (as a rule), and you avoid contractions (such as *don't* or *they'll*). The following short passage illustrates consistently formal diction:

> This search leads to a symbolist axiom: the artist disappears in his artifact. Though art does not reproduce the objective world, the work itself must be objective, not subjective. Flaubert would have the writer be like God, implicitly everywhere in his creation but totally invisible as a person. Rilke's praise of his favorite painter, Cezanne, for his "unlimited objectivity," aloof from private memories and immediate concerns, falls into the same pattern. . . . The objective image becomes increasingly palpable until it reaches the stage of epiphany or complete aesthetic existence, while by a reverse process the artist's personality recedes from sight. The perfect literary artifact is static, as against the dynamic experience of ordinary life, and it is objectively dramatic, as against the lyrical expression of more naive art.
>
> —Richard Ellmann and Charles Feidelson, Jr.,
> from the Introduction to *The Modern Tradition:*
> *Backgrounds of Modern Literature*

Everyday words consist of the vocabulary that you might expect any educated person to understand and use. If you are writing an informal argument for your rhetoric class, for instance, you use everyday words (but not slang), you sometimes write in the first person, and you may use an occasional contraction. The next passage illustrates consistently informal diction:

> My children had a pet goldfish that was a favorite of many of the kids in the diverse Washington, D.C., neighborhood where we lived. Of the children playing in our house the day the goldfish died, two were Hindu, one an Orthodox Jew, one a Catholic and three were Protestants. We decided to have a burial ceremony for the fish.
>
> As we walked together down the woodland path in our back yard, with flowers and a carefully prepared coffin, I wasn't sure what to say over the grave that wouldn't conflict with the children's varying religious beliefs. One girl sensed my uncertainty. "I know," she said. "Let's sing 'My Country 'Tis of Thee.' "
>
> We did, and I smiled to think that it took the funeral of a goldfish to teach me what the great melting pot of America is all about.
>
> —Martha W. Helgerson, from *Reader's Digest*, Jan. 1993

Colloquial words include regionalisms (a frappe in Boston is a milk shake in Denver) and slang. Colloquial diction has no place in most of the writing you will undertake in college and beyond. But if you write a note to your roommate, telling him to return a call from his Aunt Glenda, you may well use slang, first and second person pronouns, and contractions—as this example shows:

> I haven't had a chance to work through the examples and appendices, and won't until after the first. But I wanted to get this much off to you right away—hope your deadline isn't already past. Best to Bob and the kids.
>
> —From a colleague's note

	Levels of Diction	
Formal	*Informal*	*Colloquial*
May use some technical terms	Uses ordinary words	May use regionalisms and slang
Uses mostly third person pronouns	May use first and second person pronouns	Uses first and second person pronouns
Uses no contractions of verbs	May use some contractions of verbs	Uses contractions of verbs

EXERCISE 9–6

Revise the following paragraph with a particular eye to word choices. Correct any inappropriately formal or colloquial words and phrases. Replace unhelpfully vague or abstract language with specific illustrations and precise nouns. Change "to be" and similar verbs to verbs of action where doing so would strengthen the passage.

There is a lot printed about the right to privacy. To the news media and most ordinary people, it is important to maintain people's privacy about their own personal affairs. But people who are in the news a lot have no privacy. Whatever transpires in their lives is printed. It is not right for something to be revealed in the press against a person's specific injunction. The press is prevaricating when reporters clamor for the right to privacy but don't give a flip about people's feelings.

Avoiding Wordiness and Pointless Repetition   As we have seen, an important question writers must ask as we reread and relish the fruits of our toil is this: Have I said all I should? And the corollary to that question is this one: Where have I used more words than I needed to express a point? Paradoxically, it is possible for writing to be both underdeveloped and wordy. Consider the following passage, for example. It drones on like the next-door neighbor's home movies, full of sound but signifying nothing:

Poetry is written in many forms and meters, and sometimes in arrangements that appear meterless and very nearly formless as well. Of course, that variety of form and meter, even the lack of both, makes poetry what it is. Every poet is entitled to his or her own artistic freedom, as long as he or she is true to the vision that inspires a particular poem. Variety is naturally a feature of this freedom. Any poet can write any length of line or any variety of stanzaic patterns, and many succeed in writing good poems in a variety of forms, with and without meter. Variety is important in poetry.

—Student essay

Do you hear the pointless repetition of words and thought? This writer says little (what she does say could be reduced to "Variety in form and meter, and even the lack of both, are important elements of the poet's artistic freedom of expression") while missing the chance to illustrate her point with examples that would make it clearer and more convincing. After she prunes away the unneeded words, she will see the unanswered questions more clearly: *Why* is variety in form and meter so important? And if it is, how can we say that the lack of form and meter can be valuable, too? The writer now has an issue to define and focus.

Wordiness occurs often enough even when we do have something to say. The general fuzziness of first drafts nearly always gives rise to it. To eliminate underbrush of this sort from your own prose, look for and strike out unnecessary words, phrases, or sentences. Wordiness is not determined by the number of words, but by the number of useless words: verbal deadwood. It can take several forms, ranging from needless repetition to unnecessary passive voice. When you find anything that appears to be merely decorating the page or taking up space, strike it out. It will not add to the persuasiveness of your prose. Here are some strategies for pruning deadwood:

- **Reduce clauses to phrases.** For example, you can cut "The reason that President Bush lost the 1992 election was that the promised economic recovery had failed to materialize by election time" to "President Bush lost the 1992 election because the promised recovery. . . . " The revision contains one less clause with no meaning lost.

- **Avoid using impersonal constructions.** Impersonal constructions include *there is, there are, it is,* and the like. A sentence such as "It is widely believed that the Loch Ness monster exists" easily reduces to "Many people believe that the Loch Ness monster exists." Or consider this sentence: "There are many ideas about modern art that malign it unfairly." You can improve the sentence by eliminating the impersonal construction: "Many ideas about modern art malign it unfairly."

- **Change passive voice to active voice.** In passive voice, the object of the action becomes the subject of the sentence, as in "The bill was voted on at the last student senate meeting." In active voice, the subject of the action is also the subject of the sentence: "The student senate voted on the bill at its last meeting." Unless you need to emphasize the object rather than the subject, use the less wordy, more efficient active voice.

- **Replace empty modifiers with specific detail.** Avoid words like *different, various,* and *diverse,* as in "Art is different things to different people," or "Diverse factors contributed to the worldwide flu epidemic of 1919." Such empty modifiers can make you think you have said something when you haven't.

- **Eliminate redundancies.** Lawyers have worked in recent years to eliminate the redundancies that plague legal language, as in "will and testament" or "cease and desist." You may find pointless repetition in your own drafts as well. Eliminate redundancy from such sentences ("People often form and develop wrong opinions about others") and you lose nothing ("People often form wrong opinions about others").

The student who wrote the paragraph about the poet's freedom of form and meter later revised it to a less wordy and more specific passage:

> How could both e. e. cummings and John Milton be called by the same designation, poet? How could Lord Tennyson, Geoffrey Chaucer, and Gerard Manley Hopkins share it as well? Some of these poets, notably Milton, use strict stanzaic patterns and formal meter; their sonnets always look and sound like sonnets and their odes are recognizably odes. Others, like Hopkins, depart from standard meters, and some, like William Carlos Williams, seem to abandon meter altogether. And yet they are all poets, for what makes a poem is not wholly form, nor is it meter. What makes a poem is a special perspective of life, or of a red wheelbarrow, that strikes a chord of recognition—even reverence—that the reader had not known he possessed.

This writer had ideas she was not even aware of until she stripped away the undergrowth of wordiness in her first version and cleared a place for real content. Her first version lacks specifics; in the second, she names poets and describes their conventions and their idiosyncracies. She alludes to a famous line by a poet she has mentioned, William Carlos Williams, in the phrase "a red wheelbarrow." She discovers the point she really wants to argue: "[W]hat makes a poem is not wholly form, nor is it meter. What makes a poem is a special perspective . . . that strikes a chord of recognition [in a reader]." The revision has fifteen words more than the original paragraph, but it is far less wordy.

Revising for Conciseness

- Have I reduced clauses to phrases where possible?
- Have I changed passive verbs to active verbs unless I have a specific reason for emphasizing the object of the action rather than the subject?
- Have I replaced "to be" verbs with verbs that show specific action?
- Have I begun most sentences with the subject or a sentence opener rather than with an impersonal construction (*it is, there are*, etc.)?
- Have I avoided pointless repetition by combining clauses and phrases and by eliminating redundancies?

EXERCISE 9–7

Reduce the following paragraph to its core meaning by eliminating all the deadwood and other wordy constructions. Then add real content.

> Freshmen in college probably should not attempt to declare a major during their freshman year. The first year is a year of beginnings, so a student should not feel

forced to make such an important decision at that time. There is plenty of time for declaring a major later; the freshman should not feel pressure to do so too soon.

EXERCISE 9–8

The writers of the following passages, a research scientist and a psychologist, have paid attention to their subjects but not to their readers' needs. What specific problems do you find in the two paragraphs? Write revisions to improve the style of each.

(1)

It can be seen from this summary of the analysis that even the relatively restricted question of paper versus polyfoam for hot drink cups is complex. But for single-use applications it would appear that polystyrene foam cups should be given a much more even-handed assessment as regards their environmental impact relative to paper cups than they have received during the past few years.

—Conclusion to an article in *Science,* 1 Feb. 1991

(2)

In what follows, I'm going to venture an answer [to an adoptee's question, "Who am I?"]—a rather hollow one, admittedly . . . —but an answer, nonetheless. Better said, I'm going to describe a way of encouraging answers that we have developed as part of the work of the Adoption Therapy Guild. I call it a subtlety where others, I'm sure, would use the word technique or strategy, but though there is a mass of theory behind the substitution, accept merely the expression of a personal disposition that shies away from anything unpoetic or anti-philosophical.

—Draft of a essay paragraph, *Adoption Therapist* newsletter, May 1990

EXERCISE 9–9

Try your hand at combining the following material (which is given in no particular order) into a coherent and persuasive paragraph. Combine, subordinate, and rephrase clauses as you see fit, as long as you preserve their meaning. You may add to what is given here, but you must include all this information. Then write a paragraph explaining the reasons for your choices of arrangement and emphasis, and detailing your stylistic choices.

This is not to say that white-collar criminals should not be closely monitored.
Imprisoning people convicted of white-collar crimes is senseless.
People who have written hot checks or embezzled money are no threat to the physical safety of others.
Imprisonment does not rehabilitate such criminals.
Imprisonment does not pay back the victims of white-collar crime.
White-collar crime usually involves money.
Such criminals should be compelled to work to pay back their victims.

They should do work that brings income to the state, and their victims should receive part of the pay from their work.
Prison externships could offer a solution.
Imprisoning white-collar criminals in minimum security facilities only costs the taxpayer.
Convicted persons could work in government facilities or in private facilities, such as factories and hospitals, under state government contract.
They should pay for their crime.
Imprisoning white-collar criminals does nothing for the victims.
Imprisoning white-collar criminals is a waste of the inmates' abilities.
Those abilities could be put to profitable use by the state.

EXERCISE 9–10

Read the letters to the editor in several recent daily editions of a local newspaper or your campus newspaper. Select a letter that seems to you to have merit in its argument but also to fail in its expression of that argument. Improve the style of the letter by rewriting it. Add and delete material as necessary, but retain the essential argument of the original. Attach the original letter to your revision of it. What kinds of stylistic improvements (clause combining, elimination of pointless repetition, and so on) did you make?

EXERCISE 9–11

Describe your room, house, or apartment in such a way that the reader will be persuaded of its attractiveness, shabbiness, inconvenience, or menace to public health. Optional: Assume the distinctive style of Ernest Hemingway, William Faulkner, J. D. Salinger, James Joyce, or another writer with whose work you are acquainted.

Tropes

Figures of speech are words employed in special ways for emphasis and variety. Some figures alter the usual arrangement of words in sentences: These are called **schemes,** some of which you have already encountered in this chapter under the heading "Syntactical Patterns." Schemes include parallelism, antithesis, inverted order, and other deliberate arrangements of words.

But now we will consider some figures of speech that require even more careful thought when you use them, for they play on the *meanings* of words. These are called **tropes,** and such tropes as metaphor, understatement, and paradox can bring dry arguments to life. Some, like simile or the rhetorical question, you may already use in your writing; others you should try occasionally as you experiment with revising drafts of your arguments. Effective figures of speech will not make those arguments more logically convincing, but they can make them more enjoyable—and hence more persuasive—for your readers.

   Metaphor and Simile   Metaphor and simile are comparisons of unlike things that unexpectedly share certain characteristics. Metaphors say that one thing *is* another; similes say that one thing *is like* another. Because the two are so closely related, many people use *metaphor* to mean either. Normally a metaphor compares one thing that is familiar to readers with another that is less familiar, in order to illuminate the less-understood idea. Metaphors and similes create images in readers' imaginations.

Metaphor:

True art is a conduit between body and soul, between feeling unabstracted and abstraction unfelt.

> —John Gardner, *On Moral Fiction*

Simile:

Laws are like cobwebs, which may catch small flies, but let wasps and hornets break through.

> —Jonathan Swift, "A Critical Essay Upon the Faculties of the Mind"

   Metaphor (including its variant, simile) centers on relationships, but the relationships, unlike those in literal analogies, surprise the reader with unexpected and figurative connections. Metaphor is:

If the writing of history resembles architecture, journalism bears comparison to a tent show. The impresarios of the press drag into their tents whatever freaks and wonders might astonish a crowd; the next day they move their exhibit to another edition instead of to another town four miles farther west.

> —Lewis Lapham, "Sculptures in Snow"

Metaphor is not:

The writing of history is like the writing of fiction in that both history books and novels depend heavily upon the selective imaginations of their authors, and both contain fiction and reality in very nearly equal doses.

In the first case the writing of history is compared to something completely unlike it in every sense except a symbolic or pictorial one: a traveling tent show. In the second the writing of history is compared to another form of writing, and the resemblances, however cynically depicted, are offered as literal resemblances.

   The following three statements contain metaphor:

History is a bath of blood.

> —William James, "The Moral Equivalent of War"

With this new line of attack, we should gain ground against the competition.

Appealing to reason as we do, we are in a sort of a forlorn hope situation, like a small sand-bank in the midst of a hungry sea ready to wash it out of existence. But sand-banks grow when the conditions favor; and weak as reason is, it has the unique advantage over its antagonists that its activity never lets up and that it presses always in one direction, while men's prejudices vary, their passions ebb and flow, and their excitements are intermittent.

—William James, "War and Reason"

The first metaphor is as much an argumentative assertion as it is an image: History is the story of violence, death, and war. The metaphor is powerful for all its brevity. The second metaphor also hints of militarism, but it is familiar stuff, not fresh and no longer particularly vivid. The third offers a visual image—the sandbank, which, although daily buffeted by the tide, steadily increases in size and strength nonetheless—an image that clarifies the abstract relationship between reason and prejudices.

Since the power of metaphor lies in its ability to suggest fresh and unexpected figurative associations between unlike things, beware the metaphor that has grown stale with overuse—the cliché. The first metaphor that suggests itself often will be a cliché:

I think we ought to hire McDuff. He's fit as a _____ and eager as a _____ to work. Your objections amount to nothing more than a _____ in a teapot, because I know he'll keep his shoulder to the _____ and get the job done as fast as greased _____ .

Any writer is occasionally tempted to write, "That was the straw that broke the camel's back," or "He had the Midas touch," or the like. Try to resist the temptation. However, sometimes you can revive a cliché for humorous effect. In 1992 presidential candidate Ross Perot, known for his large ears, announced his willingness to listen to suggestions by reviving what would have been a tired cliché from anyone else: "I'm all ears." The real danger of clichés arises when you mix incompatible metaphors together. During the Democratic presidential primary of 1984, candidate Gary Hart was ridiculed in the press for declaring, "We have brought the [Walter] Mondale juggernaut to its knees." Such mixed metaphors can damage a writer's credibility with readers and can render a serious argument ludicrous.

Careful writers are forever plucking clichés and mixed metaphors from their own prose, and still, like weeds, the pesky things pop up again in unexpected places.

Despite these cautions, do not let the fear of looking ridiculous with inappropriate, clichéd, or mixed metaphors deter you from experimenting with metaphor in your own arguments. The ability to write with fresh and effective metaphors may well be, as rhetorician F. L. Lucas has suggested, the single greatest skill a writer can cultivate. Just keep plucking the weeds.

EXERCISE 9–12

Create persuasive metaphors to describe the following:

1. The sound of chalk scraping across a blackboard
2. Telephone solicitors

3. An old person's hands
4. A five-year-old in a toy store
5. The last snow before spring
6. The difference between writing and typing
7. Social Security
8. Making a first job application
9. The current political situation in the Middle East (or the former Soviet Union)
10. The stock market

EXERCISE 9–13

The following paragraphs are taken from the same editorial, "The Purpose of Presidents," which appeared in *The Wall Street Journal* on November 21, 1986. Both paragraphs use metaphor. Which uses it more effectively? Explain why.

(1)

President Reagan's occasionally disjointed performance at his news conference Wednesday evening appears to have caused dissatisfaction all around. The president quickly became enveloped by a miasma over who did what, where, when, with whom and by the way how does all this square with the National Security Act of 1977? This vaporous bog was predictable and partly of the president's own making. Mr. Reagan and his staff understand well enough the geostrategic importance of Iran, but by failing to elaborate this crucial point in his opening remarks he effectively made it a nonsubject.

(2)

Nobody is in fact being shut out of the foreign-policy process. Washington is a vast funnel of diverse opinions about what the foreign policy of this country ought to be. At the bottom of the funnel, someone has to act, someone has to decide what U.S. policy will be. Our reading of Article II for the Constitution says that the president is the person at the bottom of the foreign policy funnel. And when the president decides or acts, some of the people in the funnel become winners and some become losers.

Rhetorical Question The rhetorical question is asked to make a point, not to seek information. It does not really question; it asserts.

Was it for this—these computer markings on a slip of paper—that I gave up a social life and buried myself in the library for a semester?

Can we hope to learn if we dare not question?

The rhetorical question, because it invites assent, can provide a persuasive conclusion to an argument. Just be careful not to overdo rhetorical questions, or to ask them when the answer really is in doubt.

Overstatement   Also called *hyperbole,* overstatement calls attention to a point through obvious exaggeration.

> The war on poverty, that monstrous insult to the rippling muscles in a black man's arms, is an index of how men actually sit down and plot each other's deaths, actually sit down with slide rules and calculate how to hide bread from the hungry.
> —Eldredge Cleaver, "Domestic Law and International Order"

> Four hostile newspapers are more to be feared than a thousand bayonets.
> —Attributed to Napoleon Bonaparte

Overstatement is a trope to be used with restraint. Overdo overstatement, and your arguments will sound like ravings. To make a critically important point memorable, you may choose overstatement, but the hyperbole must be clearly that. A reader must not think that you mean it literally. Overstatement makes an emotional point; it does not convey literal information.

Irony   Irony takes a number of forms, but typically it involves saying one thing while clearly implying the opposite.

> Although students in past years have received generous help from their instructors in maintaining and developing poor writing habits, the current clamor for "writing across the curriculum" threatens to make poor writing passé.
> —John Keenan, "A Professor's Guide to Perpetuating Poor Writing Among Students"

> In my own case [as a writer] there are days when the result is so bad that no fewer than five revisions are required. However, when I'm greatly inspired, only four are needed before, as I've often said, I put in that note of spontaneity which even my meanest critics concede.
> —John Kenneth Galbraith, "Writing and Typing"

Effective irony is subtle, and it may be missed by unsophisticated readers. But careful readers are united with the writer in the shared understanding of an ironic statement: "You and I understand I mean just the opposite" is the message irony sends. If your audience and your purpose would be well served by the tart flavor of irony, do not be afraid to try it.

Paradox   A paradox (which we discussed on a larger scale in Chapter 2) is an apparent contradiction, both parts of which are nevertheless true.

> Last fall I had an advanced graduate student, bright, energetic, well-informed, whose papers were almost unreadable.
> —Wayne Booth, "The Rhetorical Stance"

> Being frustrated is disagreeable, but the real disasters in life begin when you get what you want.
> —Irving Kristol, "Pornography, Obscenity, and the Case for Censorship"

Paradox gives a reader something to really think about. How can two conditions, so opposed, exist at the same time? Human fondness for paradox is reflected in the many books of quotations—you cannot turn a page without finding at least one pithy statement of a paradox. When you use paradox, you make your readers think.

EXERCISE 9–14

A. Identify any metaphor, simile, rhetorical question, overstatement, irony, or paradox in the following sentences and passages.

B. Read aloud the sentences and passages in the list. Pick two or three that you either like or feel you could improve on. Then write sentences of your own with the same subject matter as those you have picked—but completely new tropes. For example, if you choose the last item—"Art is the lie that enables us to realize the truth"—you will write a sentence about art that uses paradox. One such sentence is, "Art is all around us, but few recognize it."

1. He will never furnish the house of his own mind.

　　　　　　　　　　　　　　　　　　　　　　　—John Ciardi

2. Lawton "borrowed" paper, pencil, and paper clips from the office; he "forgot" to return the change when a clerk gave him too much; he claimed as business expenses his lunches with his best friend; and he lectured his son regularly on the importance of honesty.

3. A slight injection of knowledge may hurt our feelings, but it may save our lives.

　　　　　　　　　　—Sinclair Lewis, "Gentlemen, This Is Revolution"

4. God would have us know that we must live as men who manage our lives without him.

　　　　　　　　　　—Dietrich Bonhoeffer, *Letters and Papers from Prison*

5. Our high school colors were purple and gold, a combination so garish the colors were no doubt chosen to startle our athletic opponents into dropping the ball.

6. Brian De Palma walked right off a cliff when he made his version of the Tom Wolfe novel *The Bonfire of the Vanities.*

　　　　　　　　　　　　　　　　　　　　　　　—Pauline Kael

7. A lawn "is the decent, respectably dull necktie we knot around our houses."

　　　　　　　　　　　　　　　—John Skow, "Can Lawns Be Justified?"

8. The Strunk book [*The Elements of Style*], which is a "right and wrong" book, arrived on the scene at a time when a wave of reaction was setting in against the permissive school of rhetoric, the Anything Goes school where right and wrong do not exist and there is no foundation all down the line. The little book climbed on this handy wave and rode it in.

　　　　　　　　　　　　　　　　　　　—E. B. White, "Will Strunk"

9. In modern times, it has become fashionable for a young woman, upon reaching the age of eighteen, to signify her membership in adult society by announcing that she refuses to make a debut.

—Judith Martin, *Miss Manners' Guide
to Excruciatingly Correct Behavior*

10. Art is the lie that enables us to realize the truth.

—Pablo Picasso

EXERCISE 9–15

The following student paragraph is intelligible and competent, but boring and unpersuasive. Could one or more tropes enliven it without being silly or flippant? Experiment with a trope or two in the passage—and compare versions with your classmates. Has anyone improved the paragraph's persuasiveness by making it more interesting for readers?

Adoption has changed during the last twenty years. There is a lot more openness now. Birthparents often pick the adoptive parents for their babies, and sometimes they meet. The children grow up knowing that they are adopted. They get letters from their birthparents, and sometimes they meet them. This openness in adoption does have some good effects on all the parties involved.

READINGS

WAR AND REASON

William James

1   I am only a philosopher, and there is only one thing that a philosopher can be relied on to do. You know that the function of statistics has been ingeniously described as being the refutation of other statistics. Well, a philosopher can always contradict other philosophers. In ancient times philosophers defined man as the rational animal; and philosophers since then have always found much more to say about the rational than about the animal part of the definition. But looked at candidly, reason bears about the same proportion to the rest of human nature that we in this hall bear to the rest of America, Europe, Asia, Africa, and Polynesia. Reason is one of the very feeblest of Nature's forces, if you take it at any one spot and moment. It is only in the very long run that its effects become perceptible. Reason assumes to settle things by

weighing them against one another without prejudice, partiality, or excitement; but what affairs in the concrete are settled by is and always will be just prejudices, partialities, cupidities, and excitements. Appealing to reason as we do, we are in a sort of a forlorn hope situation, like a small sand-bank in the midst of a hungry sea ready to wash it out of existence. But sand-banks grow when the conditions favor; and weak as reason is, it has the unique advantage over its antagonists that its activity never lets up and that it presses always in one direction, while men's prejudices vary, their passions ebb and flow, and their excitements are intermittent. Our sand-bank, I absolutely believe, is bound to grow—bit by bit it will get dyked and break-watered. But sitting as we do in this warm room, with music and lights and the flowing bowl and smiling faces, it is easy to get too sanguine about our task, and since I am called to speak, I feel as if it might not be out of place to say a word about the strength of our enemy.

2   Our permanent enemy is the noted bellicosity of human nature. Man, biologically considered, and whatever else he may be in the bargain, is simply the most formidable of all beasts of prey, and, indeed, the only one that preys systematically on its own species. We are once for all adapted to the military *status*. A millennium of peace would not breed the fighting disposition out of our bone and marrow, and a function so ingrained and vital will never consent to die without resistance, and will always find impassioned apologists and idealizers.

3   Not only men born to be soldiers, but non-combatants by trade and nature, historians in their studies, and clergymen in their pulpits, have been war's idealizers. They have talked of war as of God's court of justice. And, indeed, if we think how many things beside the frontiers of states the wars of history have decided, we must feel some respectful awe, in spite of all the horrors. Our actual civilization, good and bad alike, has had past wars for its determining condition. Greatmindedness among the tribes of men has always meant the will to prevail, and all the more so if prevailing included slaughtering and being slaughtered. Rome, Paris, England, Brandenburg, Piedmont—soon, let us hope, Japan—along with their arms have made their traits of character and habits of thought prevail among their conquered neighbors. The blessings we actually enjoy, such as they are, have grown up in the shadow of wars of antiquity. The various ideals were backed by fighting wills, and where neither would give way, the God of battles had to be the arbiter. A shallow view, this, truly; for who can say what might have prevailed if man had ever been a reasoning and not a fighting animal? Like dead men, dead causes tell no tales, and the ideals that went under in the past, along with all the tribes that represented them, find to-day no recorder, no explainer, no defender.

4   But apart from theoretic defenders, and apart from every soldierly individual straining at the leash, and clamoring for opportunity, war has an omnipotent support in the form of our imagination. Man lives *by* habits, indeed, but what he lives *for* is thrills and excitements. The only relief from Habit's

tediousness is periodical excitement. From time immemorial wars have been, especially for noncombatants, the supremely thrilling excitement. Heavy and dragging at its end, at its outset every war means an explosion of imaginative energy. The dams of routine burst, and boundless prospects open. The remotest spectators share the fascination. With that awful struggle now in progress on the confines of the world, there is not a man in this room, I suppose, who doesn't buy both an evening and a morning paper, and first of all pounce on the war column.

5   A deadly listlessness would come over most men's imagination of the future if they could seriously be brought to believe that never again *in saecula saeculorum* would a war trouble human history. In such a stagnant summer afternoon of a world, where would be the zest or interest?

6   This is the constitution of human nature which we have to work against. The plain truth is that people *want* war. They want it anyhow; for itself; and apart from each and every possible consequence. It is the final bouquet of life's fireworks. The born soldiers want it hot and actual. The noncombatants want it in the background, and always as an open possibility, to feed imagination on and keep excitement going. Its clerical and historical defenders fool themselves when they talk as they do about it. What moves them is not the blessings it has won for us, but a vague religious exaltation. War, they feel, is human nature at its uttermost. We are here to do our uttermost. It is a sacrament. Society would rot, they think, without the mystical blood-payment.

7   We do ill, I fancy, to talk much of universal peace or of a general disarmament. We must go in for preventive medicine, not for radical cure. We must cheat our foe, politically circumvent his action, not try to change his nature. In one respect war is like love, though in no other. Both leave us intervals of rest; and in the intervals life goes on perfectly well without them, though the imagination still dallies with their possibility. Equally insane when once aroused and under headway, whether they shall be aroused or not depends on accidental circumstances. How are old maids and old bachelors made? Not by deliberate vows of celibacy, but by sliding on from year to year with no sufficient matrimonial provocation. So of the nations with their wars. Let the general possibility of war be left open, in Heaven's name, for the imagination to dally with. Let the soldiers dream of killing, as the old maids dream of marrying. But organize in every conceivable way the practical machinery for making each successive chance of war abortive. Put peace-men in power; educate the editors and statesmen to responsibility—how beautifully did their trained responsibility in England make the Venezuela incident abortive! Seize every pretext, however small, for arbitration methods, and multiply the precedents; foster rival excitements and invent new outlets for heroic energy; and from one generation to another, the chances are that irritations will grow less acute and states of strain less dangerous among the nations. Armies and navies will continue, of course, and will fire the minds of populations with their potentialities of greatness. But their officers

will find that somehow or other, with no deliberate intention on any one's part, each successive "incident" has managed to evaporate and to lead nowhere, and that the thought of what might have been remains their only consolation.

8   The last weak runnings of the war spirit will be "punitive expeditions." A country that turns its arms only against uncivilized foes is, I thin, wrongly taunted as degenerate. Of course it has ceased to be heroic in the old grand style. But I verily believe that this is because it now sees something better. It has a conscience. It knows that between civilized countries a war is a crime against civilization. It will still perpetrate peccadillos, to be sure. But it is afraid, afraid in the good sense of the word, to engage in absolute crimes against civilization.

QUESTIONS AND IDEAS FOR DISCUSSION

1. How effective is James's introduction? When you read the first three sentences, do you want to read on? How would you describe James's tone at the outset of his essay? Comment.

2. This essay is just eight paragraphs long, but the paragraphs themselves are long and complex. To make sure you have followed the author's argument, outline its major points. Would you have organized these points as James does? Comment on any changes you would make in ordering and developing the argument if this were your own draft.

3. James uses not only the logical appeal of reason to support his argument in this essay but also the emotional appeal of style. Characterize the features that distinguish James's style, giving examples from the text. For example, James's sentences are often heavily parenthetical and subordinated, as in the second sentence of the second paragraph: "Man, biologically considered, and whatever else he may be in the bargain, is simply the most formidable of all beasts of prey, and, indeed, the only one that preys systematically on its own species." What is the stylistic effect of so much subordination?

4. Do you agree that the analogy between war and love is startling—and attention-getting? James limits the analogy to one element; might a cynic add others?

5. Comment on James's proposed solution to the problem of war. Do you find the solution reasonable?

SCULPTURES IN SNOW

Lewis Lapham

1   At random intervals in the nation's history one or another of the liberal occupations attracts a claque of admirers eager for simple answers. In the 1950s it was thought that psychoanalysis could resolve the enigma of human nature; in the 1960s it was the physicists who were going to steal the fires of heaven and the lawyers who were going to reform the laws and manage the nation's foreign policy; the most recent surge of hyperbole has placed the mantle of omniscience on the profession of journalism. For the last fifteen years journalists have enjoyed a reputation for knowing how the world works. This is silly. Reporters tend to show up at the scenes of crimes and accidents, and they take an imbecile's delight in catastrophe. Few of them know enough about the subject under discussion—whether politics, music, or the structure of DNA—to render a definitive opinion about anything other than the menu at the nearest Marriott Inn. But to concede the shallowness and ignorance of the press does nothing to diminish its usefulness or importance. Even the most mean-spirited criticisms fail to answer the question as to why anybody would bother to read or write the news. Why not wait a hundred years, until the archives have been opened and the historians have had time to arrange events in an orderly and patriotic sequence?

2   Any plausible defense of journalism rests on a modest presumption of what it provides. As follows:

3   • If the writing of history resembles architecture, journalism bears comparison to a tent show. The impresarios of the press drag into their tents whatever freaks and wonders might astonish a crowd; the next day they move their exhibit to another edition instead of to another town four miles farther west. Their subject matter is the flux of human affairs, and they achieve their most spectacular effects by reason of their artlessness and lack of sentiment.

4   The press makes sculptures in snow; its truth dwells in the concrete fact and the fleeting sound of the human voice.

5   • Journalists hire themselves out as journeymen, not as immortal artists. It would be fair to compare them to a troupe of medieval stonemasons traveling the circuit of unfinished cathedrals with a repertoire of conventional forms. They can carve figures of the saints fifty feet above the nave, but nobody would expect them to impart expression to the face.

6   Or, to take a metaphor more likely to recommend itself to the Republicans now in Washington, journalists possess the social graces of Pony Express riders—resolution, ingenuity, punctuality. They bring the news from Ghent or California, and they do their readers no favor if they try to shape it into a

work of literature. Maybe this is why the books that journalists feel compelled to write, about the war in Algeria or last year's election campaign, so often read like a definitive study of a formation of clouds.

7 • The critics of the press complain about its pessimism, its cynicism, its unwillingness to recommend a program of political advancement. Every now and then a reader of *Harper's* writes to say that the magazine should publish sermons. "Be more positive," says a correspondent in Oklahoma. "Imagine that you have been proclaimed king," says a correspondent in Florida, "and submit your blueprint for Utopia."

8 They send their requests to the wrong address. The reader in hope of inspiration can study the collected works of St. Augustine or Bishop Paul Moore; he can listen to Billy Graham defy the foul fiend or sit in rapturous contemplation of an elm tree or a whale.

9 William Randolph Hearst once complained to Dorothy Parker that her stories were too sad. To this objection (not very different from the admonitions circulated by vice presidents in charge of public relations), Miss Parker replied:

10 "Mr. Hearst, there are two billion people on the face of the earth, and the story of not one of them will have a happy ending."

11 If a man drinks too much and his doctor tells him that one of these days he will fall down dead in the club car on the way to Westport, is the doctor a pessimist? Is Israel a pessimistic nation because it bombs the Iraqi nuclear installation southeast of Baghdad, or is it an optimistic nation because it accepts the conditions of its existence? Is it pessimism to say that the theories of supply side economics have little basis in fact, or that American novelists don't write very good novels?

12 Journalism, like history, has no therapeutic value; it is better able to diagnose than to cure, and it provides society with a primitive means of psychoanalysis that allows the patient to judge the distance between fantasy and reality.

13 The question is never one of optimism or pessimism. It is a question of trying to tell the truth, of the emotions required of the teller and of the emotions the attempt calls forth in the reader. If the news, no matter how bad, evokes in the reader a sense of energy and hope, then it has done as much as can be said for it. The unctuous recitation of platitudes usually achieves the opposite effect, instilling in the reader a feeling of passivity and despair.

14 Great power constitutes its own argument, and it never has much trouble drumming up friends, applause, sympathetic exigesis, and a band. In his commencement address at West Point last May, President Reagan was pleased to announce that the American "era of self-doubt" had come to a satisfactory end. The rest of his speech could have been accompanied by a fanfare of trumpets and drums.

15 But a democracy stands in need of as much self-doubt as it can muster and as many arguments as possible that run counter to the governing body of

opinion. The press exerts the pressure of dissent on officials otherwise inclined to rest content with the congratulations of their retainers. From the point of view of the Soviet authorities the Soviet press is admirably optimistic; the era of self-doubt ended with the revolution of 1917.

16   • The press in its multiple voices argues that the world of men and events can eventually be understood. Not yet, perhaps, not in time for tomorrow's deadline, but sooner or later, when enough people with access to better information have had an opportunity to expand the spheres of reference. This is an immensely hopeful and optimistic assumption. Defined as means rather than an end, journalism defends the future against the past.

17   • The media offer for sale every conceivable fact or opinion. Most of these objects possess a dubious value, but it isn't the business of the journalist to distinguish between the significant and the worthless.

18   During World War II British raiding units pressed far behind German lines in the North African desert in search of stray pieces of metal. The patrols collected anything that came to hand—a shell casing, a broken axle, a button torn from the uniform of a dead corporal. The objects were sent to Cairo for analysis, and by this means British intelligence guessed at the state of German industry.

19   So also with journalism. The data are always fugitive and insufficient. To treat even the most respectable political ideas as if they were the offspring of pure reason would be to assign them, in Lewis Namier's phrase, "a parentage about as mythological as that of Pallas Athene."

20   • Without an audience, the media would cease to exist. Even if people don't read the same papers and periodicals, the media provide the connective tissue holding together the federation of contradictory interests that goes by the name of democracy. How else except through the instruments of the media could the surgeon and the labor leader, the ballerina and the stock-car driver form even a distorted image of one another? The media present a spectacle infinitely more crowded than Balzac's *Comédie Humaine*—the rumors of war on page one, followed, in random succession, by reports of strange crimes, political intrigues, anomalous discoveries in the sciences, the hazard of new fortunes.

21   Just as every nation supposedly gets "the government it deserves," so also it makes of the press whatever it chooses to imagine as its self-portrait. If the covers of all the nation's magazines could be displayed in a gallery, and if the majority of the images reflected dreams of wealth or sexual delight, a wandering Arab might be forgiven for thinking that the United States had confused itself with the Moslem vision of paradise.

22   The newspapers yield only as much as the reader brings to his reading. If the reader doesn't also study foreign affairs, or follow the money markets,

or keep up his practice of foreign languages, then what can he expect to learn from the papers?

QUESTIONS AND IDEAS FOR DISCUSSION

1. What is Lapham's thesis, and where do you find it most explicitly stated? Are you surprised that it appears where it does? Explain why or why not.

2. Much of this essay consists of bulleted items in a list of "what [journalism] provides" (paragraph 2). Briefly summarize the six items in the list. Has Lapham organized his points in a logical way? Explain. Suggest transitional sentences or phrases (for the points arranged as Lapham has written them or as you prefer) that would eliminate the need for typographical bullets to show the shift from one main point to the next.

3. This essay was written by a journalist, the editor of *Harper's,* and published in that magazine. Since the essay is a defense of journalism, not only what the journalist-author says but how well he says it must surely figure into his defense of journalism. And, indeed, the argument is offered with grace and style. Discuss Lapham's use of metaphor, parallelism, variation of sentence length, a large and precise vocabulary, and other elements of style. Give examples from the text of the essay.

4. Lapham offers a counterpoint to the criticism of journalism so common elsewhere (including in these pages). Here are some of his assertions; offer your own seconding arguments or refutations. But do as Lapham does: Give examples and draw analogies to support your points.

   Defined as means rather than an end, journalism defends the future against the past. (16)

   . . . it isn't the business of the journalist to distinguish between the significant and the worthless. (17)

   Just as every nation supposedly gets "the government it deserves," so also it makes of the press whatever it chooses to imagine as its self-portrait. (21)

Suggestions for Writing and Further Discussion

1. I used to rush to the school library and cram the subject, like a python swallowing rabbits; then, still replete as a postprandial python, I would tie myself in clumsy knots to embrace those accursed themes.
                                                        —F. L. Lucas, "What Is Style?"

   Should children, who have experienced so little of education and of life, be required to write essays? Based on your own experience, and directed to the school board or headmaster responsible for your precollege education, argue your answer to that question. Whether or not you found your early essay-writing experience as agonizing as did F. L. Lucas, try to describe yours vividly and persuasively.

2. Refute Lewis Lapham's defense of journalism, which you may choose to answer point by point. Lapham addresses his argument to the "consumers" of journalism—those who read *Harper's* and newspapers; address your argument to the same audience. Try some persuasive metaphors in your argument, as Lapham does.

3. Lewis Lapham concludes his argument about the value of the press with a challenge for the press's audience: "The newspapers yield only as much as the reader brings to his reading. If the reader doesn't also study foreign affairs, or follow the money markets, or keep up his practice of foreign languages, then what can he expect to learn from the papers?" How much of communication really depends on the participation of the audience? Is it fair to ask of readers and viewers that they be more than passive sponges, soaking up what newspapers, magazines, and television pour forth? Where is the audience supposed to study foreign affairs, anyway, if not in the pages of magazines or of the evening newspaper? Is there something of a Catch-22 in Lapham's challenge to his readers?

   a. Write an essay in which you argue, in support of Lapham's assertion, that news consumers need to educate themselves independently of the newspapers and the television in order to understand and intelligently evaluate both. Give specific examples from recent daily newspapers of information that would be difficult to understand fully without additional, prior knowledge of "foreign affairs, ... money markets, or ... foreign languages"—or some other field.

   b. Write an essay in which you argue against Lapham's assertion as being elitist or impracticable or otherwise flawed. Indicate in your essay how journalism ideally should function for its consumers.

4. Reason assumes to settle things by weighing them against one another without prejudice, partiality, or excitement; but what affairs in the concrete are settled by is and always will be just prejudices, partialities, cupidities, and excitements.

   —William James

Write an essay for which William James's assertion could serve as the thesis statement, centering on a particular incident (or several incidents) that illustrates the absence of reason in settling concrete difficulties.

10

Readings for Further Discussion

The test of a first-rate intelligence is the ability to hold two opposed ideas in the mind at the same time and still retain the ability to function.

—F. Scott Fitzgerald

When we all think alike, no one thinks very much.

—Walter Lippmann

The following selections address a variety of issues, from language to laws to human behavior, from matters of great scope to others of more modest dimensions; and they speak in a variety of voices, from that of a great leader addressing his countrymen and women to that of the person sitting next to you on the bus, smoking a cigarette. It is an unruly assemblage; some of the authors speak to each other as well as to us, and all of them attempt to persuade us of their often conflicting conclusions. Ours is to compare, evaluate, agree, disagree, or (despite the fact that several of these readings are paired as if the subject had but two sides of it) find a middle ground. If Lippman's statement is true, there is little danger of little thinking for the reader of these pages. Only Fitzgerald's challenge remains to give us pause.

VOTING

LET'S NOT GET OUT THE VOTE

Robert E. Coulson

1   Three years ago anyone who failed to vote had to face the combined scorn of both political parties, the schoolteachers, boy scouts, war veterans, chambers of commerce, and leagues of women voters. Last year bar associations, girl scouts, tavern keepers, President Eisenhower, radio and TV stations, and junior chambers of commerce joined the crusade. There is every prospect that in future elections, nonvoters will face jail sentences or fines, or be called to testify before investigating committees.

2   Before this happens, someone should come to their defense. Nonvoters are often more intelligent, more fair-minded, and just as loyal as voters. The right not to vote is as basic as the right to. If voting is made a duty, it ceases to be a privilege.

3   Let's look at the voting behavior of Mr. and Mrs. Whipcord and Mrs. Whipcord's brother Harold, on the day of the local school-board election. Mrs. Whipcord says, "I have studied the candidates and have made up my mind. I will vote for Jones." Mr. Whipcord says, "I know nothing about the candidates or the issues. I will stay home, and allow the election to be decided by the votes of those who have made a study and formed an opinion." Harold says, "I don't know anything about the candidates or the problems, but by golly, I'm going to vote. It's my duty. I'll pick the fellows with the shortest names."

4   If there is a bad citizen among these three, which one is it? Whose procedure is least likely to bring good government to the school district?

5   Non-voting, multiplied by the thousands, is said to mean voter apathy, and this is supposed to be a sin. Have we lost our sacred American right to be apathetic? Suppose Mr. Whipcord studied the candidates carefully and concluded that Candidate Jones was a boob and Candidate Smith was a thief. Is it un-American to refuse to choose between them? Or suppose he is satisfied that Jones and Smith are equally qualified, equally able, and that the school's problems are in good hands no matter which man wins. He is not apathetic; he is satisfied. Why should he be forced to choose between candidates on some esoteric basis?

6   The notion that "getting out the vote" makes for better election results is neither non-partisan, patriotic, nor logical. It is a device to favor the machines of both parties. It handicaps independent candidates, unfairly burdens the party in power, makes elections more expensive to conduct, greatly slows the tallying, and—worst of all—places the emphasis on the ritual of voting rather than the thought behind the vote.

7   If you fill in all the blank spaces on the ballot, the political machines will

steal three-fourths of your vote. Let's see how this works, in a typical primary election.

8   Here are seven offices to be filled by nomination, with two or three candidates for each office. Citizen Stringfellow is interested in seeing Jones win for Auditor. He has no information about the candidates for Attorney General, Treasurer, Superintendent of Schools, or the others. He votes for Jones and then looks on down the list. He has been persuaded that it is his duty to vote for *somebody* for each office. So for six of the seven names, he marks an X opposite the name best known to him, or the name on top, or the name suggested by his committeeman. These are machine candidates, and Citizen Stringfellow has given away six-sevenths of his vote.

9   After him, comes Citizen Stalwart, who knows the candidates for two of the seven offices. He also fills in all the blanks, letting the machine steal five-sevenths of his vote. One of his blind votes cancels out the intelligent vote cast by Citizen Stringfellow. At this rate, during a day's balloting, the candidates backed by the strongest machines with the biggest publicity budgets will win, even though not a single voter had an intelligent preference for them.

10   Is this what Thomas Jefferson had in mind?

11   "Getting out the vote" is always partisan. A calm and dignified effort benefits the party in power. An excited or hysterical effort benefits the party out of power. The Republicans were very happy to use the pressure of "neutral" groups in the 1952 elections. But they had better learn that this is a two-edged sword. Next time, the girl scouts, veterans' groups, radio stations, newspapers, and community funds may be out needling the Republicans with propaganda.

12   "Vote this time or your vote may be gone forever." "This may be your last chance." "Vote now or never." Anyone who is led to the polls by such arguments is going to vote against whoever brought us to the edge of this crevasse. As the pressure on the public increases, the party out of power is most likely to benefit in direct proportion to it.

13   All public-opinion surveys show that a certain proportion of the electorate has no opinion about many vital issues, does not know who is running for office, and does not care. A gentle campaign to bring a submissive one-third of the apathetic sheep to the polls gets out a voting majority for the candidates who have had the greatest amount of publicity—who usually belong to the party in power. A rip-snorting effort to get out all the ignoramuses tends to turn them into the rebel column, and thus benefits the outs.

14   In either event, the girl scouts should wash their hands of it. The job of getting out the vote is a partisan effort which belongs to the professionals.

15   The silliest idea of all is the notion that it is un-American or unpatriotic not to vote. "A plague on both your houses" is a fair American attitude—all too often a logical one. Stupidity does not become wisdom by being multiplied.

16   In every election not more than one-third of the people care very much

how it comes out. A certain percentage may have some sort of belief or opinion without feeling very strongly about it; another percentage may have studied the matter a little without forming an opinion; another percentage may not even have studied it; and so on, until we come to the people who are not even aware that an election is being held. The more we urge these people to clutter up the polling place, the more delay there is in voting, the more the cost of ballots and clerks, and the closer the returns.

17   If Candidate Jones would normally have won by 3,000 votes to 1,000, and we corral 10,000 more people into the polling places, won't Candidate Jones still win, by 8,000 to 6,000? Mathematically the last-minute coin flippers may make the election look close, but what patriotic purpose is accomplished?

18   And if the coin-flippers should happen to defeat the will of the informed majority, the cause of good government would emphatically not have been served.

19   Our city had a referendum recently in which the people voted for a tax increase to build an incinerator and against a tax increase to operate it. Every one of your communities has probably known referendums where the voters approved the bonds for a school but disapproved the sites, or voted for the site and against the bonds. All those voters who marked in opposite directions on the same afternoon were unwisely pressured into voting.

20   You have also seen primary elections where the boob with the catchy name ran away from the able man whose publicity was colorless. You have seen final elections where the straight party voters and the blank fillers smothered any discriminating choices which the thoughtful voters had made. You may have noticed with distress some of the undignified didos, cruel epithets, pompous verbosities, and Shakespearean gestures with which even good men become burdened early in their campaigns. All of these are caused in large measure by "get out the vote" efforts which emphasize putting a cross in half the squares.

21   Instead of urging people to vote, we ought to be urging them to study and form opinions. If thought and inspection of the candidates do not create a real desire to vote, then the citizen should be encouraged to stay at home on election day. A low vote is part of the public record and itself a significant voter reaction which ought to be preserved. Maybe neither of the candidates was worth voting for.

22   Certainly the right to vote is important and should not be curtailed. A fool who is willing to walk all the way to the polling place should be given every freedom to record every stupid impulse he feels, for these will tend to cancel each other out. But no one should pretend that marking X in a square is any proof of patriotism or even intelligence. It is not your duty to vote, but, if you choose to, then it should be your duty to be intelligent about it.

FOR COMPULSORY VOTING

Alan Wertheimer

1   As the Presidential election approaches we will no doubt be asked to recall that it was, in part, the demand for the "right to vote" that led to independence. Editorial writers throughout America will predictably bemoan the low level of participation and implore us to feel doubly guilty for failing to vote in this Bicentennial and Presidential election year.

2   Rather than conduct these ritual "get-out-the-vote" dances, why not simply make voting compulsory?

3   That we even seem compelled to urge citizens to exercise a right (what other *rights* do we need to urge citizens to exercise?) indicates that we may err in thinking of voting as a *right* to all. If citizens have a duty to vote, we should penalize those who fail to do their duty.

4   My argument for compulsory voting makes several (I think uncontroversial) assumptions: Competitive elections are desirable—for all their problems and deficiencies they are preferable to alternative methods of obtaining political leaders; it is technically possible to administer a compulsory-voting program (nonvoters would pay a tax or fine as in Belgium, the Netherlands, and Australia); compulsory voting works—it *does* increase the percentage of eligible voters who actually vote.

5   Elections can be understood as "public goods." A public good is any good that if made available to *any* member of a community must be made available to *all* members, generally because there is no feasible way to exclude noncontributors from enjoying the good. Public highways, national defense and police protection are examples of public good.

6   Now if the benefit of a public good is available to all, it is irrational for one to *voluntarily* contribute to its provision, in terms of money, time or energy. The rational citizen will attempt to "free ride," to enjoy the benefits while minimizing or avoiding the cost, as when we attempt to pay the lowest tax possible (or none at all).

7   All Americans benefit from the peaceful change of leadership and the fact that elections keep all elected officials (even those we do not support) at least somewhat responsive to our preferences. Voters and nonvoters alike receive these benefits and receive additional benefits if their preferred candidate wins. It follows that the rational citizen will not vote but will ride by avoiding the costs (including information cost) involved in voting.

8   I am not suggesting that we should not vote, merely that it is not in one's *individual interest* to vote, because no single vote will affect the outcome of the election and the electoral system will not crumble if any one of us fails to vote. We get the same benefits regardless of what we do.

9   It is not surprising that many citizens fail to vote. Rather, why do so many act irrationally (if altruistically) and vote?

10   First, some people are simply willing to sacrifice their interest for the public good.

11   Second, many people overestimate the importance of their vote. Third, many people vote to assuage their sense of guilt. But this hardly happens spontaneously. We systematically encourage citizens to overestimate the importance of their vote and to feel guilty when they do not vote—and it works.

12   What would compulsory voting do? First we would be spared the ritual propaganda campaigns in which we lie to ourselves about the significance of our individual votes and drum up our feelings of guilt. Second, we could be allowed to abstain, and thus citizens could specifically indicate that no candidate was satisfactory. Third, because it is largely the poor who tend not to vote, compulsory voting would increase their political power, as candidates would be forced to become more responsive to their interests. Fourth, since those who prefer candidates who are unlikely to win often do not vote, elections would provide a more accurate description of the nation's political preferences.

THROW THE RASCALS OUT

Meg Greenfield

1   I am cynical about the "new cynicism." I don't think it's very new or, for that matter, especially cynical either. In case you don't know, the "new cynicism" is the term that has lately come into use to describe the attitude of the 1990s voter. It is argued that the defeat in this year's primaries of a number of seemingly invincible individuals and political organizations by relative newcomers and antiestablishment types reflects an increasingly cynical electorate. This electorate is said to be hellbent on a throw-the-rascals-out policy, having become totally disenchanted with politics as usual.

2   How, I ask myself, can such an attitude of disenchantment possibly be called "new" in American society? It came over with the colonists, for starters, and has flourished in this country ever since. It may even, in fact, be considered the defining characteristic of our politics. Vast numbers of Americans have always been suspicious to the point of paranoia and irreverent to the point of slander about the reigning political order, whatever it was. Tom Paine, Mark Twain, Will Rogers, Mr. Dooley and just about everyone I have ever known outside the Beltway has to some extent shared in this same basic feeling: They're no damn good, there's not an honest one among them, throw the whole pack out. Yes, it is unfair; and yes, exceptions are always made for this one and that one among the condemned class of politicians. But by and large the premise is all but universally held: these characters are not to be

trusted. Political enthusiasts almost always portray their own candidate as an exception to the dreary political rule.

3   So much for the "new." What about the "cynicism"? Those of you who managed to stay alert through Philosophy 101a will no doubt remember what Cynicism actually is (it is something philosophical). For the rest of us, and especially in its current political meaning, I think the word connotes merely simple disillusion with what we have already been told and distrust of what we are currently being told by politicians, all this adding up to a kind of over-all disenchantment. But I wouldn't say that people who feel this way are being cynical so much as they are being practical and realistic. They are expressing disgust of a kind with what they see, with what exists. Indeed, far from hiding the techniques by which they try to manipulate the voters and play shamelessly on their passions, politicians nowadays often actually boast of their accomplishments in this vein. Your average tuned-in voter, I suspect, is likely to hear *more* about brilliant political technique than he is to hear about the substance of politics.

4   This is at least in part because, like just about every other human activity this side of chewing straws and playing Go Fish, political manipulation has lately been pronounced a discipline of the most abstruse kind that requires schooling and accreditation and which boasts its own impenetrable technical jargon and mathematical formulas that have all those funny little square-root-type signs in them. Truly. So it's not that people are *suspecting* that they are being fiddled with: they are being *told* they are. The news bursts with analyses of deceptive political ads, some critical, but almost as much boastfully put out by the perpetrators. We seem to have an insatiable appetite for postelection accounts of how this crooked ad and that misleading argument "played." And even in normal, nonelection times, we are forever being instructed as to which officials are being most clever in their posturings on taxes and pornography and other vexed subjects.

5   Why wouldn't a lot of people react by taking their first opportunity to elect someone who railed against all this, who was not part of the suspect system? I should say about here that I have my own doubts as to the sweepingness of the phenomenon that has been called to public attention as the "new cynicism." I figure, first, that by general-election time in November the trend won't seem so powerful, and, second, that some of what has happened is not related. For instance, the situation in Washington that led to the primary victory of Sharon Pratt Dixon over four other would-be successors to Mayor Marion Barry is as particular, not to say peculiar, as the situation in Massachusetts, where John Silber won the chance to become the Democratic successor to Gov. Michael Dukakis. Still, they are part of a core of cases where the electorate in recent days has pitched out the old and established order and chosen the new, the unestablished.

6   **Voter displeasure:** But is it not possible to argue that, far from being cynical, this is actually a kind of opposite reaction? Cynical despairs; it accuses and complains but does little; it chuckles and smirks and rolls its eyes

toward heaven; cynical would not think of investing its time and energy and hope in a reformist candidate—cynical in fact does not even have hope; it gives up and says, "What did I tell you?"

7   So to me, to the degree that people even as unlike as Sharon Pratt Dixon and John Silber have been elected as a message of voter displeasure with entrenchment and the hallowed political way of doing things, their victories speak of an almost touching faith that change is possible, that new people can do things new ways. I am a fan of Mrs. Dixon's and no fan of Mr. Silber, but I do think this same impulse was probably present in both situations—the utterly uncynical belief in the possibility of political redemption and renewal *through politics.* These election results are the handiwork of believers, not disbelievers.

8   There is, of course, some sense in which the voting public itself is a guilty party to the more crooked proceedings of American politics. We are not innocents in all the maneuvering to feed our less noble instincts to get our vote. We have all done more than a little over the years to reward those who pandered to us most disgustingly, who assured us that we were each the most put-upon victim class in American politics, while those in the next block or the next state or the next class (up or down) were getting all the unfair advantages. But even we have our limits. The self-satisfied and shameless promoters of mousetalk politics, of don't-say-what-you-mean and don't-mean-anything-if-you-can-help-it, have gone too far. That's what people are reacting to, not cynically, I'd say, but with a kind of optimism that there is a cure. Hope springs eternal.

CENSORSHIP

PORNOGRAPHY, OBSCENITY, AND THE CASE FOR CENSORSHIP

Irving Kristol

1 Being frustrated is disagreeable, but the real disasters in life begin when you get what you want. For almost a century now, a great many intelligent, well-meaning and articulate people have argued eloquently against any kind of censorship of art and entertainment. Within the past ten years, courts and legislatures have found these arguments so persuasive that censorship is now a relative rarity in most states.

2   Is there triumphant exhilaration in the land? Hardly. Somehow, things have not worked out as they were supposed to, and many civil-libertarians have said this was not what they meant. They wanted a world in which Eugene O'Neill's *Desire Under the Elms* could be produced, or James Joyce's *Ulysses* published, without interference. They got that, of course; but they also

got a world in which homosexual rape is simulated on the stage, in which the public flocks to witness professional fornication, in which New York's Times Square has become a hideous marketplace for printed filth.

3   But does this really matter? Might not our disquiet be merely a cultural hangover? Was anyone ever corrupted by a book?

4   This last question, oddly enough, is asked by the same people who seem convinced that advertisements in magazines or displays of violence on television *do* have the power to corrupt. It is also asked, incredibly enough and in all sincerity, by university professors and teachers whose very lives provide the answer. After all, if you believe that no one was ever corrupted by a book, you have also to believe that no one was ever improved by a book. You have to believe, in other words, that art is morally trivial and that education is morally irrelevant.

5   To be sure, it is extremely difficult to trace the effects of any single book (or play or movie) on any reader. But we all know that the ways in which we use our minds and imaginations do shape our characters and help define us as persons. That those who certainly know this are moved to deny it merely indicates how a dogmatic resistance to the idea of censorship can result in a mindless insistence on the absurd.

6   For the plain fact is that we all believe that there is a point at which the public authorities ought to step in to limit the "self-expression" of an individual or a group. A theatrical director might find someone willing to commit suicide on the stage. We would not allow that. And I know of no one who argues that we ought to permit public gladiatorial contests, even between consenting adults.

7   No society can be utterly indifferent to the ways its citizens publicly entertain themselves. Bearbaiting and cockfighting are prohibited only in part out of compassion for the animals; the main reason is that such spectacles were felt to debase and brutalize the citizenry who flocked to witness them. The question with regard to pornography and obscenity is whether they will brutalize and debase our citizenry. We are, after all, not dealing with one book or one movie. We are dealing with a general tendency that is suffusing our entire culture.

8   Pornography's whole purpose, it seems to me, is to treat human beings obscenely, to deprive them of their specifically human dimension. Imagine a well-known man in a hospital ward, dying an agonizing death. His bladder and bowels empty themselves of their own accord. His consciousness is overwhelmed by pain, so that he cannot communicate with us, nor we with him. Now, it would be technically easy to put a television camera in his room and let the whole world witness this spectacle. We don't do it—at least not yet—because we regard this as an obscene invasion of privacy. And what would make the spectacle obscene is that we would be witnessing the extinguishing of humanity in a human animal.

9   Sex—like death—is an activity that is both animal and human. There are human sentiments and human ideals involved in this animal activity. But

when sex is public, I do not believe the viewer can see the sentiments and the ideals, but sees only the animal coupling. And that is why when most men and women make love, they prefer to be alone—because it is only when you are alone that you can make love, as distinct from merely copulating. When sex is a public spectacle, a human relationship has been debased into a mere animal connection.

10   But even if all this is granted, it doubtless will be said that we ought not to be unduly concerned. Free competition in the cultural marketplace, it is argued by those who have never otherwise had a kind word to say for laissez-faire, will dispose of the problem; in the course of time, people will get bored with pornography and obscenity.

11   I would like to be able to go along with this reasoning, but I think it is false, and for two reasons. The first reason is psychological; the second, political.

12   In my opinion, pornography and obscenity appeal to and provoke a kind of sexual regression. The pleasure one gets from pornography and obscenity is infantile and autoerotic; put bluntly, it is a masturbatory exercise of the imagination. Now, people who masturbate do not get bored with masturbation, just as sadists don't get bored with sadism, and voyeurs don't get bored with voyeurism. In other words, like all infantile sexuality, it can quite easily become a permanent self-reinforcing neurosis. And such a neurosis, on a mass scale, is a threat to our civilization and humanity, nothing less.

13   I am already touching upon a political aspect of pornography when I suggest that it is inherently subversive of civilization. But there is another political aspect, which has to do with the relationship of pornography and obscenity to democracy, and especially to the quality of public life on which democratic government ultimately rests.

14   Today a "managerial" conception of democracy prevails—wherein democracy is seen as a set of rules and procedures, and *nothing but* a set of rules and procedures, by which majority rule and minority rights are reconciled into a state of equilibrium. Thus, the political system can be fully reduced to its mechanical arrangements.

15   There is, however, an older idea of democracy—fairly common until about the beginning of this century—for which the conception of the quality of public life is absolutely crucial. This idea starts from the proposition that democracy is a form of self-government, and that you are entitled to it only if that "self" is worthy of governing. Because the desirability of self-government depends on the character of the people who govern, the older idea of democracy was very solicitous of the condition of this character. This older democracy had no problem in principle with pornography and obscenity; it censored them; it was not about to permit people to corrupt themselves.

16   But can a liberal—today—be for censorship? Yes, but he ought to favor a liberal form of censorship.

17   I don't think this is a contradiction in terms. We have no problem contrasting *repressive* laws governing alcohol, drugs and tobacco with laws *regu-*

lating (that is, discouraging the sale of) alcohol, drugs and tobacco. We have not made smoking a criminal offense. We have, however, and with good liberal conscience, prohibited cigarette advertising on television. The idea of restricting individual freedom, in a liberal way, is not at all unfamiliar to us.

18   I therefore see no reason why we should not be able to distinguish repressive censorship from liberal censorship of the written and spoken word. In Britain, until a few years ago, you could perform almost any play you wished—but certain plays, judged to be obscene, had to be performed in private theatrical clubs. In the United States, all of us who grew up using public libraries are familiar with the circumstances under which certain books could be circulated only to adults, while still other books had to be read in the library. In both cases, a small minority that was willing to make a serious effort to see an obscene play or book could do so. But the impact of obscenity was circumscribed, and the quality of public life was only marginally affected.

19   It is a distressing fact that any system of censorship is bound, upon occasion, to treat unjustly a particular work of art—to find pornography where there is only gentle eroticism, to find obscenity where none really exists, or to find both where the work's existence ought to be tolerated because it serves a larger moral purpose. That is the price one has to be prepared to pay for censorship—even liberal censorship.

20   But if you look at the history of American or English literature, there is precious little damage you can point to as a consequence of the censorship that prevailed throughout most of that history. I doubt that many works of real literary merit ever were suppressed. Nor did I notice that hitherto suppressed masterpieces flooded the market when censorship was eased.

21   I should say, to the contrary, that literature has lost quite a bit now that so much is permitted. It seems to me that the cultural market in the United States today is awash in dirty books, dirty movies, dirty theater. Our cultural condition has not improved as a result of the new freedom.

22   I'll put it bluntly: if you care for the quality of life in our American democracy, then you have to be for censorship.

DEFENDING INTELLECTUAL FREEDOM

Eli M. Oboler

1   The Henry Luce Professor of Urban Values at New York University, Irving Kristol, was rather less than urbane in his strictures against pornography and obscenity—or what he defines as such—in his March 23, 1971, article, "Pornography, Obscenity, and the Case for Censorship," which first appeared in the *New York Times* magazine and was recently reprinted in two issues of this *Newsletter* (September and November, 1971). He has exhumed a great many

of the tired old pro-censorship arguments, but added a new dimension; he has coined a new phrase, "liberal censorship," which, despite all protestations to the contrary, is clearly a contradiction in terms.

2   Indeed, his whole essay is on the hyperbolic, exaggerated level illustrated by his undocumented statement that " . . . pornography . . . is inherently and purposefully subversive of civilization and its institutions." He is even more specific and direct in this: " . . . if you care for the quality of life in our American democracy, then you have to be for censorship." Blithely, he sells creative art down the river: "There are . . . some few works of art that are in the special category of the comic-ironic 'bawdy' (Boccaccio, Rabelais). It is such works of art that are likely to suffer at the hands of the censor. *That is the price* [my italics] one has to be prepared to pay for censorship—even liberal censorship." Snick-snack! Off with Boccaccio's head! Snip-snip! Eliminate Rabelais! And Joyce and Swift and Henry Miller and—but Kristol, contrary to all factual evidence, says, "If you look at the history of American or English literature, there is precious little damage you can point to as a consequence of the censorship that prevailed throughout most of that history."

3   Let alone the gross inexactitude of this dogmatic opinion, Kristol really ought to do a little study of the hundreds of years and thousands of literary creations between the writing of *Beowulf* and the first English legal censorship, that of Edmund Curll's *Venus in the Cloister*, in 1727. During those centuries after centuries, "most" of the history of English literature occurred. The quoted statement is only one of many examples of Kristollian *obiter dicta* which have a nice, ringing sound—but are actually quite hollow of solid fact, when closely examined.

4   It is really almost incredible that he would seriously make such a statement as "very few works of literature—of real literary merit, I mean—ever were suppressed; and those that were, were not suppressed for long." The long, long list of Anne Haight's well-known *Banned Books* is a simple answer to the first claim; and it is certainly a specious, unsound argument to say that "those that were, were not suppressed for long." *Any* length of time is contrary to the fundamental tenets of freedom of speech and expression in which, presumably, "liberal" Kristol believes.

5   Incidentally, near the end of his article, he admits that "We had censorship of pornography and obscenity for 150 years," which in simple mathematical process would indicate that censorship began in 1821. This is a most interesting date, just about 93 years after it historically began! Kristol, as I said, needs at least a capsule course in the facts of the story of censorship.

6   *If* Kristol's facts were right, one might be willing to consider the logic of his argumentation, which, on the whole, is rather persuasive. But if "liberal" censorship has to be based on misinformation and exaggeration, then it is no more worth the consideration of reasonable men and women than *il*liberal censorship.

7   Admittedly, this brief reply to Kristol is itself a polemic, rather than in a reasonable vein. The reader is referred to my forthcoming book for a lengthy,

historically based, positive set of facts and arguments concerning the merits and demerits of censorship of writings about sex.* Suffice it here, in a necessarily limited space, to say that Kristol has clearly failed to consider the most basic of all issues in the censorship/noncensorship dispute.

8   In a long perspective, the fear of the word is really the fear of the human. Like reverse Terences, those who censor and favor censorship are really saying, "I am human, but everything human is alien to me."[†] Men and women are men and women *because* of their sexual drives, and denial of this fact by even a never-ending line of censors—liberal *or* illiberal!—will not eliminate maleness and femaleness and the male-female relationship. The censor will never outlast biology.

CENSORSHIP AND ITS AFTERMATH

Nadine Gordimer

1   There is not one of us writing in South Africa today who has not either begun or spent the major part of a working life under conventional censorship and the chain-mail laws that reinforce it. While most have chafed at and some fiercely fought censorship, we have got used to it. To paraphrase Graham Greene, every country becomes accustomed to its own restrictions as part of its own violence. We have defied censorship and/or found ways around it. At the same time, inevitably, it has brought about deeper reactive consequences in our writers. And what is true of us is surely true of any other country where the *very defiance* of oppression creates defining restrictions of its own. I was in Hungary at a conference last year, and the session devoted to our host Hungarian writers revealed in them what I can only call fear of freedom— fear, for a writer, meaning not knowing how you are going to write next. Although they were overjoyed, as citizens, at their new freedom, they were bewildered about its meaning at the internal level from which the transformation of the entities of living into the writer's vision takes place. With the vise on the writer's head removed, there disquietingly is revealed—an aftermath of censorship I believe we've never considered—a cramped and even distorted imagination.

2   For when I speak of the reactive consequences of censorship I am referring to the *other* pressure upon the writer that censorship calls into being. The counterpressure of resistance also, ironically, screws tight the vise. Defiance of censorship and the regime it serves calls upon the writer to cut and weld

---

Defending Intellectual Freedom (Westport, CT: Greenwood Press, 1980).
[†]Terence, a Roman playwright (185–159 B.C.), wrote in his *Heauton Timorumenos:* "I am a man, I count nothing human indifferent to me."

his work into a weapon. It is necessary. But he may have to discard much of his particular insight in the process. It is impressed upon him that certain themes are relevant; certain modes are effective. Accustomed to the confines of allegory and allusion, our Eastern European colleagues now have to teach themselves that they may choose among numerous other modes to express life experience. Accustomed to the obsessive demands of selecting every situation and word for its trajectory against apartheid, South African writers will have to open themselves to a new vocabulary of life.

3   Many are ill-prepared, particularly the young writers. For everywhere there has been censorship the counter-orthodoxy of resistance in literature has also come about. It has been an era when, in Brecht's words, "to speak of trees is treason." And to quote Albie Sachs, the African National Congress's constitutional adviser and a fine writer: "Instead of criticism, we get solidarity criticism. Our artists are not pushed to improve the quality of their work; it is enough to be politically correct. . . . It is as though our rulers stalk every page . . . everything is obsessed by the oppressors and the trauma they have imposed. . . . What are we fighting for, if not the right to express our humanity in all its forms, including our sense of fun and capacity for love and tenderness and our appreciation of the beauty of the world?"

4   We must not think that when tyrants fall and there is a new constitution in his/her country the writer regains all that has been lost. It is not a matter of not having anything left to write about. Only those who jumped on the anti-apartheid and anticommunist bandwagons, having nothing in their baggage but the right clichés, will lose their dubious inspiration and need to find some other way of selling themselves. The real writers, on the contrary, will have the less sensational, wonderfully daunting task of finding ways to deal with themes that have been set aside in second place while writing was in battle dress—the themes of "humanity in all its forms," human consciousness in all its mystery, which demand not orthodoxy of any nature but the talent and dedication and daring to explore and convey freely through the individual sensibility. Many writers, constricted by censorship on one side and the orthodoxy of the antimode on the other, have never developed the ability to deal with anything outside the events and emotions their historical situation prescribed.

5   While we rejoice at new freedom for writers in many countries long denied it, and work for freedom for writers in those countries where the many devices of censorship still prevail, we must also remember that writers are never freed of the past. Censorship is never over for those who have experienced it. It is a brand on the imagination that affects the individual who has suffered it, forever. Where censorship appears to be swept away in the rubble of toppled regimes, let us make sure that it does not rise again to the demands of some future regime, for the generations of writers who will grow up, anywhere in the new world in the making. As African National Congress Secretary of Culture Barbara Maskela has said bluntly, and surely for all of us: "We are not prepared to see culture become a case of arrested develop-

ment, frozen at the point of liberation. Nor will we be content with a culture vulnerable to becoming the fiefdom of some future oppressive ruling class."

AIDS TESTING

WE NEED ROUTINE TESTING FOR AIDS

William J. Bennett

1 The AIDS epidemic may be the most serious health threat of this century. How best to deal with it has been the subject of a vigorous national debate. And out of this debate is emerging a growing and welcome consensus on a number of issues.

2 We can all agree, for example, on the need to care for those afflicted with AIDS, by helping to ensure that families, states, localities, hospitals and others have the resources to provide adequate medical care for those suffering from this disease. We can all agree that we must prevent violations of the civil rights of those who are carriers of the AIDS virus. And we can all agree on the need to educate all of our citizens, including young people, about how the AIDS virus is transmitted and how to guard against it. Moreover, there is now nearly universal agreement on a further point: the need for more widespread AIDS testing.

3 We need more testing for several reasons:

- Testing provides important epidemiological information, allowing us to determine just how widespread the virus is.
- Testing informs individuals if they have contracted AIDS so they can seek proper medical treatment.
- If an individual tests positive, he will know that he must refrain from activities that would endanger the life of another person.
- If an individual tests positive, he or the public health authorities can alert others who may be at risk.

4 While there is general agreement on the need for more widespread AIDS testing, some balk at going about this in the most effective way. They call for more testing, but only voluntary testing. They reject out of hand proposals for routine testing of individuals upon certain occasions: for example, for some or all of those admitted to hospitals, for those being treated at clinics serving "high-risk" populations, for couples seeking marriage licenses, and for prison inmates. Some individuals are so concerned about guaranteeing privacy that they will not allow even the confidential notification of other individuals possibly infected, or at risk of being infected, by someone found to be an AIDS carrier.

5   What has emerged, then, is a troubling paradox: Confronted with this grave public health threat, with a disease that is expected to claim more American lives by 1991 than did the Vietnam and Korean wars combined,* we have failed to employ routine testing and contact notification—commonly accepted public health measures for other similarly transmitted diseases.

6   An extraordinary gap has developed, between the recognition of the magnitude of the threat of AIDS and the failure to adopt eminently reasonable and useful public health measures to respond to it, measures for which there is long precedent.

7   Opponents of routine testing offer several arguments against it. None is convincing.

8   One argument is that routine testing would drive the principal classes of AIDS victims (homosexuals and intravenous drug users) "underground," because some individuals would be so fearful of discrimination as a result of testing positive.

9   First of all, even if a few individuals did go "underground," we would have to balance this fact with the crucial information more widespread routine testing would produce for individuals, and for society. This information would save lives.

10   Second, the possibility that some individuals may avoid testing can be minimized by strong guarantees of appropriate confidentiality and nondiscrimination.

11   Third, we would not, of course, eliminate voluntary AIDS testing sites even as we adopt a policy of select, routine testing. Routine testing would serve in conjunction with, and not in lieu of, voluntary and even voluntary anonymous testing. And states and localities could, in certain circumstances, allow exceptions to routine testing.

12   It is precisely by making testing routine, by dealing with it just as we treat other similar communicable diseases, that we will go a long way toward lessening the stigma that now surrounds AIDS tests.

13   Above all, I would point out that most estimates are that the great majority of AIDS carriers are currently unaware that they are infected. Routine testing at appropriate occasions—along with much more readily available voluntary testing—would surely decrease the number of individuals who might be unwittingly spreading the disease.

14   A second argument against routine testing is that it could lead to violations of confidentiality, particularly as it relates to the notification of past sexual partners.

15   A number of precautions can be taken to guard against this. For example, in many states today, if a person tests positive for syphilis, health authorities will ask the names of people with whom that person has been intimate.

---

*According to the *Information Please 1992 Almanac,* AIDS deaths in the United States stood at 113,426 as of 31 May 1991. The combined American death toll in the Korean and Vietnam wars was 112,381.

Then, without mentioning the name of the syphilis carrier, health authorities will confidentially notify those people who may have contracted the disease and recommend that they come in and be tested. This has long been standard public health practice. It can be done for AIDS as well. To protect others, it certainly should be done.

16   The American Medical Association's Principles of Medical Ethics recognize that a physician may reveal otherwise confidential information if this is necessary to protect the welfare of another individual or the community. There has long been recognition of the need in some instances to balance a patient's right to confidentiality and a physician's obligation to protect lives. In the case of AIDS, confidentiality would be superseded only in certain circumstances, such as to inform public health officials or to inform a wife that her husband has AIDS.

17   A third argument made against routine testing is that the AIDS test is costly and unreliable.

18   In fact, experience at the Department of Defense shows that testing can be done for less than $5 a person. The additional cost of counseling those who test positive is well worth the money.

19   The AIDS tests are reliable and have been used successfully. Moreover, a proper testing program includes provisions for double-checking positive test results.

20   There is no denying that a program of routine testing and contact notification presents some challenges. Few decisions on AIDS are easy. But the difficulty of the task cannot discourage us from facing up to our responsibilities. For what is the alternative? To go on as we have been? We cannot do that.

21   By now, the facts are clear: Business as usual is not enough. If we are to contain the spread of this deadly epidemic, routine testing must play a part. The real question we face is whether we will adopt aggressive public health measures now when time is still on our side and the spread of the virus can be curbed. Objections noted, cautions observed, civil liberties protected: We must now do what is essential to save lives.

AIDS: THE LEGAL EPIDEMIC

Arthur S. Leonard

1   At the very heart of the AIDS legal epidemic is "the Test," its uses, and abuses. The test is actually a set of laboratory procedures to detect antibodies to Human Immunodeficiency Virus (HIV, also known as LAV and HTLV-III). This virus, believed by most researchers to play a central role in AIDS and related medical disorders, stimulates the lymphatic system to produce detectable antibodies, usually within a few months of the virus being introduced into the body.

2   The test currently licensed by the Food and Drug Administration (FDA) for screening blood donations, called ELISA, is a highly sensitive test for these antibodies. If they are in the blood, the test will almost always be positive. However, in order to obtain this high degree of reactivity, the test had to be designed to react positively in doubtful cases as well, and the ELISA test is known for having a significant rate of false-positive results when used for screening donations at blood banks.

3   In addition to ELISA, there is a nonstandardized test called Western blot, which is a much more specific test for HIV antibodies. Because Western blot is more expensive and difficult to perform accurately, it is normally used only as a confirmatory test. If a blood sample repeatedly tests positive on ELISA testing, a Western blot is supposed to be used to be sure the ELISA positive is not false.

4   Newer tests are under development but not yet licensed for routine use. These tests are designed to detect the presence of HIV itself, rather than antibodies, and would presumably be more accurate than an antibody test because they would detect the viral presence, regardless of whether antibodies have been formed. The shortcomings of ELISA in this regard are illustrated by some recent cases of infection where transfused blood tested negative because infection was too recent for antibodies to have formed.

5   When the FDA licensed ELISA in March, 1985, lesbian and gay rights organizations expressed great concern about potential misuses of the test, as well as its shortcomings. Intense lobbying by the National Gay & Lesbian Task Force, with legal advice and assistance from Lambda Legal Defense and Education Fund, resulted in an agreement with the FDA to label the test kits with an unequivocal statement that ELISA was *solely* for the purpose of blood screening, and was neither a diagnostic test for AIDS nor an appropriate test for screening *people.*

6   After the test became available, however, various government agencies took actions inconsistent with this labeling restriction. The military began to use the test to screen recruits and active personnel, the State Department has announced plans to test foreign service personnel and their dependents, and the Labor Department has announced it will test Job Corps employees and

program participants. Despite statements that ELISA is not a diagnostic test for AIDS, the federal Centers for Disease Control (CDC) has added a positive test result to the surveillance definition, when present in conjunction with other physical symptoms.

7   Employers, insurance companies, schools, and prisons have all been implicated in test misuse, or proposals to use the test for screening people improperly. There have been legislative proposals to use the test for marriage licensing, to justify detention of prostitutes, and to monitor individual behavior.

8   Because of reports that the test had a high false-positive rate and, as an antibody test, a significant false-negative rate (because the test will be negative for an infected person whose system has not started producing antibodies), Lambda seriously considered back in 1985 bringing a legal challenge against licensing the test. But a careful review of the law governing FDA licensing procedures, the traditional deference courts pay to decisions made by "expert" administrative agencies, and scientific data Lambda obtained from the government through filing of an information request, persuaded Lambda that a legal challenge would be a waste of scarce resources, since a successful outcome was unlikely.

9   Instead, Lambda, as well as National Gay Right Advocates (NGRA, based in San Francisco), Gay & Lesbian Advocates & Defenders (GLAD, based in Boston), and scores of lesbian and gay attorneys and American Civil Liberties Union (ACLU) cooperating attorneys in other parts of the country, have spent considerable time since March 1985 battling individual instances of misuse of the tests and advocating against large-scale misuse proposed by the insurance industry and some federal and state officials.

10   Is the test legal? Can someone by *required* to take it? The answers to these questions depend upon the context in which the test is demanded, and the uses to which the results would be put. There are some federal and state laws, as well as constitutional principles, that might restrict the use of the test under certain circumstances, and it is important that gay people in particular, as members of a so-called "high-risk group," be aware of them.

11   As a matter of constitutional law, it may be that personal privacy rights guaranteed by the 14th and 4th Amendments of the Constitution would preclude the government from requiring you to take an antibody test unless there was a good reason for the government to suspect that the test would reveal evidence of unlawful conduct or was necessary to achieve some important benefit for society. The Supreme Court has held, for example, that law enforcement officials can subject persons suspected of drunk driving to tests to detect alcohol in their blood under certain circumstances. The police, however, cannot randomly stop cars and subject drivers to blood alcohol testing in the absence of any other evidence indicating they might be driving under the influence.

12   Can police authorities routinely subject persons arrested for prostitution to ELISA testing? This is being done in some parts of the country, and legal

challenges to such practices would present an interesting new twist on the drunk driving cases. Certainly, if an infected prostitute continued to engage in unprotected sex with customers, the prostitute would be in violation of laws forbidding the knowing transmission of sexually transmitted diseases, but we should remember that prostitution itself is illegal in every state except Nevada.

13   Could government routinely test all "risk group" members as part of a program designed to prevent the spread of HIV? The answer to this is uncertain, and at some point the question may have to be posed to the courts. There are always cases pending in which government officials are trying to require antibody testing of individuals arrested under various circumstances. For example, a member of a gay marching band who allegedly bit a police officer during a scuffle on Gay Pride Day in California is contesting a court ruling that he undergo antibody testing.

14   What about the use of the test [for] a marriage license? In many states, applicants for marriage licenses are already tested for venereal diseases. Why not AIDS? Isn't there a good argument that a prospective spouse should know about the danger to him- or herself of infection by HIV? Should a positive test result preclude marriage, or merely result in counseling of the prospective spouses about "safe sex" practices? No state has yet legislated in this area, but there are a host of proposals pending in legislatures around the country. If the test is presented as a public health measure, the courts may well defer to the "expertise" of health officials who insist that testing is necessary.

15   The test has already popped up in several lawsuits involving the rights of parents to visit their children. A nurse who works with AIDS patients was required to undergo antibody testing before her ex-husband would permit her to see her kids. Gay parents are routinely demanded to take antibody tests as part of custody and visitation litigation, although not all courts agree to go along with such demands. It is hard to discern a general legal principle to control this sort of situation, other than that courts in such cases have broad discretion to take actions deemed to be "in the best interest of the child."

16   The military, prison, foreign services, and Job Corps testing programs that have been adopted or discussed raise serious constitutional and statutory issues.

17   The military tests have already been unsuccessfully challenged in federal court. Judges usually defer to statements by the military that a particular procedure is necessary for national security purposes, even though that procedure may be restrictive of rights protected in civilian life. Concern that the military was using HIV antibody testing as a way to detect gays and IV-drug users, who would then be subjected to less-than-honorable discharges, led to Congressional adoption of an amendment to a recent appropriations bill, forbidding the military from using the tests for that purpose. Recent military

pronouncements, however, indicate that attempts will be made to get around the legislative ban, and lawsuits will surely result.

18   Testing in prisons presents special concerns, due to the unusual nature of the prison environment, in which there is likely to be forcible sex under circumstances where "safer sex" practices are unlikely to be observed. Prison officials have rejected suggestions that condoms be provided for prisoners (with some exceptions being reported for conjugal visits). In a recent case, a labor arbitrator ruled that prison guards had a right, under their collective bargaining agreement, to know whether prisoners were infected, and in effect ordered the prison to require antibody testing and reveal the results to the guard union. (The collective bargaining agreement stated that guards had a right to know about dangerous infectious diseases among prisoners they were guarding.) The prison is appealing the arbitrator's decision to a court, claiming that HIV infection presents no danger to guards and that this testing thus should not be required. In some prisons, inmates with AIDS, or those who test positive, are routinely segregated from other prisoners, ostensibly to protect them from violence, rather than to protect the other prisoners from infection.

19   The foreign service and Job Corps testing programs may come under attack not only on constitutional grounds, but also based on sections 501 and 504 of the federal Rehabilitation Act, which forbid handicap discrimination in federal employment and under federal programs. Regulations interpreting this law forbid the use of medical tests to screen out "otherwise qualified handicapped persons."

20   The State Department argues that certain countries are demanding that American personnel be tested, and that postings to some parts of the world with inadequate medical facilities would be dangerous for persons likely to develop AIDS. The former argument could be seriously challenged by analogy to religious discrimination claims brought by Jewish employees against companies which exclude them from job assignments in Moslem countries on the ground that those countries would not want American Jews to work there. Several courts have upheld such lawsuits. The latter argument seems incredible, since it seems likely that American foreign service personnel who might develop symptoms indicative of AIDS or AIDS-Related Complex could be transported relatively quickly to appropriate medical facilities. While there may be some justification for the State Department wanting to know which overseas personnel might need special attention, justification for excluding antibody-positive individuals from the foreign service, as the department proposes, seems slim.

21   The Job Corps testing seems less defensible than the military or foreign service testing. Job Corps officials claim that sexual activities and IV-drug use may take place in dormitories, where the virus could be spread. Such a rationale would justify testing in every communal living setting, including college dormitories, lumber camps, and other isolated worksites but would

seem directly contrary to the Rehabilitation Act and, in private employment, state laws forbidding disability discrimination. I suspect that, as in many uses of the test, the Job Corps testing program is designed to rid the corps of sexually active gays or participants who would incur serious medical costs. There is a growing body of precedent forbidding governmental programs from discriminating on the basis of sexual orientation, and the cost-avoidance rationale would violate the Rehabilitation Act.

22   Finally, under the heading of "closing the barn door after the horses are gone," there is the emergency regulation adopted by the Immigration Service to use the test in excluding persons from entry into the country. HIV is here, and it seems unlikely that an occasional infected immigrant is going to contribute greatly to spreading the epidemic; but, once again, the regulation seems unlikely to fall to legal attack, since many of the constitutional protections which apply to persons resident in the country have been held by the federal courts not to apply to aliens seeking entry.

23   Legal ramifications of so-called "AIDS testing" will continue to play a significant role in the unfolding legal epidemic around AIDS.

HOW *NOT* TO CONTROL THE AIDS EPIDEMIC

Mathilde Krim

1 Historically, nations under military attack have first reacted by expelling undesirables and closing borders. When the enemy was an apparently transmissible disease-causing agent, boundaries were erected between the sick and the well. The sick were physically isolated, often forcibly, and the suffering caused by this approach was justified by proclamations of its effectiveness and, importantly, by the attribution of imprudent or intemperate behavior to those afflicted. Therefore, the afflicted came to be regarded as undesirables on both health *and* moral grounds, and whatever unease their misery caused in the minds of others could be dismissed on the grounds that the misfortune of the sick was largely self-inflicted.

2   In more recent times and with a better understanding of the nature of infectious agents and their mode of transmission, more rational measures could be adopted. Improvements in sanitation now prevent epidemics of cholera and typhus. Vaccination against many infectious diseases as well as antibiotics for their treatment have silenced the call for isolation or quarantine. The spectacular success of modern methods for the control of many infectious diseases has spurred great confidence in the biomedical approach.

3   However, in their newly acquired faith in the fruits of scientific determinism, Western societies have overlooked the fact that medicine is still pow-

erless with regard to the prevention of many infections caused by viruses and that no drugs or antibiotics exist, to date, that can cure *any* viral disease. Such a disease, the Acquired Immunodeficiency Syndrome, or AIDS, is now upon us. In addition, Western societies have not yet renounced loathing certain groups of human beings. And so it is that the extraordinary conjunction in our modern societies of a lethal, virally induced, transmissible disease with life-styles that are generally despised—along with those practicing them—is a recipe for social disaster. The powerlessness of medicine in the face of AIDS has elicited atavistic fears. Uninhibited talk of screening for the purpose of isolating the sick is heard once again.

4   The emergence of AIDS in many countries, in groups similar to those defined as being "at high risk for AIDS" in the United States, established in the public mind throughout the Western world the link between the deadly disease and "immorality." The fact that the first women reported to be "at high risk for AIDS" *as a group* were prostitutes or drug abusers did nothing to dispel this notion. It only helped to reinforce the link between AIDS and "immorality." This is the kind of link that has justified untold cruelties in the distant past. It has now been forged in the case of AIDS and it could throw Western societies back into the Middle Ages inasmuch as approaches to HIV infection control are concerned. Those most at risk for AIDS are justifiably fearful of the stigma that has come to be attached to the disease plaguing them.

5   The use of *any* medical test for the screening of populations is fraught with technical and other difficulties. In the case of HIV infection, any mass screening is a particularly perilous undertaking for a number of reasons in addition to the unavoidable technical shortcomings [of false positive or negative results]. To start with, the serious long-term prognosis attached to a positive test result—a diagnosis of HIV infection—constitutes psychologically devastating news. Secondly, the social stigma attached to such a diagnosis can, and often does, result in serious social and economic harm to individuals. Last but not least, awareness of one's infected status cannot lead to useful medical intervention at this time, since none exists.

6   Nevertheless, a desire to respond to the public's fear of AIDS, an urge to "do something," has already compelled some politicians to advocate the use of the HIV-antibody tests for the mandatory mass screening of various population groups. Unfortunately, little thought was given by these politicians to the cost of such an enterprise in dollars and human resources or to what is to be done, and with what resources, with those identified as infected. No provisions were made or resources allocated by these politicians to provide for the intensive, long-term counseling that alone can help individuals identified as infected live with their devastating knowledge, since medicine will certainly *not* be able to help them in any way for some time to come. No legislation has been enacted or even proposed to prevent the emergence, as a result of discrimination against them, of a class of destitute and sick pariahs in our midst.

7   Those of us who have urged caution, further reflection, and careful planning with regard to the uses to be made of the HIV-antibody tests have been told that we are putting the civil liberties of the few ahead of the protection of the public health. Whether or not this is so has been carefully considered by the surgeon general of the United States, by the scholars participating in the Hastings Center's and other studies, and by hundreds of public health officials. They all concluded, in a remarkable consensus of opinion, that not only is there no contradiction between safeguarding individual liberties and privacy on the one hand and the protection of the public health on the other but that the individual and the public good are inseparable in the AIDS epidemic. This is so for the very simple reason that the protection of the public health does *not* rest on the identification, per se, of the infected *but on their individual willingness to assume and act upon their personal responsibility not to infect others.* Testing must, therefore, be an adjunct to education—for example, the provision of factual information on the biological aspects of AIDS, on the responsibility each infected person has not to infect others, and on the responsibility each uninfected person has not to become infected. Testing cannot be separated from supportive counseling received in an environment in which respect for person is proclaimed to be of paramount value. Therefore, testing can and should be facilitated and encouraged but must remain voluntary, and its results must be protected by strict and, when necessary, legally protected assurances of confidentiality in order to avert possible discrimination or even just the fear of it.

8   It was heartening that a bioethicist was chosen to deliver the keynote address at the meeting convened by the U.S. Centers for Disease Control in April 1987. The purpose of this meeting was to discuss the possible role of HIV-antibody testing in the prevention of HIV infection. That bioethicist, Dr. Ronald Bayer, clearly set the tone of the crucial debate that followed his presentation. The humanistic approach prevailed, despite the pressure of public anxieties on all those present and despite the fact that "mandatory screening" and "isolation" are concepts inculcated, by tradition, in all public health officials. It was agreed at that meeting that the AIDS epidemic will become gradually controllable through a combination of intensive public education and research. It was also agreed that, whether this is intended or not, any form of compulsory, mandatory mass screening would inevitably carry the threat of forcible isolation for those found to be infected. Such a threat would frighten away from testing and counseling those very people who need such services most and, rather than foster responsible behavior, the fear and resentment that would result would foster irresponsible conduct.

9   The opinion of all the experts of the U.S. Public Health Service and the Centers for Disease Control, as well as that of the scholars who have given careful thought to various possible approaches to the control of the AIDS epidemic, is now that the protection of the public health from the scourge of AIDS is best served by a diligent protection of individual liberties and pri-

vacy. Mandatory testing is, therefore, clearly *not* the way to attempt to control this epidemic.

10   Let us hope for our sake and the sake of generations to come that the counsel of humanists will continue to be sought in the formulation of public health policies. And let us hope that this counsel will continue to be heard. The battle against AIDS is one humanity cannot afford to lose.

CHRISTIANITY

WHY I AM AN AGNOSTIC

Clarence Darrow

1   An agnostic is a doubter. The word is generally applied to those who doubt the verity of accepted religious creeds or faiths. Everyone is an agnostic as to the beliefs or creeds they do not accept. Catholics are agnostic to the Protestant creeds, and the Protestants are agnostic to the Catholic creed. Anyone who thinks is an agnostic about something, otherwise he must believe that he is possessed of all knowledge. And the proper place for such a person is in the madhouse or the home for the feeble-minded. In a popular way, in the western world, an agnostic is one who doubts or disbelieves the main tenets of the Christian faith.

2   I would say that belief in at least three tenets is necessary to the faith of a Christian: a belief in God, a belief in immortality, and a belief in a supernatural book. Various Christian sects require much more, but it is difficult to imagine that one could be a Christian, under any intelligent meaning of the word, with less. Yet there are some people who claim to be Christians who do not accept the literal interpretation of all the Bible, and who give more credence to some portions of the book than to others.

3   I am an agnostic as to the question of God. I think that it is impossible for the human mind to believe in an object or thing unless it can form a mental picture of such object or thing. Since man ceased to worship openly an anthropomorphic God and talked vaguely and not intelligently about some force in the universe, higher than man, that is responsible for the existence of man and the universe, he cannot be said to believe in God. One cannot believe in a force excepting as a force that pervades matter and is not an individual entity. To believe in a thing, an image of the thing must be stamped on the mind. If one is asked if he believes in such an animal as a camel, there immediately arises in his mind an image of the camel. This image has come from experience or knowledge of the animal gathered in some way or other. No such image comes, or can come, with the idea of a God who is described as a force.

4   Man has always speculated upon the origin of the universe, including himself. I feel, with Herbert Spencer, that whether the universe had an origin—and if it had—what the origin is will never be known by man. The Christian says that the universe could not make itself; that there must have been some higher power to call it into being. Christians have been obsessed for many years by Paley's argument that if a person passing through a desert should find a watch and examine its spring, its hands, its case and its crystal, he would at once be satisfied that some intelligent being capable of design had made the watch. No doubt this is true. No civilized man would question that someone made the watch. The reason he would not doubt it is because he is familiar with watches and other appliances made by man. The savage was once unfamiliar with a watch and would have had no idea upon the subject. There are plenty of crystals and rocks of natural formation that are as intricate as a watch, but even to intelligent man they carry no implication that some intelligent power must have made them. They carry no such implication because no one has any knowledge or experience of someone having made these natural objects which everywhere abound.

5   To say that God made the universe gives us no explanation of the beginning of things. If we are told that God made the universe, the question immediately arises: Who made God? Did he always exist, or was there some power back of that? Did he create matter out of nothing, or is his existence co-extensive with matter? The problem is still there. What is the origin of it all? If, on the other hand, one says that the universe was not made by God, that it always existed, he has the same difficulty to confront. To say that the universe was here last year, or millions of years ago, does not explain its origin. This is still a mystery. As to the question of the origin of things, man can only wonder and doubt and guess.

6   As to the existence of the soul, all people may either believe or disbelieve. Everyone knows the origin of the human being. They know that it came from a single cell in the body of the mother, and that the cell was one out of ten thousand in the mother's body. Before gestation the cell must have been fertilized by a spermatozoön from the body of the father. This was one out of perhaps a billion spermatozoa that was the capacity of the father. When the cell is fertilized a chemical process begins. The cell divides and multiplies and increases into millions of cells, and finally a child is born. Cells die and are born during the life of the individual until they finally drop apart, and this is death.

7   If there is a soul, what is it, and where did it come from, and where does it go? Can anyone who is guided by his reason possibly imagine a soul independent of a body, or the place of its residence, or the character of it, or anything concerning it? If man is justified in any belief or disbelief on any subject, he is warranted in the disbelief in a soul. Not one scrap of evidence exists to prove any such impossible thing.

8   Many Christians base the belief of a soul and God upon the Bible. Strictly speaking, there is no such book. To make the Bible, sixty-six books are

bound into one volume. These books were written by many people at different times, and no one knows the time or the identity of any author. Some of the books were written by several authors at various times. These books contain all sorts of contradictory concepts of life and morals and the origin of things. Between the first and the last nearly a thousand years intervened, a longer time than has passed since the discovery of America by Columbus.

9   When I was a boy the theologians used to assert that the proof of the divine inspiration of the Bible rested on miracles and prophecies. But a miracle means a violation of a natural law, and there can be no proof imagined that could be sufficient to show the violation of a natural law; even though proof seemed to show violation, it would only show that we were not acquainted with all natural laws. One believes in the truthfulness of a man because of his long experience with the man, and because the man has always told a consistent story. But no man has told so consistent a story as nature.

10   If one should say that the sun did not rise, to use the ordinary expression, on the day before, his hearer would not believe it, even though he had slept all day and knew that his informant was a man of the strictest veracity. He would not believe it because the story is inconsistent with the conduct of the sun in all the ages past.

11   Primitive and even civilized people have grown so accustomed to believing in miracles that they often attribute the simplest manifestations of nature to agencies of which they know nothing. They do this when the belief is utterly inconsistent with knowledge and logic. They believe in old miracles and new ones. Preachers pray for rain, knowing full well that no such prayer was ever answered. When a politician is sick, they pray for God to cure him, and the politician almost invariably dies. The modern clergyman who prays for rain and for the health of the politician is no more intelligent in this matter than the primitive man who saw a separate miracle in the rising and setting of the sun, in the birth of an individual, in the growth of a plant, in the stroke of lightning, in the flood, in every manifestation of nature and life.

12   As to prophecies, intelligent writers gave them up long ago. In all prophecies facts are made to suit the prophecy, or the prophecy was made after the facts, or the events have no relation to the prophecy. Weird and strange and unreasonable interpretations are used to explain simple statements, that a prophecy may be claimed.

13   Can any rational person believe that the Bible is anything but a human document? We now know pretty well where the various books came from, and about when they were written. We know that they were written by human beings who had no knowledge of science, little knowledge of life, and were influenced by the barbarous morality of primitive times, and were grossly ignorant of most things that men know today. For instance, Genesis says that God made the earth, and he made the sun to light the day and the moon to light the night, and in one clause disposes of the stars by saying that "he made the stars also." This was plainly written by someone who had no conception of the stars. Man, by the aid of his telescope, has looked out into

the heavens and found stars whose diameter is as great as the distance between the earth and the sun. We now know that the universe is filled with stars and suns and planets and systems. Every new telescope looking further into the heavens only discovers more and more worlds and suns and systems in the endless reaches of space. The men who wrote Genesis believed, of course, that this tiny speck of mud that we call the earth was the center of the universe, the only world in space, and made for man, who was the only being worth considering. These men believed that the stars were only a little way above the earth, and were set in the firmament for man to look at, and for nothing else. Everyone today knows that this conception is not true.

14   This origin of the human race is not as blind a subject as it once was. Let alone God creating Adam out of hand, from the dust of the earth, does anyone believe that Eve was made from Adam's rib—that the snake walked and spoke in the Garden of Eden—that he tempted Eve to persuade Adam to eat an apple, and that it is on that account that the whole human race was doomed to hell—that for four thousand years there was no chance for any human to be saved, though none of them had anything whatever to do with the temptation; and that finally men were saved only through God's son dying for them, and that unless human beings believed this silly, impossible and wicked story they were doomed to hell? Can anyone with intelligence really believe that a child born today should be doomed because the snake tempted Eve and Eve tempted Adam? To believe this is not God-worship; it is devil-worship.

15   Can anyone call this scheme of creation and damnation moral? It defies every principle of morality, as man conceives morality. Can anyone believe today that the whole world was destroyed by flood, save only Noah and his family and a male and female of each species of animal that entered the Ark? There are almost a million species of insects alone. How did Noah match these up and make sure of getting male and female to reproduce life in the world after the flood had spent its force? And why should all the lower animals have been destroyed? Were they included in the sinning of man? This is a story which could not beguile a fairly bright child of five years of age today.

16   Do intelligent people believe that the various languages spoken by man on earth came from the confusion of tongues at the Tower of Babel, some four thousand years ago? Human languages were dispersed all over the face of the earth long before that time. Evidences of civilizations are in existence now that were old long before the date that romancers fix for the building of the Tower, and even before the date claimed for the flood.

17   Do Christians believe that Joshua made the sun stand still, so that the day could be lengthened, that a battle might be finished? What kind of person wrote that story, and what did he know about astronomy? It is perfectly plain that the author thought that the earth was the center of the universe and stood still in the heavens, and that the sun either went around it or was pulled across its path each day, and that the stopping of the sun would lengthen the day. We know now that had the sun stopped when Joshua com-

manded it, and had it stood still until now, it would not have lengthened the day. We know that the day is determined by the rotation of the earth upon its axis, and not by the movement of the sun. Everyone knows that this story simply is not true, and not many even pretend to believe the childish fable.

18   What of the tale of Balaam's ass speaking to him, probably in Hebrew? Is it true, or is it a fable? Many asses have spoken, and doubtless some in Hebrew, but they have not been that breed of asses. Is salvation to depend on a belief in a monstrosity like this?

19   Above all the rest, would any human being today believe that a child was born without a father? Yet this story was not at all unreasonable in the ancient world; at least three or four miraculous births are recorded in the Bible, including John the Baptist and Samson. Immaculate conceptions were common in the Roman world at the time and at the place where Christianity really had its nativity. Women were taken to the temples to be inoculated of God so that their sons might be heroes, which meant, generally, wholesale butchers. Julius Caeser was a miraculous conception—indeed, they were common all over the world. How many miraculous-birth stories is a Christian now expected to believe?

20   In the days of the formation of the Christian religion, disease meant the possession of human beings by devils. Christ cured a sick man by casting out the devils, who ran into the swine, and the swine ran into the sea. Is there any question but what that was simply the attitude and belief of a primitive people? Does anyone believe that sickness means the possession of the body by devils, and that the devils must be cast out of the human being that he may be cured? Does anyone believe that a dead person can come to life? The miracles recorded in the Bible are not the only instances of dead men coming to life. All over the world one finds testimony of such miracles; miracles which no person is expected to believe, unless it is his kind of a miracle. Still at Lourdes today, and all over the present world, from New York to Los Angeles and up and down the lands, people believe in miraculous occurrences, and even in the return of the dead. Superstition is everywhere prevalent in the world. It has been so from the beginning, and most likely will be so unto the end.

21   The reasons for agnosticism and skepticism are abundant and compelling. Fantastic and foolish and impossible consequences are freely claimed for the belief in religion. All the civilization of any period is put down as a result of religion. All the cruelty and error and ignorance of the period has no relation to religion. The truth is that the origin of what we call civilization is not due to religion but to skepticism. So long as men accepted miracles without question, so long as they believed in original sin and the road to salvation, so long as they believed in a hell where man would be kept for eternity on account of Eve, there was no reason whatever for civilization: life was short, and eternity was long, and the business of life was preparation for eternity.

22   When every event was a miracle, when there was no order or system or law, there was no occasion for studying any subject, or being interested in

anything excepting a religion which took care of the soul. As man doubted the primitive conceptions about religion, and no longer accepted the literal, miraculous teachings of ancient books, he set himself to understand nature. We no longer cure disease by casting out devils. Since that time, men have studied the human body, have built hospitals and treated illness in a scientific way. Science is responsible for the building of railroads and bridges, of steamships, of telegraph lines, of cities, towns, large buildings and small, plumbing and sanitation, of the food supply, and the countless thousands of useful things that we now deem necessary to life. Without skepticism and doubt, none of these things could have been given to the world.

23   The fear of God is not the beginning of wisdom. The fear of God is the death of wisdom. Skepticism and doubt lead to study and investigation, and investigation is the beginning of wisdom.

24   The modern world is the child of doubt and inquiry, as the ancient world was the child of fear and faith.

WHAT ARE WE TO MAKE OF JESUS CHRIST?

C. S. Lewis

1 What are we to make of Jesus Christ? This is a question which has, in a sense, a frantically comic side. For the real question is not what are we to make of Christ, but what is He to make of us? The picture of a fly sitting deciding what it is going to make of an elephant has comic elements about it. But perhaps the questioner meant what are we to make of Him in the sense of "How are we to solve the historical problem set us by the recorded sayings and acts of this Man?" This problem is to reconcile two things. On the one hand you have got the almost generally admitted depth and sanity of His moral teaching, which is not very seriously questioned, even by those who are opposed to Christianity. In fact, I find when I am arguing with very anti-God people that they rather make a point of saying, "I am entirely in favour of the moral teaching of Christianity"—and there seems to be a general agreement that in the teaching of this Man and of His immediate followers, moral truth is exhibited at its purest and best. It is not sloppy idealism, it is full of wisdom and shrewdness. The whole thing is realistic, fresh to the highest degree, the product of a sane mind. That is one phenomenon.

2   The other phenomenon is the quite appalling nature of this Man's theological remarks. You all know what I mean, and I want rather to stress the point that the appalling claim which this Man seems to be making is not merely made at one moment of His career. There is, of course, the one moment which led to His execution. The moment at which the High Priest said

to Him, "Who are you?" "I am the Anointed, the Son of the uncreated God, and you shall see Me appearing at the end of all history as the judge of the Universe." But that claim, in fact, does not rest on this one dramatic moment. When you look into His conversation you will find this sort of claim running through the whole thing. For instance, He went about saying to people, "I forgive your sins." Now it is quite natural for a man to forgive something you do to *him*. Thus if somebody cheats *me* out of £5 it is quite possible and reasonable for me to say, "Well, I forgive him, we will say no more about it." What on earth would you say if somebody had done *you* out of £5 and *I* said, "That is all right, I forgive him"? Then there is a curious thing which seems to slip out almost by accident. On one occasion this Man is sitting looking down on Jerusalem from the hill above it and suddenly in comes an extraordinary remark—"I keep on sending you prophets and wise men." Nobody comments on it. And yet, quite suddenly, almost incidentally, He is claiming to be the power that all through the centuries is sending wise men and leaders into the world. Here is another curious remark: in almost every religion there are unpleasant observances like fasting. This Man suddenly remarks one day, "No one need fast while I am here." Who is this Man who remarks that His mere presence suspends all normal rules? Who is the person who can suddenly tell the School they can have a half-holiday? Sometimes the statements put forward the assumption that He, the Speaker, is completely without sin or fault. This is always the attitude. "You, to whom I am talking, are all sinners," and He never remotely suggests that this same reproach can be brought against Him. He says again, "I am begotten of the One God, before Abraham was, I am," and remember what the words "I am" were in Hebrew. They were the name of God, which must not be spoken by any human being, the name which it was death to utter.

3   Well, that is the other side. On the one side clear, definite moral teaching. On the other, claims which, if not true, are those of a megalomaniac, compared with whom Hitler was the most sane and humble of men. There is no half-way house and there is no parallel in other religions. If you had gone to Buddha and asked him "Are you the son of Brahma?" he would have said, "My son, you are still in the vale of illusion." If you had gone to Socrates and asked, "Are you Zeus?" he would have laughed at you. If you had gone to Mohammed and asked, "Are you Allah?" he would first have rent his clothes and then cut your head off. If you had asked Confucius, "Are you Heaven?", I think he would have probably replied, "Remarks which are not in accordance with nature are in bad taste." The idea of a great moral teacher saying what Christ said is out of the question. In my opinion, the only person who can say that sort of thing is either God or a complete lunatic suffering from that form of delusion which undermines the whole mind of man. If you think you are a poached egg, when you are looking for a piece of toast to suit you, you may be sane, but if you think you are God, there is no chance for you. We may note in passing that He was never regarded as a mere moral teacher. He did not produce that effect on any of the people who actually met Him. He

produced mainly three effects—Hatred—Terror—Adoration. There was no trace of people expressing mild approval.

4   What are we to do about reconciling the two contradictory phenomena? One attempt consists in saying that the Man did not really say these things, but that His followers exaggerated the story, and so the legend grew up that He had said them. This is difficult because His followers were all Jews; that is, they belonged to that Nation which of all others was most convinced that there was only one God—that there could not possibly be another. It is very odd that this horrible invention about a religious leader should grow up among the one people in the whole earth least likely to make such a mistake. On the contrary we get the impression that none of His immediate followers or even of the New Testament writers embraced the doctrine at all easily.

5   Another point is that on that view you would have to regard the accounts of the Man as being *legends.* Now, as a literary historian, I am perfectly convinced that whatever else the Gospels are they are not legends. I have read a great deal of legend and I am quite clear that they are not the same sort of thing. They are not artistic enough to be legends. From an imaginative point of view they are clumsy, they don't work up to things properly. Most of the life of Jesus is totally unknown to us, as is the life of anyone else who lived at that time, and no people building up a legend would allow that to be so. Apart from bits of the Platonic dialogues, there are no conversations that I know of in ancient literature like the Fourth Gospel. There is nothing, even in modern literature, until about a hundred years ago when the realistic novel came into existence. In the story of the woman taken in adultery we are told Christ bent down and scribbled in the dust with His finger. Nothing comes of this. No one has ever based any doctrine on it. And the art of *inventing* little irrelevant details to make an imaginary scene more convincing is a purely modern art. Surely the only explanation of this passage is that the thing really happened? The author put it in simply because he had *seen* it.

6   Then we come to the strangest story of all, the story of the Resurrection. It is very necessary to get the story clear. I heard a man say, "The importance of the Resurrection is that it gives evidence of survival, evidence that the human personality survives death." On that view what happened to Christ would be what had always happened to all men, the difference being that in Christ's case we were privileged to see it happening. This is certainly not what the earliest Christian writers thought. Something perfectly new in the history of the Universe had happened. Christ had defeated death. The door which had always been locked had for the very first time been forced open. This is something quite distinct from mere ghost-survival. I don't mean that they disbelieved in ghost-survival. On the contrary, they believed in it so firmly that, on more than one occasion, Christ had had to assure them that He was *not* a ghost. The point is that while believing in survival they yet regarded the Resurrection as something totally different and new. The Resurrection narratives are not a picture of survival after death; they record how a totally new mode of being has arisen in the Universe. Something new had

appeared in the Universe: as new as the first coming of organic life. This Man, after death, does not get divided into "ghost" and "corpse." A new mode of being has arisen. That is the story. What are we going to make of it?

7   The question is, I suppose, whether any hypothesis covers the facts so well as the Christian hypothesis. That hypothesis is that God has come down into the created universe, down to manhood—and come up again, pulling it up with Him. The alternative hypothesis is not legend, nor exaggeration, nor the apparitions of a ghost. It is either lunacy or lies. Unless one can take the second alternative (and I can't), one turns to the Christian theory.

8   "What are we to make of Christ?" There is no question of what we can make of Him, it is entirely a question of what He intends to make of us. You must accept or reject the story.

9   The things He says are very different from what any other teacher has said. Others say, "This is the truth about the Universe. This is the way you ought to go," but He says, "*I* am the Truth, and the Way, and the Life." He says, "No man can reach absolute reality, except through Me. Try to retain your own life and you will be inevitably ruined. Give yourself away and you will be saved." He says, "If you are ashamed of Me, if, when you hear this call, you turn the other way, I also will look the other way when I come again as God without disguise. If anything whatever is keeping you from God and from Me, whatever it is, throw it away. If it is your eye, pull it out. If it is your hand, cut it off. If you put yourself first you will be last. Come to Me everyone who is carrying a heavy load; I will set that right. Your sins, all of them, are wiped out; I can do that. I am Rebirth, I am Life. Eat Me, drink Me, I am your Food. And finally, do not be afraid, I have overcome the whole Universe." This is the issue.

WOMEN'S ROLES

THE CASE FOR EQUALITY

Caroline Bird

1   Is it a good idea to treat men and women exactly alike?

2   What would happen if we tried it?

3   Is it even possible?

4   "After all, men and women are different," people argue. "You can't treat them alike!"

5   Just as we formerly had laws that said that noblemen had certain privileges because of their names, so we now have laws that say that men and women have certain privileges because of their sex. If we think we can't treat men and women alike, it may only be because the law hasn't done it.

6   But it can be done. In a provocative article in *The George Washington Law Review* of December 1965, Pauli Murray and Mary Eastwood reviewed the laws affecting men and women as separate sexes and reported that all such laws would be either clearer or fairer if rewritten in terms of situations, as all other laws are written. It wouldn't be necessary, they pointed out, to say that the crime of rape could be committed only by men or that maternity benefits could be claimed only by women. By definition, these situations apply to one sex only. A woman can't commit rape. A man can't have a baby. The conditions that seem to require special treatment for men or women can all be defined without mentioning sex. If all persons were liable for military or jury service, for instance, men and women could both claim exemption because they had dependents. Women able to serve would relieve the men for whom the draft is now a real hardship.

7   There is no reason why women should not be drafted. The crack Israeli Army drafts all boys and single girls at the age of 18. Girls who marry during their draft terms, as three out of ten do, go into the reserves. Pregnant women and mothers are excused, but women officers in the regular army get four months of fully paid leave beginning with the ninth month of pregnancy. Israeli women soldiers have fought in bloody battles in the past, but they are now assigned to handle paperwork, communications, and medical services in units with men.

8   It isn't necessary to require that husbands support wives in order to protect children. Both partners to a marriage could simply be required to support each other and their children in case of need. There is nothing morally repugnant about requiring money or services from the partner best able to give them, regardless of sex. . . .

9   All these legal inequalities could be remedied, but the real question is: Do we want to do it? Do we really want to treat men and women alike? The only way to find out is to examine, as best we can, what the change would do. The most radical effects would be felt in the field of employment. If access, pay, promotion, and conditions of work for every job were open equally to men and women, as Title VII plainly requires, there would be no legal or moral basis for what Pauli Murray and Mary Eastwood call " . . . the assumption that financial support of a family by the husband-father is a gift from the male sex to the female sex, and, in return, the male is entitled to preference in the outside world."

10   Supposing individuals were hired in all occupations without regard to sex. Women would compete with men in areas now closed to them, but they would not compete with each other as much as they now do for "women's jobs." Women who stayed in "women's jobs" would win higher wages. As the wages rose, men would be attracted to these fields. Since the lowest-paying jobs are those dominated by women, equal opportunity would have the same effect as raising the minimum wage. . . .

11   If, along with sex equality, we expect all adults to work, women who could not show that they were earning their keep at home would have to find

jobs. According to one estimate, full utilization of "womanpower" would add ten million workers to the labor force. If these women could work wherever they were needed, they would free men from the obligation to earn that injures and limits some of them as grievously as the obligation to do housework now injures and limits some women. This is no idle supposition. As we have noticed earlier, under full employment many families find it makes more sense for women to work and support their menfolk.

12   If women were freer to choose where they worked, they would take a good hard look at some of the chores that now keep them at home. What, for instance, is the actual money value of staying at home all day long to do two hours of cleaning? Of hauling groceries from the supermarket? Of waiting in the pediatrician's office for an hour? In 1968, mothers expect all sorts of people to waste their time. The waste is not necessary, and it is not motherhood.

13   A woman we know solved the problem of the doctor's waiting room by arranging for a baby-sitter to take her son to the appointment. She found that she could continue working in her office for an hour or more while they waited for his turn. She could earn more at her own trade than she could have saved in cab fare and babysitting fees, even though the expense was not deductible. A working woman has to operate a home in a world that assumes that a homemaker's time is worth less than the wages of the lowest-paid worker for money. Deliveries are arranged on the assumption that she can sit home all day long and wait. No one calculates the time cost of shopping, either, especially in crowded discount houses and supermarkets, where women on budgets are forced to shop. No one counts the time cost of toting shoes to and from the repairman, or exchanging goods that may have been ordered by telephone to save time, but weren't right on arrival. Purchasing departments count the cost of the time that clerks use when they check prices and quality before buying, but housewives don't add the cost of their time to the price paid for family purchases.

14   If all adults were required to work, and free to choose the kind of work they wanted, many women would leave their homes and thereby create more paying jobs. Baby-sitters and service workers, many of them now considered unemployable because of age or lack of education, would be drawn out of their isolation and into the labor force. But all of these newcomers would not necessarily find themselves doing what housewives used to do at home. Many would find jobs in services especially organized to do housework efficiently.

15   More women could afford housekeeping services that now exist for the very rich alone. More charge-and-deliver grocers would be needed to serve the growing number of housewives who would not mind paying more to save the time they now spend shopping in self-service supermarkets. Cleaning services could contract to keep a house in shape by sending in teams of machine-equipped professionals to tidy for an hour or so every day; maintenance services employing salaried mechanics could keep all household gear operating for a flat annual fee; yard services like those run by teams of Japa-

nese gardeners in Los Angeles could contract to keep lawns mowed and garden beds weeded. Food take-out services and caterers proliferating around the country would increase to serve the growing number of women who like to entertain but don't have time to cook.

16   These new services would be cheaper in real economic terms, because specialists working at what they enjoy are more efficient than amateurs doing chores they may detest. But the big gain would be a better use of talent. If the born cooks, cleaners, and children's nurses were paid well enough so that they could make careers out of their talents, domestic services would attract women who now enjoy household arts but hesitate to practice them professionally because they don't want to be treated as "servants." Women who have never worked often have trouble with servants because they have never learned how to hold employees to objective standards. If most women worked, domestic service could become more attractive, since, hopefully, domestic workers would begin to be treated more like office workers. . . .

17   Billions of words and hours of thought have been expanded on the complexities of race relations. Progress, said the sophisticated, will have to be slow. You cannot change a way of life overnight. Yet today it is clear that however agonizing the changes have been, the problem has never been all that complicated. What we did to the blacks was just plain wrong, and everybody knew it.

18   So with the employment of women. Relations between the sexes are complicated, and change is hard, but the way women are treated is just plain wrong.

19   It is wrong to make aspiring women prove they are twice as good as men.

20   It is wrong to pay women less than men for the same work just because they will work for less.

21   It is wrong to exclude women from work they can do so that they have to work for less in the jobs open to them.

22   It is wrong to make aspiring women pay the penalty of women who are content to be used as a labor reserve.

23   It is wrong to assume that because some women can't do mathematics, *this* woman can't do mathematics.

24   It is wrong to expect women to work for their families or the nation and then to step aside when their families or the nation wants them out of the way.

25   It is wrong to deny individuals born female the right to inconvenience their families to pursue art, science, power, prestige, money, or even self-expression, in the way that men in pursuit of these goals inconvenience their families as a matter of course.

26   It is wrong to impute motives to women instead of letting them speak for themselves.

27   It is wrong to ridicule, sneer, frighten, or brainwash anyone unable to fight back.

28   It is wrong, as well as wasteful and dangerous, to discourage talent.

29   All these things are wrong, and everybody knows it. And just as "separate but equal" schools limited white children as well as black, so the doctrine that women are different but equal limits men. Mary Wollstonecraft, John Stuart Mill, George Bernard Shaw, and President Goheen of Princeton were all concerned about sex inequality in part at least because of the damage it does to men. David Riesman points out that every boundary we impose on women we impose on men also.

30   Equity speaks softly and wins in the end. But it is expedience, with its loud voice, that sets the time of victory. The cotton gin did not make slavery wrong, but it helped a lot of Southerners to *see* that slavery was wrong. The immigrant vote did not make woman suffrage right, but it frightened politicians into enfranchising women on the theory that the educated women of politically conservative old American stock would vote more readily than the submissive women of politically unpredictable ethnic groups.

31   So with equal opportunity for women. Conditions conspire to help people see the inequity and the advantages of ending it. First the pill gives women control over their fate so that they can be as responsible as men. Then modern medicine prolongs the lives of women so that all now have decades of potential working life, beyond child-rearing age, during which none of the limitations imposed on women make sense. Next, modern technology takes their work out of the home and invites them to do it elsewhere, and for pay. It frees more mothers of the work of bringing up children, and gives it to schools. Meanwhile, the new technology is less and less a respecter of old-fashioned sex differences. It eliminated the need for physical strength very rapidly and is now eliminating the need for "detail work."

32   What the new technology needs is educated manpower that can learn new skills. What is doesn't need is more ordinary people without skills. Both needs strengthen the case for equal opportunity for the underprivileged majority of Americans who were born female.

PAID HOMEMAKING: AN IDEA IN SEARCH OF A POLICY

William J. Byron, S.J.

1 Parents in the U.S. have no economic incentive to care for their children at home. If that strikes no one as strange, it is only because our nation takes it for granted that economic incentives belong in the marketplace and other motives explain behavior at home. So, full-time care for a "priceless" child by that child's natural parent in a supportive home environment is unrewarded economically.

2   . Those who know the price of everything and the value of nothing are, as Oscar Wilde said so well, cynics. What can be said of a nation that regards its children as priceless, but attaches no economic value to child-care by the person best qualified to provide it? Shortsighted will do for the moment. Further reflection might prompt us to label as both unwise and dangerous the absence of national support for parents who want to be full-time homemakers.

3   The issue is complicated. Children are our nation's greatest treasure, our most precious resource. In the vast majority of cases, children develop best in a stable family unit, in an environment of love—of parents for each other and of both for the child. Moreover, children need to experience parental love expressed in the form of presence. An attentive, affirming presence seems to work best.

4   Yet, we know that parents are often left without partners. We also know that economic necessity frequently drives both parents into the labor market. Sometimes, a desire to give full stretch to one's talents encourages mothers for whom employment is not an economic necessity to step into the job market. (Our cultural presumption that fathers can enjoy that same full stretch only in employment other than homemaking remains unchallenged, even unexamined.) Then there are those mothers who go to work only for the sake of their offspring, to supplement the family income so that the youngsters can have more—more material things, more and better education, more developmental opportunities, but less parental presence. Presence (or absence, depending on your point of view) is the coin in which the parent-child relationship pays the price for two-paycheck marriages, or for one-parent households where the parent is employed outside the home.

5   Should homemakers be paid for their services? Not housekeepers, babysitters, or day-care providers, but homemakers—parents who choose to devote full time to the task of rearing children.

6   On Nov. 24, 1983, the Vatican published a "Charter on the Rights of the Family." It is the product of worldwide consultation and a formal process of reflection and research that began in 1980. The charter speaks principally to governments. Article 10 declares:

> Families have a right to social and economic order in which the organization of work permits the members to live together and does not hinder the unity, well-being, health and the stability of the family, while offering also the possibility of wholesome recreation.
>
> a) Remuneration for work must be sufficient for establishing and maintaining a family with dignity, either through a suitable salary, called a "family wage," or through other social measures such as family allowances or the remuneration of the work in the home of one of the parents; it should be such that mothers will not be obliged to work outside the home to the detriment of family life and especially of the education of the children.
>
> b) The work of the mother in the home must be recognized and respected because of its value for the family and for society.

7   Those "other social measures" lie, for the most part, undesigned and hidden in the imaginations of academics and social theorists. Government

should be encouraging their development. Although the Vatican statement targets no specific purse from which homemakers' pay could be drawn, the only likely source is government. Neil Gilbert, in *Capitalism and the Welfare State* (Yale University Press, 1983), proposes that the full-time homemaker receive a "social credit" for each year spent at home with children who are under 17 years of age. According to this plan, accumulated credits would either pay for higher education or entitle the homemaker to preferred hiring status in the Civil Service once the youngsters are raised and the parent is ready to enter or reenter the labor market. Gilbert specifies the Federal government as the provider of this benefit, which, like a veteran's benefit, would compensate the homemaker for time spent out of the workforce, but in service to the nation.

8   In Gilbert's scheme, each unit of social credit (one child per year of full-time care) could be exchanged for either "(a) tuition for four units of undergraduate academic training, (b) tuition for three units of technical school training, (c) tuition for two units of graduate education, or (d) an award of one-fourth of a preference point on federal civil service examinations." The parent is the implied beneficiary of the tuition grant in this G.I. Bill-type scenario. The policy would surely be more attractive and effective if an option to designate the homemaker's child as the educational beneficiary were made explicit.

9   The social credit idea bars no parent, male or female, from opting for paid employment or professional activity outside the home. It doesn't even discourage outside work. It simply provides an incentive to parents who might prefer homemaking to labor market activity. It also answers the need of those parents who bring home the second paycheck just "to put the kids through college." Under this plan, they would stay home, accumulate the social credits, and eventually redeem them in tuition payments.

10   When the legislative imagination takes up this idea, as I hope will be the case before long, some constraints will have to be set. The first would be an appropriate family income limit above which neither parent would be eligible. Those who do qualify could, if the policy so directs, be required to treat as taxable income the cash value of the credits exchanged for tuition. By keeping the benefit tax-free, however, legislators would preserve for the beneficiary freedom of choice between independent and state-supported higher education. Spending the credits for tuition at the higher priced independent colleges would mean a higher cash value and thus more taxable income. It is better to keep the benefit tax-free.

11   It is conceivable that the eligible person who decides to be a fulltime homemaking parent would soon become economically active at home. "Worksteading" is the new word for this. With the arrival of the "information economy" and the installation of computers and word processors in the home, the probability of more at-home paid employment rises sharply. Protection for the integrity of the social credit program could come from the Internal Revenue Service and would have to be written into the law. It would be easy to come up with an IRS device that would decertify from social credit

eligibility the homemaker who reports earnings above a relatively low limit specified in the law. Again, the economic incentive. In this case, the threatened loss of the credit would serve as encouragement to hold firm on the homemaking commitment in the face of attractive remunerative at-home business opportunities.

12   The credits would, of course, be nontransferable from family to family. Some might argue for a limit on the number of credits one homemaker could earn (Gilbert suggests a three-child maximum), but sensitivity to parental freedom with respect to family size would be an important consideration in any public policy relating to the family.

13   The program would be more flexible, and thus more practical and attractive, if parents could alternate on the full-time homemaker responsibility. In effect, the parents would commit themselves, as a couple, to the provision of one full-time homemaker's services each year from the birth of a child until that child reaches his or her 17th birthday. This would open up the possibility for a mother (more often than not, the mother will be the parent with full-time homemaking responsibilities) to work outside the home. There would be no loss of credit so long as the father personally provides the child care. It is worth noting that a shared responsibility for earning social credits through homemaking could promote cooperation over career competition between spouses in the modern marriage.

14   The value of the credit would best be expressed as a percentage of the cost of higher education—100% of the cost of tuition, fees, and books, regardless of the college chosen. The inclusion of other expenses that complete the so-called "cost of attending" (room and board, transportation, spending money) would be a matter of legislative choice. The point of specifying the percentage, rather than an absolute sum, is to relieve the parent of anxiety concerning the erosion of the credit by inflation and the consequent inability—17 years later—to convert the credits into payment for tuition, fees, and books. It seems to me that one year's credit should be worth one-17th of the price, at the point of consumption, of tuition, fees, and books. The total cost of tuition, fees, and books ("costs of education," as distinguished from "cost of attendance") would be completely covered in those cases where a child received full-time parental home care for the first 17 years of life.

15   The proposal is clearly intended to reinforce the nuclear family unit by rewarding a parent for remaining at home. As a policy idea, it will go nowhere unless there is widespread conviction that society needs the services of full-time homemakers.

16   Such persons need not be confined to quarters all day long. They would be free to be with their youngsters in a variety of at-home and out-of-home ways and at times not possible for the busy parent burdened with a work schedule. The homemaker's schedule would focus on the child. It would promote parental presence—to the child. When one considers how such time might be spent, expressions like "creative leisure" and "shared learning" come to mind, as do thoughts of joint participation in arts, crafts, games, mu-

seum visits, sightseeing "voyages of discovery," and similar engagements. School plays and athletic contests would attract more spectators. The schools themselves would be able to draw on a larger supply of volunteer service. As the nation deplores the condition of its schools, it should notice the promise this policy holds for the promotion of the life of the mind *at home,* a development which would be nothing but good for the schools.

17   This policy proposal is open to the criticism that it envisions a middle-class program that would be unavailable to the working poor who, credits or not, could not afford not to work. The criticism is quite fair. This proposal would not meet the needs of those who absolutely have to work. They demonstrate the power of economic incentives; many—by no means all—would prefer to be homemakers. To meet their needs (and to assist others who are less pressed for funds, but most anxious to combine careers and parental responsibilities), it is important to consider for inclusion in a national family policy measures that would encourage flexible work schedules, make day-care facilities more widely available, and make child-care expenses more readily deductible.

18   In addition, Gilbert deals with an issue that will certainly be raised by many voices in this policy debate:

> For women who want a balanced family life and a full-time career, a family credit scheme would open a successive route along which both are possible. Because this route encompasses a 25-to-30 year period of employment, it may close off a few career options which require early training and many years of preparation. There must be some price for enjoying the choice of two callings in life. This is a different path from the continuous paid career line that men typically follow. It may be better.

19   I have tested the social credit idea in the op-ed forum and in conversations with friends. The strongest negative reaction chided me for trying to "bribe" people into child-care, "to shoehorn women back into the kitchen and/or the nursery."

20   On the other hand, the mother of two disabled sons applauded the idea: "The need for social reform to strengthen the family is so great that one would imagine that America as a nation and as a culture depends on the policy you advocate. It is indeed puzzling how an issue that is so fundamental—and so simply obvious—could have been overlooked for so long." The policy, by the way, might well allow for extra credits for homemakers serving handicapped children.

21   Endorsement of the idea also came from a middle-aged male who described himself as a "well-traveled parent who longs for more time in the home."

22   A public affairs director in a Federal agency offered a reflective comment which touches upon the crucial question of who will guide the formation of values in one's children:

> As a career woman who has been on both sides of the fence (I stayed home until the children were 10 and 14 and then joined the work force 10 years ago),

I think your plan has merit. It seems to me that I have been extremely lucky—I was able to start a career later in life because of extremely hard work and fortunate circumstances. Not everyone is so positioned. I would not have wanted someone else "raising" my children and giving them different views on morality and philosophy from my own. Each parent wants to pass on his basic beliefs to his children, and it is impossible for young women today to do that if they see their child for one or two hectic hours a day.

23   R. Sargent Shriver, Democratic candidate for Vice President in 1972, called my attention to a speech he gave on "The Family" during that campaign. He repeated the maxim: What is good for families is good for nations; what hurts families, hurts nations. He further remarked that "the institution that has served human beings best and disappointed them least is the family."

24   A retired obstetrician, himself a father of eight, found the proposal to be "on target." In his medical practice, he said, he "was always well aware of the importance of a mother or parent in a home at all times with growing children; there can be no substitute."

25   Recently, I talked with a 36-year-old man whose educational credentials include a doctorate and a law degree. He has worked as a college professor, as well as a lawyer. His *curriculum vitae* notes his full-time service as a "homemaker" for the past three years. His wife, also a lawyer, has been in the labor market while he cares for two young children at home. Another child was expected soon. With the birth of their third child, the lawyer-mother planned to remain at home as the professor-lawyer-father returned to paid employment in the market economy. This is easy enough for well-educated professionals, but it only happens when parents regard it as important that their children have the full-time attention of one or the other throughout childhood.

26   Less well-educated parents are no less concerned about child development, just less able, for economic reasons, to consider full-time homemaking as a real option. If the option were available, it would be just that—an option, not an enforced condition. People would be free to take it or leave it, as their values and preferences direct.

27   We have no such option in the U.S. today because of the presence of economic pressure and the absence of a national family policy. The social credit idea addresses a policy vacuum. It surely deserves some discussion and debate.

MINORITIES' RIGHTS

A CALL FOR UNITY

Members of the Birmingham Clergy

April 12, 1963

1   We the undersigned clergymen are among those who, in January, issued "An Appeal for Law and Order and Common Sense," in dealing with racial problems in Alabama. We expressed understanding that honest convictions in racial matters could properly be pursued in the courts, but urged that decisions of those courts should in the meantime be peacefully obeyed.

2   Since that time there had been some evidence of increased forebearance and a willingness to face facts. Responsible citizens have undertaken to work on various problems which cause racial friction and unrest. In Birmingham, recent public events have given indication that we all have opportunity for a new constructive and realistic approach to racial problems.

3   However, we are now confronted by a series of demonstrations by some of our Negro citizens, directed and led in part by outsiders. We recognize the natural impatience of people who feel that their hopes are slow in being realized. But we are convinced that these demonstrations are unwise and untimely.

4   We agree rather with certain local Negro leadership which has called for honest and open negotiation of racial issues in our area. And we believe this kind of facing of issues can best be accomplished by citizens of our own metropolitan area, white and Negro, meeting with their knowledge and experience of the local situation. All of us need to face that responsibility and find proper channels for its accomplishment.

5   Just as we formerly pointed out that "hatred and violence have no sanction in our religious and political traditions," we also point out that such actions as incite to hatred and violence, however technically peaceful those actions may be, have not contributed to the resolution of our local problems. We do not believe that these days of new hope are days when extreme measures are justified in Birmingham.

6   We commend the community as a whole, and the local news media and law enforcement officials in particular, on the calm manner in which these demonstrations have been handled. We urge the public to continue to show restraint should the demonstrations continue, and the law enforcement officials to remain calm and continue to protect our city from violence.

7   We further strongly urge our own Negro community to withdraw support from these demonstrations, and to unite locally in working peacefully for a better Birmingham. When rights are consistently denied, a cause should be pressed in the courts and in negotiations among local leaders, and not in

the streets. We appeal to both our white and Negro citizenry to observe the principles of law and order and common sense.

C.C.J. CARPENTER, D.D., L.L.D., Bishop of Alabama; JOSEPH A. DURICK, D.D., Auxiliary Bishop, Diocese of Mobile-Birmingham; RABBI MILTON L. GRAFMAN, Temple Emanu-El, Birmingham, Alabama; BISHOP PAUL HARDIN, Bishop of the Alabama-West Florida Conference of the Methodist Church; BISHOP NOLAN B. HARMON, Bishop of the North Alabama Conference of the Methodist Church; GEORGE M. MURRAY, D.D., L.L.D., Bishop Coadjutor, Episcopal Diocese of Alabama; EDWARD V. RAMAGE, Moderator, Synod of the Alabama Presbyterian Church in the United States; EARL STALLINGS, Pastor, First Baptist Church, Birmingham, Alabama.

LETTER FROM BIRMINGHAM JAIL

Martin Luther King, Jr.

April 16, 1963

MY DEAR FELLOW CLERGYMEN:

1   While confined here in the Birmingham city jail, I came across your recent statement calling my present activities "unwise and untimely." Seldom do I pause to answer criticism of my work and ideas. If I sought to answer all the criticisms that cross my desk, my secretaries would have little time for anything other than such correspondence in the course of the day, and I would have no time for constructive work. But since I feel that you are men of genuine good will and that your criticisms are sincerely set forth, I want to try to answer your statement in what I hope will be patient and reasonable terms.

2   I think I should indicate why I am here in Birmingham, since you have been influenced by the view which argues against "outsiders coming in." I have the honor of serving as president of the Southern Christian Leadership Conference, an organization operating in every southern state, with headquarters in Atlanta, Georgia. We have some eighty-five affiliated organizations across the South, and one of them is the Alabama Christian Movement for Human Rights. Frequently we share staff, educational and financial resources with our affiliates. Several months ago the affiliate here in Birmingham asked us to be on call to engage in a nonviolent direct-action program if such were deemed necessary. We readily consented, and when the hour came we lived up to our promise. So I, along with several members of my staff, am here because I was invited here. I am here because I have organizational ties here.

3   But more basically, I am in Birmingham because injustice is here. Just as

the prophets of the eighth century B.C. left their villages and carried their "thus saith the Lord" far beyond the boundaries of their home towns, and just as the Apostle Paul left his village of Tarsus and carried the gospel of Jesus Christ to the far corners of the Greco-Roman world, so am I compelled to carry the gospel of freedom beyond my own home town. Like Paul, I must constantly respond to the Macedonian call for aid.

4   Moreover, I am cognizant of the interrelatedness of all communities and states. I cannot sit idly by in Atlanta and not be concerned about what happens in Birmingham. Injustice anywhere is a threat to justice everywhere. We are caught in an inescapable network of mutuality, tied in a single garment of destiny. Whatever affects one directly, affects all indirectly. Never again can we afford to live with the narrow, provincial "outside agitator" idea. Anyone who lives inside the United States can never be considered an outsider anywhere within its bounds.

5   You deplore the demonstrations taking place in Birmingham. But your statement, I am sorry to say, fails to express a similar concern for the conditions that brought about the demonstrations. I am sure that none of you would want to rest content with the superficial kind of social analysis that deals merely with effects and does not grapple with underlying causes. It is unfortunate that demonstrations are taking place in Birmingham, but it is even more unfortunate that the city's white power structure left the Negro community with no alternative.

6   In any nonviolent campaign there are four basic steps: collection of the facts to determine whether injustices exist; negotiation; self-purification; and direct action. We have gone through all these steps in Birmingham. There can be no gainsaying the fact that racial injustice engulfs this community. Birmingham is probably the most thoroughly segregated city in the United States. Its ugly record of brutality is widely known. Negroes have experienced grossly unjust treatment in the courts. There have been more unsolved bombings of Negro homes and churches in Birmingham than in any other city in the nation. These are the hard, brutal facts of the case. On the basis of these conditions, Negro leaders sought to negotiate with the city fathers. But the latter consistently refused to engage in goodfaith negotiation. . . .

7   You may well ask: "Why direct action? Why sit-ins, marches and so forth? Isn't negotiation a better path?" You are quite right in calling for negotiation. Indeed, this is the very purpose of direct action. Nonviolent direct action seeks to create such a crisis and foster such a tension that a community which has constantly refused to negotiate is forced to confront the issue. It seeks so to dramatize the issue that it can no longer be ignored. My citing the creation of tension as part of the work of the nonviolent-resister may sound rather shocking. But I must confess that I am not afraid of the word "tension." I have earnestly opposed violent tension, but there is a type of constructive, nonviolent tension which is necessary for growth. Just as Socrates felt that it was necessary to create a tension in the mind so that individuals could rise from the bondage of myths and half-truths to the unfettered realm of creative

analysis and objective appraisal, so must we see the need for nonviolent gadflies to create the kind of tension in society that will help men rise from the dark depths of prejudice and racism to the majestic heights of understanding and brotherhood.

8   The purpose of our direct-action program is to create a situation so crisis-packed that it will inevitably open the door to negotiation. I therefore concur with you in your call for negotiation. Too long has our beloved Southland been bogged down in a tragic effort to live in monologue rather than dialogue.

9   One of the basic points in your statement is that the action that I and my associates have taken in Birmingham is untimely. . . . My friends, I must say to you that we have not made a single gain in civil rights without determined legal and nonviolent pressure. Lamentably, it is an historical fact that privileged groups seldom give up their privileges voluntarily. Individuals may see the moral light and voluntarily give up their unjust posture; but, as Reinhold Niebuhr has reminded us, groups tend to be more immoral than individuals.

10   We know through painful experience that freedom is never voluntarily given by the oppressor; it must be demanded by the oppressed. Frankly, I have yet to engage in a direct-action campaign that was "well timed" in the view of those whose have not suffered unduly from the disease of segregation. For years now I have heard the word "Wait!" It rings in the ears of every Negro with piercing familiarity. This "Wait" has almost always meant "Never." We must come to see, with one of our distinguished jurists, that "justice too long delayed is justice denied."

11   We have waited for more than 340 years for our constitutional and God-given rights. The nations of Asia and Africa are moving with jetlike speed toward gaining political independence, but we still creep at horse-and-buggy pace toward gaining a cup of coffee at a lunch counter. Perhaps it is easy for those who have never felt the stinging darts of segregation to say, "Wait." But when you have seen vicious mobs lynch your mothers and fathers at will and drown your sisters and brothers at whim; when you have seen hate-filled policemen curse, kick and even kill your black brothers and sisters; when you see the vast majority of your twenty million Negro brothers smothering in an airtight cage of poverty in the midst of an affluent society; when you suddenly find your tongue twisted and your speech stammering as you seek to explain to your six-year-old daughter why she can't go to the public amusement park that has just been advertised on television, and see tears welling up in her eyes when she is told that Funtown is closed to colored children, and see ominous clouds of inferiority beginning to form in her little mental sky, and see her beginning to distort her personality by developing an unconscious bitterness toward white people; when you have to concoct an answer for a five-year-old son who is asking: "Daddy, why do white people treat colored people so mean?"; when you take a cross-country drive and find it necessary to sleep night after night in the uncomfortable corners of your automobile because no motel will accept you; when you are humiliated day in

and day out by nagging signs reading "white" and "colored"; when your first name becomes "nigger," your middle name becomes "boy" (however old you are) and your last name becomes "John," and your wife and mother are never given the respected title "Mrs.;" when you are harried by day and haunted by night by the fact that you are a Negro, living constantly at tiptoe stance, never quite knowing what to expect next, and are plagued with inner fears and outer resentments; when you are forever fighting a degenerating sense of "nobodiness"—then you will understand why we find it difficult to wait. There comes a time when the cup of endurance runs over, and men are no longer willing to be plunged into the abyss of despair. I hope, sirs, you can understand our legitimate and unavoidable impatience.

12   You express a great deal of anxiety over our willingness to break laws. This is certainly a legitimate concern. Since we so diligently urge people to obey the Supreme Court's decision of 1954 outlawing segregation in the public schools, at first glance it may seem rather paradoxical for us consciously to break laws. One may well ask: "How can you advocate breaking some laws and obeying others?" The answer lies in the fact that there are two types of laws: just and unjust. I would be the first to advocate obeying just laws. One has not only a legal but a moral responsibility to obey just laws. Conversely, one has a moral responsibility to disobey unjust laws. I would agree with St. Augustine that "an unjust law is no law at all."

13   Now, what is the difference between the two? How does one determine whether a law is just or unjust? A just law is a man-made code that squares with the moral law or the law of God. An unjust law is a code that is out of harmony with the moral law. To put it in the terms of St. Thomas Aquinas: An unjust law is a human law that is not rooted in eternal law and natural law. Any law that uplifts human personality is just. Any law that degrades human personality is unjust. All segregation statutes are unjust because segregation distorts the soul and damages the personality. It gives the segregator a false sense of superiority and the segregated a false sense of inferiority. Segregation, to use the terminology of the Jewish philosopher Martin Buber, substitutes an "I-it" relationship for an "I-thou" relationship and ends up relegating persons to the status of things. Hence segregation is not only politically, economically and sociologically unsound, it is morally wrong and sinful. Paul Tillich has said that sin is separation. Is not segregation an existential expression of man's tragic separation, his awful estrangement, his terrible sinfulness? Thus it is that I can urge men to obey the 1954 decision of the Supreme Court, for it is morally right; and I can urge them to disobey segregation ordinances, for they are morally wrong.

14   Let us consider a more concrete example of just and unjust laws. An unjust law is a code that a numerical or power majority group compels a minority group to obey but does not make binding on itself. This is *difference* made legal. By the same token, a just law is a code that a majority compels a minority to follow and that it is willing to follow itself. This is *sameness* made legal.

15   Let me give another explanation. A law is unjust if it is inflicted on a minority that, as a result of being denied the right to vote, had no part in enacting or devising the law. Who can say that the legislature of Alabama which set up that state's segregation laws was democratically elected? Throughout Alabama all sorts of devious methods are used to prevent Negroes from becoming registered voters, and there are some counties in which, even though Negroes constitute a majority of the population, not a single Negro is registered. Can any law enacted under such circumstances be considered democratically structured?

16   Sometimes a law is just on its face and unjust in its application. For instance, I have been arrested on a charge of parading without a permit. Now, there is nothing wrong in having an ordinance which requires a permit for a parade. But such an ordinance becomes unjust when it is used to maintain segregation and to deny citizens the First Amendment privilege of peaceful assembly and protest.

17   I hope you are able to see the distinction I am trying to point out. In no sense do I advocate evading or defying the law, as would the rabid segregationist. That would lead to anarchy. One who breaks an unjust law must do so openly, lovingly, and with a willingness to accept the penalty. I submit that an individual who breaks a law that conscience tells him is unjust, and who willingly accepts the penalty of imprisonment in order to arouse the conscience of the community over its injustice, is in reality expressing the highest respect for law.

18   Of course, there is nothing new about this kind of civil disobedience. It has evidenced sublimely in the refusal of Shadrach, Meshach and Abednego to obey the laws of Nebuchadnezzar, on the ground that a higher moral law was at stake. It was practiced superbly by the early Christians, who were willing to face hungry lions and the excruciating pain of chopping blocks rather than submit to certain unjust laws of the Roman Empire. To a degree, academic freedom is a reality today because Socrates practiced civil disobedience. In our own nation, the Boston Tea Party represented a massive act of civil disobedience.

19   We should never forget that everything Adolf Hitler did in Germany was "legal" and everything the Hungarian freedom fighters did in Hungary was "illegal." It was "illegal" to aid and comfort a Jew in Hitler's Germany. Even so, I am sure that, had I lived in Germany at the time, I would have aided and comforted my Jewish brothers. If today I lived in a Communist country where certain principles dear to the Christian faith are suppressed, I would openly advocate disobeying that country's anti-religious laws.

20   I must make two honest confessions to you, my Christian and Jewish brothers. First, I must confess that over the past few years I have been gravely disappointed with the white moderate. I have almost reached the regrettable conclusion that the Negro's great stumbling block in his stride toward freedom is not the White Citizen's Counciler or the Ku Klux Klanner, but the white moderate, who is more devoted to "order" than to justice; who prefers

a negative peace which is the absence of tension to a positive peace which is the presence of justice; who constantly says: "I agree with you in the goal you seek, but I cannot agree with your methods of direct action"; who paternalistically believes he can set the timetable for another man's freedom; who lives by a mythical concept of time and who constantly advises the Negro to wait for a "more convenient season." Shallow understanding from people of good will is more frustrating than absolute misunderstanding from people of ill will. Lukewarm acceptance is much more bewildering than outright rejection.

21   I had hoped that the white moderate would understand that law and order exist for the purpose of establishing justice and that when they fail in this purpose they become the dangerously structured dams that block the flow of social progress. I had hoped that the white moderate would understand that the present tension in the South is a necessary phase of the transition from an obnoxious negative peace, in which the Negro passively accepted his unjust plight, to a substantive and positive peace, in which all men will respect the dignity and worth of human personality. Actually, we who engage in nonviolent direct action are not the creators of tension. We merely bring to the surface the hidden tension that is already alive. We bring it out in the open, where it can be seen and dealt with. Like a boil that can never be cured so long as it is covered up but must be opened with all its ugliness to the natural medicines of air and light, injustice must be exposed, with all the tension its exposure creates, to the light of human conscience and the air of national opinion before it can be cured.

22   In your statement you assert that our actions, even though peaceful, must be condemned because they precipitate violence. But is this a logical assertion? Isn't this like condemning a robbed man because his possession of money precipitated the evil act of robbery? Isn't this like condemning Socrates because his unswerving commitment to truth and his philosophical inquiries precipitated the act by the misguided populace in which they made him drink hemlock? Isn't this like condemning Jesus because his unique God-consciousness and never-ceasing devotion to God's will precipitated the evil act of crucifixion? We must come to see that, as the federal courts have consistently affirmed, it is wrong to urge an individual to cease his efforts to gain his basic constitutional rights because the quest may precipitate violence. Society must protect the robbed and punish the robber. . . .

23   You speak of our activity in Birmingham as extreme. At first I was rather disappointed that fellow clergymen would see my nonviolent efforts as those of an extremist. I began thinking about the fact that I stand in the middle of two opposing forces in the Negro community. One is a force of complacency, made up in part of Negroes who, as a result of long years of oppression, are so drained of self-respect and a sense of "somebodiness" that they have adjusted to segregation; and in part of a few middle-class Negroes who, because of a degree of academic and economic security and because in some ways they profit by segregation, have become insensitive to the prob-

lems of the masses. The other force is one of bitterness and hatred, and it comes perilously close to advocating violence. It is expressed in the various black nationalist groups that are springing up across the nation, the largest and best-known being Elijah Muhammad's Muslim movement. Nourished by the Negro's frustration over the continued existence of racial discrimination, this movement is made up of people who have lost faith in America, who have absolutely repudiated Christianity, and who have concluded that the white man is an incorrigible "devil."

24   I have tried to stand between these two forces, saying that we need emulate neither the "do-nothingism" of the complacent nor the hatred and despair of the black nationalist. For there is the more excellent way of love and nonviolent protest. I am grateful to God that, through the influence of the Negro church, the way of nonviolence became an integral part of our struggle.

25   If this philosophy had not emerged, by now many streets of the South would, I am convinced, be flowing with blood. And I am further convinced that if our white brothers dismiss as "rabble-rousers" and "outside agitators" those of us who employ nonviolent direct action, and if they refuse to support our nonviolent efforts, millions of Negroes will, out of frustration and despair, seek solace and security in black-nationalist ideologies—a development that would inevitably lead to a frightening racial nightmare.

26   Oppressed people cannot remain oppressed forever. The yearning for freedom eventually manifests itself, and that is what has happened to the American Negro. Something within has reminded him of his birthright of freedom, and something without has reminded him that it can be gained. Consciously or unconsciously, he has been caught up by the *Zeitgeist*, and with his black brothers of Africa and his brown and yellow brothers of Asia, South America and the Caribbean, the United States Negro is moving with a sense of great urgency toward the promised land of racial justice. If one recognizes this vital urge that has engulfed the Negro community, one should readily understand why public demonstrations are taking place. The Negro has many pent-up resentments and latent frustrations, and he must release them. So let him march; let him make prayer pilgrimages to the city hall; let him go on freedom rides—and try to understand why he must do so. If his repressed emotions are not released in nonviolent ways, they will seek expression through violence; this is not a threat but a fact of history. So I have not said to my people: "Get rid of your discontent." Rather, I have tried to say that this normal and healthy discontent can be channeled into the creative outlet of nonviolent direct action. And now this approach is being termed extremist.

27   But though I was initially disappointed at being categorized as an extremist, as I continued to think about the matter I gradually gained a measure of satisfaction from the label. Was not Jesus an extremist for love: "Love your enemies, bless them that curse you, do good for them that hate you, and pray for them which despitefully use you, and persecute you." Was not Amos an

extremist for justice: "Let justice roll down like waters and righteousness like an everflowing stream." Was not Paul an extremist for the Christian gospel: "I bear in my body the marks of the Lord Jesus." Was not Martin Luther an extremist: "Here I stand; I cannot do otherwise, so help me God." And John Bunyan: "I will stay in jail to the end of my days before I make a butchery of my conscience." And Abraham Lincoln: "This nation cannot survive half slave and half free." And Thomas Jefferson: "We hold these truths to be self-evident, that all men are created equal . . . " So the question is not whether we will be extremists, but what kind of extremists we will be. Will we be extremists for hate or for love? Will we be extremists for the preservation of injustice or for the extension of justice? In that dramatic scene on Calvary's hill three men were crucified. We must never forget that all three were crucified for the same crime—the crime of extremism. Two were extremists for immorality, and thus fell below their environment. The other, Jesus Christ, was an extremist for love, truth and goodness, and thereby rose above his environment. Perhaps the South, the nation and the world are in dire need of creative extremists.

28   I had hoped that the white moderate would see this need. Perhaps I was too optimistic; perhaps I expected too much. I suppose I should have realized that few members of the oppressor race can understand the deep groans and passionate yearnings of the oppressed race, and still fewer have the vision to see that injustice must be rooted out by strong, persistent and determined action. I am thankful, however, that some of our white brothers in the South have grasped the meaning of this social revolution and committed themselves to it. They are still too few in quantity, but they are big in quality. Some—such as Ralph McGill, Lillian Smith, Harry Golden, James McBride Dabbs, Ann Braden and Sarah Patton Boyle—have written about our struggle in eloquent and prophetic terms. Others have marched with us down nameless streets of the South. They have languished in filthy, roach-infested jails, suffering the abuse and brutality of policemen who view them as "dirty nigger-lovers." Unlike so many of their moderate brothers and sisters, they have recognized the urgency of the moment and sensed the need for powerful "action" antidotes to combat the disease of segregation. . . .

29   I hope the church as a whole will meet the challenge of this decisive hour. But even if the church does not come to the aid of justice, I have no despair about the future. I have no fear about the outcome of our struggle in Birmingham, even if our motives are at present misunderstood. We will reach the goal of freedom in Birmingham and all over the nation, because the goal of America is freedom. Abused and scorned though we may be, our destiny is tied up with America's destiny. Before the pilgrims landed at Plymouth, we were here. Before the pen of Jefferson etched the majestic words of the Declaration of Independence across the pages of history, we were here. For more than two centuries our forebears labored in this country without wages; they made cotton king; they built the homes of their masters while suffering gross injustice and shameful humiliation—and yet out of a bottomless vitality

they continued to thrive and develop. If the inexpressible cruelties of slavery could not stop us, the opposition we now face will surely fail. We will win our freedom because the sacred heritage of our nation and the eternal will of God are embodied in our echoing demands.

30   Before closing I feel impelled to mention one other point in your statement that has troubled me profoundly. You warmly commended the Birmingham police force for keeping "order" and "preventing violence." I doubt that you would have so warmly commended the police force if you had seen its dogs sinking their teeth into unarmed, nonviolent Negroes. I doubt that you would so quickly commend the policemen if you were to observe their ugly and inhumane treatment of Negroes here in the city jail; if you were to watch them push and curse old Negro women and young Negro girls; if you were to see them slap and kick old Negro men and young boys; if you were to observe them, as they did on two occasions, refuse to give us food because we wanted to sing our grace together. I cannot join you in your praise of the Birmingham police department.

31   It is true that the police have exercised a degree of discipline in handling the demonstrators. In this sense they have conducted themselves rather "nonviolently" in public. But for what purpose? To preserve the evil system of segregation. Over the past few years I have consistently preached that nonviolence demands that the means we use must be as pure as the ends we seek. I have tried to make clear that it is wrong to use immoral means to attain moral ends. But now I must affirm that it is just as wrong, or perhaps even more so, to use moral means to preserve immoral ends. Perhaps Mr. Connor and his policemen have been rather nonviolent in public, as was Chief Pritchett in Albany, Georgia, but they have used the moral means of nonviolence to maintain the immoral end of racial injustice. As T. S. Eliot has said: "The last temptation is the greatest treason: To do the right deed for the wrong reason."

32   I wish you had commended the Negro sit-inners and demonstrators of Birmingham for their sublime courage, their willingness to suffer and their amazing discipline in the midst of great provocation. One day the South will recognize its real heroes. They will be the James Merediths, with the noble sense of purpose that enables them to face jeering and hostile mobs, and with the agonizing loneliness that characterizes the life of the pioneer. They will be old, oppressed, battered Negro women, symbolized in a seventy-two-year-old woman in Montgomery, Alabama, who rose up with a sense of dignity and with her people decided not to ride segregated buses, and who responded with ungrammatical profundity to one who inquired about her weariness: "My feets is tired, but my soul is at rest." They will be the young high school and college students, the young ministers of the gospel and a host of their elders, courageously and nonviolently sitting in at lunch counters and willingly going to jail for conscience' sake. One day the South will know that when these disinherited children of God sat down at lunch counters, they were in reality standing up for what is best in the American dream and for the most sacred values in our Judaeo-Christian heritage, thereby bringing our

nation back to those great wells of democracy which were dug deep by the founding fathers in their formulation of the Constitution and the Declaration of Independence.

33   Never before have I written so long a letter. I'm afraid it is much too long to take your precious time. I can assure you that it would have been much shorter if I had been writing from a comfortable desk, but what else can one do when he is alone in a narrow jail cell, other than write long letters, think long thoughts and pray long prayers?

34   If I have said anything in this letter that overstates the truth and indicates an unreasonable impatience, I beg you to forgive me. If I have said anything that understates the truth and indicates my having a patience that allows me to settle for anything less than brotherhood, I beg God to forgive me.

35   I hope this letter finds you strong in the faith. I also hope that circumstances will soon make it possible for me to meet each of you, not as an integrationist or a civil-rights leader but as a fellow clergyman and a Christian brother. Let us all hope that the dark clouds of racial prejudice will soon pass away and the deep fog of misunderstanding will be lifted from our fear-drenched communities, and in some not too distant tomorrow the radiant stars of love and brotherhood will shine over our great nation with all their scintillating beauty.

Yours for the cause of Peace and Brotherhood,
MARTIN LUTHER KING, JR.

THE MIDDLE EAST

SHARING THE LAND AND THE LEGACY

Rami Khouri

1 When the state of Israel was created in 1948, the Jewish people realized a dream they had carried in their hearts since the destruction of the Second Temple, some 2,000 years ago. Their years of wandering, persecution and struggle had come to an end. Or so it was thought to be.

2   The reality is rather different, for since the establishment of Israel in 1948 Israel and the Arabs have fought five major wars. Israel has not had genuine peace and security. It has, thanks to massive American aid and the fervor of its own people, only enjoyed a military advantage. It has been able to defend itself, but not to find a place among the nation-states of the Middle East.

3   For the four million Palestinian people, the establishment of Israel as a Jewish state in 1948 marked the start of the Palestinian diaspora, of Palestinian homelessness and political disenfranchisement.

4   Let us forget, for the moment, the rights and wrongs of the past, and

apportion neither guilt, nor righteousness, in the history of Arab-Israeli warfare.

5   The challenge before the people of the Middle East today is not how to ascribe blame for the horrors of the past, but rather how to reconcile conflicting Arab and Israeli claims in order that we may all share the land of Palestine—and the promise of the future.

6   On the surface, political circumstances in the Middle East and further afield suggest that Arab-Israeli reconciliation is a distant and naive dream. But beneath the surface, things may be slightly less discouraging.

7   Consider the following:

1. In 1967, the Arab summit at Khartoum rejected negotiations, recognition or coexistence with Israel. In the 1982 Arab summit at Fez, the Arab world proposed a peace plan based on negotiations with Israel, leading to ultimate coexistence on the basis of an Israeli state living side-by-side with a Palestinian state. The shift in the Arab peace posture since 1967 has been dramatic, but insufficiently appreciated in the West.

8   2. In Israel, public opinion polls since 1967 have shown a consistent trend toward more and more Israelis who are willing to make peace with the Palestinians and the other Arab states on the basis of an Israeli withdrawal from parts or all of the occupied West Bank and Gaza. A small but growing number of Israeli politicians and peace groups have accepted the principle of the mutual and simultaneous self-determination of Israelis and Palestinians. The Israelis have realized most recently in Lebanon that military force can never resolve political disputes.

9   3. In the United States, the traditional concern for Israel's security has been increasingly matched by an appreciation of Palestinian rights. The Reagan initiative of September 1982 was a step forward in this respect, though it was immediately rejected by the Israeli government, and also failed to satisfy the Arab demand for Palestinian self-determination.

10   Efforts now taking place in the Middle East again aim to reinvigorate the forces of peace on both sides. Jordan and the Palestine Liberation Organization (PLO) reached agreement on February 11, [1985,] on a joint position that envisages a peaceful settlement of the Arab-Israeli conflict, based on Israeli statehood and security, and Palestinian self-determination. Egypt has made some specific proposals. Israel's response has left the door open for direct talks with a Jordanian-Palestinian team. The United States has tried to keep the momentum for peace alive.

11   The prospects for direct negotiations between Arabs and Israelis are distant, as always, but perhaps less distant than they were a few years ago. The opportunity that now challenges us all is nothing less than peace among all the children of Abraham—Christians, Moslems and Jews.

12   The Jewish people have secured their state, and fortified it militarily. But they have not secured that which should be more dear to them than any-

thing else in this world—the acceptance of their Arab brothers and sisters, their Semitic cousins, their Abrahamic family.

13   History has taught us all that genuine security does not come from the strength of guns, but rather from the mercy, forgiveness and acceptance of one's adversary. There are increasing numbers of Israelis and Arabs who have become convinced that warfare cannot resolve the Arab-Israeli conflict. It can only be resolved by assuring the rights of both Israelis and Palestinians, in the historical land of Palestine they both covet. . . .

14   An international consensus has emerged in recent years that envisages the resolution of the Arab-Israeli conflict through the satisfaction of Israeli demands for recognition and security, and of Palestinian demands for self-determination and security. In the Fez peace plan and the Jordan-PLO accord, the Arab world has outlined its vision of a Middle East at peace, with security guaranteed for Israel, a Palestinian state confederated with Jordan, and all the other Arab states.

15   The people of Israel and their many supporters in the West must soon decide: Is their objective the false security that comes from occupying Arab lands and denying Palestinian rights? Or is their objective the genuine security that can only emanate from a peace that satisfies Palestinian as well as Israeli demands?

16   For the first time since 1948, the Arab world is talking in terms of a negotiated, peaceful and permanent resolution of the conflict with Israel. We are talking about international guarantees for the security of all states in the region, including an Israeli and a Palestinian state.

17   The opportunity before us today will not remain on the table for very long. The history of the Arab-Israeli conflict is one of short-lived opportunities that have been missed because of inflexible political attitudes, and invariably replaced by a resurgent extremism on both sides.

18   A new opportunity now presents itself: An opportunity to satisfy Palestinian demands for the promise of national self-determination that Woodrow Wilson articulated for all the people of the free world in 1918. An opportunity for Israel and the Jewish people to enjoy the kind of genuine security they have sought unsuccessfully for two millennia. An opportunity for the Arab states to get on with the challenges of nation-building and fulfilling the vast potential of their people.

19   If this opportunity is to be seized, reasonable people on all sides will have to reinforce the conviction that peace, security and the right of self-determination, like liberty, are indivisible, and must be granted to both Israelis and Palestinians. If balance and reciprocity are our guidelines, the dream of a just peace can be attained. And the legacy of Abraham can be realized at last.

MAPS OF REVENGE

Meron Benvenisti

1   A little while ago, just before the Passover vacation, my son Yuval came home with the itinerary for his school outing. My father, who was there at the time, asked to see it. Glancing through it, I could see something was making him angry. "Why are all the place names in Arabic?" he demanded. "Don't they know in the Scouts that these places have Hebrew names?" His reaction was not surprising. My father, eighty-seven, a teacher and a geographer, has devoted his whole life to one thing: creating a new Hebrew map of Eretz Israel and instilling in young people a love of country. For years he has been a member of the official "naming committees" whose task it was to Hebraize all the names on the ordinance map of Eretz Israel and to name new Jewish settlements. His maps can be seen on the walls of classrooms throughout Israel. In fact the huge blue-brown-and-green wall map he drew is imprinted in the visual memory of hundreds of thousands of Israelis. . . .

2   Changing place names in order to arrive at a Hebrew map of Eretz Israel was considered by my father a sacred task. He was one of Israel's first geographers—awarded the Israel Prize for his life's work. And now, after sixty years, that his own grandson should come to him with Arab names instead of Hebrew ones seemed to him tantamount to sacrilege. Like all immigrant societies, we attempted to erase all alien names, but here the analogy becomes complicated because we were not simply an immigrant society or an army of conquerors. At our coming, we reestablished contact with those same landscapes and places from which we had been physically removed for two thousand years but whose names we had always preserved. We carried around with us for centuries our *geographia sacra,* not only biblical names but all the mishnaic and talmudic names. Wherever we were dispersed—in France, Germany, Egypt, Persia—we would study texts and learn about the rosters of priestly duty in the Temple enumerating by turn their home villages in the Galilee. People who knew nothing about the physical reality of those villages knew their names by heart. So when we returned to the land it was the most natural thing to seek out those ancient places and identify them. . . .

3   From a very early age, perhaps four or five, I and my brother would accompany my father on his Sabbath expeditions. And so it was that the Arab names of villages and mountains, groves and springs became those of my childhood. I remember the names perfectly—they became second nature to me—and when I travel around the country I unfailingly recall the previous names. The Arab names. I have a friend who lives in a Jewish village in the Jerusalem corridor. When he mentions the Hebrew name Shoevah, I immediately think of it as Saris, the Arab name. . . .

4   The Hebrew map of Israel constitutes one stratum in my consciousness,

underlaid by another stratum of the previous Arab map. Those names turn me and anyone who was born into them into sons of the same homeland—but also into mortal enemies. I can't help but reflect on the irony that my father, by taking me on his trips and hoping to instill in me the love of our Hebrew homeland, imprinted in my memory, along with the new names, the names he wished to eradicate.

5   This bring me, strangely enough, to the Lebanon war. I was aware for quite some time that Palestinian research institutes in Beirut were compiling files on each Palestinian village in Israel. Since the beginning of the war I wondered about the fate of those files. I was fairly sure that General Sharon and General Eitan would search them out, seize them, and destroy them in order to complete the eradication of Arab Palestine. This is what eventually happened when the Israeli Army entered West Beirut. I knew that some of the information in those files was purely imaginary and was used as propaganda against my country. Every refugee, even the lowliest, is convinced that he used to own at least a hundred acres of orchards and a large house in Israel. It is an understandable tendency to magnify the scale of what they lost. But the point is—and there lies the irony and the tragedy—that they have created their own *geographia sacra,* just as we did in our Diaspora. Their map-making is the answer to our Hebrew, Israeli map. They are trying by an act of will to recreate and preserve the old reality, the one we erased in order to create our own. Their map-making is as far removed from reality as our memorizing the list of villages of the priestly roster.

6   Not only are the refugee camps organized by sections according to the villages in Palestine from which the refugees originated, their children are taught exclusively with reference to the pre-1948 map of Palestine. On their maps hundreds of Palestinian villages, long since destroyed, are shown, but the Jewish cities, settlements, roads, and ports are omitted. Everything that happened subsequent to their departure is perceived as an aberration. Their refusal to cope with the stark and cruel reality causes them to believe that what the Jews print on their maps is sheer fiction. . . .

7   At this point in our conflict, maps cease being geographical and turn into an act of faith, a call for action, for revenge. I'll destroy your map as you have destroyed mine. A zero-sum game that is played out not only in words and symbols, but in concrete deeds of destruction.

8   There is no point in asking who started. It is true that my father had started his Hebrew map to gain symbolic possession of his ancestral land. But he believed that he was doing so peaceably, not disinheriting anybody. Indeed he and most of his generation genuinely believed that there was enough room in the country for everybody. The Palestinians did not take him seriously. For them he was a romantic Westerner, just like the British and German explorers who came before him and left, with their strange compasses, sextants, and theodolites. They did not realize that his map-making was of a different sort, that he intended to settle down and teach his children the names he invented, and by so doing, to perpetuate them and thus transform

symbolic possession into actual possession. When the Arabs realized the danger, it was too late. They tried to destroy my father physically, but they failed. He offered them compromises, but they rejected them. Finally an all-out war decided the issue; they were driven out, and his map triumphed. Then we set out to transform the land, to construct our own edifices, to plan our own orchards. But we also deliberately destroyed the remnants our enemies left lest they come back and attempt to lay claim to it. We knew that had they won they would have destroyed our work. But we won, so we became the destroyers. Who is the victim? Who is the culprit? Who is the judge? . . .

9　　Almost two million Palestinians still live on their land, cherish it, and are determined to preserve their own map and physical forms. It is impossible to erase their contribution to the landscape of our shared homeland, no matter how hard people try. Someone, someday, will raise the question and will demand an answer. Are we ready to merge the two maps? Are we ready to stop eradicating each other's names? When such questions can be asked, perhaps the dissonance and conflict that plague so many Israelis will be resolved.

10　　When at a certain stage I left my own immediate surroundings to seek out a more universal dimension to my experiences, I found myself in the Grand Opera House of Belfast. The first performance of Brian Friel's *Translations* was given in the Opera House—rebuilt after twenty-four bombing incidents—to an all-Catholic audience. The play dealt with the substitution of an English map of Ireland for the original, the ultimate symbolic expression of possession. When the play ended, I said to my friend, a Catholic, "You know what? We've been doing the same thing all along—translating, changing names, creating a new reality." My friend regarded me for a moment with an expression of the utmost sadness and said at last, "Well, if that's the case, may God have mercy on you all!"

Selected References

Chapter 1

Aristotle. *The Rhetoric of Aristotle.* Trans. Lane Cooper. Englewood Cliffs, NJ: Prentice-Hall, 1960.

Booth, Wayne C. *Now Don't Try to Reason with Me.* Chicago: The University of Chicago Press, 1972.

Brooks, Cleanth, and Robert Penn Warren. *Modern Rhetoric.* New York: Harcourt, Brace & World, 1970.

Corbett, Edward P. J. *Classical Rhetoric for the Modern Student.* 3rd ed. New York: Oxford University Press, 1990.

Jordan, John E., ed. *Questions of Rhetoric.* New York: Holt, Rinehart, & Winston, Inc., 1971.

Mannes, Marya. "How Do You Know It's Good?" In *But Will It Sell?* Philadelphia: J. B. Lippincott Co., 1964.

Plato. *Apology, Crito,* and *Phaedrus.* Trans. Jowett. *Dialogues of Plato,* Ed. Justin D. Kaplan. New York: Washington Square Press, 1950. (And various other editions.)

Pospesel, Howard, and David Marans. *Arguments: Deductive Logic Exercises.* 2nd ed. Englewood Cliffs, NJ: Prentice-Hall, 1978.

Robinson, James Harvey. "On Various Kinds of Thinking." *The Mind in the Making.* New York: Harper & Bros., 1921.

Weaver, Richard M. *Language Is Sermonic.* Baton Rouge, LA: Louisiana State University Press, 1970.

Chapter 2

Baker, Sheridan. *The Complete Stylist and Handbook.* 3rd ed. New York: Harcourt, 1989.

Booth, Wayne C. "The Rhetorical Stance." *Now Don't Try to Reason With Me: Essays and Ironies for a Credulous Age.* Chicago: The University of Chicago Press, 1972.

Burke, Kenneth. *A Rhetoric of Motives.* Berkeley and Los Angeles, CA: University of California Press, 1969. 43–65.

Enos, Richard Leo. "Ciceronian *Disposito* as an Architecture for Creativity in Composition: A Note for the Affirmative." *Rhetoric Review* 4.1 (September 1985): 108–110.

Green, Lawrence D. "Enthymemic Invention and Structural Prediction." *College English* 41 (February 1980): 623–34.

Larson, Richard L. "Discovery Through Questioning: A Plan for Teaching Rhetorical Invention." *College English* 30 (November 1968): 132–33.

Long, Russell C. "Writer-Audience Relationships: Analysis or Invention?" *College Composition and Communication* 31 (May 1980): 221–26.

Lucas, F. L. "Party of One" ("What Is Style?"). *Holiday,* March 1960: 11, 14–16, 18–21.

Ong, Walter J. "The Writer's Audience Is Always a Fiction." *PMLA* 90 (1975): 9–21.

Park, Douglas B. "The Meaning of 'Audience.'" *College English* 44 (March 1982): 247–57.

Chapter 3

Charlton, James, ed. *The Writer's Quotation Book*, 3rd ed. Yonkers, NY: The Pushcart Press, 1991.

Copi, Irving. *Introduction to Logic,* 7th ed. New York: Macmillan, 1986. 127–73.

Langer, Susanne K. "The Lords of Creation." *Fortune,* Jan. 1944.

Munson, Ronald. *The Way of Words: An Informal Logic.* Boston: Houghton Mifflin, 1976. 98–140.

Runkle, Gerald. *Good Thinking: An Introduction to Logic.* 3rd ed. New York: Harcourt, 1991.

Sindler, Allan P. *Bakke, DeFunis, and Minority Admissions.* New York: Longman, 1978.

Stevens, Wallace: "The Noble Rider and the Sound of Words." In *The Necessary Angel: Essays on Reality and the Imagination.* New York: Random House-Vintage, 1951.

Szasz, Thomas. *The Second Sin.* Garden City, NY: Anchor Press, 1973.

Chapter 4

Barzun, Jacques, and Henry Graff. *The Modern Researcher*, 4th ed. New York: Harcourt, 1985.

Gibaldi, Joseph, and Walter S. Achtert. *MLA Handbook for Writers of Research Papers.* 3rd ed. New York: The Modern Language Association of America, 1988.

Harris, Sherwood, ed. *The New York Public Library Book of How and Where to Look It Up.* New York: Prentice, 1991.

Kraus, Keith. *Murder, Mischief, and Mayhem: A Process for Creative Research Papers.* Urbana, IL: National Council of Teachers of English, 1978.

Newman, Robert P., and Dale R. Newman. *Evidence.* Boston: Houghton Mifflin, 1969.

Tryzna, Thomas. "Approaches to Research Writing: A Review of Handbooks with Some Suggestions." *College Composition and Communication* 34 (May 1983): 202–7.

van Leunen, Mary-Claire. *A Handbook for Scholars.* 2nd ed. New York: Knopf, 1992.

Chapter 5

Ayer, Alfred Jules. *Language, Truth, and Logic,* 2nd ed. New York: Dover, 1946.

Beardsley, Monroe C. *Thinking Straight: Principles of Reasoning for Readers and Writers,* 4th ed. Englewood Cliffs, NJ: Prentice-Hall, 1976.

———. *Writing With Reason: Logic for Composition.* Englewood Cliffs, NJ: Prentice-Hall, 1976.

Cohen, Morris R. *A Preface to Logic.* New York: Holt, Rinehart & Winston, Inc., 1965.

Harris, Sydney J. *For the Time Being.* Boston: Houghton Mifflin Co., 1972.

Watson, James. *The Double Helix.* New York: Atheneum, 1968.

Winterowd, W. Ross. *Rhetoric: A Synthesis.* New York: Holt, Rinehart & Winston, Inc., 1968.

Chapter 6

Beardsley, Monroe C. *Thinking Straight: Principles of Reasoning for Readers and Writers,* 4th ed. Englewood Cliffs, NJ: Prentice-Hall, 1976.

———. *Writing With Reason: Logic for Composition.* Englewood Cliffs, NJ: Prentice-Hall, 1975.

Castaneda, Hector Neri. "On a Proposed Revolution in Logic." *Philosophy of Science* 27 (1960): 279–92.

Cooley, J. C. "On Mr. Toulmin's Revolution in Logic." *Journal of Philosophy* 56 (1959): 297–319.

Copi, Irving R. *An Introduction to Logic,* 7th ed. New York: Macmillan, 1988.

Corbett, Edward P. J. *Classical Rhetoric for the Modern Student.* 3rd ed. New York: Oxford UP, 1990.

Emmet, E. R. *Handbook of Logic: The Use of Reason.* Totowa, NJ: Littlefield, Adams & Co., 1974.

Fulkerson, Richard. "Logic and Teachers of English?" *Rhetoric Review* 4.2 (January 1986): 198–207.

Johnson, Ralph H. "Toulmin's Bold Experiment." *Informal Logic Newsletter.* 3.2 (1981): 16–27 and 3.3 (1981): 13–20.

Plato. *Plato: Five Dialogues.* Trans. G. M. A. Grube. Indianapolis: Hackett Publishing Co., 1982.

Salmon, Wesley C. *Logic.* 3rd ed. Englewood Cliffs, NJ: Prentice-Hall, 1984.

Toulmin, Stephen C. *The Uses of Argument.* Cambridge: Cambridge University Press, 1964.

Weaver, Richard M. *Composition.* New York: Henry Holt, 1957.

Chapter 7

Kahane, Howard. *Logic and Contemporary Rhetoric: The Use of Reason in Everyday Life,* 6th ed. Belmont, CA: Wadsworth 1, 1992.

Kilgore, William. *An Introductory Logic,* 2nd ed. New York: Holt, Rinehart & Winston, 1979. 11–29.

Munson, Ronald. *The Way of Words: An Informal Logic.* Boston: Houghton Mifflin Co., 1976. 260–314.

Rank, Hugh. "Teaching about Public Persuasion: Rationale and a Schema." Ed. Daniel Dieterich. *Teaching about Doublespeak.* Urbana, IL: National Council of Teachers of English, 1976.

Roll, Charles W., and Albert H. Cantril. *Polls: Their Use and Misuse in Politics.* Cabin John, MD: Seven Locks Press, 1972.

Chapter 8

Brostoff, Anita. "Coherence: 'Next to' Is Not 'Connected to.' " *College Composition and Communication* 32 (October 1981): 278–94.

Gibson, Walker. *Persona: A Style Study for Readers and Writers.* New York: Random House, 1969.

———. *Tough, Sweet, and Stuffy.* Bloomington, IN: Indiana UP, 1966. 28–54.

Winterowd, Ross, "The Grammar of Coherence." *College English* 31 (May 1970): 828–35.

Zinsser, William. *On Writing Well,* 4th ed. New York: Harper, 1990.

Chapter 9

Altick, Richard D. and Andrea Lunsford. *Preface to Critical Reading,* 6th ed. New York: Harcourt, 1984.

Corbett, Edward P. J. *Classical Rhetoric for the Modern Student,* 3rd ed. New York: Oxford UP, 1990.

Gibson, Walker. *Persona: A Style Study for Readers and Writers.* New York: Random House, 1969.

Lakoff, George, and Mark Johnson. *Metaphors We Live By.* Chicago: The University of Chicago Press, 1980.

Lucas, F. L. "Party of One" ("What Is Style?"). *Holiday,* March 1960. 11, 14–16, 18–21.

Strunk, William, and E. B. White. *The Elements of Style,* 3rd ed. New York: Macmillan, 1979.

Zinsser, William. *On Writing Well,* 4th ed. New York: Harper, 1990.

Acknowledgments

Chapter 1

p. 1: Extract from "Language Is Sermonic" by Richard Weaver. Reprinted by permission of Louisiana State University Press.

p. 3: Raphael, *The School of Athens.* Alinari/Art Resource.

pp. 23–24: Debbie Sapp, "What So Proudly We Hailed?" (student essay). Reprinted by permission of the author.

pp. 25–26: Lindsay Moran, "Thinking and Rethinking" (student essay). Reprinted by permission of the author.

pp. 27–28: Ellen Goodman, "Celebrate Free Speech: Say What You Think." Copyright 1991. Reprinted by permission of the *Boston Globe.*

Chapter 2

p. 31: Extract from Mark Van Doren, *Liberal Education.* Reprinted by permission of Dorothy Van Doren. Copyright held by Dorothy G. Van Doren.

pp. 53–54: Erik Johnson, "Group Discussions Are Beneficial" (student essay). Reprinted by permission of the author.

pp. 55–57: Linda Chavez, "Pay Equity Is Unfair to Women." Reprinted by permission of *Fortune,* Inc. Copyright © 1985.

Chapter 3

p. 66: Extract from Allan P. Sindler, *Bakke, DeFunis, and Minority Admissions.* Copyright © 1978 by Longman, Inc. Reprinted by permission.

pp. 69–70: Linda Waddle, "If It Isn't Censorship, What Is It?" Reprinted by permission of the author.

pp. 71–72: Amy Taylor Haun, "What Lasts" (student essay). Reprinted by permission of the author.

pp. 73–76: Paul Rudnick, "Born to be Mild." *Spy* reprinted by permission of UFS, Inc.

Chapter 4

p. 82: Excerpt from the Ann Landers column. Reprinted by permission of News America Syndicate. Copyright by Ann Landers and News America Syndicate.

pp. 112–113: Extract from Lynn Quitman Troyka, *Simon & Schuster Handbook for Writers.* Copyright © 1987 by Lynn Quitman Troyka. Reprinted by permission of Prentice Hall.

pp. 114–119: Excerpt from S. I. Hayakawa and Alan Hayakawa, *Language in Thought and Action,* 5th ed. Copyright © 1989 by S. I. Hayakawa and Alan R. Hayakawa. Reprinted by permission of Harcourt Brace & Co., Inc.

pp. 120–131: Dequa Thompson, "The Problems with Television News" (student essay). Reprinted by permission of the author.

Chapter 5

pp. 139–140: Extract from Sydney J. Harris, "How to Keep the Air Clean." Reprinted from *For the Time Being* by Sydney J. Harris. Copyright © 1982 by Sydney J. Harris. Copyright © 1969, 1970, 1971, 1972 by Publishers-Hall Syndicate. Reprinted by permission of Houghton Mifflin Company.

pp. 153–155: Excerpt from Albert Z. Carr, "Is Business Bluffing Ethical?" *Harvard Business Review,* January/February 1968. Copyright © 1968 by the President and Fellows of Harvard College; all rights reserved. Reprinted by permission of *Harvard Business Review.*

pp. 156–158: Judy (Syfers) Brady, "Why I Want a Wife," *Ms.,* Spring 1972. Reprinted by permission of the author.

pp. 159–161: Suzanna Gratia, "Concealed Weapons Can Save Lives." Reprinted by permission of the author.

Chapter 6

pp. 185–187: Barbara Tuchman, "Should We Abolish the Presidency?" Reprinted from *Practicing History* by Barbara Tuchman. Copyright © 1981 by Alma Tuchman, Lucy T. Eisenberg, and Jessica Tuchman Matthews. Reprinted by permission of Alfred A. Knopf, Inc.

pp. 190–195: Arthur C. Clarke, "We'll Never Conquer Space." Reprinted by permission of the author and the author's agents, Scott Meredith Literary Agency, Inc., 845 Third Avenue, New York, New York 10022.

pp. 196–198: Hosea L. Martin, "A Few Kind Words for Affirmative Action." Reprinted by permission of the author.

Chapter 7

pp. 219–220: T. J. Stone, "Lies, Fallacies, and Santa Claus" (student essay). Reprinted by permission of the author.

pp. 221–226: Jeffrey Schrank, "The Language of Advertising Claims." Reprinted by permission of *Media and Methods,* America's Magazine of the Teaching Technologies.

p. 228: True cigarette advertisement. Reprinted by permission of Lorillard, Inc.

p. 229: North by Northeast advertisement. Copyright © 1981 by North by Northeast Co. Reprinted by permission.

p. 230: Instant Memory advertisement. Reprinted by permission of the Institute of Advanced Thinking.

p. 231: Bost gold ball advertisement. Copyright © 1987 by Bost Enterprises, Inc. Reprinted by permission.

pp. 232–240: Max Shulman, "Love Is a Fallacy." Copyright © 1951, 1979 by Max Shulman. Reprinted by permission of Harold Matson Company, Inc.

Chapter 8

pp. 275–276: Kathy Taylor, "Conformity and Nonconformity: The Prices Paid for Each" (student essay). Reprinted by permission of the author.

pp. 276–278: Kathy Taylor, "Nonconformity: The Price and the Payoff" (student essay). Reprinted by permission of the author.

Chapter 9

pp. 306–309: Excerpt from William James, "Remarks at the Peace Banquet." Copyright by the Atlantic Monthly Company. Reprinted by permission.

pp. 310–313: Excerpt from Lewis Lapham, "Sculptures in Snow." Copyright © 1981 by *Harper's Magazine.* All rights reserved. Reprinted from the August issue by special permission.

Chapter 10

pp. 316–318: Robert E. Coulson, "Let's Not Get Out the Vote." Copyright © 1955. Reprinted by permission of Rose S. Coulson, Executor of the Estate of Robert E. Coulson.

pp. 319–320: Alan Wertheimer, "For Compulsory Voting." Copyright © 1976 by The New York Times Company. Reprinted by permission.

pp. 320–322: Meg Greenfield, "Throw the Rascals Out" ("The Handiwork of Believers"). From *Newsweek,* © 1990, Newsweek, Inc. All rights reserved. Reprinted by permission.

pp. 322–325: Specified abridgment of Irving Kristol, "Pornography, Obscenity, and the Case for Censorship." Copyright © 1971 by Irving Kristol. Reprinted by permission of Irving Kristol.

pp. 325–327: Eli M. Oboler, "Defending Intellectual Freedom." Reprinted by permission of the American Library Association from *Newsletter of Intellectual Freedom* 21(1): 30 (Jan. 1972).

pp. 327–329: Nadine Gordimer, "Censorship and Its Aftermath." Reprinted by permission of the author.

pp. 329–331: William J. Bennett, "We Need Routine Testing for AIDS." Reprinted by permission of *The Wall Street Journal,* Dow Jones & Co., Inc. Copyright © 1986. All rights reserved.

pp. 332–336: Arthur S. Leonard, "AIDS: The Legal Epidemic." Copyright © 1987 by *The New York Native.* Reprinted by permission of *The New York Native.*

Index

A

Abstracts, 87
Achtert, Walter S., 374
Adams, John, 94
Additional information transition, 271
Ad hominem, 202, 207
Ad misericordiam, 202
Adoption Therapist, 299
Ad populum, 202
Advertising claims, 222–226
Almanacs, 87
Alternative (or disjunctive) argument, 180–181,
   182–183
Altick, Richard D., 376
American Heritage Dictionary, 64
Analogy, 134, 265
   argument from, 137–142
      evaluating, 138–139
   faulty, 202, 204–205
   literal, 135, 137–138
   metaphorical, 136, 138
Anaphora, 287
Angelou, Maya, 289
Antecedent clause, 181
Antithesis, 287–288
Appeal to pity fallacy, 201–203
Appeal to popular sentiments fallacy, 202, 203
A priori premises, 4–5, 22
Argument(s), 1–30
   from analogy, 137–142
   categorical, 180
   from cause or effect, 135, 142–147

creating, 31–58
development of, 59–78, 79–133
   checking, 245–257
dimensions of, 14, 22
distinguished from persuasion, 1–2
either/or (alternative or disjunctive), 180–181,
   182–183
from examples, 148–152
fallacy in, 201–205
focusing, 43
if/then (hypothetical), 180–181, 181–182
invention of, 38
limiting, with qualifiers, 11–12
need for, 4–5
parameters of, 32
point-by-point, 254
relationships in, 5–14
revising, 242–279, 280–314
rhetorical context of, 32–37
roles of definition in, 65–69
shaping, 50–53
testing, 134–162, 163–199, 200–241
verbal signals of, 7–8
Argumentative edge, 80
Aristotle, 63, 288, 373
Assertion, 5–6
   arguable, 6
Association, guilt by, 174, 202, 205
Assumptions, 9–10, 22
Audience, 33–35
   analysis of, 36
Austen, Jane, 152

Authoritative testimony, 81–83
Ayer, Alfred Jules, 374

B

Baker, Sheridan, 40, 80, 373
Barber, Benjamin R., 184
Barnes, Fred, 13
Barnouw, Erik, 147
Barthes, Roland, 64
Barzun, Jacques, 374
Beardsley, Monroe C., 374, 375
Begging the question, 174, 175–176, 202, 204
Bennett, William J., 250, 329–331
Benvenisti, Meron, 255, 370–372
Bibliographies, 86
Bird, Caroline, 347–351
Birmingham clergy, 357–358
Black or white fallacy, 183, 204
Blanchard, Keith, 64
Blinder, Alan S., 84
Bloom, Allan, 64
Bonaparte, Napoleon, 304
Bonhoeffer, Dietrich, 305
Boorstin, Daniel, 152
Booth, Wayne, 304, 373
Brady, Judy, 156–158
Brandt, Siegmund, 64
Brimelow, Peter, 11, 83–84
Brinkley, David, 132
Brooks, Cleanth, 373
Brostoff, Anita, 375
BRS Information Technologies, 89
Bruner, Jerome Seymour, 134
Buckley, William F., Jr., 288
Bulletins, 88
Burke, Kenneth, 373
Burnam, Tom, 136
Business Week, 84
Byron, William J., 351–356

C

Caldwell, Christopher, 184
Cantril, Albert H., 84, 375
Carpenter, C.C.J., 358
Carr, Albert Z., 153–155, 161, 279
Carr, Edward Hallet, 141

Carroll, Lewis, 59
Castaneda, Hector Neri, 375
Categorical arguments, 180
Causal arguments, 135, 142–147
    evaluating, 144–146
Causes
    false, 205
    necessary, 143
    necessary and sufficient, 144
    sufficient, 143–144
Charged language, 16
Charlton, James, 374
Chavez, Linda, 55–56
Chesterton, G. K., 80
Churchill, Winston, 289
Ciardi, John, 305
Circular reasoning, 174, 202, 204
Citations
    in humanities, 109–112
    legal, 112
    in natural sciences, 113–114
    in social sciences, 112–113
Claiborne, Robert, 265
Claims, 5, 7, 22
    in advertising, 222–226
Clarity, 243
Clarke, Arthur C., 190–195, 199, 249
Classes, 7
Cleaver, Eldridge, 304
Climactic order, 288
Cohen, Morris R., 374
Coherence, 243, 271
    revising for, 265–268, 272
Colloquial diction, 292, 296
Colloquial words, 295
Common knowledge, body of, 108
Comparison, 61
Comparison transitions, 271
Completeness, 243
    paragraph, revising for, 263–265
    testing for, 244–245
"Compliment the consumer" claim, 226
CompuServe Information Services, Inc., 89
Computerized information sources, 89
Concession transitions, 271
Conciseness, revising for, 298
Conclusion, 5, 7, 245, 255–257
Conclusion transitions, 271
Conditions for use, 61

Confirmation, 245, 252–253
Consequences, 44–46
Consequent clause, 181
Context, rhetorical, 32–37
Contradictions, finding and resolving, 41–43
Contrast, 61
Contrast transitions, 271
Cooley, J. C., 375
Copi, Irving, 68, 374, 375
Corbett, Edward P. J., 373, 375, 376
Cordes, Helen, 151
Coulson, Robert E., 316–318
Counterargument, fallacy in, 202, 206–209
Craig, Will, 262, 263
Creativity, in research, 79–81
Creedon, Jeremiah, 65

D

Dahmen, Hans Dieter, 64
Dallas Morning News, 13, 179, 180, 211
Darrow, Clarence, 254, 339–344
Database of Databases, 89
Databases, 89
  selected sources, 89–90
Data Informer, 89
Day, Clarence, 106
Deane, Nancy Hilts, 108
Deduction, 134, 164–165, 184
  in fiction and fact, 163–164
Definitions, 60–62
  to clarify, 66–67
  to control, 67–68
  how to judge, 62–63
  persuasive, 68–69
  questions of, 40
  reportive, 60–61
  roles of, in argument, 65–69
  standards of clarity and completeness, 62
  stipulative, 60, 61–62
DeRogatis, Jim, 18
Development, 59–78, 79–133
  checking, 245–257
  enthymeme, guidelines for, 50
  thesis, 37–46
Diagrams, 168–170
Dialog Information Services, Inc., 89
Diction, 282
  colloquial, 292, 296

formal, 292, 296
  informal, 292, 296
  levels of, 292–298
Didion, Joan, 287
Disagreement, apparent, 43
Disjunctive argument, 180–181, 182–183
Documented essays, evidence in, 102–107
Downing, Colette, 21
Doyle, Arthur Conan, 163
Durick, Joseph A., 358

E

Either/or fallacy, 204
Either/or arguments, 180–181, 182–183
Ellipsis, 270, 287
Ellmann, Richard, 295
Emerson, Ralph Waldo, 287
Emmet, E. R., 141, 375
Emotional appeal, 14, 15–17, 22
Emphasis transitions, 271
Encyclopedias, 85–86
Endorsements, 225
Enos, Richard Leo, 373
Enthymeme, 47, 171, 177–178
  evaluating, 52
  guidelines for developing, 50
  rules for constructing, 47–49
  as thesis, 46–50
Epstein, Joseph, 273
Equivocation, 174
Ethical appeal, 14, 18–20, 22
Ethics, of persuasion, 2–4
Ethos, 19, 243
Etymology, 61
Evidence, 42, 43, 265. *See also* Research
  background and historical, locating, 85–86
  contrary, lack of, 202, 206
  current, locating, 86–89
  in documented essays and research papers,
    102–107
  evaluating, 94–99
  finding, 81–93
  kinds of, 81–85
  primary, 95–96
  recent, 95
  representative, 95, 98
  secondary, 95
  selection of, 16

Evidence *(cont.)*
  sufficient, 95, 99
  unbiased, 95, 96–98
Examples, 61, 81, 135, 265
  arguments from, 148–152
    evaluating, 148–150
Example transitions, 271
Explanation, 43
Exposition, 245, 252

F

Fact(s), 42, 95
  conflicting, 43
  questions of, 40
  statements of, 6
Fallacy, 200–201. *See also specific fallacy*
  in arguments, 201–205
  common, 202
  in counterarguments, 202, 206–209
  detecting, 209–210
  formal, 173–176
  kinds of, 201
False cause, 205
False dilemma, 202, 204
Faulty analogy, 202, 204–205
Feidelson, Charles, Jr., 295
Figures of speech, 300–301
Fikes, Stacy, 253
Fitzgerald, F. Scott, 315
Forbes, 83–84
Formal diction, 292, 296
Frank, T. C., 16
Freud, Sigmund, 94
Fulkerson, Richard, 375

G

Galbraith, John Kenneth, 147, 283, 304
Gallup Poll of Public Opinion, 100, 101
Gambler's fallacy, 149
Gardner, John, 301
Generalizations
  considerations for, 150
  hasty, 202, 205
  limiting, 151
Geronimus, Arline T., 84
Gibaldi, Joseph, 374

Gibran, Kahlil, 77
Gibson, Walker, 376
Goodman, Ellen, 27–28, 249
Gordimer, Nadine, 327–329
Gould, Stephen Jay, 288
Graff, Henry, 374
Grafman, Milton L., 358
Grammatical patterns, repetition of, 267–268
Granger's Index to Poetry, 101
Gratia, Suzanna, 159–161
Gray Panthers, 203
Green, Lawrence D., 374
Greenfield, Meg, 320–322
Gregory, Dick, 211
Grounds, 5
Guilt by association, 174, 202, 205

H

Hacker, Andrew, 64
Halberstam, David, 97–98
HALT (Help Abolish Legal Tyranny), 203
Hardin, Paul, 358
Harmon, Nolan B., 358
Harris, Sherwood, 374
Harris, Sydney J., 140, 375
Harvard Dictionary of Music, 100
Hayakawa, S. I., 43, 114–119, 132
Helgerson, Martha W., 295
Holmes, Sherlock, 198
Holoway, Marguerite, 265
Howitt, Mary, 200
Huan, Amy Taylor, 71–72
Huff, Darrell, 92
Hyperbole, 304
Hypothetical argument, 180–181, 181–182

I

Ideas
  conflicting, 43
  topic, 264
If/then arguments, 180–181, 181–182
Illustration, 43
Indexes, 87–88
Induction, 134, 164–165
  patterns of, 134–137
  scientific, 135

Influences, 44–46
Informal diction, 292, 296
Information Please Almanac, 100
Introduction, 245–246
    autobiographical, 246, 251
    categories of, 246
    concession, 246, 250–251
    corrective, 246, 248–249
    inquisitive, 246, 247–248
    kinds to be avoided, 251–252
    major premise, 246, 249–250
    narrative, 246, 248
    paradoxical, 246, 249
    preparatory, 246, 247
Invented reader, 35–37
Irony, 304
Isaac Asimov's Book of Facts, 101

J

James, William, 301, 302, 306–309, 314
Jefferson, Thomas, 288
Johnson, Mark, 376
Johnson, Ralph H., 375
Johnson, Samuel, 62, 210
Joint Method of Agreement and Difference, 145
Jordan, John E., 373
Jordan, Suzanne Britt, 278

K

Kael, Pauline, 305
Kahane, Howard, 375
Keenan, John, 304
Kennedy, Edward, 64
Kennedy, John F., 105, 288
Kennedy, X. J., 150
Key terms, 264
    repetition of, 267
Khouri, Rami, 367–369
Kilgore, William, 375
Kimble, Gregory A., 92
King, Martin Luther, Jr., 251, 254, 358–367
Knowledge, personal, 90–91
Korenman, Sanders D., 84
Kraus, Keith, 374
Krim, Mathilde, 336–339

Kristol, Irving, 212, 255, 279, 304, 322–325
Kuhn, Thomas, 63
Kuhse, Helga, 105
Kushner, Harold S., 21

L

Labels, conflicting, 43
Lakoff, George, 376
Landers, Ann, 82
Langer, Susanne K., 374
Language, charged, 16
Lapham, Lewis, 257, 279, 301, 310–313
Larson, Richard L., 374
Larson, Roy E., 210
Legal citations, 112
Leonard, Arthur S., 332–336
Lewis, Bill, 281
Lewis, C. S., 344–347
Lewis, Sinclair, 305
Library of Congress Subject Headings, 85
Lichter, Linda, 83
Lichter, Robert, 83
Lippmann, Walter, 270–271, 315
Lists of works cited, forms for, 111–112
Literal analogy, 135, 137–138
Logic
    limitations of, 176–177
    sentence, 290–291
Logical appeal, 14–15, 22
Logical clause transition, 271
Logical outcome transition, 271
Long, Russell C., 374
Lucas, F. L., 35, 287, 302, 313, 374, 376
Lunsford, Andrea, 376

M

Mabry, Marcus, 11
Macauley, Thomas, 105
Macro-revision, 244–262
Major premise introduction, 246, 249–250
Mannes, Marya, 28, 287, 373
Marans, David, 373
Marks, Albert, Jr., 214
Martin, Hosea L., 196–198, 199
Martin, Judith, 306

Marvell, Andrew, 65
McCabe, Casey, 147
McClelland, Doug, 148
McLuhan, Marshall, 241
Mencken, H. L., 287
Metaphor, 301–302
Metaphorical analogy, 136, 138
Method of Agreement, 144
Method of Difference, 144–145
Micro-revision, 262–272
Middle term, undistributed, 175–176, 205
Mill, John Stuart, 144
Miller, Arthur, 20
Milli Vanilli, 26
Mill's Methods, 144
Momaday, N. Scott, 106
Moran, Lindsay, 25–26
Morgan, Robin, 213
Munson, Ronald, 374, 375
Murphey, Gib, 280
Murray, George M., 358
Myers, Miles, 141

N

Nabokov, Vladimir, 210
Nadler, Morton, 97
Naison, Mark, 18
National Right to Life Committee, Inc., 203
New Hampshire Supreme Court, 15
Newman, Dale, 83, 374
Newman, Robert, 83, 374
Newsweek, 13, 17, 264
Nixon, Richard M., 215–218, 241
Non sequitur, 201
Notable American Women, 100

O

Objections, trivial, 202, 208–209
Oboler, Eli M., 257, 325–327
Ong, Walter, 35, 374
Organization, 243
  checking, 245–257
O'Rourke, P. J., 64, 179
Overgeneralization, 175
Oversimplification, 202, 206
Overstatement, 304

P

Palmer, Pam, 142
Paradox, 43, 304–305
Paragraph completeness, revising for, 263–265
Paragraph unity, revising for, 262–263
Parallelism, 267–268, 269, 270, 287–288
Paraphrasing, 102–103
Parenthetical citations
  punctuation in, 110–111
  what to include in, 110, 112–113
Park, Douglas B., 374
Pavlov, Ivan Petrovich, 79
Penthouse, 212
Persona, 2, 19–20
Personal attack, 202, 207
Personal knowledge, 90–91
Personal research, 90–93
  guidelines for, 91
Personal statements, 19
Persons, 168
Persuasion, 1–30
  distinguished from argument, 1–2
  ethics of, 2–4
Persuasive definitions, 68–69
Picasso, Pablo, 306
Pickering, Miles, 64, 141
Pity, appeal to, 201–203
Plagiarism
  avoiding, 107–109
  definition of, 108
Planned Parenthood Federation of America, Inc., 203
Plato, 2, 209, 210, 373, 375
Point-by-point argument, 254
Policy
  question of, 45, 46
  verbs of, 49
Polls, 92–93
  developing questions for, 92
  picking sample population for, 92–93
Popular sentiments, appeal to, 202, 203
Porter, Katherine Anne, 53, 283
Pospesel, Howard, 21, 373
Post hoc ergo propter hoc, 146, 202, 205
Post hoc fallacy, 145–146, 202, 205
Predicate term, 168

Premises, 5
  major, 47
  a priori, 4–5, 22
Pronouns, repetition of, 266, 267, 268
Proper names, 168
Pruning strategies, 297–298
Pseudo-formality, avoiding, 293
Punctuation, in parenthetical citations, 110–111
Purpose, 33
Putney, Gail J., 107
Putney, Snell, 107

Q

Qualification transitions, 271
Qualifiers, 11
  limiting arguments with, 11–12
Quarrel, 1
Questions. *See also* Begging the question
  rhetorical, 226, 303
Quotations, 102–103
  additions, 107
  changes, 104–106
  direct, 103
  incorporating, 103–107
  omissions, 106–107

R

Ramage, Edward V., 358
Random House Dictionary, 64
Rank, Hugh, 375
Raphael, *The School of Athens*, 2
Reader, invented, 35–37
Reader's Guide to Periodical Literature, 87
Reason, 100
Reasoning
  circular, 174, 202, 204
  deductive, 134, 164–165, 184
  inductive, 134–137, 164–165
  scientific method of, 135
Redefinition, 43
Reference list, guidelines for, 113
Refutation, 245, 253–254
Register, Cornelius, 68
Repetition
  of key terms, sentence structure, or pronouns,
    266, 267–268

pointless, avoiding, 296–298
Repetitiousness, avoiding, 268–271
Report, 6
Reportive definitions, 60–61
Research. *See also* Evidence
  creativity in, 79–81
  personal, 90–93
Research papers
  evidence in, 102–107
  example, 120–131
Resneck-Sannes, Helen, 64
Restatement transitions, 271
Revision, 242–243, 262
  aims of, 243–244
  for coherence, 265–268, 272
  for conciseness, 298
  for paragraph completeness, 263–265
  for paragraph unity, 262–263
Rhetorica ad Herennium, 38
Rhetorical context, 32–37
Rhetorical questions, 226, 303
Robinson, James Harvey, 28, 373
Roll, Charles W., 84, 375
Rothman, Stanley, 83
Rudnick, Paul, 73–76
Runkle, Gerald, 60, 374

S

Salmon, Wesley, 165, 375
Samplings, considerations for, 150
Samuelson, Robert J., 10
Sapp, Debbie, 23–24
Schemes, 300
Schildwachter, Gregory T. M., 65
Schrank, Jeffrey, 141, 200–201, 221–226, 240–241
Science, 299
Scientific claims, 225–226
Scientific induction, 135
Scientific method of reasoning, 135
Sentence(s)
  complex, 284
  compound, 284
  compound-complex, 284
  length of, 285
  logic, 290–291
  openers for, 286
  recasting, 168

Sentence(s) *(cont.)*
  simple, 284
  structure of, repetition of, 266, 267–268
  style, 284–292
  types of, 284–285
Sentiments, popular, appeal to, 202, 203
Shakespeare, William, quoted, 242, 289
Shared characteristic, fallacy of, 174
Shaw, George Bernard, 280
Shenkman, Richard, 10, 14, 141
Shifting ground, 202, 207–208
Shulman, Max, 201, 232–240, 288
Sidey, Hugh, 63
Siegfried, Tom, 63
Simile, 301–302
Simon, Paul, 147
Sindler, Allan P., 66–67, 374
Singer, Peter, 105
Skow, John, 305
Slanting, 16–17
Socrates, 2, 210
Sophocles, 152
Soundness, 166–167
Sources
  citing, 103, 107–114
  computerized, 89
  selected databases, 89–90
"So what" claim, 224
Spatial relationship transition, 271
Spurgin, Sally De Witt, 100
Stallings, Earl, 358
Starr, Roger, 251
Statements
  of fact, 6
  personal, 19
Statistical claims, 225–226
Statistics, 83–85
Stein, Gertrude, 138
Stereotypes, 34–35
Stevens, Wallace, 374
Stipulative definitions, 60, 61–62
Stock issues, 40
Stone, Judith, 11, 247, 248
Stone, T. J., 219–220, 256
Straw man fallacy, 202, 208
Strunk, William, 376
Style, 243
  definition of, 280–282
  elements of, 282

sentence, 284–292
Subject term, 167
Subordination, 266–267, 269
Summarizing, 102–103
Summary or conclusion transitions, 271
Swift, Jonathan, 301
Syllogism, 171–172
Synonyms, 60–61
Syntactical patterns, 287–288
Synthesis, 43
Szasz, Thomas, 67, 374

T

Taney, Roger Brooke, 82
Taylor, Kathy, 247, 276–278
Teacher, Lawrence, 272
Teacher, Stuart, 272
Terms, 167
  defining, 59–78
  distributed, 167
  distribution of, 167–170
  key, 264
    repetition of, 267
  undistributed, 167
Testimonials, 225
Testimony, authoritative, 81–83
Texas Trial Lawyers Association, 210
Thesis, 37
  developing, 37–46
    questions to consider, 39
  enthymeme as, 46–50
  invention strategy, 38–40, 41–43, 44–46
  working, 46, 50, 52
Thesis statement, 257
Thompson, Dequa, 120–131, 256
Time, 18, 141, 211
Time sequence transition, 271
Tolstoy, Leo, 20
Topical checklists, 38–40
Topic idea, 264
Topics, 38
Torrey, Fuller, 101
Toulmin, Stephen, 177, 375
Toulmin's corrective, 176–177
Transitions, 266, 270–271
  common, 271
Tropes, 300–305
Troyka, Lynn Quitman, 112

Truth, 166–167
Tryzna, Thomas, 374
Tuchman, Barbara, 185–189
Tu quoque, 207

U

Unfinished claims, 223
Unity, 243
  paragraph, revising for, 262–263
  testing for, 244–245
Updike, John, 289
U.S. News & World Report, 17
Utne Reader, 16

V

Vague claim, 225
Validity, 166–167
  six rules of, 173, 174–176
  testing, 171–172
Value, question of, 45, 46
Van Doren, Mark, 31
Van Leunen, Mary-Claire, 374
Verbal signals, 7–8
Verbs
  active, 48–49
  of policy, 49

W

Waddle, Linda, 69–70
Wainwright, Loudon, 266, 278
Wall Street Journal, 98, 212, 303

Ward, Andrew, 248
Warrant, 47
Warren, Robert Penn, 373
"Water is wet" claim, 224
Watson, James, 135, 375
Weasel claim, 222–223
Weaver, Richard M., 1, 373, 375
"We're different and unique" claim, 223–224
Wertheimer, Alan, 319–320
White, E. B., 288, 305, 376
Whitehead, Alfred North, 267, 278
Williams, Vanessa, 212
Williams, Walter, 142
Wills, Christopher, 21
Wilson, Edmund, 106
Wilson, Woodrow, 20
Winterowd, Ross, 375, 376
Wordiness, avoiding, 296–298
  strategies for, 297–298
Word order, inverted, 288
Words, 292–306
  choosing, 293–295
  colloquial, 295
  connotation of, 294
  denotation of, 294
  everyday, 295
  technical, 295
Working thesis, 46, 50
  enthymeme as, evaluating, 52

Z

Zinsser, William, 376